Army Generals and Reconstruction

Philip H. "Little Phil" Sheridan

Army Generals and Reconstruction

Louisiana, 1862–1877

JOSEPH G. DAWSON III

Louisiana State University Press
Baton Rouge and London

Designer: Joanna Hill
Typeface: Bembo
Typesetter: G&S Typesetters, Inc.
Printer and binder: Thomson-Shore, Inc.

Chapter III was originally published in slightly different form as "General Phil Sheridan and Military Reconstruction in Louisiana," in *Civil War History*, XXIV (June, 1978), 133–51, copyright © Kent State University Press. Parts of Chapter IV appeared as "Army Generals and Reconstruction: Mower and Hancock as Case Studies," in *Southern Studies: An Interdisciplinary Journal of the South*, XVII (Fall, 1978), 255–72, and "General Lovell H. Rousseau and Louisiana Reconstruction," in *Louisiana History*, XX (Fall, 1979), 373–91.

LIBRARY OF CONGRESS CATALOGING IN PUBLICATION DATA
Dawson, Joseph G., 1945–
  Army generals and Reconstruction.

  Bibliography: p.
  Includes index.
    1. Reconstruction—Louisiana. 2. Louisiana—
Politics and government—1865–1950. 3. Louisiana—
Politics and government—Civil War, 1861–1865.
I. Title.
F375.D27   976.3'061   81-11735
ISBN 0-8071-0896-9 (cloth)   AACR2
ISBN 0-8071-1960-1 (paper)

Louisiana Paperback Edition, 1994
03 02 01 00 99 98 97 96 95 94   5 4 3 2 1

To Bev
and to the memory of T. Harry Williams

Contents

Illustrations

Abbreviations Used in the Notes

AAAG	Acting Assistant Adjutant General
AAG	Assistant Adjutant General
AG	Adjutant General
AGO	Adjutant General's Office, Washington, D.C.
CG	Commanding General
CO	Commanding Officer
C/S	Chief of Staff
Dept Gulf	Department of the Gulf (Records of)
Dept La	Department of Louisiana (Records of)
Dept La&Texas	Department of Louisiana and Texas (Records of)
Dept South	Department of the South (Records of)
Dept Texas	Department of Texas (Records of)
Dist La	District of Louisiana (Records of)
DSL	Department of the South-Late: designation given to bound letter-book volumes in the National Archives which were formerly filed with the Dept South, but transferred to the Dept Gulf records
5 MD	Fifth Military District (Records of)
GO	General Order
HQ/USA	Headquarters, United States Army
Lafourche Dist	Lafourche District (Records of)—subdistrict in southern Louisiana
MilDivGulf	Military Division of the Gulf (Records of)
MilDivMo	Military Division of the Missouri (Records of)
MilDivSouth	Military Division of the South (Records of)
MilDivSW	Military Division of the Southwest (Records of)
NA	National Archives
Recd	Received
RG	Record Group
SO	Special Order
SW	Secretary of War

Acknowledgments

Several persons gave of their time, knowledge, and support, helping to bring this book to completion. I would particularly like to thank John L. Loos for his valuable suggestions concerning organization and style, and for his own special brand of wry humor; Thomas E. Schott, who reacquainted me with the English language; Mark Leutbecker, who helped with the selection of photographs from the National Archives and spent some of his own time tracking down some elusive information there; and James E. Sefton, who tendered helpful advice all along the way, in addition to closely reading the manuscript and offering worthwhile criticisms and suggestions. Thanks are also in order to Roger J. Spiller, who took time out from his own projects to provide an encouraging word; and to George C. Rable, with whom I often discussed the Reconstruction era.

I would like to acknowledge the assistance of several archivists and librarians, including Elaine Everly, Michael Musick, and Jimmy Walker of the National Archives and Stone Miller, Margaret Dalrymple, and Merna Whitley of the Louisiana State University Department of Archives and Manuscripts.

I am pleased to acknowledge the assistance and encouragement of those at the Louisiana State University Press, including Director L. E. Phillabaum, Executive Editor Beverly Jarrett, Managing Editor Martha L. Hall, and Editor Judy Bailey.

I also wish to mention my debt to Joe Gray Taylor for his monumental book *Louisiana Reconstructed*, which did much to clear the muddy waters of Louisiana's postwar politics.

Words of appreciation are inadequate to describe completely the role of my wife, Bev. She gave comments, asked questions, made recommendations, listened to my complaints, deciphered my handwriting, and typed the manuscript many times. It could not have been done without her.

With deep gratitude, I must express my debt to T. Harry Williams for his encouragement and wise counsel.

Army Generals and Reconstruction

Introduction

The United States Army and its generals did not always act at the beck and call of Republicans in Louisiana during Reconstruction. Some generals, including Philip H. Sheridan, Joseph A. Mower, and Joseph J. Reynolds, were Radicals or strongly favored the Republican party and its causes. But other senior commanders, specifically Winfield S. Hancock, Lovell H. Rousseau, and Christopher C. Augur, were Democrats or opposed Radical Reconstruction for one reason or another. On another tack, some generals who commanded soldiers in Louisiana made every effort to carry out national policy in a fair-minded manner without showing favoritism toward either political party. Robert C. Buchanan and William H. Emory best exemplify the officers who tried to remain unbiased. Accordingly, there was no stereotype of a military commander in Louisiana—or the South—during Reconstruction.

In fact, considering the difficult, thankless, and sometimes hazardous jobs that three presidents gave the army during the years 1862–1877, the generals and their soldiers performed remarkably well. Generals and lesser offices ruled on matters of justice, finance, transportation, education, labor, and charity. Under the circumstances that existed in 1865— southern governments disrupted or deposed, millions of ex-slaves uncertain of their rights and responsibilities, and thousands of ex–Confederate soldiers returning to their homes—the army was the only agency of the federal government that could have policed the South.

Although the military occupation was obviously necessary, many Americans naturally found unpalatable the idea that any part of the nation should be divided and regulated by army generals. This period of military domination over a section of the nation was unique in American history. No previous events had prepared Americans to endure the stigma of defeat followed by occupation and military government.[1]

1. C. Vann Woodward, *The Burden of Southern History* (rev. ed.; Baton Rouge, 1968), 19.

Moreover, the United States Army had had little experience with military government. For nine months in 1848, following the Mexican War, the army had occupied parts of Mexico, including the capital, Mexico City, while the representatives of the two nations considered the ratification of the Treaty of Guadalupe Hidalgo. Acting under martial law, United States soldiers supervised Mexican elections, regulated saloons, and enforced curfews. Courts-martial decided cases involving Mexican citizens and American soldiers. Most army officers viewed the Mexican episode with distaste, and when the army withdrew, it was just as glad to leave as the Mexicans were to see it go.[2]

Another type of military occupation grew out of the Mexican War, one which had even more similarity to the army's later role in Louisiana. The United States acquired almost one-half of the Republic of Mexico as a result of the fighting. California, Arizona, New Mexico, Nevada, and Utah would later be cut from this new land. Rather than simply occupying these captured territories temporarily, the army administered them as a prelude to United States civil government. The army's control was so complete and so pervasive that it was more than just martial law; it was military government. Theodore Grivas has best explained the difference in his study of California territory. Martial law is usually temporary, brought on during a time of "disaster or enemy invasion" when civil law may be "suspended" but not cancelled. In contrast, military government is designed to replace civil government and is usually used in hostile enemy territory or captured lands that will later be annexed. Grivas concluded: "Martial law supports civil government; military government supplants it."[3] Civilians in California did not take full control until more than four years after American forces arrived. Civil authorities, such as mayors, judges, and city councils, existed, but all served on the approval of the military commander, who often replaced civilian officials with men more acceptable to the United States occupation. For easier administration, the senior general subdivided California into districts, where subordinate officers exercised control. Finally, in 1849 the army commander registered voters and called for a constitutional convention to prepare California for statehood. Unfortunately, the War Department did

2. Justin H. Smith, "American Rule in Mexico," *American Historical Review*, XXIII (January, 1918), 288–98.

3. Theodore Grivas, *Military Governments in California, 1846–1850* (Glendale, Cal., 1963), 13–16. See also *ibid.*, 86–89, 92–93, 105–108, 112, 141–45, 214, 218–20, 222.

not require the army officers in California, nor those who had served in Mexico, to prepare a handbook for future generals who would have to deal with martial law, occupation, and military government in the South during Reconstruction.

Reconstruction was a contemporary term of the 1860s that meant generally the procedure or requirements demanded for the states of the southern Confederacy to return to the Union. The debate over Reconstruction started almost as soon as southern soldiers occupied Fort Sumter. President Abraham Lincoln held that these states had never left the Union and needed only to be restored to "their proper relationship" with their sister states. Other politicians disagreed, believing that the eleven wayward states had actually seceded and that stiff conditions should be set for the Confederates to meet before they could return to the Union. All parties to this debate reckoned that any Reconstruction plan must abide by the Constitution, but the debaters often disagreed because the Constitution contained no provisions regarding either secession or reconstruction.[4]

Radical Republicans in Congress hoped to achieve certain goals in the South during Reconstruction. Many northerners, particularly Republicans, wanted blacks to vote in elections, hold elective and appointive offices, serve on juries, pay taxes, receive education at public expense, choose their own jobs, and rest safely in their homes—that is, the North wanted the South to acknowledge that the freedmen would have basic civil and political rights. The Republicans proposed various laws and constitutional amendments to make their goals binding. However, the hostility of southerners toward blacks, Republicans, and the United States Army made it impossible to attain these goals quickly. Instead, decades of supervision were needed, but the Radicals' crusade lasted less than ten years in most southern states.

In Louisiana, Reconstruction began in 1862 and ended in 1877, lasting longer than in any other state. The actions of the army in the state can be divided into two parts. During the first period, 1862–1869, the army exercised its greatest influence. During these years, the rulings of generals who commanded troops in the state often overshadowed the actions of the state's civil officials, and especially under the leadership of Sheridan and Mower, the goals of the Radical Republicans were partially met. Moreover, from 1866 to 1869 the army was more capable of responding

4. Herman Belz, *Reconstructing the Union: Theory and Policy During the Civil War* (Ithaca, N.Y., 1969), 1–14 and *passim*.

to Republican requests for aid than in the 1870s because the War Department stationed an average of 21,000 soldiers per year in the South.[5]

During the second phase, 1870–1877, the influence of the army was sometimes less apparent, but continued to be extremely important to both the Republicans and the Democrats. During the 1870s the average size of the entire army was only 29,000, and only about 7,500 soldiers per year served in the South.[6] Consequently, the generals had fewer troops at their disposal. It became more difficult to guarantee the newly won rights of the Negro, and sometimes the commanders refused or neglected to use their full powers. Furthermore, during the 1870s Louisiana's Democrats boldly used violence against Republicans and blacks in an effort to subvert the Republican government in the state. Out of necessity, Ulysses S. Grant and the army sometimes had to intercede on behalf of the legally elected government in Louisiana or to protect defenseless civilians against the violent acts of the Democrats.

I will approach Reconstruction in Louisiana mainly from the perspective of the generals who commanded soldiers in the state. The army worked closely with the Freedmen's Bureau, an organization that has been ably treated by Howard A. White.[7] Some attention will be given to the enlisted soldier, and I will discuss politics and politicians, but the attitudes, actions, ideas, and influence of the generals will stand above the other subjects.

---

5. James E. Sefton, *The United States Army and Reconstruction, 1865–1877* (Baton Rouge, 1967), 260–61.

6. *Ibid.*, Russell F. Weigley, *History of the United States Army* (New York, 1967), 567.

7. Howard A. White, *The Freedmen's Bureau in Louisiana* (Baton Rouge, 1970).

CHAPTER I

The Beginnings Under
Butler and Banks

On the night of April 24, 1862, Flag Officer David Glasgow Farragut of the Union navy prepared final orders for his fleet, which was embarking on a hazardous assignment. Several days of sporadic fighting had failed to reduce Forts Jackson and St. Philip on the Mississippi River, which were the keys to the defense of New Orleans. Farragut decided that he would attempt to run by the forts under cover of darkness and then steam upriver to capture the "Queen City of the Confederacy." The Union vessels got underway by 3:30 A.M., and as they drew opposite the twin forts, southern batteries and gunboats opened fire. The battle lasted about three hours. Heavy Confederate fire scored hits on the Union vessels, but the attackers sank most of the Confederate gunboats. Vulnerable now from two directions, the forts surrendered. Farragut's gamble had succeeded.

Learning that the Union navy was fighting its way past the forts, Confederate General Mansfield Lovell ordered his troops to evacuate New Orleans. The general left the city without detailing an officer to represent the Confederate government at the surrender, and consequently, Farragut had to negotiate with Mayor John T. Monroe and the city council. By noon on April 26 familiar red-and-white-striped flags were whipping in the breeze over the Federal mint, the post office, the Custom House, and the city hall. Farragut waited patiently while General Benjamin F. Butler brought up his troops, and on May 1, 1862, the navy turned over command of the city to the army. The long ordeal of the United States Army in Louisiana Reconstruction had begun.[1]

Although he had been sent to do a soldier's job, General Benjamin Franklin Butler was not a professional soldier. Actually, he was a rotund, jowly politician who had served as a Democrat in the Massachusetts legislature for several years. President Lincoln, to gain support for the war effort,

---

1. John D. Winters, *Civil War in Louisiana* (Baton Rouge, 1963), 95–102.

began appointing politicians, including Butler, to the rank of general. At a time of few Union victories, Butler's main tasks were to defeat Confederate armies and capture more Confederate territory, but he devoted equal time to pacifying New Orleans, thus beginning Reconstruction.

From the 18,000-man expeditionary force that invaded Louisiana, Butler assigned 2,500 troops to garrison New Orleans and issued a lengthy proclamation declaring martial law in the city and throughout the surrounding area. The pronouncement was based on Butler's recent experiences on the Virginia coast, where he had served before going to New Orleans. It listed several regulations. Proper respect was demanded for the United States flag. The killing of any Union soldiers by civilians would be considered murder and not acts of war. All saloon owners were to register their businesses with the army, provost marshal.[2]

Before its capture, New Orleans was the largest and most cosmopolitan city in the Confederacy. More than 170,000 residents had been busy in a variety of private and commercial enterprises. Several thousand of these had left to fight in the war or to avoid the Federal occupation. Despite its surface appearances of civilization, General Butler thought that the city was "untamed." In the confusion of the first days after the surrender, a host of administrative matters awaited his attention. Hundreds of persons were destitute and hungry. Butler saw to it that captured Confederate rations and Federal supplies were distributed to the needy. The general prohibited the use of Confederate money after May 27, 1862, and required that banks and businesses switch to United States currency. Several ministers in the city refused to substitute the phrase "President of the United States" for "President of the Confederate States" in their regular prayers. Therefore, Butler closed some churches, preventing some pastors from preaching until they changed their supplications.[3]

A more worldly matter next captured the Louisiana commandant's attention. Many women in New Orleans had repeatedly shown disrespect for the army by unladylike words or deeds, including spitting on soldiers as they walked on the streets. Butler believed that such indiscretions might encourage more cohesive opposition if allowed to continue. Ac-

2. "Proclamation by Benjamin F. Butler, May 1, 1862," in War Department, *War of the Rebellion: A Compilation of the Official Records of the Union and Confederate Armies* (128 parts in 70 volumes; Washington, D.C., 1880–1901), Series I, vol. VI, 717–20, hereinafter cited as *Official Records*. All citations are to Series I unless otherwise indicated.

3. Joe Gray Taylor, *Louisiana Reconstructed, 1863–1877* (Baton Rouge, 1974), 2, 5–6; Benjamin F. Butler, *Butler's Book* (Boston, 1892), 373–74, 387–88, 392–93; Hans L. Trefousse, *Ben Butler: The South Called Him Beast!* (New York, 1957), 108–119.

Benjamin F. Butler

cordingly, on May 15 Butler issued an order specifying that whenever a woman insulted troops "by word, gesture, or movement," such a "female" would "be regarded and held liable to be treated as a woman of the town plying her avocation." The citizens of New Orleans were outraged by this pronouncement and condemned it as barbaric. Butler was vilified in the southern press and castigated by the foreign consuls in Louisiana. However, after soldiers posted the order, such insulting incidents noticeably declined.[4]

The mayor's reaction to the "woman order" and recalcitrance on the part of several municipal officials prompted Butler to reorganize the government of New Orleans. Mayor Monroe protested against the "woman order" in a strongly worded letter to Butler. In fact, Monroe had repeatedly hindered the city's administration since the surrender, and his letter provided the general with the reason he needed to remove the mayor from office. Butler designated Colonel George F. Shepley of the 12th Maine Infantry acting mayor. Following Monroe's ouster, Butler dismissed most of the city council, the police chief, and a judge for failure to cooperate with military authorities. Some of these men were confined at Fort Jackson. Butler made Captain Jonas H. French temporary police chief, and until civil trials resumed, a military commission presided over most court cases.[5]

Butler believed that issuing the "woman order" and removing pro-Confederate civil officials were necessary, but his next controversial act probably ruined his chances to effectively carry out Reconstruction. On April 26, before Butler took command of New Orleans, William B. Mumford, a local gambler, had torn the United States flag from its staff atop the mint building, ripped the flag to shreds, and distributed the pieces to an appreciative crowd. Learning of the escapade, Butler promised to have Mumford severely punished. Federal authorities arrested the gambler, and a military court sentenced him to be hanged. In spite of the public outcry against the verdict, Mumford was executed on June 7, 1862, as an example that Federal authority or its symbols could not be

4. GO No. 28, Dept Gulf, May 15, 1862, in *Official Records*, XV, 426; Winters, *Civil War in Louisiana*, 132.

5. John T. Monroe to Butler, May 16, 1862, XLIII, 526, GO No. 24, Dept Gulf, May 10, 1862, VI, 724, both in *Official Records*; Robert J. Futrell, "Federal Military Government in the South, 1861–1865," *Military Affairs*, XV (Winter, 1951), 182, 186–87; John S. Kendall, *History of New Orleans* (3 vols.; Chicago, 1922), I, 293–94; Howard P. Johnson, "New Orleans Under General Butler," *Louisiana Historical Quarterly*, XXIV (April, 1941), 497–99.

violated. Swiftly responding to Mumford's hanging, emotional Louisianians branded the man who authorized the execution with the nickname "Beast" Butler.[6]

After that, it mattered little that Butler and his officers gave Louisiana months of fair and reasonable government. One of the first projects to benefit the city was a massive cleanup operation. July marked the start of the dreaded three-month yellow fever season. The unacclimated Union troops were especially vulnerable to this deadly disease, which, over the years, had killed thousands of people in Louisiana. Butler detailed unemployed whites and Negroes to thoroughly scrape and clean streets, gutters, ditches, and canals, greatly improving city sanitation. Some local officials, who failed to cooperate in the project by taking an oath of loyalty to the United States, were removed from office and replaced by army officers or local citizens who supported the Union. Butler's sanitation and quarantine program succeeded, and neither citizens nor occupation forces suffered from an outbreak of the terrible "yellow jack."[7]

Having ensured the city's health, Butler set out to change its loyalty. According to an agent of the Treasury Department, Butler boasted "that in six months New Orleans should be a Union City or—a home of the Alligator." On June 10 Butler stipulated that all public officials in occupied Louisiana must take an oath of loyalty to the Union or leave office. Faced with this requirement, many summarily resigned their posts. Butler also decreed that any resident (foreigner or citizen) desiring to use the courts in civil or criminal cases had to pledge his fidelity to the United States. Three months later only about 14,000 persons had taken the oath. Prompted further by the threatened confiscation of their property (under the congressional Confiscation Act of July 12, 1862), some 68,000 people renewed their allegiance. However, Butler's predictions of a change in Louisiana's loyalty were overly optimistic. For instance, several newspaper editors remained opposed to the Union, and their irreconcilable attitudes showed clearly in print. Between May and November, 1862,

6. There are many treatments of the Mumford case. See, for example, Richard S. West, Jr., *Lincoln's Scapegoat General: A Life of Benjamin F. Butler, 1818–1893* (Boston, 1965), 149–52.

7. Butler to Mayor & Council, May 9, 1862, VI, 723–24; Butler to George Shepley & Council, June 4, 1862, XV, 462–63, both in *Official Records*; Gerald M. Capers, *Occupied City: New Orleans Under the Federals, 1862–1865* (Lexington, 1965), 66, 73, 88, 91; Jo Ann Carrigan, "Yankees Versus Yellow Jack in New Orleans, 1862–1866," *Civil War History*, IX (September, 1963), 248–60.

Butler suspended the publication of six Crescent City papers and one in Baton Rouge.[8]

Even as Butler pressured Louisianians into renewing their loyalty, he lost some of his power over the state. On June 10 Lincoln appointed George Shepley, recently promoted to brevet brigadier general, military governor of Louisiana. This split the responsibilities of command in the Gulf Department, apparently leaving tactical military operations to Butler while Shepley dealt with political Reconstruction. These assignments were never made clear, however, and inevitably, there was friction between the two generals.[9]

Butler was unsuccessful on the battlefield, but he made an important contribution to the Union war effort by enlisting large numbers of blacks into the Federal army. At first blacks were hired only as laborers. Later, Butler made plans to induct Negro slaves into a special military unit. Butler argued with General John W. Phelps over how the black troops would be recruited, but eventually Butler reaped the credit for raising three regiments of a "Corps d'Afrique" in Louisiana. Other states, including those in the North, raised similar units, which fought in several battles and played an important role as garrison troops after the war.[10]

Butler's next controversial actions led to his transfer. Foreigners in New Orleans, most of whom were prosouthern, strenuously objected to orders that required them to swear an oath of loyalty to the Union. Then Butler set out to confiscate all Confederate funds. Since many foreigners had concealed Confederate money and supplies when the city fell, Butler sometimes had to enter European consulates. His high-handedness in this matter not only alienated the New Orleans European community but simultaneously antagonized Secretary of State William H. Seward. A move was soon afoot in Washington to have the troublesome general replaced, and in early November, President Lincoln chose Major General Nathaniel P. Banks as the new commander of the Department of the Gulf.[11]

8. George S. Denison to Mrs. E. S. Denison, June 10, 1862, in James A. Padgett (ed.), "Some Letters of George S. Denison, 1854–1866: Observations of a Yankee on Conditions in Louisiana and Texas," *Louisiana Historical Quarterly*, XXIII (October, 1940), 1,183; Capers, *Occupied City*, 92–94; Butler to Edwin M. Stanton, June 28, 1862, XV, 502–503, SO No. 513, Dept Gulf, November 14, 1862, XV, 595–96, both in *Official Records*.

9. Stanton to Butler, June 10, 1862, XV, 471, Stanton to Shepley, June 10, 1862, Ser. III, vol. II, 141, both in *Official Records*.

10. Dudley T. Cornish, *The Sable Arm: Negro Troops in the Union Army, 1861–1865* (New York, 1966), 17, 24, 57–66.

11. Trefousse, *Butler*, 124–27, 132–33.

Before Banks arrived, a congressional election was scheduled in Louisiana. Bypassing Butler, Lincoln sent orders concerning the election to General Shepley. Some symbols of Louisiana's unionism were needed, and new representatives in Congress seemed appropriate. Prior to the election on December 2, Butler encouraged loyal voters to support the proadministration candidates, Michael Hahn, who had been born in Bavaria in 1831 and had settled in Louisiana in 1840, and Edward H. Durell. Hahn was a winner, but a treasury agent named Benjamin F. Flanders defeated Durell for the second seat. Lincoln thought if Congress accepted these representatives, it might encourage some states to leave the Confederacy. A few days after the election, General Banks arrived in Louisiana. On December 17 Butler relinquished command, but General Shepley retained his post as military governor.[12]

Louisiana was gladly rid of Ben Butler. The questionable honesty of his administration, stories of which were later exaggerated, received justifiable criticism. Several army officers and treasury agents made personal fortunes in cotton dealings in 1862. Among others, Andrew Jackson Butler, the general's brother, profited from inside information. Southerners accused the general himself of stealing a variety of personal and state property, but the charges were never proven. These and other revelations did nothing to improve Butler's image. It would have made little difference to southerners if he had had the honesty of a saint. Butler's list of "sins" was too long for his redemption, and for years after the war the "Beast" was roundly criticized by the state's newspapers. Although villified for decades, however, Butler's administration was not nearly so bad as it was sometimes portrayed.[13] Admittedly, his methods were distasteful—even harsh—but his task had been to convince Louisiana that Federal authority had returned permanently. This required oaths of loyalty, removal of civil officials, and even sterner measures in some cases. The experience of Butler's successors demonstrated that the unmarked path to Louisiana's Reconstruction was thorny and difficult to follow. Indeed, it became even more twisted and complex.

Nathaniel Prentiss Banks, like Ben Butler before him, had left Massachusetts politics to wear the stars of a Union general. However, Banks

12. Abraham Lincoln to Shepley, November 21, 1862, in Roy P. Basler (ed.), *The Collected Works of Abraham Lincoln* (9 vols., New Brunswick, N.J., 1955), V, 504–505; Belz, *Reconstructing the Union*, 106–110; GO No. 17, Dept Gulf, December 17, 1862, in *Official Records*, XV, 611.

13. Willie M. Caskey, *Secession and Restoration of Louisiana* (Baton Rouge, 1938), 66–69;

possessed broader political experience, including service as a state legislator, Speaker of the House in Congress, and governor of Massachusetts. He had a handsome face graced by a mustache and goatee, and his head was topped with graying, fashionably long hair. By 1861 Banks was an ambitious and influential Republican and, thus, rated consideration for a high military appointment. It soon became evident that Lincoln had not chosen a military expert to replace Butler. On the contrary, in his campaigns in the Shenandoah Valley, the new general had earned the epithet "Nothing Positive" Banks.

Banks had been sent to Louisiana to give the North victories in the field, but his background naturally made him interested in Reconstruction. He quickly learned that the army was operating "an immense military government, embracing every form of civil administration, the assessment of taxes, fines, punishments, charities, trade, regulation of churches, confiscation of estates, and the working of plantations, in addition to the ordinary affairs of a military department." Banks continued most of Butler's public works programs and the food distributions to the needy, but he departed from the firm and, naturally, unpopular methods of his predecessor, in the hope that a relaxation of the severity of the military occupation would win support for Louisiana's reconstruction. For example, a new order reopened all churches previously closed by Butler, even if the minister refused to pray for President Lincoln. Banks also released several civilian prisoners held in confinement on Butler's order. Furthermore, noting, in a Christmas Eve proclamation, that Lincoln's Emancipation Proclamation did not apply to occupied Louisiana, he declared that the war was not a war on slavery, but a struggle to preserve the Union. He added, however, that many unexpected results could come from such a great Civil War, and at its end the institution of slavery would probably cease to exist.[14]

Banks apparently had ulterior motives for making the process of reconstruction easier in Louisiana. If he were successful both militarily and politically, the resulting fame would enhance his chances for high national office, perhaps even the presidency. Banks's desire to control reconstruction placed him directly at loggerheads with Military Governor

---

Capers, *Occupied City*, 83–84, 87; Trefousse, *Butler*, 122–24; Taylor, *Louisiana Reconstructed*, 18.

14. GO No. 118, Dept Gulf, December 24, 1862, XV, 624, Nathaniel Banks to Henry W. Halleck, January 7, 1863, XV, 639–40, SO No. 66, Dept Gulf, March 7, 1863, XV, 1,111, all in *Official Records*; Fred H. Harrington, *Fighting Politician: Major General N. P. Banks* (Philadelphia, 1948), 93–94, 99, 104.

Nathaniel P. Banks

Shepley, who believed that everything of a political nature was his responsibility. An argument erupted over command of the provost marshal's office, which Shepley had theretofore directed. In a special order, Banks shifted the provost marshal's operations to his own headquarters. He further decreased Shepley's power by ordering all future civil cases to be brought before the Louisiana Provisional Court, established by Lincoln in December, 1862, to lessen the responsibility of the courts-martial. With these orders, Shepley's prestige in the state slowly declined.[15]

In contrast, the political and economic influence of Banks became more pervasive, and this was especially true in matters concerning Negro labor and black troops. The new commander quickly began recruiting qualified blacks into regiments of all arms. By the end of the war, more Negro regiments had been raised in Louisiana than in any other state. Enlisting black soldiers into the army was a truly radical act and indicated that the role of blacks in society would be different after the war. On the other hand, Banks instituted a moderate Negro labor program. Previously, Butler had dabbled in making rules for plantation workers and had posted troops to guard some plantations near Union lines. Thinking they were free, many blacks had left the plantations and were wandering unregulated in the countryside. On January 29, 1863, Banks issued a lengthy order on Negro labor that required blacks to sign a yearly contract with an employer of their choice. The contract called for a ten-hour workday for the laborer; for his part, the plantation owner had to furnish adequate food, clothing, and shelter and to pay the worker in wages or part of the crop. The army provided supervisors to monitor the agreements and see that blacks were not mistreated. Flogging was outlawed. The order threatened vagrants with arrest and a term of unpaid labor on public works. Banks drew criticism from many Radical Republicans who thought that his programs needlessly catered to slave-holding conservatives. The general, apparently, designed his program to avoid alienating plantation owners, for he believed them to be essential to his reconstruction plan.[16]

15. Banks to Shepley, January 27, 1863, in *Official Records*, XV, 1097–98; Futrell, "Military Government in the South," 183. Banks's motives have been reexamined by Peyton McCrary, *Abraham Lincoln and Reconstruction: The Louisiana Experiment* (Princeton, 1978), 209–210.

16. On black troops see Cornish, *Sable Arm*, 103, 126–29, 247–48. Modern historians also have criticized Banks's labor program on the grounds that it hurt the chances for truly radical changes, *i.e.*, complete equality for blacks, immediately following the war. See es-

Meanwhile, in Washington, Louisiana's new representatives Hahn and Flanders were given seats in Congress, but only for the remainder of the existing term, which expired on March 3, 1863. Therefore, they enjoyed their positions for less than one month. Even so, the recognition of the southerners pleased Lincoln. The president held that these men were due their seats in Congress because Louisiana had never really been out of the Union. Many Republicans and several Democrats disagreed with this idea. Furthermore, in the opinion of many congressional leaders of both parties, Hahn and Flanders had been improperly elected because an army general (in this case Shepley) had conducted Federal elections in a state that did not have a civilian governor.[17]

Back in Louisiana the political factions that formed during Butler's short tenure now gathered into a shaky alliance. All of the factions initially belonged to the pro-Union Free State party, virtually the state's only functioning political party. The Democrats had been so discredited by secession and war that, temporarily, no politician in occupied Louisiana carried that label. The Moderates, led by Michael Hahn and supported by Lincoln and Banks, formed the largest faction of the Free State party. The Moderate wing was composed of old Louisiana Whigs and Union men, who favored the destruction of slavery but did not advocate immediate civil rights or political privileges for blacks. The second faction, comprising the Radicals, was guided by Benjamin Flanders and Thomas J. Durant, a skilled lawyer from New Orleans. The Radicals not only wanted slavery abolished but also demanded civil and political rights for blacks as soon as possible. Flanders and Durant were among the very few native New Orleanians or long-term residents that adhered to the Radical wing, which was largely composed of agents of the Treasury Department, other recent arrivals to the state, and a handful of army officers, among them General Shepley. The Conservative Unionists, primarily native planters and businessmen who preferred retaining the institution of slavery, made up the third group. Obviously, most Conservatives did not want blacks to be given any rights. One of the most prominent Conservatives was J. Q. A. Fellows. Although all three fac-

pecially Louis S. Gerteis, *From Contraband to Freedman: Federal Policy Toward Southern Blacks, 1861–1865* (Westport, Conn., 1973), 5, 7, 82–83, and C. Peter Ripley, *Slaves and Freedmen in Civil War Louisiana* (Baton Rouge, 1976), 48–49, 200–202. Banks's program is GO No. 12, Dept Gulf, January 29, 1863, XV, 666–67, and he revised it with GO No. 23, Dept Gulf, February 23, 1864, XXXVI, Pt. 2, pp. 227–28, both in *Official Records*.

17. Belz, *Reconstructing the Union*, 110–15.

tions supported the Union and wanted Louisiana fully reinstated, their views on slavery and Negro rights forced them to drift apart through the summer of 1863.[18]

In August, Lincoln ordered Banks to create a new constitution for Louisiana. The president wanted the state to abolish slavery on its own since a new constitution that disallowed slavery would help convince the North that Louisiana was sincerely redressing its own faults. Of course, the constitution had to be written by civilians, but Lincoln urged Banks to expedite the process as much as possible. Shepley had appointed Durant attorney general and made him responsible for registering voters, and Lincoln assumed that a registration drive was under way.[19]

But Lincoln was mistaken, or misled, about the voter registration. Despite additional orders from Secretary of War Stanton, Shepley did not press or assist Durant, who hesitated to enroll voters until the Radicals gained additional strength. Banks learned that few new voters were on the rolls, and he cancelled the congressional election scheduled for November. In a straw vote, two Conservative Unionists claimed to have been elected anyway, but neither Banks nor Shepley acknowledged the voting as valid, and Congress did not seat them. Lincoln wrote to Banks that he was "bitterly" disappointed over Louisiana's political difficulties.[20]

Early in December, Lincoln issued a "Proclamation of Amnesty and Reconstruction," better known as his 10-percent plan, though it was really a set of guidelines designed to entice the southern states away from the Confederacy. The president offered amnesty to all Confederates except high civil and military leaders. To receive amnesty, southerners were required to swear an oath of future loyalty and agree to abide by all wartime measures on slavery. When a number equal to 10-percent of the voters in the 1860 presidential election in any one state had sworn this oath, a new loyal state government could be formed, and once this government abolished slavery, the chief executive would consider the state reconstructed. Any congressmen or senators elected by these states would still require the approval of Congress itself before they were seated. This proclamation indicated that Lincoln believed the executive

18. Caskey, *Secession and Restoration*, 97–103; Taylor, *Louisiana Reconstructed*, 21–22; T. Harry Williams, "General Banks and the Radical Republicans in the Civil War," *New England Quarterly*, XII (June, 1939), 268–80; McCrary, *Lincoln and Reconstruction*, 159–85.

19. Lincoln to Banks, August 5, 1863, in Basler (ed.), *Works of Lincoln*, VI, 365; Harrington, *Fighting Politician*, 108–10.

20. Stanton to Shepley, August 24, 1863, in *Official Records*, XXVI, 694–95; Taylor, *Louisiana Reconstructed*, 22; Lincoln to Banks, November 5, 1863, in Basler (ed.), *Works of Lincoln*, VII, 1.

was responsible for leading the Reconstruction process. But in no way did the president demand congressional recognition of any new governments that might come into being. Lincoln was relying primarily on General Banks and Louisiana to demonstrate the feasibility of his proposal.[21]

To do all that the president wanted, Banks claimed that he needed control over all facets of Reconstruction in Louisiana. He requested that Shepley be transferred and Durant relinquish his duties as registrar. Lincoln soothingly replied that all along he had intended for Banks to be the civil and military "master" of Louisiana. Shepley was there simply to "assist" the department commander, and Durant must stay in his job to allow representatives of all factions to participate in the "free state reorganization of Louisiana." Banks, reassured by Lincoln's letter, began a voter registration drive and designated February 22, 1864, as the election date for governor, lieutenant governor, and other executive offices. Prospective voters were required to take the oath of future loyalty contained in Lincoln's proclamation. Furthermore, Banks declared that on March 28, delegates to a constitutional convention would be chosen in a separate canvass.[22]

At the Free State party convention on February 1, 1864, the Radical and Moderate Republicans split over their nominee for the governorship. The Radicals angrily quit the hall and, convening separately, nominated Benjamin Flanders. Michael Hahn easily obtained the Moderates' endorsement. In an unusual effort to attract broad support, both groups selected James Madison Wells, a native Louisiana planter from Rapides Parish, for lieutenant governor. The obvious division of the Free-Staters fired the hopes of the Conservatives, who put forth their own candidate for governor, J. Q. A. Fellows.[23]

When the votes were tabulated, Hahn had won the election. To the surprise of some, Fellows finished second, and Flanders trailed in third place. Wells was handily elected lieutenant governor. Banks was quite pleased with these results, especially with Hahn's victory. Moreover, the number of votes cast was more than 20 percent of the number of ballots cast in Louisiana's 1860 presidential election and thus exceeded the re-

21. Presidential Proclamation, December 8, 1863, in Basler (ed.), *Works of Lincoln*, VII, 53–66.

22. Lincoln to Banks, December 24, 1863, in Basler (ed.), *Works of Lincoln*, VII, 89–90; Proclamation by Banks, January 11, 1864, Series III, vol. IV, 22–23, GO No. 35, Dept Gulf, March 11, 1864, Series III, vol. IV, 170–72, both in *Official Records*.

23. Belz, *Reconstructing the Union*, 190–91; Taylor, *Louisiana Reconstructed*, 27–28.

quirements of Lincoln's 10-percent plan. Banks wrote Lincoln that Louisiana "will become in two years, under a wise and strong government, one of the most loyal and prosperous States that the world has ever seen." Unfortunately, like his predecessor, Banks underestimated Louisiana's resistance to reconstruction.[24]

Hahn was inaugurated as civil governor on March 4, and eleven days later he took Shepley's place as military governor.[25] He found the duality of his civil-military governorship cumbersome. The 10-percent plan gave Louisiana a semblance of civil administration, but the army still controlled the state. As long as the war continued, it was impossible to arrange it any other way.

The next step was the drafting of a new constitution. In the election of constitutional convention delegates, voters overwhelmingly supported the Moderates, but several Conservatives and a few Radicals were also selected. At the opening session on April 6, the convention chose Edward H. Durell, a Moderate, as president. A Harvard graduate, Durell had been a lawyer and judge in Louisiana since 1834. From the opening gavel until adjournment on July 23, 1864, the convention delegates debated several important issues. Most of the delegates, a few conservatives excepted, agreed that the institution of slavery would be abolished, but there was a great deal of debate over what rights to grant the new freedmen. After lengthy dispute, a proposal for black suffrage was defeated, but the constitution provided that Negroes could be granted the right to vote by an act of the legislature in the future. Other clauses in the constitution increased representation for New Orleans in the legislature, provided for segregated public schools, and established hours and minimum wages for laborers on public works. The document then faced approval or rejection by the voters. It appeared possible the charter might be rejected, and that the convention might have to meet again to consider revisions or to write another constitution. Therefore, as an afterthought, the delegates passed a resolution that empowered President Durell to reconvoke the convention. They gave slight consideration in July, 1864, to the legality of this unusual procedure, which later had ominous consequences for the army, Louisiana, and presidential Reconstruction.[26]

24. For results of the election see Taylor, *Louisiana Reconstructed*, 30; Banks to Lincoln, February 25, 1864, in *Official Records*, Series III, vol. IV, 133–34.

25. Lincoln to Michael Hahn, March 15, 1865, in *Official Records*, Series III, vol. IV, 182.

26. The most thorough account of the convention is McCrary, *Lincoln and Reconstruction*, 253–67.

Soon after the convention sat for its first meeting, Confederate forces defeated General Banks's army in north Louisiana. Grand strategy, as planned by President Lincoln and Major General Henry W. Halleck, called for the Red River campaign of 1864 to be one in a series of successes on all fronts for Union arms that might end the war in that year. Instead, Confederate General Richard Taylor trounced Banks at Mansfield and forced the northerners to retreat to the lines held at the start of the campaign, still leaving a considerable portion of Louisiana in Confederate hands.[27]

Upon hearing the results of the campaign, Lincoln, with Grant's approval, decided to appoint a new field commander in the Southwest. The president chose Major General Edward R. S. Canby, a West Point graduate and Mexican War veteran, to command the new Military Division of West Mississippi, which included Arkansas, the Texas coast, and all of Louisiana west of the big river. Banks remained in a subordinate capacity as commander of the Department of the Gulf. Canby assumed command on June 9, 1864, and focused his attention primarily on field operations.[28]

Meanwhile, Lincoln ordered Banks to prepare an election for state legislators, congressmen, and ratification or rejection of the new constitution. On September 5 Louisiana conducted its fourth election under military supervision since 1862. The constitution was approved by a six-to-one margin, and the voters selected three congressmen and a new state legislature. After the election, the president ordered Banks to Washington to lobby in Congress for the acceptance of Louisiana's congressmen and the recognition of the new state constitution. He remained there for six months.[29]

To replace Banks as commander in the Department of the Gulf, Lincoln chose Major General Stephen A. Hurlbut, a native South Carolinian who had moved to Illinois, where he prospered as a lawyer and Republican politician. He had led volunteers at Shiloh and later commanded the Memphis garrison under Major General William T. Sherman. Upon taking command, Hurlbut attempted to increase his powers and immediately ran afoul of Governor Hahn. For example, Hurlbut placed restric-

27. Ludwell H. Johnson, *Red River Campaign: Politics and Cotton in the Civil War* (Baltimore, 1958), 128–62.

28. Halleck to E. R. S. Canby, May 7, 1864, in *Official Records*, XXXIV, Pt. 3, pp. 491–92; Max L. Heyman, *Prudent Soldier: A Biography of Major General E. R. S. Canby, 1817–1873* (Glendale, Cal., 1959), 206–233.

29. Lincoln to Banks, August 9, 1864, in Basler (ed.), *Works of Lincoln*, VII, 486; McCrary, *Lincoln and Reconstruction*, 267–69, 282.

Edward R. S. Canby

tions on gambling halls and required licenses for all houses of prostitution in the Crescent City. Moreover, he closed all amusement and gaming places on Sundays. Governor Hahn objected to Hurlbut's orders and claimed that the army had needlessly invaded the domain of civil government. The real core of the dispute was the status of Louisiana's government. In a letter to Canby's headquarters, Hurlbut called Louisiana's civil government "an experiment liable to be cut short at any time by military orders." Until "approved and received by Congress," the state was "wholly within the scope of martial law." For his part, Canby recognized the need for both practical and political judgment when dealing with Louisiana's peculiar government, supported as it was by the president. But Canby concluded that "all attempts at civil government, within the territory declared to be in insurrection, [were] the creation of military power, and of course subject to military revision and control."[30]

The presidential election of 1864 confirmed the opinions of the two military commanders. Lincoln received Louisiana's electoral votes, but when it became clear that the president did not need them to be reelected, Congress neglected to count these votes, casting great doubts on the validity of Louisiana's government. Canby and Hurlbut continued to operate a military government rather than implementing the Constitution of 1864. Governor Hahn's powers were so weak that he could not fill vacancies on a public works commission, and Hurlbut did so instead. If wartime Reconstruction was to succeed, an end to bickering was imperative. Lincoln wanted Louisiana "into proper practical relations with the nation." The president concluded that "much good work [was] already done, and surely nothing can be gained by throwing it away." Unfortunately for Lincoln and his followers, however, a majority of Congress did not find "much good work" in Louisiana. In February, 1865, after heated debate over the issues, the national legislature refused to seat the Pelican State representatives. Presidential Reconstruction remained incomplete.[31]

In spite of this setback, Louisiana Free State leaders behaved as if it

30. Capers, *Occupied City*, 117–18; Futrell, "Military Government in the South," 191; Stephen A. Hurlbut to AAG C. T. Christensen, October 22, 1864, Canby to Hurlbut, October 29, 1864, both in *Official Records*, XLI, Pt. 4, pp. 412–13.

31. Taylor, *Louisiana Reconstructed*, 54; Lincoln to Hurlbut, November 14, 1864, Lincoln to Canby, December 12, 1864, both in Basler (ed.), *Works of Lincoln*, VIII, 107, 164; Hahn to Hurlbut, and reply, both December 1, 1864, in *Official Records*, XLI, Pt. 4, pp. 735–38. See also Amos E. Simpson and Vaughn B. Baker, "Michael Hahn: Steady Patriot," *Louisiana History*, XIII (Summer, 1972), 229–53.

were only a matter of time before Congress accepted Lincoln's ideas on restoration. Governor Hahn quit the anomalous governorship, and the Louisiana legislature elected him to a vacant seat in the U.S. Senate. The solons refused Hahn admission, however, just as the representatives had turned down Louisiana's congressmen-elect, and without the influence of either office, Hahn's importance faded. James Madison Wells replaced "Senator" Hahn as governor of Louisiana on March 4, 1865, and quickly gauged the shifting political winds in the state. Returning Confederate veterans had about them an air of determination; an unquenched defiance remained in the hearts of many ex-soldiers. Slavery was gone, and the Confederates understood this. Yet they refused to admit that the social fabric woven over so many decades in the South had been irrevocably ripped apart. Southern leaders, Wells among them, knew that, unless Congress passed extraordinary legislation to deprive the Confederates of their voting rights, these veterans were the constituency of the future.[32]

After Wells had been in office a few days, General Hurlbut permitted him to appoint Dr. Hugh Kennedy mayor of New Orleans. Kennedy was the first civilian to hold the office since the military had arrived in 1862. The mayor's pro-Confederate sympathies soon became evident. Wells, who had at first associated with the Moderates, gradually gravitated toward the Conservatives. By the time the war was in its final agonies, he had become the neo-Democrat governor of the southern state that had been longest under Federal occupation.[33]

General Hurlbut unsettled matters further when he decided to resign from the army. Obviously, Louisiana needed a new commander. Canby had recently been concentrating his efforts on the capture of Mobile, Alabama, which eventually fell on April 12. He knew that Louisiana needed evenhanded leadership with emphasis on firmness. Lincoln disappointed Canby, however, by reassigning Nathaniel Banks to the Pelican State.[34]

Before Banks reached New Orleans, exhilarating and shocking news struck the country. On April 9, 1865, the Army of Northern Virginia, led by General Robert E. Lee, surrendered at Appomattox. A few days later, as the North celebrated, John Wilkes Booth mortally wounded President

32. Walter M. Lowrey, "The Political Career of James Madison Wells," *Louisiana Historical Quarterly*, XXXI (October, 1948), 1,023; Michael Perman, *Reunion Without Compromise: The South and Reconstruction, 1865–1868* (Cambridge, 1973), 3–53.

33. Taylor, *Louisiana Reconstructed*, 58–59; Lowrey, "Career of Wells," 1,024–30.

34. Canby to Ulysses S. Grant, March 5, 1865, XLVIII, Pt. 1, p. 1,092, SO No. 132, AGO, March 18, 1865, XLVIII, Pt. 1, p. 1,206, Hurlbut to Canby, April 23, 1865, XLVIII, Pt. 2, p. 163, all in *Official Records*.

Lincoln in Ford's Theater. An uneasy feeling gripped many northerners as Andrew Johnson, a former Democrat and former slave-owner from Tennessee, was sworn in as president. The new chief executive was heartened by the surrender of General Joseph E. Johnston's tired Confederates in North Carolina. Only one major southern field force, General Edmund Kirby Smith's army in Louisiana and Texas, then remained.

Meanwhile, Banks resumed command of the Department of the Gulf on April 22. Following Hahn's resignation, Banks had to work with a new governor who showed himself at odds with the government Banks had patched together over many months. Wells's conservative appointees displeased Banks, and he replaced several of them, including Mayor Kennedy, with army officers and cooperative civilians. Kennedy protested his removal, and Canby allowed him to be reinstated over Banks's lame objections. Banks thereupon resigned from the army. He remained in Louisiana for several months, practicing law and seeking support for the Moderates, but his impact was negligible, and his advice was often disregarded. Finally, in disgust, Banks returned to Massachusetts in September, 1865.[35]

Banks had failed both as a general and as a director of Reconstruction. Actually, his failure as a Reconstruction leader can be attributed, in part at least, to his military defeats. Had Banks overwhelmed the Confederate armies and occupied the rest of Louisiana, he could have followed a firmer program of reconstruction. Instead, he combined Lincoln's directives with his own moderate labor program, and relaxed Butler's restrictions, expediently endeavoring to cement Confederate sympathizers to an uncertain alliance of Unionists. The result was an ineffectual civil government dominated by the army. Indeed, so long as the war lasted, most white Louisianians were unlikely to cast aside their loyalty to the Confederacy. Until the Union army conquered most of the state and even afterwards, army generals would make most of the political decisions in Louisiana. In fact, Banks watched professional soldiers grapple with postwar problems, and he could easily have concluded that the challenges of Louisiana politics were no easier for West Pointers to master than they had been for him and Butler.

35. GO No. 42, Dept. Gulf, April 22, 1865, *ibid.*, XLVIII, Pt. 2, pp. 156–57; Kendall, *History of New Orleans*, I, 297; Harrington, *Fighting Politician*, 166–69.

CHAPTER II

The Seed of the Rebellion

The month after Banks resigned, on May 26, 1865, the last Confederate soldiers in Louisiana capitulated to General Canby, and those in Texas surrendered on June 2. The War of the Rebellion had ended. In view of this fact, it appeared that Americans could turn their full attention to Reconstruction. However, General in Chief Ulysses S. Grant concluded that "before all the seed of the rebellion can be regarded as crushed out" the French armies of Emperor Napoleon III must be expelled from the Republic of Mexico.[1]

Invading Mexico in 1861, the French had seated Austrian Archduke Maximilian on the throne of a new "empire." The United States, caught in the throes of Civil War, had been unable to stop this violation of the Monroe Doctrine. Making matters worse, Maximilian had established cordial relations with the Confederacy. But by May, 1865, the situation had changed. Large veteran American armies stood ready to drive Maximilian from Mexico if he would not leave voluntarily.

Putting aside questions of Reconstruction for the moment, General Grant considered several officers for the tasks of protecting the Rio Grande frontier and possibly invading Mexico. For several reasons, he selected Major General Philip Henry Sheridan. Born to Irish immigrants on March 6, 1831, in New York, Sheridan had spent his boyhood in Ohio. In 1848 he had received an appointment to the Military Academy at West Point. Swarthy, mustachioed, with closely trimmed, receding hair, "Little Phil" stood only five feet, five inches tall, but he was an aggressive fighter. In fact, he was naturally combative; after fighting with a cadet sergeant, Phil had been suspended for a year from West Point and was graduated in 1853. But he was an instinctive horseman, a skilled tactician, and an inspiring leader. Sheridan had revamped and spurred the Cavalry Corps of the Army of the Potomac to victory over Jeb Stuart's

1. Ulysses S. Grant to Philip H. Sheridan, August 13, 1865, in *Official Records*, XLVIII, Pt. 2, p. 1,180.

hearty Confederates. Later, Grant had ordered him to lay waste the rich Shenandoah Valley, "Breadbasket of the Confederacy." Sheridan's soldiers put the fertile fields to the torch, so that, as the saying went, even a crow had to carry its own rations when flying over the valley. This smashing campaign made Sheridan a hero in the North. Whatever Sheridan lacked in height, he made up in grit: he was a determined—even ruthless—combat soldier. Moreover, friendship bound Grant and Sheridan, a comradeship built upon mutual respect and nurtured through battles from Lookout Mountain to Appomattox. Little more than a month after the surrender ceremonies there, Grant ordered Sheridan to command the vast domain of the Military Division of the Southwest.[2]

"Little Phil" and Grant saw eye to eye on the problem of French forces south of the Rio Grande, and Sheridan ordered his staff to prepare elaborate plans for an invasion of Mexico. Grant had given him plenty of troops for the task. More than 30,000 soldiers had been ordered to Louisiana and Texas, in addition to the 25,000 troops that Canby already commanded in the Bayou State and the 12,000 men in Arkansas under the command of General Joseph J. Reynolds. In early June, Sheridan established his headquarters in New Orleans and made an inspection tour of his division.[3]

Soon conflicts caused by overlapping commands developed. This was a vexing problem that Sheridan and other officers had experienced during the Civil War. Sheridan's Military Division of the Southwest included all of the area west of the Mississippi River and south of the Arkansas River, roughly consisting of southwest Arkansas, the Indian Territory, Texas, and most of Louisiana. However, Louisiana also belonged to Canby's Department of the Gulf, which additionally contained Mississippi, Alabama, and Florida. Canby never hindered the operation of the division, but he sometimes responded to Sheridan's orders with the tone of an equal rather than a subordinate. Therefore, Sheridan requested outright control over Canby's department. In July, 1865, the War Depart-

2. Richard O'Connor, *Sheridan the Inevitable* (Indianapolis, 1953), 18–38 and *passim*. Grant to Sheridan, May 17, 1865, *ibid.*, 476. Originally, Grant also ordered him to defeat Kirby Smith, but the Confederate surrendered to Canby before Sheridan arrived in the Southwest.

3. Grant to Sheridan, May 31, 1865, Sheridan to John A. Rawlins, June 4, 28, 1865, all in *Official Records*, XLVIII, Pt. 2, pp. 691, 767, 1,014; Manuscript Returns, Dept Gulf, June, 1865, Records of the Adjutant Generals Office, in RG 94, NA; Carl C. Rister, *Border Command: General Phil Sheridan in the West* (Norman, 1944), 9, 11; William L. Richter, "The Army in Texas During Reconstruction, 1865–1870," (Ph.D. dissertation, Louisiana State University, 1970), 43–47.

ment responded by creating a new conglomerate called the Military Division of the Gulf, composed of Indian Territory, Arkansas, Mississippi, Florida, Texas, and Louisiana, but eventually this unwieldy arrangement was discarded, and the division was reduced to Florida, Texas, and Louisiana. Sheridan held supreme command over all troops in these three states. Canby, who had previously directed a department with four states, commanded hereafter in only one, Louisiana.[4]

Adjusting the command arrangements to his liking, Sheridan seldom intervened in Louisiana Reconstruction during the following weeks. He devoted his main attention to the Texas frontier. He and Grant frequently communicated about the French forces in Mexico and their ties to the defunct Confederacy. After reading a letter from Sheridan at a cabinet meeting on July 14, 1865, the president and his advisors discussed the possibility of war because of the Mexican crisis.[5]

In the meantime, Sheridan left General Canby to enforce martial law in Louisiana and wrestle with the sticky political questions of military government. Born in Kentucky and educated in Indiana, Edward Richard Sprigg Canby had been a professional soldier since graduating from the Military Academy in 1839. During the Rebellion, he campaigned in New Mexico Territory and held various staff assignments before being ordered to replace Banks in Louisiana. From his record, it appears that diligence was Canby's outstanding trait; he was noted neither for tactical brilliance nor mesmerizing personality. Instead, contemporaries remarked about his professional demeanor and obliging nature. Square-jawed, hiding large ears under a fringe of hair, but disdaining sideburns, Canby had little about his person to mark him as extraordinary.[6]

Since 1862 the army, as a matter of course, had dominated Louisiana's politics and economy. Canby had no preconceptions about restoration, but he had inherited a variety of de facto powers from his predecessors, Butler and Banks. Martial law was commonplace throughout the South, but the army had not given its generals any clearly defined mission. Sol-

4. GO No. 95, AGO, May 17, 1865, Sheridan to Rawlins, July 3, 1865, GO No. 1, MilDivGulf, July 17, 1865, all in *Official Records*, XLVIII, Pt. 2, pp. 475, 1,042, 1,087; GO No. 59, AGO, August 6, 1866, in Philip H. Sheridan Papers, Manuscript Division, Library of Congress.

5. Many of the Sheridan-Grant exchanges, June through August, can be found in *Official Records*, XLVII, Pt. 2, pp. 875–1,192; Howard K. Beale (ed.), *Diary of Gideon Welles* (3 vols.; New York, 1960), II, 332–33. See also Jack A. Dabbs, *The French Army in Mexico, 1861–1867* (The Hague, 1963).

6. Ezra J. Warner, *Generals in Blue: Lives of the Union Commanders* (Baton Rouge, 1964), 67–68.

diers worked intimately with treasury agents and other bureaucrats, who carried out the important task of confiscating cotton and other property owned by the Confederate government. Butler had started the confiscation of Confederate holdings, but Banks relaxed enforcement of the Confiscation Act of 1862. Working under this law, special agents of the Treasury Department seized millions of dollars worth of derelict property. Benjamin F. Flanders, the Radical political leader, became one of the most active treasury agents, collecting more than five million dollars worth of materials for the Federal government. Assigned by the provost marshal, soldiers routinely protected confiscated property both in transit and at storage depots.

Canby believed that the trouble caused by cotton outweighed the value of the revenue it brought to the government. The "cotton question in Louisiana," Canby told Secretary of War Edwin M. Stanton, was "hopelessly complicated by the frauds of speculators," not to mention the conflicting interests of grasping treasury agents and despairing planters, and the resulting confusion was demoralizing for the army. Canby favored returning cotton to local planters who presented reasonably honest claims, thus disassociating the cotton business from the army and the Treasury Department, but his opinion went unheeded.[7]

A new organization, the Bureau of Refugees, Freedmen, and Abandoned Lands, supplemented the activities of the army and the Treasury Department. On March 3, 1865, Congress established the Freedmen's Bureau to find jobs for blacks, regulate their wages, and take legal action against employers who mistreated freedmen. Bureau agents distributed food to the needy of both races and provided assistance to Negro schools. The army enforced the rules and regulations of the bureau, and military officers served as assistant commissioners (i.e., state superintendents) and local agents. In August, 1865, Brigadier General Absalom Baird replaced a civilian appointee as Louisiana's superintendent. Eventually, six of Louisiana's eight superintendents were generals on active duty. By late 1866 the army had only a few officers attached to the Freedmen's Bureau, although many former soldiers were employed as local agents.[8]

7. James G. Randall, *Constitutional Problems under Lincoln* (rev. ed.; Urbana, 1964), 275–92; White, *The Freedmen's Bureau*, 48; SO Nos. 90 and 93, Dept Gulf, April 23, 27, 1866, DeWitt Clinton to Benjamin F. Flanders, May 1, 1866, all in Benjamin F. Flanders Papers, Department of Archives and Manuscripts, Louisiana State University Library, Baton Rouge; E. R. S. Canby to Edwin M. Stanton, August 12, 1865, in Dept Gulf, vol. 79, "Records of U.S. Army Continental Commands," RG 393, NA.

8. White, *The Freedmen's Bureau, passim.*

For a short period of time, until early 1866, Canby divided Louisiana into two parts to facilitate administration of the state. The Eastern District, commanded by Major General Thomas W. Sherman, included all land east of the Mississippi River, plus the Bayou Teche country roughly from Bayou Goula to New Iberia and south to Brashear City (later renamed Morgan City). District headquarters were in New Orleans. The Western District comprised the rest of the state. Its headquarters were located in Alexandria, a town General George A. Custer's wife, Elizabeth, thought was "a hundred years behind the times." The site of a cavalry training depot as well as district headquarters, Alexandria experienced a short-lived economic boom.[9]

In contrast, the economy of New Orleans suffered because the city attracted the unemployed and destitute of both races. Throughout 1865 and 1866 the army quartermaster and commissary regularly distributed food, wood, and coal to the city's needy, including those living in charitable institutions such as the New Orleans Orphan Asylum, the Convent of the Good Shepherd, and the Soulé Asylum for Colored Children. The army made similar distributions in other towns.[10]

Soldiers also acted in the arena of business and finance. Butler, Banks, and Canby had appointed army officers to serve on or supervise the boards of directors of local financial institutions. By January, 1866, Canby had returned most of the banks to civilian directors, but a few remained under military control until later that year. A similar situation existed with regard to several railroad companies, which had been managed for several months by panels of military officers. Canby held meetings with businessmen, civil officials, and the army officers who temporarily operated the railroads to determine when and how the lines would return to private control.[11]

Thus, in the summer and fall of 1865, Canby was directing Louisiana's military government in a manner similar to that of Banks, with the exception that Canby was trying to decrease the army's responsibilities in

9. GO No. 4, Dept La and Texas, July 20, 1865, in *Official Records*, XLVIII, Pt. 2, pp. 1094–95; Elizabeth B. Custer, *Tenting on the Plains* (New York, 1887), 74.

10. Wickham Hoffman to Robert A. Cameron, June 7, 1865, in Lafourche Dist, Letters Recd, Hoffman to CO, Baton Rouge, November 30, 1865, E. R. Ames to Quartermaster, Dept La, December 6, 1865, both in Dept Gulf, vol. 79, George Lee to C. G. Sawtelle, August 30, October 1, 1866, in Dept Gulf, vol. 258, all in RG 393, NA.

11. Grant to Canby, June 3, 1865, in *Official Records*, XLVIII, Pt. 2, p. 743; Canby to James Forsyth, November 30, 1865, in Dept Gulf, vol. 79, GO No. 2, Dept La, January 5, 1866, in GO, Dept La, both in RG 393, NA. See also Stephen A. Caldwell, *A Banking History of Louisiana* (Baton Rouge, 1935), 97–98.

some matters. Actually, no orders from Sheridan, the War Department, or the president had changed ultimate military control over civilians. In a few parts of the state, the army's protection was still necessary, but Canby found it impossible to patrol every parish thoroughly. There were scattered reports of lawless, armed riders—called jayhawkers—who attacked and robbed defenseless civilians. General Thomas Sherman issued a circular in the Eastern District warning all "Guerillas and Jayhawkers" to cease their criminal activities or suffer the severest consequences. Colonel Charles L. Norton, commanding the 98th U.S. Colored Infantry at New Iberia, believed that "beyond the immediate vicinity of U.S. troops lawlessness prevails to a great extent." Canby sent out additional patrols, and gradually, as returning Confederate veterans found jobs, jayhawking disappeared.[12]

Canby's responsibility to protect civilians seemed clear, but his relationship with Governor Wells was still ill defined. Secretary of War Stanton instructed Canby "not to interfere with its [the state's] action further than it may be necessary for the peace and security of the department." The governor believed that he ought to be allowed to exercise his full executive powers since the war was over, and he asked Canby to remove all civil officials appointed by military orders prior to March 4, 1865, the day Wells was inaugurated. The governor claimed that many of these appointees had disobeyed his directives and obstructed the orderly return to complete civil control of the state government. This was true, at least from Governor Wells's point of view. Many of the Unionist or Republican officeholders had used Wells's pro-Confederate sympathies to justify disregarding his orders. After giving the matter "serious consideration," Canby responded that all military appointments would stand unless the governor demonstrated just causes for removal, such as malfeasance or some criminal offense. Of course, incumbents could be turned out if authorized elections were held. Otherwise, Canby advised, any substitution had to be ordered by himself, not by Wells. The general did not mean to discourage the governor by this reply. In fact, Canby said he hoped to give up "all questions of civil administration," and pledged to help Wells resume the full powers of the governorship.[13]

12. Cameron to Hoffman, June 26, 1865, in *Official Records*, XLVIII, Pt. 2, p. 997; Circular No. 1, July 11, 1865, Dist Eastern La, Charles L. Norton to B. B. Campbell, June 30, 1865, in Letters Recd, Lafourche Dist, both in RG 393, NA.

13. Stanton to Canby, May 28, 1865, J. Madison Wells to Canby, June 10, 1865, Canby to Wells, June 19, 1865, all in *Senate Executive Documents*, 39th Cong., 1st Sess., No. 2, p. 56, 54–55.

However, by September, 1865, Canby grew worried about the number of ex-Confederates that Wells was bringing into his administration.
In his executive capacity, Wells appointed several temporary officeholders in parishes that had been under Confederate control at the time
of the surrender in May. Most of the governor's appointees were ex-
Confederates. Moreover, Wells had become the fulsome friend of Hugh
Kennedy, the pro-Confederate mayor of New Orleans. Canby recognized that Wells was preparing a base of support for himself in the statewide elections to be held in November.[14]

To solidify his position, Wells ordered a new registration of voters
throughout Louisiana, based on President Johnson's Proclamation of Pardon and Amnesty. Johnson's proclamation, which formed the basis for
his own executive plan of southern Reconstruction, recognized the Wells
government in Louisiana, similar ones begun under Lincoln in Tennessee
and Arkansas, and Virginia's reestablished pro-Union government. For
each of the remaining seven states of the former Confederacy, Johnson
appointed a provisional governor, who would register voters and see that
the state adopted a new constitution that abolished slavery, repudiated
Civil War debts, and voided the ordinance of secession. The president
gave pardon and amnesty "to all persons who participated in the . . . Rebellion." Upon taking a simple oath of future loyalty to the United
States, similar to the one in Lincoln's old 10-percent plan, a former Confederate could regain his political rights. Johnson excluded civil and dip-
lomatic officials of the Confederate government, all governors and other
important southern civil officials, and all officers above the rank of colonel in the army or lieutenant in the navy from the amnesty just as Lincoln
had. He also excluded anyone who "voluntarily participated in said rebellion and the estimated value of whose taxable property [was] over
$20,000," thereby snubbing his longtime personal foes, the rich southern
planters. However, anyone initially denied a pardon could receive one if
he applied individually to the president. Thousands of Confederate veterans took advantage of Johnson's proclamation, and under its mandate,
Wells called for voters to register.[15]

Louisiana's prospective voters took the required loyalty oath, registered to vote, and prepared to support Wells in November. The old Mod-

14. Canby to Carl Schurz, September 8, 1865, *ibid.*, 56; Taylor, *Louisiana Reconstructed*,
61.
15. James D. Richardson (comp.), *A Compilation of the Messages and Papers of the Presidents, 1789–1897* (10 vols.; Washington, D.C., 1896–1899), VI, 310–312; James E. Sefton,
Andrew Johnson and the Uses of Constitutional Power (Boston, 1980), 108–109.

erate Unionists and the Democrats, once again respectable, both nominated Wells for governor. The old Conservatives nominated former Confederate governor Henry Watkins Allen, who was self-exiled in Mexico and in no position to protest his unwanted candidacy. These contestants left the Radicals without a candidate to support. They showed their dissatisfaction by holding a separate, unauthorized election for a special "territorial delegate" to Congress, explaining that, because Louisiana had seceded, it must be considered a territory once again. The Radicals planned to allow blacks to vote in this "territorial" election. Their nominee for "delegate" was a flamboyant ex-Union colonel from Missouri named Henry Clay Warmoth.[16]

Canby ordered the commanders of all posts and camps to be prepared "to keep the peace at the polls," but his forebodings were not justified. The election of November 6 passed off quietly, and Wells easily retained the governorship. So many former Confederates won seats in the legislature that its next meeting promised to look like a convention of regimental reunions. The disgruntled Radicals tried to be jubilant over Warmoth's election to the ineffectual position of "territorial delegate," but although Warmoth favorably impressed Republican leaders in Washington, Congress predictably refused him a seat. Warmoth was only twenty-two years old, but he was popular with unenfranchised Louisiana blacks, whose support had propelled him into the front ranks of southern Republican politicians.[17]

Governor Wells called the legislature into special session on November 23. The most important laws passed in this session were statutes, known collectively as the black code, that forced Negroes to work as agricultural labor and closely restricted their personal rights. The black code, patterned in part on Banks's old labor program, attempted to put blacks under the planters' supervision, instead of that of the Freedmen's Bureau and the army. Although Canby did not like the laws, he did not believe that he was empowered to void acts of the state legislature. One by one, other southern states each passed similar black codes, which northerners commonly viewed as devices to reenslave the freedmen.[18]

Wells's victory in the recent canvass gave the state an elected governor and legislature, but the New Orleans municipal government continued

16. Taylor, *Louisiana Reconstructed*, 65, 71–77.
17. *Ibid.*, 73, 78; GO No. 59, Dept La, October 21, 1865, in GO, Dept La, RG 393, NA.
18. Taylor, *Louisiana Reconstructed*, 39, 100–101; Eric L. McKitrick, *Andrew Johnson and Reconstruction* (Chicago, 1964), 10.

to operate through a combination of military appointees and elected officials. Therefore, in January, 1866, Sheridan authorized Canby to schedule a municipal election for the Crescent City. Sheridan was more concerned about a border skirmish involving American troops and, thus, left the preparations and conduct of the balloting entirely up to Canby. Since he was aware that Mayor Kennedy and some of the city councilmen had been receiving graft and were involved in a variety of illegal activities, Canby, quite logically, prohibited any incumbent from selling city property or granting any work contracts until after the election, which he set for March 12. Wells claimed that Canby's interference infringed on the legitimate operation of the city's business. Nevertheless, Canby's order was obeyed.[19]

Wells, Kennedy, and their cronies nominated Joseph H. Moore for mayor. Moore's opponent was none other than former Mayor John Monroe, who had held the position when General Butler arrived in 1862. Monroe won the election, but because he had not been pardoned by President Johnson, Canby refused to allow him to take office. Instead, the general appointed the chairman of the city council acting mayor. Undaunted, Monroe immediately applied for the necessary pardon, and President Johnson obligingly complied with the request. On May 15, 1866, Monroe again became mayor of New Orleans. Canby then faced a state government dominated by men who only a few months before had been opposed to the Union.[20]

During all of the foregoing events, Sheridan had concentrated mainly on activities in Mexico and along the Rio Grande, but in the fall of 1865 he began to concern himself with Reconstruction matters. In October, for example, he had issued a directive concerning freedmen to each of his departmental commanders. Thenceforth, civil authorities would be allowed to make decisions pertaining to Negroes that did not violate the ex-slaves' rights. The army and the Freedmen's Bureau could intervene in contested cases, but Sheridan concluded that it was "hard to enforce martial law after war has ended and a form . . . of civil Government" exists. In November Sheridan wrote to President Johnson, suggesting

19. Sheridan to Grant, January 5, 1866, Sheridan to Cyrus B. Comstock, March 2, 1866, in Ulysses S. Grant Papers, Manuscript Division, Library of Congress (microfilm copy in Louisiana State University Library, Baton Rouge); Heyman, *Prudent Soldier*, 283–85. John Trowbridge, a Massachusetts novelist touring the southern states who visited Sheridan's headquarters in January, 1866, noticed that Sheridan spent most of his time on Mexican matters, rather than southern affairs. See John T. Trowbridge, *A Picture of the Desolated States and the Work of Restoration, 1865–1868* (Hartford, 1868), 402.

20. Heyman, *Prudent Soldier*, 286; Caskey, *Secession and Restoration*, 201–202.

that legislation alone would not solve the South's postwar problems. In the general's opinion, because of the great investment of Yankee capital in the South, the nation needed to "wait and trust to a little time and the working of natural causes" to heal the wounds of civil war.[21]

Gradually, Sheridan had to face a problem that affected his capability to deal with Reconstruction and the border situation. This was the staggering logistical nightmare of mustering out volunteer regiments. Hostilities in the Southwest had ended more quickly than anticipated, leaving dozens of infantry, artillery, and cavalry units under Sheridan's command, with even more regiments on their way from the East. Acting on orders of the War Department, Sheridan had mustered out a few units as early as June, 1865, even if their terms of enlistment had not expired. Impatient volunteers, sweltering in the Texas heat and Louisiana humidity, announced that they had enlisted to fight Johnny Rebs, not police rural towns, chase jayhawkers, guard cotton depots, or patrol the Mexican border. These were jobs for the regular army. Although worried about Maximilian, Sheridan expedited the disbanding of volunteer regiments as much as he dared and requested that regulars replace them. In January, 1866, Grant gave Sheridan permission to discharge any units under his command. In Louisiana from September, 1865, through March, 1866, Sheridan mustered out twenty infantry regiments (fourteen of them black), along with two volunteer cavalry regiments and three artillery batteries. The number of soldiers in the Military Division of the Gulf dropped drastically. By April, 1866, only 19,112 men served in the entire division, as compared to 77,874 in September, 1865.[22]

On April 5, 1866, Napoleon III of France announced that he would gradually remove his troops from Mexico during the next year. Napoleon's decision was proof of the efficacy of the Monroe Doctrine. Secretary of State William Seward's diplomacy, the internal pressure of the Mexican rebels, Sheridan's theatrics on frequent trips to the border, and his widely publicized, but never used, plans of invasion had persuaded the French to withdraw their support for Maximilian. Napoleon's announcement speeded the mustering-out process. General Grant ordered

21. Sheridan to Grant, October 7, 1865, in Grant Papers; Sheridan to Johnson, November 26, 1865, in Autograph Letters, Sheridan Papers.

22. Ida M. Tarbell, "How the Union Army Was Disbanded," *Civil War Times Illustrated*, VI (December, 1967), 4–9, 44–47; Harry W. Pfanz, "Soldiering in the South During the Reconstruction Period, 1865–1877" (Ph.D. dissertation, Ohio State University, 1958), 24–26; Sefton, *Army and Reconstruction*, 261; Manuscript Returns, Dept La, April, 1866, in Records of AGO, RG 94, NA; Grant to Sheridan, January 22, 1866, in Grant Papers; Sheridan to Thomas Vincent, March 1, 1866, in Dept Gulf, vol. 248, RG 393, NA.

Sheridan to muster out more soldiers in Texas and Louisiana, indicating that for all practical purposes the Mexican crisis had ended. But Maximilian refused to abdicate his perilous throne. Because he still feared the "emperor's" disruptive powers, Sheridan made a trip to Texas in April. Later, he warned Grant's chief of staff that the French had "not yet abandoned the idea that they have a strong sympathy in the southern states."[23]

In the midst of these developments, personal and professional antipathy between Sheridan and Canby, which had smoldered for many weeks, flamed into the open. General Canby complained to Sheridan that the present troop level in Louisiana was "scarcely sufficient for the ordinary requirements of the service" even though he well knew that Sheridan had been ordered by the War Department to discharge large numbers of soldiers. Ill feelings had existed between the two generals since July, 1865, when Sheridan had insisted on complete domination of the Gulf area. In February, 1866, Sheridan aggravated the situation by suggesting to Grant that Canby should be mustered out of the army along with several lesser volunteer officers. This snub obviously wounded Canby's pride. Sheridan also criticized Canby for devoting too much effort to civil affairs, an odd complaint from someone who gave only a modicum of his time to this potentially volatile matter. Canby became even more exasperated when he learned that members of Sheridan's staff had investigated the Louisiana provost marshal's office and its actions in the cotton-rich parishes along the Red River. The staff officers uncovered a variety of improper and apparently illegal activities in cotton trading by civilians, some of which had been approved or supervised by the provost marshal. The investigators also accused several plantation owners in the Red River area of mistreating Negroes just as if slavery still existed. Moreover, ex-Confederates routinely persecuted and insulted white Unionists. Finally, an officer described Shreveport, the most important town in northwest Louisiana, in terms befitting a Kansas cowtown. Gambling in all of its various forms appeared to be the town's major industry, the best gambler served as Shreveport's mayor, and the inspector warned that it was "dangerous to be on the streets after dark." Major James Forsyth, of Sheridan's staff, concluded that Union men would be driven from north Louisiana were "it not for the presence of United States troops."[24]

23. Dexter Perkins, *A History of the Monroe Doctrine* (Boston, 1955), 132, 134–35; Sheridan to Grant, April 27, 1866, Sheridan to Rawlins, July 16, 1866, both in Grant Papers.
24. Sheridan to Grant, February 20, 1866, in Grant Papers; Canby to AAG, Mil-DivGulf, March 24, 1866, in Dept Gulf, vol. 80, James Forsyth to Sheridan, January 11,

Appalled by these revelations about north Louisiana, Sheridan advised Canby to correct all discrepancies "at once, even if it requires your own presence in that section." But some weeks later Sheridan informed the War Department that almost everywhere he looked in Louisiana he "found fraud and abuses," which existed because of Canby's inattention. Under the circumstances, one general or the other had to leave the state.[25]

His patience expiring, on May 5, 1866, Canby requested a transfer from Louisiana, ostensibly "on the score of health." A few days later the War Department granted him a temporary leave and ordered him to Washington for consultations with the secretary of war. On May 28 Sheridan replaced Canby as commander of Louisiana with the superintendent of the Freedmen's Bureau, General Absalom Baird.[26]

Upon Canby's departure, Sheridan took a new interest in Louisiana's problems and closely examined various reports from the state's post commanders. Some accounts mentioned contented freedmen hard at work in the fields and civilian officials whose attitude and efficiency in office recently had improved. However, widespread bitterness over the war persisted among much of the white population, and the people were "orderly and respectful through compulsion." One officer reported that "respect for the 'lost cause'" was common, and anyone who showed deference for the army or northern men risked "all social and political relations with their former friends and neighbors." Several officers cited "cases of cruelty to freedmen" in their area. In an unusual incident, two whites in Alexandria tried to persuade a Negro corporal of the 80th Colored Infantry to work in their fields. The regiment's commander arrested the pair and gave "them a good lecture on the altered condition of affairs, and the absurdity of attempting to treat colored soldiers as slaves."[27]

Sheridan strongly concurred with his lieutenants in the belief that the army must remain in Louisiana to protect "Northern capital and Union people," including freedmen. He even thought it best to ask for an additional regular cavalry regiment for mobile patrol duty in the interior of the state. Sheridan believed that over time, with the army alert to prevent

1866, A. D. Nelson, Inspection Report, February 25, 1866, both in Letters Recd, MilDiv-Gulf, all in RG 393, NA.

25. Sheridan to Canby, January 19, 1866, in Dept Gulf, vol. 248, RG 393, NA; Sheridan to Rawlins, April 5, 1866, in Sheridan Papers.

26. Canby to AGO, May 5, 1866, in Dept Gulf, vol. 80, GO No. 50, Dept La, May 28, 1866, in GO, Dept La, both in RG 393, NA; Sheridan to Edward Townsend, May 22, 1866, in Sheridan Papers.

27. *House Executive Documents*, 40th Cong., 2nd Sess., No. 57, pp. 49–51, 131–36 contains reports of post commanders.

racial fighting, the Negro, "by the logic of the necessity for his labor," would gain an important and rightful place in the South. To this end, Sheridan thought blacks deserved and needed voting rights as insurance for their freedom. These beliefs obviously marked Sheridan as an adherent to many of the ideals of the Radical Republicans in Congress. Sheridan publically professed that the great majority of Louisiana's white citizens "earnestly" wanted "a perfect Union with the other states;" but he privately told Republican leader Henry Wilson that southerners would "chafe and be restless for a long time" and that the army needed to remain strong and vigilant.[28]

Events soon confirmed the need for such vigilance. In June, 1866, Radical and Unionist members of the Constitutional Convention of 1864, which had met under the direction of General Banks, attempted to reconvoke the convention. The issue of Negro suffrage had been avoided by the conservative legislatures under Wells, but the time had come when Louisiana Radicals would have no power in the state unless they enfranchised the Negro. To save themselves from political extinction, the Radicals decided that a new constitution must grant voting rights to blacks. Naturally, controversy surrounded the move to revitalize the convention. A preliminary meeting on June 26 lacked a quorum because several of the members, doubting the legality of the procedure, declined to attend. Governor Wells, a remarkable political chameleon, now switched from his pro-Confederate position to a pro-Union one and approved the reconvening of the convention. The governor's support stimulated the gasping convention like a transfusion, and July 30 was set as the date for its next meeting in New Orleans.[29]

With one eye on Mexico, Sheridan undoubtedly watched these proceedings with misgivings. He must have noticed the formation of two distinct factions, one opposed to the convention and the other in favor of it. Just as it appeared that Louisiana had finally captured Sheridan's attention, trouble erupted on the Mexican border again. In late June the important town of Matamoros, under siege for many months, fell to Mexican forces opposing Maximilian. Great excitement rippled through

28. New York *Times*, May 3, 1866; Sheridan to Rawlins June 23, 1866, in Sheridan Papers; Sheridan to Henry Wilson, June 29, 1866, in Henry Wilson Papers, Manuscript Division, Library of Congress. The regiment was not sent.

29. Donald E. Reynolds, "The New Orleans Riot of 1866 Reconsidered," *Louisiana History*, V (Winter, 1964), 5–8; New Orleans *Daily Picayune*, June 27, 1866; Lowrey, "Career of Wells," 1,075–80.

northern Mexico, and rumors reached New Orleans that the Mexican reaction to Matamoros' fall might prevent the planned departure of French
forces from the country. In Sheridan's words, all this added up to "the
diablo to pay." He decided he must go to Texas.[30]

Sheridan's reasons for making this decision are obscure. During his
dispute with Canby, Sheridan had been backing into the job of Reconstruction. Apparently, he realized that it was a significant responsibility
with national implications. Then suddenly he chose to charge off, leaving
New Orleans troubled by Radical agitation and demands for black suffrage. For months the general had been fascinated by the prospects of the
border: a full-scale war seemed unlikely, but the president might order
him to lead a punitive expedition across the Rio Grande, giving him another chance to command troops in the field. Evidently, Sheridan believed that Reconstruction could wait until he returned.

The tension that had been evident among the New Orleans population
increased after Sheridan's departure. It was apparent to the Radicals that
the old quorum of seventy-six delegates could not be obtained by the
Constitutional Convention until after the election of new members on
September 3, still more than a month away. Nevertheless, the Radicals
decided to hold another meeting on July 30, but clearly this gathering had
no more chance for making binding legal decisions than the unproductive June 26 session. On the evening of July 27 the Radicals staged a mass
rally in New Orleans to promote the cause of black rights.[31]

The highly charged atmosphere of New Orleans made General Absalom Baird's position no easier. Baird's credentials, which looked substantial, made him seem a good choice for department commander. Appointed from his home state of Pennsylvania, he had been graduated
from West Point in 1849. At the outbreak of the Civil War, he occupied a
comfortable chair in mathematics at his alma mater. Baird held staff positions with the Army of the Potomac, but later wartime assignments sent
him to field duty. He commanded a division in Sherman's "march to the
sea" and won the Medal of Honor for gallantry in an engagement near
Atlanta. Despite his conduct in this phase of the war, staff work seemed
more suitable to Baird, and he ably administered the Louisiana Freed-

30. Sheridan to Grant, July 3, 1866, Sheridan to Rawlins, July 16, 21, 1866, all in Grant
Papers.
31. Reynolds, "New Orleans Riot," 8–10; John R. Ficklen, *History of Reconstruction in
Louisiana (Through 1868)*, Johns Hopkins University Studies in Historical and Political Science, XXVIII (Baltimore, 1910), 157.

men's Bureau. He sported a large mustache and side whiskers, adding a touch of flair to his otherwise academic appearance.[32]

The reconvoked convention created an extraordinary crisis for Baird, the army, and the national government. Though not a Radical, Baird saw no reason to prevent the reconvocation unless he received orders to that effect from his superiors in Washington. Andrew Herron, Louisiana's attorney general, feared that Baird might send troops to guard the convention and thereby give it the sanction of the federal government. Consequently, he petitioned the state courts to declare the old assembly illegal and sought an injunction to stop it from meeting. In the meantime, Herron and Louisiana's lieutenant governor, Albert Voorhies, both conservatives bitterly opposed to political advancement for the Negro, telegraphed President Johnson, asking him to clarify Baird's position. Actually, they hoped that Johnson would order the army to remain uninvolved.[33]

Johnson's reply cheered Voorhies and Herron, but did not really specify orders for Baird. "The Military," declared the president, "will be expected to sustain and not to obstruct or interfere with the proceedings of the Courts." Heartened by this response, the state officials took the telegram to General Baird, who, they now supposed, must see his proper course of action and prevent the convention from meeting. The general remained unyielding: the convention could meet unless he received orders to the contrary. Nevertheless, however firm he had appeared to the Louisiana politicians, Johnson's message had given Baird doubts, and he dispatched an inquiry about the whole matter to Secretary of War Stanton. For reasons never fully explained, Stanton did not answer Baird's plea for orders. Therefore, after July 28 Baird had to act on his own initiative.[34]

On July 29 Baird alerted the small New Orleans headquarters staff of about twenty officers and men and warned the commander of the 860-man 1st Infantry Regiment to prepare his troops to move at a moment's

32. Warner, *Generals in Blue*, 15–16; John A. Baird, Jr., *Profile of a Hero: Absalom Baird, His Family, and the American Military Tradition* (Philadelphia, 1977), *passim*.

33. Albert Voorhies and Andrew Herron to Andrew Johnson, July 28, 1866, in Andrew Johnson Papers, 1865–1869, Manuscript Division, Library of Congress (microfilm copy in Louisiana State University Library, Baton Rouge).

34. Johnson to Voorhies and Herron, July 28, 1866, Absalom Baird to Stanton, July 28, 1866, both *ibid*. McKitrick is especially good on this point in *Johnson and Reconstruction*, 423–24. See also Benjamin P. Thomas and Harold M. Hyman, *Stanton: the Life and Times of Lincoln's Secretary of War* (New York, 1962), 489, 495–97.

notice. The regiment occupied Jackson Barracks, located three miles below the city. In July, 1866, more troops were stationed in Louisiana than in any other southern state except Texas. Baird commanded more than five thousand men in Louisiana, of which two thousand were within a few hours call of New Orleans. The rest garrisoned nine forts and camps across the state. The situation did not appear to warrant a call for outside assistance. In fact, the general might have averted any violence had he stationed a few companies of soldiers at a point within the city from which they could be ordered in a few minutes to quell any trouble. But a tragic flaw marred Baird's protective plans for the convention. Somehow he misunderstood the proposed meeting time. The Radicals intended to convene at noon, but the general thought the appointed hour was 6:00 P.M.[35]

Early on the morning of July 30 the newspapers printed a special proclamation from Mayor John Monroe to the people of New Orleans. Monroe advised everyone "to avoid with care all disturbances and collision" and particularly warned young people against gathering near the Mechanics' Institute, site of the convention. Instead of calming the city's population, Monroe's proclamation read like a prediction of things to come.[36]

Dozens of young men and boys congregated near the Mechanics' Institute that morning. Nevertheless, at noon the Radicals met as planned, but the quorum they had hoped for did not materialize. At about this time a column of two hundred Negroes marched through the city in support of the convention. When the blacks arrived at the hall, they confronted the large crowd of whites already gathered there. The two mobs exchanged taunts and shouts. Paving stones and other missiles filled the air, several shots rang out, and a bloody riot resulted.

Once the fighting began, large numbers of uniformed police quickly appeared. The police normally carried only nightsticks, but this group was armed. They began firing their pistols indiscriminately into the mass of milling blacks. Then the combined force of uniformed officers and white civilians charged the Mechanics' Institute in an attempt to drive the convention members and their supporters from the building. The white

35. Sefton, *Army and Reconstruction*, 261, 85–87, *House Reports*, 39th Cong., 2nd Sess., No. 16, pp. 5–6, 440–64.

36. New Orleans *Bee*, New Orleans *Crescent*, New Orleans *Times*, New Orleans *Daily Picayune*, all July 30, 1866.

mob overpowered and outgunned the blacks and the Radicals, who possessed only a few firearms and fought mainly with clubs and brickbats.[37]

The New Orleans headquarters commander sent an aide to inform Baird of the tumult downtown, and the general immediately dispatched the soldiers from Jackson Barracks. Because of the poorly chosen route, the infantry took twice the normal time to reach the city. When they finally reached the institute at 3:00 P.M., the riot had almost run its course. The official report of the U.S. Army surgeon in New Orleans listed thirty-eight persons killed in the fighting, thirty-four of whom were blacks. The surgeon recorded 146 men wounded, including 119 blacks, 10 policemen, and 17 white civilians. Only one white rioter was killed.[38]

The riot stigmatized President Johnson's lenient Reconstruction plan and shattered his hopes for an early return of southern representatives to Congress. All of those involved had to share the blame for the riot. The Radicals convened an assembly of dubious legality whose existence only invited public wrath. General Baird laid incomplete plans and was poorly prepared to deal with the unsettled conditions either to protect the convention or to prevent a riot. Secretary of War Stanton neglected the cry for help from one of his generals in a dangerous situation. City and state officials, particularly Mayor Monroe, Governor Wells, and Lieutenant Governor Voorhies, failed to maintain order. Many New Orleans citizens disregarded the advice of the mayor and vigorously engaged in mob violence. The police lost all discipline and helped to turn the streets into a battlefield. Because he needlessly left the state at a troubled time General Sheridan bore considerable responsibility for the riot. Even Mayor Monroe concluded that Sheridan had chosen an "imaginary and bloodless campaign" in Texas rather than face the predicament in New Orleans.[39]

While Sheridan hurried back to Louisiana, Baird worked to improve the unstable situation in the Crescent City. On the evening of July 30, he declared martial law and ordered two infantry regiments and a battery of

---

37. New Orleans *Bee, Crescent, Times* and *Daily Picayune,* all July 31, 1866; Reynolds, "New Orleans Riot," 11–13.

38. *House Reports,* 39th Cong., 2nd Sess., No. 16, pp. 12, 16, 19, 464–66; Caskey gives a highly partisan southern account of the riot in *Secession and Restoration,* 223.

39. Interview with Monroe, New Orleans *Daily Picayune,* March 5, 1871. The impact of the riot has been well chronicled by historians. See, for example, John Hope Franklin, *Reconstruction after the Civil War* (Chicago, 1961), 63–65, Philip H. Sheridan, *Personal Memoirs of P. H. Sheridan* (2 vols.; New York, 1888), II, 251.

artillery into New Orleans to ensure against any further disturbances. On July 31 Baird formed a special military commission to investigate the riot. When Sheridan arrived in the capital on August 1, he found little to do. Rumors predicted new troubles, but Sheridan felt confident that, because he had returned, no other violence would occur. "You need feel no uneasiness about the condition of affairs here," Sheridan wired Grant, "I think I can arrange matters without difficulty." [40]

Later, however, Sheridan told Grant that there was "quiet in the city, but considerable excitement in the public mind." Nevertheless, the army would not interfere with the state government unless it became absolutely necessary. Sheridan described the Radical leaders of the convention as "agitators and revolutionary men," but as he obtained more information, he began to suspect that high Louisiana civil officials had conspired to cause the riot. He accused the mayor and the city police of behaving "in a manner so unnecessary and atrocious as to compel one to say it was murder." Accordingly, Sheridan remained suspicious of Lieutenant Governor Voorhies and Attorney General Herron, and suggested that the civil government would benefit from the removal of Mayor Monroe and Governor Wells. In the meantime, Sheridan decided to continue martial law indefinitely while the military commission investigated the riot. Grant replied that martial law should be continued, but discouraged the idea of removing elected officials. [41]

President Johnson, meanwhile, impatient over the daily onslaught in the newspapers against his Reconstruction policies, demanded all of Sheridan's information on the riot. Sheridan's reply came in a long coded telegram. Contrary to his first impressions, Sheridan had come to believe that Louisiana officials had not planned the violence against the convention. The recall of this assembly had created much ill will among opposing political groups, and he gave this as the "immediate cause" of the fighting. Sheridan could not specify who fired the first shot because of the confusion in the opening minutes of the riot, but he accused Mayor Monroe of inflaming hostile feelings and failing to supervise the police force. Sheridan concluded by citing Governor Wells for his complete lack of leadership during the crisis. By August 21, some of the soldiers who

40. Baird to Stanton, July 30, 1866, Sheridan to Grant, August 1, 1866, both in Johnson Papers.
41. Sheridan to Grant, August 2, 1866, *ibid.*; Sheridan to Grant, August 1, 3, 1866, Grant to Sheridan, August 3, 1866, all in Sheridan Papers.

had been brought into New Orleans after the riot returned to their base at Jackson Barracks, but elements of the 1st Infantry remained in the city as a precautionary measure.[42]

During August, Sheridan and his staff temporarily turned their attention away from politics to an unusual military task. On July 28, 1866, the War Department had authorized six regular regiments of black troops, the 38th, 39th, 40th, and 41st Infantry and the 9th and 10th Cavalry. Adjutant General Edward D. Townsend in Washington ordered that the Department of the Gulf serve as the recruiting and training area for the 39th, 41st, and 9th. Aside from blacks who had served with George Washington's revolutionary army, the creation of these regiments marked the first time in American history that blacks had been officially inducted into the regular army. Recruits were found by enlisting recently discharged Negro volunteers or by transferring some black volunteers who had not yet been mustered out. Special recruiting advertisements also encouraged new enlistees. After forming and training, the 41st occupied posts in Texas, the 9th joined its sister regiment, serving in Texas and at other points on the western frontier, and the 39th remained on duty for several years in Louisiana.[43]

Since returning to New Orleans after the riot, Sheridan had become dissatisfied with Absalom Baird's performance of his duties—dissatisfied to the point where a change in state commanders was expected. Newspaper editorials also had criticized Baird for his awkward handling of recent events. Later, the New Orleans *Republican* characterized Baird as "an amiable but irresolute subordinate." On September 8, perhaps under pressure from Sheridan, Baird resigned his post as assistant commissioner of the Louisiana Freedmen's Bureau. Sheridan took his place temporarily. On September 17, Baird received an extended leave from the service and left the state.[44]

After Baird departed, Brevet Major General Joseph A. Mower of the recently formed 39th Infantry, who had served as chairman of Baird's

42. New York *Tribune*, July 31–August 7, 1866; Johnson to Sheridan, August 4, 1866, Sheridan to Johnson, August 5, 6, 1866, all in Johnson Papers; New Orleans *Daily Picayune*, August 22, 1866.

43. Edward Townsend to Sheridan, August 4 and 12, 1866, in Sheridan Papers; Baton Rouge *Tri-Weekly Advocate*, August 17, 1866; New Orleans *Daily Picayune*, September 23, 1866; Sefton, *Army and Reconstruction*, 96; William H. Leckie, *The Buffalo Soldiers: A Narrative of the Negro Cavalry in the West* (Norman, 1967), 7–11.

44. New York *Times*, August 2, 8, 1866; New Orleans *Daily Picayune*, September 5, 1866, New Orleans *Republican*, September 6, 1867.

commission, submitted the panel's report on the riot. The document revealed no new facts. Ardent opposition to the Convention of 1864 by a majority of New Orleans citizens was listed as the cause of the riot. Contradictory testimony and statements of witnesses left the officers unable to say who fired the first shot on July 30. Without equivocation, Mower roundly condemned the unwarranted participation in the riot by the police.[45]

In view of the military commission's report, it came as no surprise that Sheridan selected General Mower to command Louisiana. Mower was originally from Vermont, and though not a college graduate, he had attended Norwich Academy for two years. He had fought as an enlisted man in the Mexican War and in 1855 obtained a lieutenant's commission in the regular army. In the Civil War, he had earned a praiseworthy record and eventually commanded a corps. Most of his duty was in the western theater, including several months in Louisiana, but he had also served in Sherman's "march to the sea." Sheridan once commented that Louisiana needed a "decisive and shrewd" commander, and both he and Grant believed Mower fitted the description admirably.[46]

Following Mower's appointment, Sheridan made two trips to Texas, one in November and the other in December. Texas reconstruction politics, Indian attacks on settlers, and Maximilian's moribund dictatorship all demanded his attention. In fact, earlier Sheridan had wanted to devote more time to Texas affairs, but he told Grant that he felt "handcuffed to New Orleans." By December Sheridan had returned to the Crescent City, celebrating Christmas there for the second time. Then in January, with prospects of momentous political activities in the offing for the spring session of Congress, Grant summoned Sheridan to Washington for consultations.[47]

Several factors influenced the attitude of the next Congress. Southerners had committed a variety of indiscretions, such as the riots in Memphis and New Orleans, the adoption of the black codes, and the election of former important Confederate military and civilian leaders. President Johnson's own actions, including his frequent vetoes of Republican bills, also had been detrimental to the South, which looked to

45. *House Executive Documents*, 39th Cong., 2nd Sess., No. 68, pp. 36–43.

46. Sheridan to Grant, October 4, November 3, 1866, in Grant Papers; Grant to Sheridan, November 3, 1866, in Sheridan Papers; Warner, *Generals in Blue*, 338–39.

47. Sheridan to Grant, August 22, 1866, in Sheridan Papers; Richter, "Army in Texas," *passim*; Sheridan to Grant, January 19, 1867, in Grant Papers.

Johnson for leadership and advice. These factors helped to produce a strong Republican showing in the fall congressional elections. When the new Congress met, the Republicans would have more than enough strength to pass legislation over presidential vetoes. Republicans found common ground in opposition to Johnson, a desire to protect the political and economic gains of the Civil War years, and the belief that some form of protection should be accorded to the southern freedmen. Therefore, the Republican party was unified enough to pass a series of laws that gave Congress great influence over the Reconstruction process.

The Republicans passed the first of these acts on March 2, 1867, over President Johnson's veto. The law declared that the southern governments fostered by the president were provisional and held no legal authority. Congress divided the South into five military districts, whose commanders had to be either brigadier or major generals. These generals, once selected by the president, would hold all power over civilian governments and courts. The law also required the southern states within these districts to draft new constitutions in constitutional conventions. The right to vote for delegates to these conventions was granted to all adult males, except those disfranchised for service to the Confederacy. Furthermore, each of these new constitutions must contain a provision that, in effect, would enfranchise black men. When the voters in each state accepted the new constitution, they were to elect a new governor and legislators. After the legislature ratified the proposed Fourteenth Amendment to the Constitution, the state's congressmen would be considered for readmission to Congress. Upon readmission, military control would end, and the duly elected civil authorities would resume their proper roles. The passage of this law was a watershed in Reconstruction, for by it the congressional Republicans seized the initiative from the executive, and the army became the agent of social and political change.[48]

The traumatic circumstances of the post–Civil War era appeared to demand such a radical departure from the usual American process of debate and compromise. What other part of the government but the army could compel a large percentage of the population to abide by laws many considered repugnant? The Civil War had been fought to keep the Union from breaking apart. Now the army was called on to help bind the nation together. Thereafter, assignment to the South made some soldiers long

48. Sefton, *Army and Reconstruction*, 109–110.

for the trans-Mississippi plains where Indian fighting at least had some glory, some professional reward or recognition. Service in the South held the prospect of neither glory nor honor, only duty of the most confusing and frustrating kind—military government.

CHAPTER III

Sheridan Sees His Duty

On March 11, 1867, President Johnson chose the generals for the newly organized southern military districts. With the exception of John Pope, the appointees all had served varying lengths of Reconstruction duty in the South. Pope had been commanding part of the Indian-fighting army west of the Mississipppi River. He came east and took charge of the Third Military District, containing Georgia, Alabama, and Florida, the last state formerly a part of the old Division of the Gulf. Sheridan retained command of Louisiana and Texas, together called the Fifth Military District. The extent of Grant's influence on Johnson's choices is not known. Sheridan had spoken out in favor of Radical Republican ideas, and Grant's desire to retain the experienced general in the Southwest was probably decisive for Johnson.[1]

In General Order No. 1, March 19, 1867, Sheridan emphasized to the people of Louisiana and Texas that their civil governments were provisional. The army held veto power over all actions of civilian officials in the states. A carefully worded paragraph of the order stated that there would be no wholesale removals of civilian officeholders. However, if any individual should "impede . . . or delay" reorganization of the states according to the new Reconstruction law, his action would be considered grounds for dismissal from office. By this order, Sheridan warned state politicians to expect that the laws of Congress would be rigorously enforced.[2]

On March 23 Congress overrode another of President Johnson's ineffective vetoes and passed the second Reconstruction Act. This act set September 1, 1867, as the date when all qualified southern voters should be registered. Furthermore, the statute contained details of election procedures, which had been omitted from the first law enacted earlier in the

1. Grant to Sheridan, March 13, 1867, in Johnson Papers; Sefton, *Andrew Johnson*, 154.
2. New Orleans *Daily Picayune*, March 20, 1867; Sheridan, *Personal Memoirs*, II, 252.

month. For example, the number of delegates to the constitutional conventions scheduled for the fall was to equal the membership of the largest branch of the state legislature in 1860. Each district commander would decide how to apportion the delegates in the states he commanded and then designate the site of the convention.[3]

As Sheridan interpreted the congressional Reconstruction Acts, he was vested with the power, and even the obligation, to make adjustments in Louisiana's government. On March 27 he removed from office several of his antagonists, Mayor John Monroe of New Orleans, Attorney General Andrew Herron, and Judge Edmund Abell. All three men had irritated Sheridan by their actions before, during, and after the New Orleans riot of the previous July. Monroe was by implication responsible for the violent behavior of the city's police force. Herron had failed to indict white citizens who had violated the law. Abell had refrained from prosecuting those who had been arrested, and had publicly advocated that New Orleans residents ignore the Reconstruction laws. Sheridan believed that the shortcomings of these men justified replacing them with Republicans who would properly carry out the laws.[4]

Removal of important public officials did not enhance Sheridan's reputation with Louisiana's citizens, and the New Orleans *Daily Picayune* feared that this act presaged a "sweep from office of the civil authorities of State and city." Nevertheless, the general, having endured months of antagonism and inactivity on the part of these functionaries, saw no other course to take. Grant supported and approved Sheridan's actions, believing that under the circumstances the removals were necessary. But Grant misjudged the result of Sheridan's order if he thought it would produce quieting effects on Louisiana.[5]

In late March and early April, Sheridan took action regarding elections and voter registration. On March 28 he issued a directive that prohibited all local elections in Louisiana until the state complied with the provisions of the congressional laws. Until the district commander scheduled new elections, all local officeholders were to continue in their positions. Next, Sheridan turned his attention to the registration of voters for the upcoming fall election. He formulated his plans early so that the Fifth District

3. Sefton, *Army and Reconstruction*, 113.
4. GO No. 5, 5 MD, March 27, 1867, Sheridan to Grant, April 19, 1867, both in *Senate Executive Documents*, 40th Cong., 1st Sess., No. 14, pp. 240, 201; Sheridan, *Personal Memoirs*, II, 254–55.
5. Grant to Sheridan, March 29, 1867, quoted in Adam Badeau, *Grant in Peace* (Hartford, 1887), 102; New Orleans *Daily Picayune*, March 28, 1867.

would be the first to begin registration. However, the Reconstruction Acts did not clearly specify who was eligible to register. Sheridan asked Grant for "an authoritative decision" on this subject. His request passed in turn through the hands of Grant, Secretary of War Stanton, and the president. Johnson apparently ordered Attorney General Henry Stanbery to formulate a reply that would erode the authority of the Reconstruction Acts. During the interim, Grant advised Sheridan to "go on giving your own interpretation to the law" until Stanbury handed down an opinion.[6]

Meanwhile, as Sheridan and other commanders awaited Stanbery's decisions, uncooperative civil officials continued to worry the generals. For example, General Charles Griffin, commander of the Department of Texas under Sheridan, informed his superior that it seemed that all officeholders in Texas were "disloyal." Griffin advised the "immediate removal" of several officials, particularly Governor James W. Throckmorton. Sheridan had no doubts about the sincerity of Griffin's suggestion. Although he had already removed three important Louisiana officials, Sheridan told Grant that he intended "to make but few removals." However, he stressed, unless Governor Wells and Governor Throckmorton became more responsive to the wishes of Congress, they would have to be replaced by men who would properly enforce federal laws. Grant ordered "that no removals of governors of States be made at present." As for lower ranking officials, he pointedly admonished Sheridan to "make no more removals than you find absolutely necessary" and only for "the grossest disregard of the law." Nevertheless, if a serious situation demanded the removal of an official, Grant firmly believed that district commanders had the power to act, even if it was not spelled out in the Reconstruction Acts.[7]

Apparently hoping that he would not have to remove any other officeholders, Sheridan continued with his registration plans in Louisiana. He initiated his program in New Orleans on April 12, earlier than any other southern state. Registration went well in the big city. The 20th Infantry Regiment dispatched several companies to towns in north Loui-

6. Sheridan to Grant, April 1, 1867, in *House Executive Documents*, 40th Cong., 1st Sess., No. 14, p. 193; SO No. 7, 5 MD, March 28, 1867, Grant to Sheridan, April 7, 1867, both in *Senate Executive Documents*, 40th Cong., 2nd Sess., No. 209, pp. 25, 196. See also Sefton, *Andrew Johnson*, 156.

7. Charles Griffin to George A. Forsyth, March 28, 1867, Sheridan to Grant, April 2, 1867, both in *House Executive Documents*, 40th Cong., 1st Sess., No. 20, pp. 62–63; Grant to Sheridan, April 3, 1867, in *Senate Executive Documents*, 40th Cong., 1st Sess., No. 14, p. 195; Grant to Sheridan, April 5, 1867, in Autograph Letters, Sheridan Papers.

siana to prepare for the arrival of the registrars, while the 1st and 39th Infantry Regiments supplied soldiers to protect registrars in the southern part of the state. On April 20 Sheridan appointed civilian registrars of voters in forty-seven parishes. Ten army officers served as supervisors-at-large to ensure that registrars complied with all laws, and as a safeguard against improper registrations, Sheridan tried to appoint at least one ex-Union officer to each registration board. On April 21 statewide registration began. Sheridan anticipated no violence during the process, and he told Grant that his "only desire [was] to faithfully carry out the law as a military order." In this statement to his friend, Sheridan revealed his basic concept of the whole Reconstruction process.[8]

Sheridan followed Grant's advice and carried out his own ideas on enrolling voters. Although Attorney General Stanbery had not made a ruling, Sheridan's orders disfranchised hundreds of Louisianians. The Reconstruction Acts prohibited unspecified "executive and judicial" officers of the Confederacy from registering. Sheridan interpreted the phrase broadly to include governors, mayors, judges, policemen, school board members, city councilmen, and even public auctioneers. Apparently, men who had held these and various other offices, knowing they could not register, made little attempt to do so. Many other men in the New Orleans area and, presumably, elsewhere were unable to register on the standard grounds that they had performed Confederate military service.[9]

Sheridan carefully supervised the progress of voter enrollment. During one of his frequent investigations into the procedure he found that Thomas A. Boylan, an aide to the New Orleans chief of police, had intimidated Negroes and prevented them from registering. Sheridan suspended Boylan from duty, and when full inquiry revealed the gravity of his offense, Boylan was removed from the police force.[10]

8. Sheridan to Grant, April 6, 21 (quotation), 1867, in *House Executive Documents*, 40th Cong., 1st Sess., No. 20, pp. 79, 83; Sheridan to Grant, April 12, 1867, in Johnson Papers; Sheridan to Grant, April 19, 1867, SO No. 23, 5 MD, April 20, 1867, both in *Senate Executive Documents*, 40th Cong., 1st Sess., No. 14, pp. 202, 244; Monroe *Ouachita Telegraph*, April 25, May 16, 1867; AAAG Lewis Spalding to COs 20th and 1st Infantry regiments, April 15, 1867, Spalding to CO, 39th Infantry, May 5, 1867, all in Dept Gulf, vol. 274, RG 393, NA.

9. For example, see "Memorandum of those refused registration, April 24–July 31, 1867," (manuscript in Joseph P. Hornor Collection, Department of Archives and Manuscripts, Louisiana State University Library). See also Sheridan to Grant, April 16, 1867, with attached memoranda, in *Senate Executive Documents*, 40th Cong., 1st Sess., No. 14, p. 200; Sefton, *Army and Reconstruction*, 130; William A. Russ, "Disfranchisement in Louisiana (1862–1870)," *Louisiana Historical Quarterly*, XVIII (July, 1935), 573.

10. New York *Times*, April 29, 1867; SO No. 25, 5 MD, April 23, 1867, in *Senate Executive Documents*, 40th Cong., 1st Sess., No. 14, p. 246.

Following Boylan's dismissal, Sheridan acted to reorganize the New Orleans Police Department. Actually, the general had been dissatisfied with the department since its participation in the 1866 riot. He nullified a state law passed in 1866 designed to prevent former Federal soldiers from becoming policemen. The law held that all applicants for the police force must have resided in New Orleans for five years. Sheridan issued an order that set the residency requirement at only two years. Furthermore, he required that thenceforth at least half of the 250-man police force be ex-Union soldiers. Sheridan now believed that he had a reliable municipal police department.[11]

The next conflict between the civil government and the army arose over the Louisiana levee board. This important state agency spent large sums of money to construct and repair the levees along the Mississippi River. A committee of the state legislature had appointed the board of levee commissioners, bypassing Governor Wells in the process. When the legislature appropriated four million dollars for levee construction and maintenance, Wells abolished the legislative board and selected his own panel of commissioners. Each board questioned the legality of the other and asked Sheridan to decide which was the legitimate one. Rather than choose between them, he formed an entirely new board and discharged both of the others. This, of course, left neither side satisfied, but the politicians involved did notice that Sheridan had not taken sides in the dispute. The New Orleans *Crescent* described Sheridan's appointees as "well-known citizens" who were expected to do their jobs "honestly and conscientiously." The New Orleans *Times* criticized Wells and concluded that Sheridan's actions were "justified by the facts" of the situation.[12]

After the levee board controversy, Sheridan kept an even closer watch on all levels of state politics. When fifty St. Landry Parish citizens accused their sheriff, James T. Hays, of dereliction of duty, Sheridan removed Hays and selected a new sheriff. Next, he announced the appointment of a Republican politician to fill a vacancy on the Pointe Coupee Parish police jury. He also deposed a New Orleans clerk of court for issuing false certificates of U.S. citizenship to foreigners and ex-Confederates

11. SO No. 33, 5 MD, May 2, 1867, in *House Executive Documents*, 40th Cong., 2nd Sess., No. 342, p. 165; Sheridan, *Personal Memoirs*, II, 261-64.
12. SO No. 34, 5 MD, May 3, 1867, in *House Executive Documents*, 40th Cong., 1st Sess., No. 20, p. 16; Sefton, *Army and Reconstruction*, 140–41; Sheridan, *Personal Memoirs*, II, 265–66; New Orleans *Times*, May 14, 1867; New Orleans *Crescent*, May 4, 1867.

to enable them to sign the voting rolls. Registration proceeded quietly, though many whites refused to register because they opposed the Reconstruction Acts.[13]

In May the general had to deal with a crisis in New Orleans that might have caused another riot. Horse-drawn streetcars had operated for many years in the Crescent City with separate coaches for white and black passengers. Blacks used cars marked with a painted star, and white patrons rode in unmarked vehicles. The segregated streetcars had proved troublesome to Generals Butler, Banks, and Canby, none of whom could resolve the problem. Trouble began in April when blacks insisted on traveling in the cars usually reserved for whites. Policemen forced blacks to continue riding in the "star cars," which prompted Negroes to stage a more unified protest against the discriminatory practice. Eventually the army became involved when black soldiers of the 39th Infantry also attempted to ride unrestricted on the urban transit. At this point Sheridan intervened. He held a meeting with the officers of the streetcar companies and persuaded them to integrate their businesses. Sheridan "advised the companies to make no distinction" between white and black passengers in the future, implying that he would, otherwise, ban the horse-drawn coaches from the streets.[14]

Sheridan had won one of the earliest victories for black civil rights in the South, but his motive had been practical rather than idealistic. Like most of the white men of his time, Sheridan believed that the colored races were inferior to the white. However, he would not tolerate a situation where U.S. soldiers, regardless of color, were discriminated against on public conveyances. If he had permitted the star cars to continue operating, it would have been damaging to troop morale. Moreover, such a circumstance might lead to an outbreak of violence in his district. These practical reasons, rather than ardent civil rights fervor, dictated the general's course of action.

Black success in the star car issue may have stimulated protests on

13. "Loyal Citizens of Opelousas and St. Landry" to Sheridan, April 18, 1867, in 5 MD, Letters Recd, Civil Affairs, RG 393, NA; SO No. 35, 5 MD, May 4, 1867, Sheridan to Grant, May 4, 1867, both in *Senate Executive Documents*, 40th Cong., 1st Sess., No. 14, p. 251; SO No. 41, 5 MD, May 11, 1867, in *House Executive Documents*, 40th Cong., 2nd Sess., No. 342, p. 166.

14. See Roger A. Fischer, *The Segregation Struggle in Louisiana, 1862–1877* (Urbana, 1974), 30–38, and Fischer, "A Pioneer Protest: The New Orleans Street Car Controversy of 1867," *Journal of Negro History*, LIII (July, 1968), 219–33. In neither of his writings does

other questions. While Sheridan was inspecting voter registration preparations in Texas from May 12 to May 17, a large crowd of black ste-
vedores assembled on the New Orleans riverfront and conducted a wild-
cat strike for better working conditions and higher wages. Before any
violence occurred, General Joseph Mower went down to the docks and
spoke to the excited blacks. Supported by a troop of mounted cavalry,
Mower urged the workers to return to their jobs and threatened to bring
in troops and break the strike if the strikers caused the slightest disturbance. Mower's speech and the knowledge that more soldiers had been
ordered to the scene persuaded the crowd to disperse, and the strike
ended. Sheridan returned to a peaceful city.[15]

On May 24, 1867, Attorney General Stanbery announced his decision
on voting qualifications. In Stanbery's judgment, state "executive and judicial officers" who had sworn to support the U.S. Constitution in the
line of their jobs and then accepted an office under the Confederacy
should be disqualified. Stanbery also excluded high state officials, such
as governors, state treasurers, state attorney generals, and other upper-
echelon leaders. Compared to Sheridan's blanket order, the Attorney
General's ruling disfranchised only a few men. Like Sheridan, district
commanders John Pope and Edward O. C. Ord had already issued directives that disfranchised a variety of citizens whom the attorney general
considered qualified to vote. Adjutant General Edward Townsend urged
the district commanders to use Stanbery's ruling as the basis for registration. However, the military officers regarded his ruling as only an opinion without force of law. Each district commander continued to make his
own decisions on voting qualifications.[16]

A few days after Stanbery issued his opinion on voting, Sheridan
learned that the Radicals and blacks in New Orleans were planning a
public parade for May 29. Since the organizers anticipated a large crowd,
Sheridan decided to bring several companies of soldiers into the city and

---

Fischer stress Sheridan's ultimate influence over the crisis. See also New Orleans *Daily Picayune*, May 7, 8, 1867; New Orleans *Republican*, May 7, 1867; Sheridan to Grant, May 10,
1867, in *House Executive Documents*, 40th Cong., 1st Sess., No. 20, p. 75.

15. Sheridan to Grant, May 11, 18, 1867, in Grant Papers; New York *Times*, May 18,
1867; New Orleans *Bee*, May 17, 1867; New Orleans *Daily Picayune*, May 12, 14, 17, 1867;
Edward Heath to George Hartsuff, May 15, 1867, in 5 MD, Letters Recd, RG 393, NA.

16. Sefton, *Army and Reconstruction*, 130–31; Stanbery's opinion is in *Senate Executive
Documents*, 40th Cong., 1st Sess., No. 14, pp. 275–87; Edward Townsend to Military District Commanders, June 20, 1867, in James D. Richardson (comp.), *Messages and Papers*, VI,
552–56.

place them near the parade route. Additional units remained on alert at Jackson Barracks. On the evening of May 29 a crowd of one thousand blacks and a few of their white supporters enjoyed a torchlight procession in downtown New Orleans. Sheridan believed it was "the largest political assembly" in Louisiana since 1865. Negroes "paraded the streets without the slightest disturbance," wrote Sheridan to Grant. The rally concluded peacefully, making it unnecessary to call the troops stationed nearby.[17]

Sheridan had successfully weathered another crisis, but his high-level confrontation with Governor Wells continued. For a month following the levee board dispute, Sheridan tried to tolerate the uncooperative governor. Finally, after many weeks of misunderstanding, Sheridan decided to remove Wells from office on June 3. The removal order offended Wells's sensibilities because it was wedged between two others concerning ordnance inspection and street cleaning. The New York *Times* branded Sheridan's move as the act of an "impetuous cavalry leader, rather than the calm, wise administrator," but Louisiana newspapers generally applauded the removal. Several editors and many politicians had been alienated by Wells's changing political loyalties from pro-Democrat to pro-Republican. The New Orleans *Times*, no friend of the governor, quipped, "All's well that ends Wells." Obviously pleased by Wells's misfortune, the Shreveport *South-Western* declared that whoever replaced Wells would do a better job. Other state newspapers offered similar comments.[18]

Defending his action to his superiors in Washington, Sheridan labeled Wells a "political trickster and a dishonest man" whose "conduct has been as sinuous as the mark left in the dust by the movement of a snake." Wells's "subterfuge and political chicanery" could be tolerated no longer in the Fifth Military District. Wells protested his removal to President Johnson, called Sheridan's action a "usurpation of power," and demanded that he be allowed to remain in the office to which he had been elected. Andrew Herron, the former Louisiana attorney general previously re-

17. Sheridan to Grant, May 30, 1867, in *Senate Executive Documents*, 40th Cong., 1st Sess., No. 14, p. 211; New Orleans *Crescent*, May 30, 1867; AAAG Spalding to W. H. Wood and Maurice Maloney, May 25, 1867, Spalding to Wood, Maloney, and Benjamin Abrahams, May 29, 1867, both in Dept Gulf, vol. 274, RG 393, NA.

18. SO No. 59, 5 MD, June 3, 1867, in Johnson Papers; Sheridan, *Personal Memoirs*, II, 266–67; Lowrey, "Career of Wells," 1090–92; New Orleans *Times*, June 4, 1867; Shreveport *South-Western*, June 12, 1867. See also New Orleans *Crescent*, June 4, 1867; Baton Rouge *Tri-Weekly Advocate*, June 7 and 10, 1867; Alexandria *Democrat*, June 12, 1867.

moved by Sheridan, supported Wells in his fight to stay in office. In a letter to the president, Herron strongly criticized Sheridan and recommended that the general be relieved of his command.[19]

Former state attorney general Thomas Durant, Sheridan's first choice as a replacement for Wells, refused to accept the governorship. Sheridan then appointed Benjamin Flanders, a former treasury agent who had confiscated great amounts of cotton for the federal government after the war. Flanders had been a Louisiana resident for twenty-three years, having come to the state after his graduation from Dartmouth College in 1842. He had served as a Louisiana congressman before the Civil War, but had left the state during the conflict. Returning to New Orleans with the Federal occupation, he resumed his political career as a Radical Republican, but had lost to Wells in the gubernatorial election in 1864. Such ideological opponents as the Alexandria *Democrat* and the New Orleans *Republican* both complimented Sheridan on his choice of a new governor. However, Wells stubbornly refused to surrender his post. The obstinate Louisianian locked himself in the governor's office in the Mechanics' Institute. On June 7 Sheridan's aide, Major James W. Forsyth, personally delivered an ultimatum to Wells: leave the building peaceably or be dragged out. Under this threat, Wells finally relinquished the office, and Flanders moved in the next day.[20]

Meanwhile, the registration of voters that began on April 21 proceeded rapidly. Many whites managed to register in spite of the barriers that Sheridan maintained. The state paid the registrars twenty-five cents for each person who signed the voting rolls. Apparently some registrars accepted the signatures of Confederate veterans and others Sheridan had excluded from eligibility. Blacks had been encouraged to register and, by the end of June, 1867, made up more than half of the 87,941 registered voters. Most Unionists had also signed the rolls. Sheridan had planned to end registration on June 30, but as the other four military districts had been ordered to continue the process until August, the president asked

19. Sheridan to Stanton, June 3, 1867, Sheridan to Grant, June 4, 1867, both in *House Executive Documents*, 40th Cong., 1st Sess., No. 20, pp. 65, 7; J. Madison Wells to Johnson, Herron to Johnson, both June 4, 1867, in Johnson Papers.
20. SO No. 62, 5 MD, June 6, 1867, in Johnson Papers; New Orleans *Times*, June 7, 9, 1867; Shreveport *South-Western*, June 19, 1867; Alexandria *Democrat*, June 12, 1867; New Orleans *Republican*, June 7, 1867; New York *Times*, June 9, 1867; Sheridan to Grant, June 8, 1867, in *House Executive Documents*, 40th Cong., 1st Sess., No. 20, p. 94; Sheridan to Wells, June 7, 1867, in U.S. Army Letterbook, 1867–1868, Fifth Military District Papers, 1867–1868, Duke University Library, Durham.

that Louisiana keep its books open until the same date. In late June, Sheridan informed Grant that registration in Louisiana was nearly complete; continuing it would create "a broad macadamized road for perjury and fraud to travel on." In other words, even more undesirables might find a way to register. Nevertheless, to placate Johnson, Sheridan grudgingly consented to extend registration to mid-July.[21]

Grant advised Sheridan to comply fully with Johnson's request to extend registration until August 1, a course, he said, that would avoid public disclosure of ill will between Sheridan and the president. Grant further suggested that Sheridan should not interpret Stanbery's ruling as an order, but that he should enforce his "own construction of the military bill until ordered to do otherwise." Sheridan, thus persuaded, informed Adjutant General Townsend that the Fifth District would conform to the president's wishes—registration would be prolonged until August 1. Despite Sheridan's belief that the registrars would have little to do after the end of June, thousands flocked to the parish courthouses. Almost forty thousand men signed the rolls between July 1 and August 1, many of whom came forward when they learned that simple service in the Confederate army no longer meant disfranchisement. Registration ended with 127,639 Louisianians on the rolls, 82,907 of them blacks.[22]

On July 19 Congress, over Johnson's veto, passed the third Reconstruction Act. The new law permitted a district commander to remove any civil official in his jurisdiction if he believed that such a move would benefit the district and the process of Reconstruction. Any appeals from politicians so removed were to go to General Grant and Congress for review, bypassing President Johnson. This third act gave registrars final authority over any individual who desired to register. The Radicals included a barb directed at Attorney General Stanbery, a provision that military personnel were not required to obey any "opinion of any civil officer of the United States." This act increased Sheridan's confidence because it confirmed a policy he had followed since April.[23]

21. Sheridan to Grant, June 18 and 21, 1867, Townsend to Sheridan, June 21, 1867, all in *Senate Executive Documents*, 40th Cong., 1st Sess., No. 14, pp. 227, 237, 235–36; Sheridan to Grant, June 22, 1867, in Johnson Papers; Sheridan, *Personal Memoirs*, II, 269–70; Rembert W. Patrick, *The Reconstruction of the Nation* (New York, 1967), 101.

22. Grant to Sheridan, June 24, 1867, in Autograph Letters, Sheridan Papers; Sheridan to Grant, and reply, June 28, 1867, in *House Executive Documents*, 40th Cong., 1st Sess., No. 20, pp. 92–93; Sheridan to Townsend, June 29, 1867, in Johnson Papers; Sheridan to Grant, July 2, August 5, 1867, both in Grant Papers; Ficklen, *Reconstruction in Louisiana*, 191.

23. Sefton, *Army and Reconstruction*, 135–36.

Grant had attempted earlier to cover up the antagonistic relationship between President Johnson and Sheridan, but Sheridan's removal of state officials and his disregard for the opinions of the U.S. attorney general had further irritated the president. When the third Reconstruction Act was passed, Johnson became fearful that Sheridan might become completely unrestrained, and he made it clear how little he trusted the commander of the Fifth District. In July the president sent Brigadier General Lovell Harrison Rousseau to New Orleans as his special representative. Rousseau had no official powers, but Johnson wanted Sheridan to know that he was under observation. For about a month the president received reports on Louisiana conditions from Rousseau.[24]

Not intimidated by Rousseau's presence in Louisiana, Sheridan continued to exercise his authority. On July 30 Sheridan removed James W. Throckmorton, the governor of Texas, whom he considered to be an impediment to Reconstruction. In his place the general appointed a Unionist, Elisha M. Pease, whom Throckmorton had soundly defeated only a few months before in the gubernatorial election. Following the removal of Throckmorton, Louisiana newspapers printed rumors that Sheridan's transfer from the district was imminent.[25]

Undaunted, Sheridan proceeded to reorganize the governments in three Louisiana communities. On August 1 he removed twenty-two New Orleans city councilmen. Evidence indicated that the council had badly mismanaged city finances and increased the city's indebtedness. The editor of the New Orleans *Bee* commended most of the new councilmen chosen by Sheridan and remarked on the "favorable character" of the blacks who had been appointed. On the other hand, the New Orleans *Times* and the *Daily Picayune* disapproved of the new councilmen, especially of Oscar J. Dunn, a prominent black politician. Next, the district commander dismissed the New Orleans treasurer for complicity in the misuse of municipal funds and selected a former army major, J. J. Williamson, to be the Crescent City's new chief of police. Finally, acting on the recommendation of Governor Flanders, Sheridan replaced the mayor and two city councilmen in the town of Lake Charles, and acting on his own, deposed the mayor and board of aldermen of Shreveport.

24. Beale (ed.), *Diary of Welles*, III, 141–42; Lovell H. Rousseau to Johnson, July 24, 1867, in Sheridan Papers; New Orleans *Daily Picayune*, August 20, 1867.

25. Sheridan to Grant, July 20, 23, 1867, both in Sheridan Papers; Sheridan to Grant, August 3, 1867, in Johnson Papers. See also Sefton, *Army and Reconstruction*, 144; New Orleans *Bee* and New Orleans *Republican*, both July 30, 1867; Baton Rouge *Tri-Weekly Advocate*, July 31, 1867; New Orleans *Crescent*, August 1, 1867.

Clearly, Sheridan expected the new officeholders to cooperate with the military government and facilitate Louisiana's reconstruction.[26]

President Johnson viewed all of this activity with increasing alarm. He feared that if the general were not curbed, Sheridan might replace every civil officer in Louisiana and Texas. Johnson had already asked the cabinet members for their opinions on transferring Sheridan out of the Fifth Military District. The cabinet divided equally on the ticklish subject. Meantime, Sheridan's aide-de-camp Major James Forsyth, temporarily visiting in Washington, sent a telegram warning the general of his impending transfer.[27]

Despite this warning, Sheridan struggled over the draft of a memorandum on juries, hoping to have it put into law before he left the state. He believed that jurors should be selected from the state's registered voters, including blacks who had never exercised this responsibility. On the other hand, many whites who had been disfranchised would not be considered for jury duty, previously the exclusive task of their race. Grant agreed with Sheridan that jury members should be picked from the voting lists, but he left this decision to the district commander. Grant strongly recommended that Sheridan plan a schedule for the fall elections. In the event that Sheridan were transferred, the job of beginning a Republican state government would already be started.[28]

On August 17, 1867, after many days of agonizing over the situation, Johnson removed Sheridan as commander of the Fifth Military District. General Grant, then serving as acting secretary of war, told Johnson that the removal of an officer of Sheridan's stature would only encourage southerners to violate the Reconstruction Acts. Taking an extreme stand to defend his old friend, Grant claimed that Sheridan's dismissal was "contrary to the wishes of the American people." The president replied that he had not heard the northern people express such an opinion. In fact, Johnson believed Sheridan's "rule" had "interfered with" the Reconstruction Acts. Another general must be found who would do a better job and repair the disruption in Louisiana.[29]

26. Sheridan, *Personal Memoirs*, II, 270; New Orleans *Times*, August 2, 6, 9, 1867; New Orleans *Bee*, August 3, 6, 1867; New Orleans *Daily Picayune*, August 2, 1867; W. R. Rutland to Flanders, July 9, 1867, in 5 MD, Letters Recd, Civil Affairs, RG 393, NA; New Orleans *Crescent*, August 6, 9, 1867; Shreveport *South-Western*, August 28, 1867.

27. Sheridan to Grant, August 5, 1867, in Grant Papers; Beale (ed.), *Diary of Welles*, III, 149; Forsyth to Sheridan, August 12, 1867, in Sheridan Papers.

28. Sheridan to Grant, August 15, 1867, Grant to Sheridan, August 16, 21, 1867, all in Grant Papers.

29. Executive Order, August 17, 1867, Grant to Johnson, August 17, 1867, Johnson to

Johnson's choice to replace the Radical Sheridan was Major General George H. Thomas, hero of the battle of Chickamauga and commander of the Department of the Cumberland. To get Sheridan out of the South, Johnson intended to assign him to the important Department of the Missouri, where he would replace Major General Winfield Scott Hancock. In turn, Hancock would assume Thomas' command over Kentucky and Tennessee. However, Alexander B. Hasson, an army physician, reported that Thomas was suffering from a liver ailment and recommended that the general retain command of the Cumberland. Johnson concurred with the surgeon's advice and ordered all commanders to hold their posts until further notice. Grant cautioned Sheridan, "Relax nothing in consequence of probable change of commands." Johnson soon made his decision. Since it was inadvisable to transfer Thomas, on August 26 the president simply ordered Sheridan and Hancock to switch commands. Sheridan would proceed "at once" to the Department of the Missouri, and Hancock would report to the Fifth District.[30]

The announcement of Sheridan's removal dismayed and angered the Radical Republicans, who called loudly for the president's impeachment, but it brought mixed reactions from Louisiana's newspapers. Some were glad to see him go. The Alexandria *Democrat* was overjoyed and severely criticized the general's administration in a scalding editorial. The New Orleans *Times* condemned Sheridan's "close adherence to the partisan 'requirements of Congress.'" The Baton Rouge *Tri-Weekly Advocate* judged that Sheridan's rigorous enforcement of "the law entrusted to him" had created a gulf of bitterness between him and the majority of Louisiana citizens.[31]

On the other hand, two prominent New Orleans newspapers viewed Sheridan's removal in a different light. The *Bee* ran a long editorial, remarking that the work of Reconstruction would be done no matter

Grant, August 19, 1867, all in *House Executive Documents*, 40th Cong., 2nd Sess., No. 57, pp. 3, 1–2, 4–6; Beale (ed.), *Diary of Welles*, III, 174; New Orleans *Times*, August 20, 21, 1867; St. George L. Sioussat (ed.), "Notes of Colonel W. G. Moore, Private Secretary to President Johnson, 1866–1868," *American Historical Review*, XIX (October, 1913), 110; Hans L. Trefousse, *Impeachment of a President: Andrew Johnson, the Blacks, and Reconstruction* (Knoxville, 1975), 82, 101–102.

30. A. B. Hasson to Grant, August 21, 1867, Executive Order, August 22, 1867, Grant to Sheridan, August 24, 1867, Executive Order, August 26, 1867, all in *House Executive Documents*, 40th Cong., 2nd Sess., No. 57, pp. 6–7.

31. Trefousse, *Impeachment of a President*, 105; Alexandria *Democrat*, September 4, 1867; New Orleans *Times*, August 28, 1867; Baton Rouge *Tri-Weekly Advocate*, August 28, 1867; see also New Orleans *Daily Picayune*, August 21, 1867, Monroe *Ouachita Telegraph*, August 29, September 5, 12, 1867, Shreveport *South-Western*, August 28 and September 11, 1867.

which general commanded the Fifth Military District; using a "bold style," Sheridan had done the work "promptly," as the Radicals in Congress expected. "For this, then, we must blame Congress and not Sheridan," the *Bee* concluded. The New Orleans *Crescent* considered it "fulsome hypocrisy to pretend that the great majority of our citizens have not looked with aversion and alarm upon the partisan leanings of Gen. Sheridan." Nevertheless, the *Crescent* admitted, he had acted with "candor, directness and vigor," and some of his appointments actually had been "judicious." Therefore, the *Crescent* concluded, "the change of commanders will recall the question, 'whether it were not better to bear the ills we have, than to fly to others that we know not of.'" [32]

Even after he received Johnson's orders directing him to report "at once" to the Indian frontier, Sheridan lingered in New Orleans. Perhaps he intended to remain until Hancock relieved him. Until then, Sheridan calmly proceeded to make adjustments in civil government. He removed the New Orleans surveyor, two city attorneys, and the city coroner for unsuitably performing their jobs and impeding the Reconstruction Acts. He cashiered the New Orleans city controller and the St. Tammany Parish tax collector for improperly handling public funds. Sheridan annulled $103,000 worth of public works contracts on the grounds that they were fraudulent. Learning that a Rapides Parish sheriff had failed to arrest the accused murderer of a black man, Sheridan removed the sheriff from office. Furthermore, he set September 27 and 28 as the dates for the election of delegates to the constitutional convention. Lastly, he drafted the final version of a special order that declared only registered voters were qualified for jury duty. [33]

Then Sheridan received permission from Grant to take a long leave in Washington as soon as he had transferred his headquarters to the West. This was the signal for which he had been waiting. On September 1, Sheridan designated General Charles Griffin the interim commander of the Fifth District. Four days later, controversial "Little Phil" departed for his new assignment on the Missouri. On September 11, he detrained at Fort Leavenworth, Kansas, headquarters of his new department. Hancock yielded the seat of command the following day. Within two weeks

32. New Orleans *Bee*, August 6, 1867; New Orleans *Crescent*, August 20, 1867.

33. Sheridan, *Personal Memoirs*, II, 271–75; SO Nos. 125 and 129, 5 MD, August 24 and 29, 1867, in *House Executive Documents*, 40th Cong., 2nd Sess., No. 342, p. 172; New Orleans *Times*, August 25, 30, 31, 1867; New Orleans *Crescent*, August 21, 23, 25, 28, 30, 31, 1867.

Sheridan began his trip east to Washington, and all across the North big crowds accorded the diminutive general a hero's welcome. At a gala reception in New York he sat as guest of honor. Sheridan was pleased to be back among people who appreciated him.[34]

Unquestionably, Phil Sheridan found it unnatural to shift from the theater of war to the arena of politics. When he first arrived in the Southwest, war, or at least the possibility of a field campaign across the Rio Grande, had distracted him from attending to political matters. However, his idea of the methods that would be needed to carry out Reconstruction had evolved from that June day in 1865 when he first set foot in Louisiana. His military training and experience made Sheridan easily displeased with two things: negligence in the performance of duty and failure to follow orders. By early 1867, Sheridan concluded that "nearly every civil officer within my command was either openly or secretly opposed to the law and to myself." Consequently, he hit upon "only one sensible course to pursue and that was to remove every civil officer who did not faithfully execute the law, or who put any impediment in the way of its execution." Sheridan considered the Reconstruction Acts as valid as any order from a military superior; in April, 1867, he had written as much to Grant. Sometimes generals issued incomplete or unclear orders which lent themselves to interpretation by subordinates. Likewise, Congress at times vaguely phrased a law as it did with regard to the removal powers of a district commander in the Reconstruction Act of March 2, 1867. With no qualms, Sheridan filled in the missing details, granting to himself powers Congress later formalized in the third Reconstruction Act.[35]

Sheridan helped establish the army as the agent by which the Reconstruction Acts would be enforced. Most importantly, if the whole unprecedented process were to succeed, voter registration had to be handled competently and thoroughly. Sheridan did this, giving encouragement to the freedmen and logically putting up as many barriers as possible to former Confederates. Determination to do a thorough job prompted him to investigate suspicious individuals and situations at all levels of Louisiana

---

34. Grant to Sheridan, August 30, 1867, Sheridan to Grant, September 11, 1867, both in Grant Papers; Sheridan, *Personal Memoirs*, II, 275–77; New York *Times*, September 24, 26, 27, 29, October 1, 1867.

35. Sheridan to Grant, April 21, 1867, in *House Executive Documents*, 40th Cong., 1st Sess., No. 20, p. 83; Sheridan to Grant, September 15, 1867, in Sheridan Papers; Sheridan, Report on the 5 MD, September 20, 1867, in *House Executive Documents*, 40th Cong., 2nd Sess., No. 1, pp. 379–80.

politics. Sheridan had definitely failed to grasp the serious implications of
the events leading to the 1866 riot in New Orleans. However, in several
episodes thereafter, such as the levee board dispute and the matter of the
judicious appointments to office, especially the replacement of the con-
fused, uncooperative Governor Wells, Sheridan carried out the laws
fairly, strictly, but not harshly. All the while, he labored under the burden
of knowing that every time he, an army officer, removed or installed a
civil official, he went against a hundred years of American tradition and
law. He replaced administrators who he believed to be genuine impediments to Reconstruction or who had overtly violated federal statutes. He
put men into office whose dedication was needed to make Reconstruction
successful.

But Sheridan found it difficult to make Reconstruction prevail. He
usually dealt with southerners of limited capabilities, men of secondary
quality, mere politicians, not statesmen. The South needed gifted men
during Reconstruction, leaders who knew how to compromise, how to
make the best of an unpleasant situation, and how to adjust to a tremen-
dous change in their society. Louisiana had too few men of this type, and
those few made little impression on the many who took the path of defiance, resistance, and violence. Losing the Civil War had filled these
stubborn, individualistic southerners with sadness, frustration, and hostility. At various times during Reconstruction these complicated emotions inspired hostile actions directed against Sheridan and other soldiers,
who were primarily responsible for the South's defeat and subjugation. It
would have been difficult for any federal commander to receive cooperation from men motivated by such emotions, no matter how discreet, re-
strained, and tactful the officer might have been.[36]

Sheridan believed he saw at least one positive result of his tenure in
Louisiana. He witnessed "some improvement in the tone of the public in
reference to the rights and privileges of the freedmen." It became apparent during the next several years that if the freedmen were to keep these
rights and privileges the army would have to stand guard over them.
However, in a relatively short time Sheridan had integrated New Orleans
streetcars, registered thousands of black voters, and directed them to
serve on juries like any other enfranchised citizen. Moreover, several
blacks had been appointed to public office. Sheridan's orders did not res-

36. Paul H. Buck, *The Road to Reunion, 1865–1900* (Boston, 1937), x, 31–38; Wilbur J.
Cash, *The Mind of the South* (New York, 1941), 106–108, 112–16, 121; Perman, *Reunion
without Compromise,* 3–38.

cue blacks from discrimination and intimidation, but he attempted to lay the groundwork for their participation in democracy.[37]

Shortly before Sheridan left Louisiana in 1867, the New Orleans *Bee* editorialized, "We must blame the General for being too ready to carry out the Congressional measures, and for displaying too much alacrity in its service, but at the same time no man believes he is acting contrary to order[s]." Twenty years later Sheridan wrote in his *Memoirs*, "I simply tried to carry out, without fear or favor, the Reconstruction Acts as they came to me." A modern authority condenses the subject in a similar fashion, "Whatever they [the military commanders] might have thought privately of the federal policy, they enforced it, as was their duty."[38] Philip H. Sheridan carried out his duty as he saw it.

---

37. Sheridan, Report on the 5 MD, September 20, 1867, in *House Executive Documents*, 40th Cong., 2nd Sess., No. 1, p. 379; *House Reports*, 39th Cong., 1st Sess., No. 30, Pt. 4, p. 123.

38. New Orleans *Bee*, August 6, 1867; Sheridan, *Personal Memoirs*, II, 278; Sefton, *Army and Reconstruction*, 253.

CHAPTER IV

Impediments to Reconstruction

Brevet Major General Charles Griffin, who became the interim commander of the Fifth Military District when Sheridan left Louisiana on September 5, 1867, had gained considerable experience in handling Reconstruction in Texas. He had been Sheridan's commander of Texas, with headquarters at Galveston, since November, 1866, and had consistently supported Sheridan's ideas on Reconstruction. Unfortunately, however, Griffin contracted yellow fever on September 12 and died three days later at the age of forty-one.[1]

Griffin's place was taken by Joseph A. Mower, commander of the 39th Infantry and senior officer in Louisiana. Having served in the Southwest since 1865, Mower was familiar with the problems in Texas and particularly Louisiana. He had a brooding countenance, a straight nose separated steady eyes, and he wore a rich full beard that partly hid a firm mouth. Overall, his appearance gave him an air of determination that accorded with his well-earned reputation as an excellent battle-tested division commander during the war. Perhaps his upbringing in Vermont and Massachusetts had influenced his firmly held belief in black rights. In any case, it quickly became apparent that Mower and Phil Sheridan had kindred personalities and shared similar ideas on Reconstruction.

Immediately upon assuming full control of his office, Mower requested that additional troops be stationed in Louisiana to guard against violence in the upcoming election for the constitutional convention. However, since unacclimated troops were particularly vulnerable to yellow fever, which in recent months had caused the death of seven hundred persons in Louisiana, Mower actually wanted permission to postpone the election until the fever abated and reinforcements could be used to protect the polls.[2]

1. William L. Richter, "Tyrant and Reformer: General Griffin Reconstructs Texas, 1865–1866," *Prologue*, X (1978), 224–41.
2. Joseph A. Mower to Grant, September 16, 1867, in Grant Papers; New York *Times*, September 24, 1867.

Joseph A. Mower

The new commander expected election violence in Louisiana because of the excitement evident among all classes of citizens. Increasing numbers of black semimilitary organizations annoyed white citizens by frequent drilling and unnecessary shooting practice. White organizations, styled "gunclubs," intimidated local Negroes, white Unionists, and settlers from the North. For example, Circuit Judge John Ilsley informed Louisiana Supreme Court Justice James G. Taliaferro that a "panic throughout the whole" countryside was preventing government men from traveling in the vicinity of Opelousas. To forestall trouble, Mower issued an order prohibiting any extralegal gatherings of armed men, black or white.[3]

Mower's edict sufficiently quieted the state to enable preparations for the election to proceed on schedule, and the general marshaled his forces to guard against violence during the balloting itself. Mower ordered twelve infantry companies, nine of the 1st Infantry and three of the 39th Infantry, brought into New Orleans. An artillery battery and a cavalry troop accompanied the foot soldiers. Altogether, Mower had more than one thousand soldiers in the capital. Outside of the New Orleans vicinity, 665 men in ten companies of the 20th Infantry were distributed among the important towns of Alexandria, Baton Rouge, Monroe, and Shreveport. The regiment's colonel, West Pointer George Sykes, had served before the war at Fort Jesup, near Natchitoches. Although other officers of the regiment had no previous experience in Louisiana, the 20th acquired a reputation for friendliness and cooperation with the people. For instance, the Shreveport *South-Western* cited the good conduct of the companies assigned to that town, commenting that it had "no cause for complaint" against the soldiers of the 20th Infantry.[4]

Thus, in the event of trouble Mower could depend on three infantry regiments, two troops of the 4th Cavalry, and one battery of the 1st Artillery, a total of 2,400 men. There had been more than 5,000 soldiers in

3. John Ilsley to James G. Taliaferro, September 4, 1867, in James G. Taliaferro and Family Papers, Department of Archives and Manuscripts, Louisiana State University Library, Baton Rouge; GO No. 11, 5 MD, September 16, 1867, in *Appleton's Annual Cyclopedia and Register of Important Events, 1867* (New York, 1868), 462–63; Mower to AAG George L. Hartsuff, September 15, 1867, in Dept Gulf, vol. 274, RG 393, NA; New Orleans *Times*, September 17, 18, 1867.

4. Mower to Grant, September 19, 1867, in Grant Papers; SW, "Annual Report, 1867–1868," in *House Executive Documents*, 40th Cong., 2nd Sess., No. 1, pp. 472–73; George W. Cullum, *Biographical Register of the Officers and Graduates of the United States Military Academy at West Point, New York, 1802–1867* (2 vols.; New York, 1868), II, 62–63; Shreveport *South-Western*, April 17, July 24, 1867.

the state during the previous year, but few reenlistments, the mustering out of the last black volunteer regiments, and the transfer of another regiment had depleted the ranks. However, Grant apparently believed that Mower had enough troops to maintain order, and the reinforcements that Mower had requested earlier were not sent. In 1867 Louisiana ranked third among the southern states, behind Texas and Virginia, in the number of soldiers located within its borders.[5]

Prior to the election, Mower sent out detachments of troops to several parish seats throughout the state with orders to protect the polls and prevent intimidation of the voters. Despite widespread rumors predicting riots, the election on September 27 and 28 passed with only minor disturbances. When the polls closed, more than 75,000 men had voted in favor of a constitutional convention and elected ninety-eight delegates. Slightly more than 4,000 negative votes were cast. The army had done a good job preserving order.[6]

In the days after the election, Mower followed Sheridan's approach to Reconstruction in the Fifth District by issuing orders concerning elections and by removing uncooperative officials. He began by ordering that all Texas jury members be registered voters, copying Sheridan's similar ruling for Louisiana. On the recommendation of Governor Flanders, Mower removed a justice of the peace in St. Charles Parish on October 9. A few days later, Mower removed five members of the Jefferson board of aldermen for violating Sheridan's order prohibiting any elections for public office until the state had drafted a new constitution. The aldermen had passed an ordinance for the election of city officials in Jefferson.[7]

Mower's approach to the state's problems disappointed the New Orleans *Crescent*. In the editor's opinion, the district commander had needlessly dismissed the Jefferson councilmen. Perhaps a more reasonable course would have been to invalidate the improper election and issue a warning reminding the aldermen of Sheridan's order. Local Democrats found it even more disturbing that Mower also removed a sheriff and a

5. SW, "Annual Report, 1868–1869," in *House Executive Documents*, 40th Cong., 3rd Sess., No. 1, p. 310; Manuscript Returns, Dept Gulf, January, 1867, AGO, RG 94, NA; SW, "Annual Report, 1867–1868," 472–73; Sefton, *Army and Reconstruction*, 261.

6. Mower to Grant, September 19, 24, 28, 29, 1867, in Grant Papers; SO No. 116, 5 MD, October 21, 1867, in *House Executive Documents*, 40th Cong., 2nd Sess., No. 342, p. 174; AAG Nathaniel Burbank to COs at Shreveport, Monroe, Alexandria, Vidalia, Baton Rouge, and Amite, September 18, 1867, in Dept Gulf, vol. 274, RG 393, NA.

7. SO No. 151, 5 MD, September 28, 1867, in *House Executive Documents*, 40th Cong., 2nd Sess., No. 342, p. 173; New Orleans *Daily Picayune*, October 10, 17, 1867; SO No. 162, 5 MD, October 15, 1867, in Johnson Papers.

clerk of court in St. John the Baptist Parish on the vague grounds that they were "impediments to Reconstruction" without giving any specific reasons for the removals. In only one month, he had replaced eight public officials.[8]

Meanwhile, the yellow fever epidemic slackened about halfway through October. By November the incidence of the disease among both soldiers and civilians had slowed down considerably.[9] Once the yellow fever had subsided, Louisiana waited expectantly for the arrival of General Hancock. Most citizens expected Hancock to wield his authority less arbitrarily than Mower. Even Sheridan had normally accompanied his removals with explanations.

Mower sought out ways to use his powers of removal and appointment. On November 12 the general appointed a well-known Republican, R. King Cutler, to an Orleans Parish judgeship recently vacated by a resignation. At the same time, Governor Flanders approved the removal of a Jefferson Parish justice of the peace. Within a few days, on November 16, Mower removed Orleans Parish Sheriff Harry Hays, a former Confederate officer, as an "impediment to Reconstruction." Although Sheridan had reorganized the police department, he had not removed Hays. In the same order Mower also deposed an Orleans clerk of court for malfeasance and dismissed three members of the town council of Brashear, but no reasons were given. In the next few days, Mower displaced six more civil officials, including a judge and a state tax collector, calling them "impediments to Reconstruction." Since Sheridan's departure, twenty officials had been removed from office.[10]

For his next political targets, Mower chose higher appointees than constables and city councilmen. Apparently motivated by a desire to finish the process begun by Sheridan, Mower removed Lieutenant Governor Albert Voorhies, the secretary of state, the state treasurer, the superintendent of public education, the state auditor, and yet another tax collector. As before, Mower used the phrase "impediment to Reconstruction" to justify the dismissals. Governor Flanders strenuously objected to this latest flurry of removals, calling them "inexpedient" and noting that some of the new appointees were unsuitable for their posi-

8. New Orleans *Crescent*, October 22, 1867.
9. *Ibid.*, November 1, 1867; Mower to Cyrus B. Comstock, October 21, 1867, in Grant Papers.
10. SO Nos. 184, 188, and 191, 5 MD, November 12, 16, and 20, in *House Executive Documents*, 40th Cong., 2nd Sess., No. 342, p. 177; Mower to Grant, November 17, 1867, in Grant Papers.

tions. The governor broke friendly relations with Mower and suggested that Grant nullify all of his orders since November 10, leaving Hancock to make the ultimate determinations concerning these personnel matters. Grant quickly agreed. He ordered Mower to suspend all of these removals pending the arrival of General Hancock, who would then decide each case individually. The district commander promptly complied with Grant's demand.[11]

On November 23 the constitutional convention opened in New Orleans. Blacks occupied half of the ninety-eight seats in the convention. Many of these black delegates were well educated, and most were respected businessmen and landowners. The delegates selected Judge James Taliaferro as chairman. Under Taliaferro's direction the convention took four months to draw up a new constitution for the state.[12]

As the convention was beginning its deliberations, General Hancock was expected to arrive in New Orleans at any moment. Disregarding the fact that Hancock would soon take command, Mower threw aside caution and good judgment and requested specific authority from Grant to remove Governor Flanders. Mower complained that the governor had blocked the removal of officials who were not properly doing their jobs. But before Grant replied, General Hancock reached New Orleans by riverboat on the evening of November 28.[13]

Mower had directed Louisiana through the potentially violent election period with no significant disturbances. For this he earned neither affection nor respect from Louisiana's white citizens. Many of them had been pleased by Sheridan's departure, only to find his successor even more Radical than "Little Phil." A northern newspaper commented that Mower "out Sheridan's Sheridan." Speaking for most whites, the New Orleans *Daily Picayune* was particularly gratified that Mower had been shunted off to the regimental headquarters of the "dusky 39th" at Greenville, where command could not require either "bodily or mental exertion." Luckily, he had done nothing drastic to dislocate the foundation that Sheridan had built, but Mower's impolitic and ill-considered re-

11. SO Nos. 192 and 193, 5 MD, November 21 and 22, 1867, in *House Executive Documents*, 40th Cong., 2nd Sess., No. 342, pp. 177–78; Benjamin F. Flanders to Grant, November 21, 1867, and Grant to Mower, November 22, 1867, in Grant Papers; Mower to Grant, November 22, 1867, in Johnson Papers.

12. Charles Vincent, *Black Legislators in Louisiana During Reconstruction* (Baton Rouge, 1976), 48–67; Taylor, *Louisiana Reconstructed*, 147–55.

13. AAG Nathaniel Burbank to CG, Dist La, November 22, 1867, in 5 MD, vol. 1, RG 393, NA; Mower to Grant, November 25, 1867, in Grant Papers.

movals marred his record. Although he adopted Sheridan's attitude and approach to Reconstruction problems, Mower's solutions lacked the reasonableness and soundness of the senior general's.[14]

Winfield S. Hancock, well known in army circles as a Democrat, assumed command on November 29, 1867, and on that same day he issued his important General Order No. 40, an order which pleased most of the white people of Louisiana and Texas. Hancock declared that "the military power should cease to lead and the civil administration resume its natural and rightful dominion." The military would thenceforth leave purely civil offenses and problems to the responsible elected officials. The rights of trial by jury, *habeas corpus*, and freedom of speech and of the press were all reconfirmed. In fact, Hancock did not make any extraordinary change in policy. His order did no more than spell out the conditions that legally existed under Sheridan and Mower. Nevertheless, as was soon evident, he did institute a change in attitude. Friendly messages of welcome from New Orleanians filled the mail trays in Hancock's office and the post box at his home in the Garden District. Newspapers carried editorials lauding Order No. 40. President Johnson complimented Hancock in a special message to Congress. Hancock's wife later wrote that "the gratitude was universal."[15]

Hancock, who was forty-three years old in 1867, had had experience in both combat and administration. Appointed to West Point from Pennsylvania, he was graduated in 1844. His combat record in the Civil War was crowned by his outstanding leadership at the battle of Gettysburg, where his corps had repulsed several important Confederate assaults, including Pickett's Charge. Hancock received a severe wound, and Congress awarded him a special vote of thanks for his actions in the pivotal battle. After the war he served on two special army commissions and then resumed field duty against the Indians in the Department of the Missouri. Honored and valiant, Hancock looked the part of the heroic general he was. His combed hair revealed a broad forehead, and his aquiline nose slightly bowed over an important-looking mustache, goatee, and chin whiskers. Subsequent to being assigned to the Southwest, he had had

14. New Orleans *Republican*, October 25, 1867 (Brooklyn *Union* quoted), November 23, 30, 1867; New Orleans *Daily Picayune*, December 5, 1867.

15. Winfield S. Hancock to Grant, November 29, 1867, in Grant Papers; SW "Annual Report, 1868–1869," 210; Glenn Tucker, *Hancock the Superb* (Indianapolis, 1960), 279–80; New Orleans *Daily Picayune*, November 30, 1867; New Orleans *Bee*, November 30, 1867; Baton Rouge *Tri-Weekly Advocate*, December 2, 1867; New Orleans *Times*, December 7, 1867; Richardson, *Messages and Papers*, VI, 595–96; Almira R. Hancock, *Reminiscences of Winfield Scott Hancock* (New York, 1887), 124–25.

time to think about ways to bring the Fifth District's radical government more in tune with the president's concept of restoration.[16]

Hard on the heels of General Order No. 40, Hancock began to deal with Mower's appointments and removals. Usually Hancock replaced Radicals with Conservatives. After reviewing their cases, Hancock reinstated three men Mower had removed—a clerk of court, the state auditor, and the state treasurer.[17]

Besides replacing Mower's appointees with more conservative officials, Hancock canceled Sheridan's order of August 24, 1867, which allowed blacks to qualify as jurors simply by being registered voters. Hancock ruled that determination of "who shall and who shall not be jurors" belonged to the state legislature. The New Orleans *Times* praised the order in an editorial bearing the headline "No More Negroes on Juries." Indeed, although it did not immediately eliminate blacks, Hancock's cancellation of Sheridan's edict was the first step toward virtual exclusion of blacks from juries. New Orleans residents roared their approval of Hancock's new policy by cheering him when he appeared at an opera house.[18]

Using his authorized powers, Hancock continued his crusade to displace the Radicals. On December 14 he replaced the mayor of Shreveport and the town council as well, all of whom had been appointed to office only four months before by General Sheridan. Five days later, Hancock reinstated nine more men who had been removed by Mower, including Lieutenant Governor Albert Voorhies, the secretary of state, and the director of public education. Hancock appointed thirteen other minor officials, such as police jurors and constables, to fill vacancies around the state. Most of these new appointees, to the delight of the State's Democratic press, were Conservatives.[19]

From the time of Hancock's arrival in Louisiana, Republicans and Democrats from various parts of the state had inundated him with letters requesting troops. A recurring theme of these letters was the fear that blacks might revolt around Christmastime. The threat of such a holiday

16. Warner, *Generals in Blue*, 202–204.
17. SO Nos. 200, 202, 205, 5 MD, December 2, 4, 7, 1867, in *House Executive Documents*, 40th Cong., 2nd Sess., No. 342, pp. 179–81.
18. SO No. 203, 5 MD, December 5, 1867, *ibid.*, 180–81; New Orleans *Times*, December 6, 8, 1867.
19. SO No. 210, 5 MD, December 14, 1867, in New Orleans *Times*, December 14, 1867; SO No. 214, 5 MD, December 19, 1867, in *House Executive Documents*, 40th Cong., 2nd Sess., No. 342, p. 184; Alexandria *Democrat*, December 18, 1867.

B-2022

Winfield S. Hancock

rebellion had constantly worried southerners during the prewar years, although none had ever occurred. Hancock responded to these requests by asking General Grant for more troops—specifically white ones. "A few soldiers at various posts under discreet commanders, to represent the Federal Authority and maintain the laws, are in my opinion absolutely necessary," Hancock wrote, "but they must be white: black troops are unsuited for the performance of this peculiar service." Grant's secretary, Cyrus B. Comstock, replied that three or four companies of white troops would probably be sent to Louisiana from the Third Military District. This reply must have disappointed Hancock, for he had hoped for at least another regiment.[20]

Before these reinforcements arrived, important changes took place in the command structure of the Louisiana department. Hancock requested that Brevet Major General Robert Christie Buchanan, commanding officer of the 1st Infantry, replace Mower as the commander of Louisiana and superintendent of the Freedmen's Bureau. Grant approved Hancock's request, although Mower retained command of the 39th Infantry. On January 2, 1868, Buchanan assumed his duties. Originally from Maryland, Buchanan was an alumnus of West Point, having graduated in 1830. Notations of battlefield service filled his military file. He had fought against the Seminoles in 1837 and had earned promotion to brevet lieutenant colonel in the Mexican War. He had experienced some of the roughest fighting in the eastern theater during the Civil War and had also served for a few months in New Orleans. From 1865 to 1867 Buchanan held assignments in Washington, D.C., on three army boards.[21]

In addition to a new commander, Louisiana also got a new governor in 1868. Sheridan's appointee, Benjamin Flanders, resigned from office because he and Hancock could not cooperate on running the state. To replace Flanders, Hancock chose Joshua Baker, a sixty-nine year old planter. Baker had lived in Louisiana for fifty-seven years and had received one of the state's earliest appointments to West Point, graduating

20. James M. Eddy to Hancock, December 2, 1867, and A. R. Whitney to Hancock, December 2, 1867, in Dept Gulf, vol. 274, Hancock to AGO, December 18, 1867, in 5 MD, vol. 1, "Petition of Citizens of Tensas and Madison Parishes" to Hancock, December 18, 1867, George W. Green to Hancock, December 27, 1867, both in 5 MD, Letters Recd, all in RG 393, NA; Hancock to Grant, December 23, 1867, Comstock to Hancock, December 27, 1867, both in Grant Papers.

21. Hancock to Grant, November 30, 1867, in U.S. Army Letterbook, Fifth Military District Papers; Grant to Hancock, December 3, 1867, in Grant Papers; SO No. 1, 5 MD, January 2, 1868, in *House Executive Documents*, 40th Cong., 2nd Sess., No. 342, p. 180; Warner, *Generals in Blue*, 48–49.

in 1819. After only one year in the army, Baker had returned to Louisiana to open a law practice and operate a plantation. Eventually, he obtained a judgeship and a seat in the state senate. A firm Unionist, but not a Radical, Baker supported Andrew Johnson's mild Reconstruction requirements.[22]

The new year seemed a propitious time to announce other changes. Hancock declared that it was no longer the place of the commanding general, simply by virtue of his rank, to assume "judicial functions in civil cases." In the future, questions of civil law and procedure would be handled as much as possible by the appropriate branch of the state government. Furthermore, agreeing with Attorney General Stanbery's opinion on voter registration, Hancock voided another of Sheridan's rulings. School board members, town councilmen, and several other minor officials who had been disqualified by Sheridan's order were to be allowed to vote. Louisianians and most registrars realized that many of the men denied registration under Sheridan were free now to come forward and sign the rolls. By this action, Hancock influenced the voter registration process as much as Sheridan had, but in a negative way. Sheridan had wanted to prevent as many ex-Confederates as possible from participating in government, so that the Republican party could take root and grow. In contrast, Hancock's action speeded the recovery of the Democratic party and the eventual demise of the Republicans.[23]

In February, Hancock made his final strike against the Radicals, removing nine New Orleans city councilmen from office. Two of the councilmen were white, seven were black, and all had been appointed by Sheridan. The councilmen had voted to fill a vacant municipal office, thereby violating the national Reconstruction Act, which prohibited elections to any office until the state was readmitted by Congress. Hancock had warned the councilmen that such an action was illegal, and he had, as a precedent to support him, General Mower's removal of some Jefferson aldermen for holding a similar election. Hancock dispatched a brief report on the changes in the council to Grant, who, less than pleased with Hancock's action, responded with a terse telegram that reached New Or-

22. Cullum, *Register of West Point*, I, 187–88; New Orleans *Times*, January 3, 4, 12, 1868; Flanders to Hancock, December 18, 1867, in 5 MD, Letters Recd, Civil Affairs, Joshua Baker to Hancock, January 4, 1868, in 5 MD, Telegrams Recd, both in RG 393, NA.

23. GO No. 1, 5 MD, January 1, 1868, in *The Civil Record of Major General Winfield S. Hancock During His Administration in Louisiana and Texas* (New Orleans[?], 1871), 22–23; Tucker, *Hancock*, 284; SO No. 3, 5 MD, January 11, 1868, in SW, "Annual Report, 1868–1869," 219–21; Baton Rouge *Tri-Weekly Advocate*, March 16, 1868.

leans on February 8: "suspend your order removing city council of New Orleans until full report is sent." Hancock replied that he believed an adequate summary of the situation had already been forwarded, and the state's Democratic newspapers supported him. Grant then retreated. If the new appointees had been installed, he said, then Hancock was to let them keep their positions. Indeed, several of the council seats had already been filled.[24]

This last exchange of telegrams appeared to solve the problem, but ten days later on February 21, a wire unexpectedly arrived that called on Hancock to reinstate Sheridan's old councilmen. Grant had changed his mind and decided that the councilmen had not done anything illegal. Hancock permitted Sheridan's councilmen to reoccupy their seats as ordered, but he did so with "serious apprehension." Upon reflection, Hancock wired Grant, reiterating all his previous arguments for his initial decision, and asked Grant to reconsider his orders, but Grant stood firm. He did not want a misunderstanding, he said, but Hancock's reasons did not warrant the removal of the councilmen.[25]

The council dispute prompted Hancock to request a transfer from the Fifth District, "where it is no longer useful or agreeable for me to serve." He planned to leave as soon as possible to discuss a new assignment with President Johnson in Washington. Hancock assumed that Brevet Major General Joseph J. Reynolds of the Department of Texas was the senior officer in the district and made him acting commander. When Hancock departed from New Orleans on March 16, 1868, citizens and newspaper editors speculated about the permanence of the absence; even Hancock himself was unsure if he would return to Louisiana. Within a few days after the meeting between the general and the president, Hancock received orders to report to the Division of the Atlantic under Major General George G. Meade.[26]

Hancock's approach to Reconstruction in Louisiana was a marked de-

24. SO No. 28, 5 MD, February 7, 1868, in SW, "Annual Report, 1868–1869," 222; Hancock to Grant, February 7, 9, 11, 1868, Grant to Hancock, February 8, 11, 1868, all in *House Executive Documents*, 40th Cong., 2nd Sess., No. 172, pp. 1–3; New Orleans *Times*, February 8, 9, 11, 1868; Baton Rouge *Tri-Weekly Advocate*, February 10, 1868.

25. Rawlins to Hancock, February 21, 1868, and Hancock to Grant, February 27, 1868, in *House Executive Documents*, 40th Cong., 2nd Sess., No. 209, pp. 10–13.

26. Hancock to AG Lorenzo Thomas, February 27, 1868, in SW, "Annual Report, 1868–1869," 223; Tucker, *Hancock*, 287; Baton Rouge *Tri-Weekly Advocate*, February 28, March 18, 1868; New Orleans *Times*, March 17, 1868; New Orleans *Daily Picayune*, March 9, 1868; Grant to Hancock, March 14 and 15, 1868, Hancock to Grant, March 15, 1868, endorsed by Johnson, both in Grant Papers.

parture from that of Sheridan and Mower. Under those two officers, the direct military influence on the state reached its zenith. Hancock diluted the effect of the Radical generals by a series of orders. Taken together, General Order No. 40, the directive on jury selection, and the change in voter registration greatly damaged Sheridan's efforts to aid the Republican party and hindered his program to force equal opportunity for blacks. Hancock relaxed voter registration requirements, enabling some deserving whites to register, but also opening the way for registrars to bar blacks from signing the rolls solely on racial grounds.

Hancock's departure came as the result of his conflict with Grant over the removal of the New Orleans councilmen, a legal act entirely within the authority of a district commander. However, Grant disapproved of Hancock's action because the councilmen had been appointed by Sheridan. Although Grant was well within his powers as general in chief on this matter, he undermined Hancock's position as an independent commander and ruled against a law Sheridan strongly supported. Democrats saw Hancock as a savior from Radical devils like Sheridan and Mower. Republicans feared that all political advances and advantages built up so laboriously during the previous few years would be ruined and discarded in only a few months of an administration like Hancock's.[27] In carrying out the Reconstruction Acts, army generals played political chess, improvising the rules as the game progressed. The generals were not simply interchangeable political pawns. District commanders more closely resembled the bishop in a game of chess: they were very powerful in narrow lanes of command. A district commander could help either Republicans or Democrats, depending on which party he favored.

To the surprise of both parties, Hancock's successor was perhaps the most objective and fair-minded commander to serve in the state during the postwar years. Before General Reynolds could even locate a residence in New Orleans, General Robert C. Buchanan replaced him as district commander on March 25. Buchanan succeeded to the position because he had received his brevet rank of major general ahead of Reynolds. Hancock had mistakenly assumed that Reynolds was the senior of the two officers. The adjutant general in Washington announced that Buchanan's assignment was only temporary, although he did not specify when a permanent commander would be named.[28]

27. For an excellent summary of Hancock's time in Louisiana, see Sefton, *Army and Reconstruction*, 176–78.
28. Joseph J. Reynolds to AGO, March 24, 1868, in Telegrams Sent, 5 MD, GO No. 16,

Buchanan was fifty-seven years old in 1868, making him the second oldest officer to command Louisiana between 1865 and 1877. But Buchanan's age did not hinder him in carrying out his duties. Four previous assignments in Louisiana both before and during the Civil War had given him a familiarity with the state that no other postwar commander could equal. He had the demeanor of a strict uncle: graceful gray mustaches accompanied a well-trimmed beard, and dark brows arched over intent eyes. Buchanan had a reputation as a martinet, and in the antebellum years he had been the scourge of junior officers, applying army regulations and rules of etiquette with equal force. In fact, Buchanan had been Grant's superior at two different military posts before the Civil War. Apparently, great antagonism built up between the two men because of Grant's drinking habits. Buchanan, supposedly, had goaded Grant into submitting his resignation from the service in 1854. However, these past difficulties did not appear to have any adverse effect on their relations when Buchanan was commander of Louisiana and Grant was general in chief.[29]

Buchanan assumed control over Louisiana at a crucial time. The new state constitution, which had taken four months to draft, had just been completed. This document was to go before the voters for ratification or rejection on April 17 and 18. In this same election, Louisiana voters would cast ballots for new state officers and congressional representatives.[30]

Buchanan wanted an honest and peaceful election. Using an order Hancock had issued before leaving Louisiana, Buchanan directed that registrars revise the voting rolls by striking off the names of men who had died or moved away. He designated April 3 to April 7 as registration dates for new applicants. While this was being done, he received permission from Washington to retain three infantry companies from the Third District (sent previously at Hancock's request), increasing the number of soldiers available to guard the polls. Buchanan issued a special proclamation that notified the public that every man's right to vote would be protected and that the army would be quickly dispatched to any area troubled by violence. Furthermore, military orders prohibited any nighttime

---

5 MD, March 25, 1868, in GO, 5 MD, both in RG 393, NA; New Orleans *Daily Picayune*, March 25, 1868.

29. Cullum, *Register of West Point*, I, 373–74; Lloyd Lewis, *Captain Sam Grant* (Boston, 1950), 329–32.

30. SO No. 55, 5 MD, March 11, 1868, in SW, "Annual Report, 1868–1869," 237; Grant to Hancock, March 13, 1868, in Grant Papers.

political parades or rallies until the election was completed. Only author-ized law enforcement officers or soldiers were allowed to carry firearms in public. Special detachments of soldiers marched into normally ungar-risoned towns. As election eve neared, Buchanan held a public review of the troops in New Orleans and put the soldiers there on a forty-eight-hour alert. The quartermaster hired a steamboat docked near Jackson Barracks that was capable of moving an additional 250 soldiers to New Orleans on short notice. After all these preparations, Buchanan was ready for the voting to begin.[31]

Running for governor on April 17 and 18 were two Republicans, Hen-ry Clay Warmoth and James G. Taliaferro. Warmoth was the young Rad-ical who had achieved recognition in 1865 as the unofficial and unrecog-nized "territorial delegate" from Louisiana. Since then he had practiced law and presided over the Louisiana chapter of the Grand Army of the Republic, a partisan veterans' organization. Taliaferro had recently gained prominence by serving as the chairman of the state constitutional convention. Taliaferro received some support from the Democrats, who did not nominate a candidate for governor and appeared to prefer the old resident Unionist over the brash Missourian who had come to the state only a few years earlier. Warmoth was obviously the more Radical of the two candidates.[32]

The election produced the ratification of the new constitution and a win for Warmoth, but John R. Conway, a Democrat, was elected mayor of New Orleans. The tabulation revealed that 66,152 Louisiana men voted for the constitution, 48,739 against it. Warmoth defeated Taliaferro by 26,895 votes—64,941 to 38,046. The election had been a calm one by Louisiana standards. Buchanan called it "the most peaceful, quiet, and orderly of any that had taken place in the State of Louisiana for a great many years." There were no reports of violence associated with the elec-tion even though blacks reportedly voted in large numbers. Within a few days, Buchanan ordered the three companies of soldiers on loan from the Third District to return to their posts in Mississippi.[33]

31. Robert C. Buchanan to Grant, April 6, 1868, Rawlins to Buchanan, April 8, 1868, both in Grant Papers; AAG George Baldey to Chief Quartermaster, Dist La, April 16, 1868, in Dept Gulf, vol. 274, RG 393, NA; New Orleans *Times*, March 31, April 15, 1868; SW, "Annual Report, 1868–1869," 313.

32. Wynona G. Mills, "James Govan Taliaferro: Louisiana Unionist and Scalawag" (M.A. thesis, Louisiana State University, 1969), 73–85. The best treatment of Warmoth's career is F. Wayne Binning, "Henry Clay Warmoth and Louisiana Reconstruction" (Ph.D. dissertation, University of North Carolina, 1969).

33. Buchanan, Departmental Report, in SW, "Annual Report, 1868–1869," 314; Bu-

Despite the peaceful election, charges that Buchanan was being lax in the performance of his duties came unexpectedly from Stephen B. Packard, a Republican serving as chairman of the state board of voter registration. A native of Maine and a former Union army captain, Packard had established a law practice in New Orleans after the Civil War, hoping to profit from the state's unsettled political and economic conditions. Following the gubernatorial election, Packard wrote General Grant a grim description of the situation in Louisiana. "Revenge and murders are rampant in our state," the board chairman claimed. He accused Buchanan of failure to investigate the crimes because of his mistaken assumption that the civilian authorities were able to protect the citizens of Louisiana. Such a statement from a Radical Republican disturbed Grant, who demanded that Buchanan forward as soon as possible a detailed report on "the state of affairs" in the district. Replying promptly, Buchanan reported that there had been only seventeen murders in the state in the month following Warmoth's election. The civil authorities had investigated these crimes, and most of the murders had not been associated with politics. This report satisfied Grant.[34]

Having failed to make good on his charges of disorder in Louisiana, Packard next criticized Buchanan from a different angle. Packard wanted Warmoth inaugurated quickly, but it appeared to him that Buchanan was taking longer than necessary to promulgate the April election results. Buchanan had previously informed Grant that the new officeholders would be installed sometime after military officers tabulated the results of the election; they completed the count on June 2. He issued an order notifying the public that the new officials would take their posts on the first Monday in November, or whenever Congress approved the new state constitution, whichever came first. Most Republicans opposed such a long wait for Warmoth's inauguration. Packard attempted to nullify Buchanan's order by issuing an illegal proclamation that called for the swearing in of the new state officials before November.[35]

Buchanan decided Packard's actions violated an army order prohibiting

---

chanan to Grant, May 9, 1868, in Grant Papers; Baton Rouge *Tri-Weekly Advocate*, April 29, 1868; New Orleans *Times*, May 14, 1868; Donald W. Davis, "Ratification of the Constitution of 1868—Record of Votes," *Louisiana History*, VI (Summer, 1965), 301–305; F. Wayne Binning, "Carpetbaggers' Triumph: The Louisiana State Election of 1868," *Louisiana History*, XIV (Winter, 1973), 21–39.

34. Stephen B. Packard to Grant, May 14, 1868, Grant to Buchanan, May 15, 1868, Buchanan to Grant, May 16, 1868, all in Grant Papers; Binning, "Henry Clay Warmoth," 193.

35. Buchanan to Grant, May 22, 1868, Packard to Grant, May 21, June 4, 1868, both in

anyone in the state from issuing proclamations contrary to the rulings of the district commander. On June 6 soldiers arrested Packard, and Buchanan arranged for a speedy trial by military commission. Then, perhaps under pressure because of Packard's comments, Buchanan suddenly declared that all newly elected municipal officials would be allowed to take office on June 8, except those in New Orleans, who would be installed on June 10. All state officials had to wait investiture until Congress approved the state constitution.[36]

Grant ordered Buchanan to drop the case against Packard. Congress was considering a bill that would allow Louisiana and five other southern states to regain their representation in Congress pending each state's ratification of the Fourteenth Amendment. With this important step so close, Grant did not want divisive activities between Buchanan and Packard to endanger the reentry of Louisiana's representatives to Congress. Army Chief of Staff John Rawlins reprimanded Packard and commanded the registrar not to issue any more illegitimate proclamations.[37]

Despite the knowledge that civilian control was only a few weeks away, Packard disregarded Rawlins' directions and seized the first opportunity after his release from jail to call for the installment of all state civil officials by June 15. He also declared that the legislature should meet on June 22 regardless of any orders from Buchanan. State officials paid no heed to Packard's carping, but waited, instead, for orders from the army. However, Radical Mayor Edward Heath of New Orleans refused to allow Mayor-elect John R. Conway to move into the office. Buchanan ordered Heath's removal, and the conservative Conway established himself as the new mayor.[38]

On June 26 Buchanan learned that Congress had approved Louisiana's new constitution and that the state's representatives would be seated when the legislature ratified the Fourteenth Amendment. Accordingly, on June 27 Warmoth was inaugurated as governor. Oscar J. Dunn, a black Union army veteran and New Orleans councilman, took the oath as lieutenant governor. In an extraordinary move, using his powers as

Grant Papers; New Orleans *Republican*, June 7, 1868; SO No. 121, 5 MD, June 2, 1868, in New Orleans *Times*, June 3, 1868.

36. Buchanan to Grant, June 6, 1868, in Grant Papers; SO No. 125, 5 MD, June 6, 1868, in New Orleans *Times*, June 7, 1868.

37. Grant to Buchanan, June 8, 1868, Rawlins to Packard, June 9, 1868, both in Grant Papers.

38. Buchanan to Grant, June 10, 1868, Edward Heath to Grant, June 10, 1868, both *ibid.*; New Orleans *Daily Picayune*, June 10, 11, 12, 1868.

district commander, Buchanan appointed the elected officials to their new positions by military order, making it clear that the army endorsed the Republican administration. Warmoth scheduled the opening of the state legislature for June 29, a Monday.[39]

The convening of the legislature immediately created a crisis that alarmed Buchanan. The Republicans held an edge in both legislative chambers: twenty to sixteen in the senate and fifty-six to forty-five in the house. Lieutenant Governor Dunn, presiding officer in the senate, demanded that all the senators take a strict "test oath" before they could be seated, although this extra oath was not a part of the new constitution. The test oath, like the old "iron clad" oath used during the Civil War and earlier in Reconstruction, required the new senators to swear that they had not fought against the United States or aided those who did. Robert H. Isabelle, also a black Union army veteran, now acting chairman of the house, cooperated with Dunn and refused to seat representatives in the lower chamber unless they too took the oath. By 1868 all Democrats elected to the legislature had received pardons or had been granted amnesty. The standard oath required by the new constitution asked only that the legislator swear to uphold the laws of the state. The legislature adjourned after an abbreviated first session, with most of the sixty-one Democrats still unseated. Fearing trouble because of this unexpected turn of events, Buchanan wired Grant for instructions.[40]

Shortly after daylight on the morning of June 30, Buchanan learned of a Conservative plot to disrupt the legislature because the Democrats had been denied their seats. A motley crowd of two thousand persons had gathered in front of the legislature's meeting hall at the Mechanics' Institute, site of the bloody riot in 1866. Acting swiftly on the general's orders, a detachment of the 1st Infantry arrived at the institute and formed a cordon around the building. The soldiers permitted only legislators and reporters to pass through the line. Buchanan stationed a horse-drawn artillery battery and G Troop of the 6th Cavalry a few blocks away from the meeting site. The crowd grew to an estimated three thousand persons, but it did not become disorderly. At noon the rap of the gavel brought the legislature into session without interruption, and the crowd

---

39. Grant to Buchanan, June 26, 27, 1868, in Grant Papers; AAAG Thomas Neill to Baker, June 27, 1868, in 5 MD, Telegrams Sent, RG 393, NA; New Orleans *Times*, June 27, 1868; New Orleans *Daily Picayune*, June 28, 1868; Ficklen, *Reconstruction in Louisiana*, 203.
40. Buchanan to Grant, June 27, 1868, in Grant Papers; New Orleans *Times*, June 30, 1868.

dispersed shortly thereafter. Inside the building the representatives and senators listened while a clerk read a letter from Grant to Buchanan. Grant declared that the only oath required of new legislators was the one in the Louisiana constitution. This statement settled the controversy, and the Republicans permitted the Democrats to occupy their seats. However, on Buchanan's order, troops remained near the institute for several days.[41]

Buchanan's swift and decisive action prevented a civil disturbance that could have turned into a major riot, repeating the terrible events of July 30, 1866. The New Orleans *Daily Picayune* complimented Buchanan on his decisiveness. The editor said it was a pleasant contrast to Absalom Baird's ineffective actions two years before.[42] If another riot had erupted in the summer of 1868, it probably would have canceled Louisiana's impending readmission to Congress, and military government would have continued indefinitely.

Some areas of the state apparently still needed the firm hand of military government. Army detachments from Monroe and Shreveport had to be sent into Claiborne and DeSoto parishes to investigate allegations of intimidation and acts of violence against blacks. Captain William W. Webb reported that the civil authorities in the town of Homer in Claiborne Parish were capably handling their responsibilities. The Freedmen's Bureau agent in the area told Webb that most violence in the parish involved personal quarrels and not political rivalries. In contrast, Lieutenant Charles O. Bradley reported from Mansfield in DeSoto Parish that the whites appeared to be holding blacks in "a system of terrorism." In Bradley's opinion, "the presence of a small military force would give the Agent of the [Freedmen's] Bureau the moral support which he needs." With such conflicting reports in hand, Buchanan did not alter the arrangement of his soldiers, who, with few exceptions, remained stationed in the larger towns. From these centers troops could be dispatched to locations where violence threatened.[43]

On July 13, 1868, after Warmoth officially notified him that the legislature had ratified the Fourteenth Amendment, Buchanan announced "to the people of the state, and to the troops under [this] command, that the

41. Buchanan, Departmental Report, 315; New Orleans *Times*, July 2, 1868; William E. Highsmith, "Louisiana During Reconstruction" (Ph.D. dissertation, Louisiana State University, 1953), 237; Grant to Buchanan, June 30, 1868, in Grant Papers.
42. New Orleans *Daily Picayune*, July 2, 1868.
43. William W. Webb to AAAG, Dist La, July 1, 1868, Charles O. Bradley to Capt. Charles E. Farrand, July 21, 1868, both in Dist La, Letters Recd, RG 393, NA.

provisions of the Reconstruction acts of Congress cease[d] to operate in Louisiana." Buchanan further stated that "military authority will no longer be exercised . . . unless upon a proper application by the civil authorities to preserve the peace." Concluding his remarks, Buchanan congratulated the people of Louisiana for regaining their civil government, gave them good wishes for the future, and ended by saying that "civil law was once more supreme."[44]

Florida, Alabama, and the two Carolinas also regained their representation in Congress during the summer of 1868, and since these states were again operating under civilian governments, the adjutant general's office had to reorganize the military districts. On July 28 the Second and Third Districts were discontinued. Georgia, Alabama, Florida, North Carolina, and South Carolina were placed in the new Department of the South with headquarters in Atlanta. Virginia kept its designation as the First Military District. In the Southwest, Mississippi continued to be called the Fourth District. Texas retained the title of Fifth District, and Joseph Reynolds remained in command. Arkansas and Louisiana were joined to form the new Department of Louisiana, and Brevet Major General Lovell H. Rousseau was assigned as the commander. Buchanan remained in charge until Rousseau transferred his headquarters from Washington Territory to New Orleans.[45]

Before the new commander arrived, Buchanan had to deal with problems growing out of the 1868 presidential campaign. The Republicans nominated Ulysses S. Grant, general in chief of the northern armies. Opposing Grant was the Democratic war governor of New York, Horatio Seymour. Most white Louisianians favored Seymour, and organizations of former Confederate soldiers paraded in the streets in support of the Democrat. The Republicans, too, scheduled marches and rallies on behalf of their candidate. Governor Warmoth believed that the Democrats were not restricting themselves to parades, but were also using violence and murder to intimidate Republicans. There had been twenty-five confirmed homicides in Louisiana since Warmoth's election, and many others had been reported. Despite Warmoth's pleas for more troops, Adjutant General Edward Townsend made no plans to send extra soldiers to

44. Henry C. Warmoth to Buchanan, July 13, 1868, in 5 MD, Letters Recd, Civil Affairs, RG 393, NA; GO No. 154, 5 MD, July 13, 1868, in New Orleans *Times*, July 14, 1868; New Orleans *Daily Picayune*, July 11, 14, 1868; SW, "Annual Report, 1868–1869," 316.

45. GO No. 55, HQ/USA, July 28, 1868, in SW, "Annual Report, 1868–1869," 316; New Orleans *Times*, August 4, 1868; Sefton, *Army and Reconstruction*, 186, 256.

Louisiana. After considering the governor's expressions of concern, Buchanan issued a proclamation announcing that he and his troops would act decisively in the event of a major disturbance anywhere in the state.[46]

Early in September the Radicals scheduled a huge torchlight parade in New Orleans for Saturday, September 12. On September 11, Colonel Edward Hatch, superintendent of the Louisiana Freedmen's Bureau, telegraphed Secretary of War John M. Schofield requesting that Buchanan be specifically ordered to protect the large number of Negro marchers expected on the streets the next night. Schofield complied with the request. When Buchanan received the order, he replied that in his estimation the blacks might cause serious property damage if allowed to march unrestricted through the city, so he planned to place guards along the parade route. On the evening of the parade the general dispersed soldiers from seven companies of the 1st Infantry to several locations within the city, including the United States Mint. More than 6,500 Radicals and blacks participated in the rally and parade, creating a carnival atmosphere that lasted until late Saturday night. Buchanan was relieved to learn that no violence or property damage occurred. Once again Buchanan's planning and his ample use of troops had prevented a potentially violent situation from getting out of hand.[47]

Buchanan kept the peace in Louisiana during months filled with potentially dangerous situations. Despite the heated political controversy that was commonplace, the state had held a gubernatorial election, convened a new legislature, and regained its congressional representation. Never waiting until a crisis exploded into violence, Buchanan acted objectively, judiciously posting soldiers to key locations in New Orleans when danger threatened. Even the *Picayune*, a Democratic newspaper, called Buchanan a "distinguished old soldier" who had "wisely and delicately performed the novel and difficult duties imposed on him" in Louisiana.[48] His successors would find it difficult to do as well.

46. Alexandria *Democrat*, August 5, 1868; Buchanan to Edward Townsend, August 19, 1868, in Dept Gulf, vol. 266, GO No. 3, Dept La, August 13, 1868, in GO, Dept La, both in RG 393, NA; AAG J. C. Kelton to Buchanan, August 25, 1868, in *Senate Executive Documents*, 41st Cong., 3rd Sess., No. 16, Pt. 1, p. 32.

47. Baldey to W. M. Graham, September 12, 1868, in Dept Gulf, vol. 274A, RG 393, NA; Hatch to John M. Schofield, September 11, 1868, Schofield to Hatch, September 12, 1868, Kelton to Buchanan, Septemer 12, 1868, and reply, all in SW, "Annual Report, 1868–1869," xxxiii–xxxiv; New Orleans *Bee*, September 13, 1868; New Orleans *Times*, September 13, 1868.

48. New Orleans *Daily Picayune*, July 2, 1868.

On September 15, 1868, relinquishing command in a brief ceremony to Brevet Major General Lovell Rousseau, who had just arrived in New Orleans, Buchanan assumed command of the 1st Infantry Regiment. The new commander of the Department of Louisiana was a Kentuckian, born near Stanford in 1818. He moved to Indiana in 1840, practiced law, and later served in both houses of the Indiana legislature. In the Mexican War, Rousseau raised and commanded a volunteer infantry company. In 1849 he returned to Kentucky, and there in 1860 he won a seat in the state senate. Unswervingly loyal to the Union, he resigned his senate seat in 1861 and raised a Kentucky regiment for service in the Federal army. Colonel Rousseau led his regiment in the battles of Shiloh and Perryville and was promoted to major general of volunteers. He subsequently commanded part of occupied Tennessee. After the war, he resigned from the army, returned to Kentucky, and won election to the U.S. House of Representatives.

While in Congress, Rousseau became friends with President Johnson, voting against the Freedmen's Bureau Bill and other Radical legislation and consistently sustaining the president's Reconstruction policies. In March, 1867, Johnson made Rousseau a brigadier general in the regular army and picked him to lead the official delegation that took possession of Alaska, which had been purchased from Russia. On his return from Alaska, Rousseau inspected conditions in Louisiana before taking command in Washington Territory. He was there when he received orders in 1868 to take charge of the Louisiana department. Rousseau had thinning hair, long, thick sideburns, a matching mustache, and an openness about his appearance that matched his personality. Louisiana Republicans immediately recognized his political inclination. Governor Warmoth astutely described the general as "a Kentucky Democrat, with all of the prejudices against Reconstruction, and a supporter of President Johnson's policy." [49]

Rousseau came to Louisiana just as the 1868 presidential campaign was mounting in intensity and threats of violence were becoming more frequent. The greatest danger appeared to come from the Democrats. Voter registration was reopened, allowing many unsigned Democrats to register. The Democrats not only began to gain in voter strength but also began to use their powers of intimidation. All over the state Democrats

49. Warner, *Generals in Blue*, 412–13; *Dictionary of American Biography*, XVI, 194–95; New Orleans *Times*, September 16, 1868; Henry C. Warmoth, *War, Politics, and Reconstruction: Stormy Days in Louisiana* (New York, 1930), 78.

Lovell H. Rousseau

organized political clubs, including the "Cadets," "Southrons," "Sentinels," and "Knights," and paraded noisily for their ticket. The demonstrators usually attended rallies and other political events well armed.[50]

On the night of September 22, two rival political processions, one white and the other black, clashed in downtown New Orleans. In a short but deadly fight, three blacks were killed, and an undetermined number on both sides were wounded. Before the incident could mushroom, soldiers from the New Orleans garrison and city police restored order. The following day the Democrats, as if celebrating a victory, held a large and enthusiastic political rally under the watchful eyes of additional troops brought in from Jackson Barracks.[51]

Rousseau penned a gloomy report on the situation to President Johnson on September 26. The "condition of affairs here . . . could not be much worse," wrote the general in dismay. Rousseau expressed little faith in the strength of the civilian authorities alone to maintain order. He believed that most citizens still looked to the army to keep the peace. Although it seemed premature to do so, Rousseau predicted a Democratic victory for Seymour in November. The general promised Johnson that he would do his best to ensure law and order, but he concluded that he could "compare the population here to nothing so apt as a volcano ready for an explosion at any moment."[52]

Just two days later Rousseau's "volcano" erupted violently in St. Landry Parish. Three local Democrats assaulted and caned Emerson Bentley, Radical editor of the Opelousas St. Landry Progress. Local Radicals, who had been organizing St. Landry blacks into political clubs, sent out messengers to gather the clubs together and demanded punishment for Bentley's attackers. Responding to what they saw as a black uprising, well-armed whites quickly assembled, and gunfire was exchanged between the rival groups. The shots killed one Negro and wounded three whites and several blacks. The sheriff and white vigilantes arrested several blacks, locked them in jail, and charged them with disturbing the peace. The following night all but a few of the freedmen were removed from jail and murdered. For the next two weeks, armed whites rode

50. New Orleans *Times*, September 18, October 23, 1868.

51. Baldey to CO, Jackson Barracks, September 23, 1868, Baldey to W. H. Wood, September 23, 1868, both in Dept Gulf, vol. 274A, Lovell H. Rousseau to AGO, September 23, 1868, in Dept Gulf, vol. 266, all in RG 393, NA; Rousseau, District Report, in SW, "Annual Report, 1868–1869," 303.

52. Rousseau to Johnson, September 26, 1868, in Johnson Papers.

through the parish terrorizing the Negro population. The New Orleans *Times* reported that more than one hundred blacks were killed in St. Landry during the reign of terror. When Rousseau finally dispatched a squad of soldiers to Opelousas several days after the riot started, the troops found that white vigilantes were patrolling the town and the surrounding countryside. The violence accomplished its purpose—the complete intimidation of all St. Landry Republicans on election day in November. Grant received no votes in that parish, which had given more than 2,500 votes to Warmoth in April.[53]

Rousseau made no concerted effort to quell the violence that ripped through several parishes, including St. Mary, Caddo, Bossier, Carroll, and Rapides. Rampaging Democrats destroyed two Republican newspapers and killed several Republicans. The need for the use of troops was manifest, and eventually detachments did reach areas troubled by violence, but Rousseau's response was not decisive. Publicly, the general spoke before a gathering of Democratic clubs in New Orleans and advised them not to riot because the army would strictly enforce all laws. Privately, Rousseau wrote President Johnson that the "ascendance of the negro in this state is approaching its end" and that "A Fair vote will give the state to the democrats." Rousseau probably based his prediction on the increased registration of whites and also on the effect of the Democrats' terrorism. Notwithstanding the general's opinion, however, the number of votes cast for Warmoth six months before indicated that a "fair vote" would be very close and might yield another Republican victory.[54]

Because of continuing violence, Rousseau requested that two more regiments be sent to Louisiana. A request for so many soldiers was unusual, and Rousseau knew that at most only a few companies could be spared from other departments. In response to this request, Adjutant

53. Opelousas *Courier*, October 3, 1868; Rousseau, District Report, 308–309; Carolyn E. DeLatte, "The St. Landry Riot: A Forgotten Incident of Reconstruction Violence," *Louisiana History*, XVII (Winter, 1976), 45–59; Capt. A. E. Hooker to AAIG R. B. Hayes, October 16, 1868, in Dept La, Letters Recd, RG 393, NA; Lt. J. M. Lee to Capt. B. T. Hutchins, October 8, 1868, in *Senate Executive Documents*, 40th Cong., 3rd Sess., No. 15, p. 17.

54. Baton Rouge *Tri-Weekly Advocate*, October 7, 1868; New York *Times*, October 6, 29, 1868; Rousseau to Johnson, October 4, 1868, in Johnson Papers; Rousseau to Grant, October 20, 1868, in Grant Papers; Rousseau, District Report, 303; Capt. C. E. Farrand (Caddo and Bossier Parishes) to Baldey, November 27, 1868, in Dist La, Letters Recd, Lt. Stanton Weaver to Baldey, October 7, 1868, in Dept La, Letters Recd, both in RG 393, NA.

General Townsend ordered Mississippi commander Major General Alvan C. Gillem to temporarily assign as many soldiers as possible to aid Rouseau in Louisiana.[55]

Meanwhile, Governor Warmoth implored Rousseau to allow him to form a state militia to control the violence in the vicinity of New Orleans. Two blacks had been murdered in Gretna on October 23, and six Negroes had been killed in street fighting on October 24. Rousseau forwarded Warmoth's letter to Secretary of War Schofield, asking for specific instructions on Warmoth's request. Schofield replied that Rousseau should take whatever action was required to "preserve peace and good order." Rousseau decided not to approve Warmoth's request for a state militia, which undoubtedly would have been composed mostly of blacks. Prodded by the increasingly dangerous situation in New Orleans, he did, however, order all unassigned troops into the Crescent City, and he beseeched General Gillem to hurry the reinforcements to Louisiana. Another violent incident, this one in St. Bernard Parish, resulted in the deaths of several more blacks and whites and heightened the urgency of Rousseau's appeal.[56]

Adding to the confusion in New Orleans area was the fact that rival police organizations might at any time challenge each other for control of the southern parishes. The state legislature, at Governor Warmoth's direction, had passed a law establishing the Metropolitan Police, composed of 375 men, two-thirds of them black, to operate in the parishes of Orleans, Jefferson, and St. Bernard. Responsibility for controlling this unusual organization was given to a board of five legislators and Lieutenant Governor Dunn, the chairman. However, Warmoth held the actual power over the Metropolitans, and he employed them like a state militia. The mayors of municipalities in the parishes naturally had no control over the special force and therefore maintained independent police departments. Rousseau claimed that the majority of citizens had no respect for the Metropolitans, whom the general called "practically worthless" because of poor organization, lack of training, and low morale. This divi-

55. Rousseau to Schofield, October 20, 1868, Townsend to Alvan C. Gillem, October 22, 1868, in SW, "Annual Report, 1868–1869," xxxiv.

56. New Orleans *Times*, October 24 and 27, 1868; Warmoth to Rousseau, October 25, 1868, in Warmoth, *War, Politics, and Reconstruction*, 76; Rousseau to Schofield, October 26, 1868, Schofield to Rousseau, October 27, 1868, both in SW, "Annual Report, 1868–1869," xxxv, 304; Neill to Buchanan, October 26, 1868, in Dist La, Letters Recd, Rousseau to Gillem, October 24, 1868, in Dept Gulf, vol. 266, both in RG 393, NA; Rousseau to Grant, October 27, 1868, in Grant Papers; Taylor, *Louisiana Reconstructed*, 169–70.

sion of authority among the police underscored the alarming situation in south Louisiana.[57]

Rousseau could not abide the possibility of a battle for supremacy between rival police departments. To forestall trouble, he held meetings with Mayor John Conway of New Orleans, the Metropolitan Police Board, and James B. Steedman, a Democrat and former Union general from Ohio now serving as collector of revenue for New Orleans. As a result of these conferences, Steedman was appointed chief of the Metropolitan Police on October 28, and Conway agreed not to appoint a new chief for the city police until after the election. Steedman's appointment calmed the several factions, especially when Rousseau announced that the army would support him. Rousseau also issued a special preelection proclamation that prohibited large assemblies and parades and forbade the carrying of firearms in public. Had he issued such a proclamation two or three weeks earlier and backed it with an appropriate show of force, he might have prevented or curtailed the violence that had occurred during October.[58]

At this point Warmoth asked for a conference with Rousseau to discuss the unstable situation. The governor said that he fully expected rioting in the streets on election day if violence continued to build at its present rate. Rousseau replied that Steedman's appointment and the army's support would discourage other disturbances. He then made an amazing request—he asked Warmoth to issue a public statement telling blacks to remain away from the polls in the interest of peace and civil order. Rousseau must have thought the situation desperate to request such a statement from the Republican governor, but the general had made no secret of his support of Johnson's policy and the Democratic party. If black voters heeded Warmoth's advice, the likelihood of a Democratic victory in Louisiana would be increased. Warmoth, of course, knew that such a proclamation would severely damage the Republicans, but concluded that the situation was dangerous enough to require a statement discouraging blacks from voting. If they voted, there might be riots; if they abstained, the Democrats would probably win the election. Warmoth was in an unenviable position.[59]

57. New Orleans *Times*, October 17, 18, 20, 1868; Rousseau, District Report, 304–306. See also Sefton, *Army and Reconstruction*, 216.

58. New Orleans *Times*, October 29, 1868; Rousseau, District Report, 306.

59. Rousseau, District Report, 307; Warmoth, *War, Politics and Reconstruction*, 76–77.

A week before the election Rousseau received the extra troops he had previously requested. Five companies of the 34th Infantry arrived from Mississippi. More than 550 soldiers were stationed in the Crescent City and its environs. Despite all the conferences, proclamations, and additional troops, Rousseau doubted his ability to keep the peace. Telegraphing Secretary of War Schofield for advice, Rousseau tried to explain the tense situation which had developed because of the rival police forces and requested orders as to how to "interpose" his soldiers between the rivals in the event of trouble. Rousseau reported that Steedman disliked his job as Metropolitan Police chief and had threatened to resign. Furthermore, Rousseau requested one or two "Men-of-War" for service along the New Orleans riverfront during the election. "Time is pressing," Rousseau concluded. "Please send a prompt reply." [60]

Schofield responded immediately that it was "impossible to give instructions in detail from this distance in the short time allowed" but that Rousseau already had ample authority to do what was "necessary to preserve the peace." As the local commander, Rousseau "must take the responsibility of action." There was no warship available, but a revenue cutter had been ordered to New Orleans. In an "unofficial" personal telegram Schofield was even more emphatic. You must act decisively to protect all citizens, the war secretary told Rousseau, and he added that, if necessary, army "troops would be a good temporary substitute for both rival police forces, but of that you must judge." [61]

Rousseau did not use his troops as a substitute for the police, but he remained fearful that, once the tenuous compromise arranged for the election ended, the New Orleans city police might openly challenge the Metropolitans for supremacy. Once again he asked Schofield's advice on the matter. This time Schofield referred Rousseau's message to President Johnson, who wrote on October 31, "You are expected and authorized to take all legitimate steps necessary and proper to prevent breaches of the peace or hostile collisions between citizens." Johnson further reminded

---

60. Rousseau, District Report, 304; Rousseau to Schofield, October 29, 1868, in SW, "Annual Report, 1868–1869," xxxv–xxxvi; Gillem to Buchanan, October 27, 1868, in Dist La, Letters Recd, Rousseau to Schofield, October 29, 1868, filed with 5 MD, Telegrams Recd, both in RG 393, NA.

61. Schofield to Rousseau, October 29, 1868 (two communications), in SW, "Annual Report, 1868–1869," xxxvi; Schofield to Rousseau, October 30, 1868, filed with 5 MD, Telegrams Recd, RG 393, NA.

Rousseau that strictly civil affairs were to be left "to the proper civil authorities for [their] consideration and settlement."[62]

That afternoon James Steedman abruptly resigned as chief of the Metropolitan Police after serving only four days in the position. Steedman probably had not expected the job to be so difficult. Warmoth had criticized his plans to reorganize the department, and there was the possibility of armed conflict with other area police forces. To add to the confusion, Mayor Conway had offered him the job of New Orleans City Police chief. Steedman decided that resigning was the best way out of a perplexing situation. One of Steedman's assistants took command of the Metropolitans during the election.[63]

During the last few days before the election Rousseau made his final preparations. By then detachments had been placed in several towns where soldiers normally were not stationed, such as Gretna and Brashear City. Rousseau also sent soldiers to the towns of St. Joseph in Tensas Parish and Franklin in St. Mary Parish to assist local authorities and protect the polls.[64]

Election day, November 3, 1868, dawned cool and gray. Most stores, shops, and cafés were closed in New Orleans. Policemen and soldiers were stationed in prominent places. The election proceeded very quietly, with an almost "Sabbath-like stillness," according to the New Orleans *Times*. Following the advice of Warmoth and other Radical leaders, few blacks voted in Louisiana. In spite of the low turnout, marauding whites murdered three freedmen near Monroe. However, reports from other parishes indicated a peaceful election.[65]

Grant won the national election handily with 3,013,421 popular votes and 214 electoral votes to Seymour's 2,706,829 popular votes and 80 electoral votes. The Democrats carried only eight states, including two in the South, Georgia and Louisiana. Seymour won Louisiana with 80,225 votes to Grant's 33,225. In the April election Warmoth had received more

62. Rousseau to Schofield, October 30, 1868, Johnson to Rousseau, October 31, 1868, both in SW, "Annual Report, 1868–1869," xxxvii.
63. New Orleans *Times*, October 30, 31, November 1, 1868.
64. Warmoth to Rousseau, October 31, 1868, Neill to Buchanan, November 2, 1868 (two communications), all in Dist La, Letters Recd, RG 393, NA.
65. Rousseau to Schofield, November 3 and 4, 1868, in SW, "Annual Report, 1868–1869," xxxviii–xxxix; New Orleans *Times*, November 4, 1868; Capt. W. W. Webb (Monroe) to AAAG Baldey, November 10, 1868, Lt. John S. Allanson (Carroll Parish) to Baldey, November 4, 1868, Capt. A. A. Harback (Tensas Parish) to Capt. William Fletcher, November 4, 1868, all in Dist La, Letters Recd, RG 393, NA.

than 69,000 votes. Thirty-two Louisiana parishes went Democratic, including parishes that had been disturbed by preelection violence, such as Orleans, Jefferson, St. Bernard, Caddo, Bossier, St. Landry, and St. Mary. Sixteen parishes recorded majorities for Grant.[66]

Although Rousseau charged that Republicans had instigated the preelection violence, it was the Democrats who succeeded in carrying Louisiana through intimidation of Republican voters, especially blacks. A subsequent congressional investigation of the election violence indicated that the Democrats were better organized than they had been during Warmoth's election and that they were determined to carry the election by whatever means necessary.[67] Rousseau's allegiance to the Democratic party was well known, but it did not excuse his actions, or lack of them. Instead of using his troops to guarantee every man's right to vote as Buchanan had done only a few months before, Rousseau had encouraged Warmoth to warn blacks away from the polls. Because he wanted to avoid a violent confrontation between the army and the Democrats, he had responded slowly to reports of riots in St. Landry and St. Bernard, waited until the eve of the election to position soldiers in other parishes where intimidation was blatant, and failed to enforce existing orders against unauthorized armed patrols, even when such vigilantes rode within the city of New Orleans itself. At various times during Reconstruction the Democrats complained loudly about the army's "bayonet rule" and "military oppression." No such complaints could be made against Rousseau. On the contrary, Rousseau had relaxed his supervision nearly to the point of negligence and had allowed the Democrats almost a free hand in several parishes.

After the tumult surrounding the election, the remainder of November passed quietly in Louisiana. Rousseau ordered the five companies of the 34th Infantry to return to Mississippi on November 5, and at about the same time, he decided to close down the posts at New Iberia and Lake Providence. The soldiers were later sent to Baton Rouge and Alexandria. December was also a placid month filled mostly with the usual social activities of the holiday season.[68]

On January 4, after visiting Governor Warmoth, Rousseu was sud-

66. New Orleans *Times*, November 25, 1868; Taylor, *Louisiana Reconstructed*, 172.
67. The congressional committee that investigated the pre-election violence reported its findings in *House Miscellaneous Documents*, 41st Cong., 2nd Sess., No. 154, see especially pp. 17–39, 177–79.
68. Rousseau to Johnson, November 10, 1868, in Johnson Papers; New Orleans *Times*, November 14, 15, 1868; Rousseau to Gillem, November 5, 1868, in Dept Gulf, vol. 266,

denly and inexplicably stricken by severe cramps and congestion of the lower intestinal tract. His condition worsened rapidly, and at 11:00 P.M. on the night of January 7, he died. "We have to record, with a regret heightened by the circumstances, a loss to the people of the United States, and a graver loss to the people of Louisiana, in the death of General Lovell H. Rousseau," intoned the editor of the New Orleans *Times*. Robert Buchanan, after sadly reporting Rousseau's death to President Johnson, temporarily assumed command.[69]

According to the New Orleans *Times*, the sky of Saturday, January 9 "assumed a dark and lowering gloom" as Rousseau's long funeral cortege assembled. It included infantry, artillery, and cavalry units, a regimental band, local Democratic officials, Mayor Conway, Governor Warmoth, and lesser dignitaries. At 2:00 P.M. almost every store and shop in the city closed its doors in honor of the departed general. Thousands of New Orleaneans lined the sidewalks, standing bareheaded in a slight drizzle, to watch as the procession passed down Canal Street on its way to Lafayette Cemetery. A reporter for the *Times* believed it was one of the largest funerals ever held in the city.[70]

During the following several days, articles appeared in state newspapers lauding Rousseau, detailing his career, and lamenting his death. The Alexandria *Democrat* voiced the praise of many when it said that Rousseau "respected the feelings and even the prejudices of our people." This comment underscored the reason behind such an outpouring of sentiment for a Union general by southerners.[71] There can be no question that Rousseau had been extremely well liked by the white citizens of the state, and his actions had catered to the white majority. To have acted otherwise would have required a complete change of personality for Rousseau. Like his friend Andrew Johnson, he had stayed with the Union in its crisis, but he did not support radical changes after the shooting stopped.

Baldey to George Sykes, November 17, 1868, in Dept Gulf, vol. 274A, both in RG 393, NA.

69. New Orleans *Times*, January 9, 1869. See similar comments in New Orleans *Crescent*, January 8, 1869, New Orleans *Daily Picayune*, January 8, 1869. Buchanan to Johnson, January 8, 1869, in Johnson Papers.

70. New Orleans *Times*, New Orleans *Crescent*, New Orleans *Daily Picayune*, New Orleans *Republican*, all dated January 10, 1869.

71. New Orleans *Daily Picayune*, January 12 and 13, 1869; Shreveport *South-Western*, January 13, 1869; Thibodeaux *Sentinel*, January 16, 1869; Lake Providence *Carroll Record*, January 16, 1869; Alexandria *Democrat*, January 20, 1869.

CHAPTER V

Interlude Under Mower and Reynolds

On January 11, 1869, Robert C. Buchanan again became commander of the Department of Louisiana. Just as before, the assignment was only temporary, but when a permanent commander might be selected or who he would be, Buchanan did not know. Even under these circumstances, Buchanan did not want to continue as state commander of Louisiana, and therefore he designated General Joseph A. Mower to fill that vacancy. Mower had supervised Reconstruction in the Fifth District for a few months in 1867. Since that time, however, he had been in near exile on Ship Island in the Gulf of Mexico, training the 39th Infantry and supervising the military prison located on the island. On January 19 Buchanan ordered Mower back to the civilized environs of the Crescent City.[1]

Mower's appointment brought a warning blast from the New Orleans *Crescent*, whose editor proclaimed that "the civil power is in the ascendency, and officials are no longer mere Jacks-in-the-box to be shoved up or down at the bidding of a military dictator." Although the *Crescent* opposed "the present bastard State government in Louisiana," it preferred that government to "the exercises of the caprice of a partisan general commanding." Accordingly, the *Crescent* expected that Mower, "who swept his scythe so unmercifully and with so little discrimination in the latter part of 1867," would now leave the civil government alone.[2]

One of Mower's first important tasks as state commander was to receive an inspection tour by the commanding general of the army, William T. Sherman. Mower had served well under Sherman during the Civil War and was on good terms with him, but the two men held opposite views on Reconstruction. Mower was a staunch Radical. In contrast, Sherman believed that the states should be left alone to find their

---

1. GO No. 1, Dept La, January 8, 1869, in GO, Dept La, RG 393, NA; New Orleans *Crescent*, January 13, 21, 27, 29, 1869.
2. New Orleans *Crescent*, January 22, 1869. A similar tone was taken by the Plaquemine *Iberville South*, January 23, 1869.

own solutions to the problems of race relations and economic recovery. Sherman spent a couple of evenings in the Crescent City, attending the opera and sightseeing. On February 10 the visiting general and his aides inspected the river defenses at Forts Jackson and St. Philip. Although improvements had been made over the years, the forts were still isolated from towns and provided few comforts or diversions for the soldiers of the 39th Infantry, who amused themselves by throwing mess hall scraps to the alligators in the moats. Sherman also went by riverboat to Alexandria, where he visited the Louisiana State University campus and talked with his old friend David F. Boyd, president of the struggling college. Before the Civil War Sherman had been superintendent of the school, and he maintained a fond attachment for the institution throughout his life. Sherman's visit seemed to be a pleasant one. However, if Buchanan and Mower expected to learn from him the identity of the permanent commander for the Department of Louisiana they were disappointed.[3]

Quite possibly Sherman knew of the bill in Congress, passed in early March, that reduced the size of the army. This reduction called for a redisposition of troops throughout the nation and greatly affected command arrangements in Louisiana. Buchanan learned from a friend in Washington that he would be leaving the state soon since his regiment, the 1st Infantry, had been assigned to Fort Leavenworth, Kansas. At about this same time, the War Department ordered the transfer of the 20th Infantry from Louisiana to Minnesota. This meant that two regiments experienced in dealing with Reconstruction problems in Louisiana were to be removed simultaneously. Reducing the number of soldiers in the army necessitated combining several infantry regiments. The 28th Infantry was integrated into the 19th, and the 39th and 40th united to form a single black regiment, the 25th. Some of the men of the 19th and 28th moved to Louisiana from Arkansas, and the 40th came to Louisiana from South Carolina.[4]

3. AAG Luke O'Reilly to CO, Fort Jackson, February 9, 1869, in Dept Gulf, vol. 274A, RG 393, NA; Pfanz, "Soldiering in the South," 408–409; New Orleans Crescent, February 9 and 10, 1869; William T. Sherman to David F. Boyd, February 22, 1869, in William T. Sherman Letters/David F. Boyd Family Papers, Department of Archives and Manuscripts, Louisiana State University Library, Baton Rouge.

4. George Gibson to Buchanan, February 19, 1869, filed with 5 MD, Telegrams Recd, RG 393, NA; Mower, Annual Report, 1869, in SW, "Annual Reort, 1869–1870," House Executive Documents, 41st Cong., 2nd Sess., No. 1, p. 97; Francis B. Heitman, Historical Register and Dictionary of the United States Army, 1789–1903 (2 vols.; Washington, 1903), I, 117; John Nankivell (comp. and ed.), History of the Twenty-fifth Regiment, United States Infantry, 1869–1926 (Denver, 1927), 8–13.

William T. Sherman

Adding to the confusion of these consolidations and troop movements were Buchanan's orders to close down the military posts at Shreveport, Alexandria, Monroe, and Amite. Apparently Congress and the War Department ordered these closings and similar ones in other states to save money. Maintaining or renting buildings at these places cost thousands of dollars each year, and supplying scattered posts in the state added to the cost. These posts were closed despite Louisiana's demonstrated need for close supervision, but no contingency plans were made to reopen them in the event of trouble.[5]

The orders closing several posts pleased most white Louisianians, but the War Department released additional orders regarding command arrangements that surprised many people in the state. President Grant asked Phil Sheridan to resume command of Louisiana, a request that disappointed Sheridan as much as Louisiana's Democrats. The little general previously had told Grant that he wanted nothing more to do with Louisiana's Byzantine politics and that he would serve there again only on Grant's direct orders. Within a few days the orders were changed. Sheridan, recently promoted to the rank of lieutenant general, was given command of the Indian-fighting army in the huge Division of the Missouri. Major General Oliver O. Howard, director of the Freedmen's Bureau, drew the Louisiana assignment. Joe Mower had assumed temporary command pending Howard's arrival when he learned that orders had been changed again. The one-armed Civil War hero would remain in Washington as superintendent of the Freedmen's Bureau. Command of the Department of Louisiana, rejected by two of the army's senior generals, fell by default to Mower.[6]

During March, Mower and his subordinates handled a routine military task, processing more than 150 white recruits who had arrived in New Orleans from depots in the North. The rookie soldiers received uniforms dispensed by the quartermaster from old stocks left over from the Civil War. The trousers and jackets rarely fitted properly, and the soldiers had to have them altered by a tailor. The paymaster deducted the cost of any

5. Mower, Annual Report, 1869, p. 96; AAAG Thomas Neill to Mower, March 1, 5, 1869, in Dept Gulf, vol. 266, O'Reilly to CO, Amite, February 26, 1869, in Dept Gulf, vol. 274A, Montgomery Meigs to Sherman, and Sherman's endorsement, March 30, 1869, in Dept La, Letters Recd, all in RG 393, NA.

6. GOs No. 10 and 18, AGO, March 5 and 16, 1869, in Edward McPherson, *The Political History of the United States of America During the Period of Reconstruction, 1865–1870* (2nd ed.; Washington, 1875; rpr. New York, 1969), 424–25; New Orleans *Crescent*, March 7, 9, 17, 1869; Sheridan to Grant, February 19, 1869, in Autograph Letters, Sheridan Papers; New Orleans *Bee*, April 2, 3, 1869.

alterations from a private's beginning pay of sixteen dollars per month. The infantrymen were assigned to deteriorating old barracks and consequently spent considerable amounts of time repairing their roofs, walls, and windows. The buildings were sparsely furnished. Rows of wooden bunks lined the walls, with footlockers and wall pegs for personal belongings and uniforms. The soldiers followed the standard training exercises: close order drill, manual of arms, guard mount, care of weapons, and target practice.[7]

Infantry units, such as those to which most of the recruits were assigned, did not always meet the commander's needs. Cavalry was more mobile and better suited than infantry to operate at some distance from regular garrisons, especially in the interior of the state, where Republicans complained of a lack of protection from criminals and vigilantes. Moreover, if called for by the civil authorities, cavalry could reach the site of a riot more quickly than infantry. Three troops of cavalry had been on duty in Louisiana, but in order to fulfill the reorganization requirements, they had been sent to the Texas frontier. Therefore, Mower requested permission of the War Department to purchase some horses and mount some of his infantry companies as cavalry.[8]

General Sherman refused Mower's request to buy horses, saying that instead he should make every effort toward "a thorough and systematic reduction in expenses" of the army in Louisiana. Giving advice on the use of soldiers, the commanding general told Mower to intervene in civil affairs only when "the Civil Authorities confess themselves powerless." Undoubtedly Sherman's reply disappointed Mower. The lack of mounted troops reduced the speed with which his orders could be carried out. Moreover, the decreasing number of seasoned soldiers in Louisiana reduced the army's effectiveness.[9]

The 20th Infantry was the next veteran regiment to leave Louisiana. On April 4 it followed the 1st Infantry to new duty stations in the North. A special citizens committee tendered its "sincere thanks" to Colonel Sykes and the soldiers of the 20th regiment for their "kindness and cour-

7. New Orleans *Bee*, March 16, 1869; Pfanz, "Soldiering in the South," 262–65, 307–308, 369–74, 378–84; Jack D. Foner, *The United States Soldier between Two Wars: Army Life and Reforms, 1865–1898* (New York, 1970), 15, 19; Inspector Thomas Neill to AAG, Dept La, February 19, 1869, Lt. Owen Sweet to AAAG, Report of Quarterly Target Practice, Dept La, December 31, 1869, both in Dept La, Letters Recd, Capt. John B. Johnson to AAIG L. P. Graham, March 23, 1868, in Dept Gulf, vol. 273, Capt. A. E. Hooker to AAAG, 5 MD, June 30, 1868, in 5 MD, Letters Recd, all in RG 393, NA.
    8. Mower to Edward D. Townsend, April 2, 1869, in Dept Gulf, vol. 266, RG 393, NA.
    9. Sherman to Mower, April 3, 1869, filed with 5 MD, Telegrams Recd, *ibid.*

tesy on the discharge of their official duties" while in Baton Rouge. The West Baton Rouge *Sugar Planter* noted that the departure of the 20th would deprive local music lovers of concerts by the regiment's "excellent amateur minstrel band." Within a few days, elements of the 19th Infantry arrived to take over the garrison at Baton Rouge.[10]

The reduced number of soldiers in the state prompted Mower to continue Buchanan's consolidation program. Mower ordered the closing of the post in New Orleans and the transfer of the troops from their rented billets in the city to Jackson Barracks. Only headquarters orderlies and staff officers would remain in the Crescent City itself. The barracks at Greenville were to be closed by the end of April. Mower ordered troops withdrawn from Shreveport on April 12, and all of the army's buildings in Shreveport, including the officers' quarters, barracks, mess hall, hospital, and stable, were sold at auction.[11]

Meanwhile, Republicans called for the army's assistance with troubles in south Louisiana. Rowdies and brigands had set upon blacks and Republicans in St. Landry Parish. Local authorities asked the governor to send in the state militia, and in turn Warmoth asked Mower to dispatch troops to Opelousas. Two years before Mower had unhesitatingly ordered soldiers to help Republican officials. In this case, however, he telegraphed General Sherman, asking both for permission to give help and for advice on how to do it. Sherman approved sending the troops and left the details to Mower.[12]

Accordingly, on April 27 Mower ordered Company H of the 25th Infantry to Opelousas, telling Captain Frank M. Coxe to keep his men "entirely aloof from the citizens" and not to interfere in civil affairs. Coxe found Opelousas citizens "laboring under great political agitation." Democrats boldly declared their disdain for the Reconstruction Acts and had intimidated most Republicans to the point where they seldom spoke their minds in public. Coxe concluded that loyal Union men lived "in hourly dread" of the army's departure. Stationing black soldiers in the Conservative stronghold of Opelousas caused tempers to flare. Several citizens ("noted debauchers and outlaws," according to Coxe) threatened some enlisted men as they walked to a dance in town. The soldiers ran

10. Baton Rouge *Tri-Weekly Advocate*, April 5, 1869; West Baton Rouge *Sugar Planter*, February 6, 1869.

11. Sherman to Mower, April 3, 1869, filed with 5 MD, Telegrams Recd, RG 393, NA; Mower, Annual Report, 1869, p. 97; Shreveport *South-Western*, April 14, 1869.

12. Mower to Warmoth, April 17, 1869, in Dept Gulf, vol. 266, Sherman to Mower, April 21, 1869, filed with 5 MD, Telegrams Recd, both in RG 393, NA.

back to camp with gunshots and catcalls ringing in their ears. When Coxe persuaded a local judge to hold a hearing on the incident, a fight almost broke out in the courtroom between spectators and soldiers. The captain quit trying to have the rowdies arrested because the case would have been "presented to a jury of men pledged to save from punishment their own Confederates."[13]

Having persuaded Mower to send troops to one town, Warmoth was emboldened to ask for similar assistance in other places. When Republicans in Franklin Parish wanted the army to enforce the peace in Winnsboro, Mower ordered Lieutenant Richard Vance and a company of the 19th Infantry from Baton Rouge to "protect, aid and sustain the civil authorities." But Mower, again unwilling to rely solely on his own judgment, requested approval from Washington. Adjutant General Edward Townsend replied that Sherman approved of the temporary garrison. Mower believed that Franklin Parish was in "the worst portion of the State, . . . infested by a gang of desperadoes and thieves, who defy and ignore the local civil authorities entirely." Corroborating Mower's opinion, Lieutenant Vance reported that whipping of black field hands was commonplace, civil law appeared to have broken down completely, and drunken citizens raced horses up and down the streets of Winnsboro.[14]

About two weeks after sending troops to Winnsboro, Mower learned that the state supreme court had declared the Metropolitan Police a legal and proper law enforcement agency, a ruling that angered the local police departments in the parishes surrounding New Orleans. Legally empowered by the court to extend their authority, the Metropolitans established a precinct station in Jefferson Parish. On May 18 the Jefferson police fired on the Metropolitans, threatening to bring on the interpolice battle that General Rousseau had feared might occur the previous year. Warmoth demanded that the army intervene. Without hesitating, Mower ordered a company of the 25th Infantry to move into the troubled area. In this case, simply the foreknowledge of a quick military response dispersed the rioters. Troops bivouacked near the precinct station for several

13. Mower, Annual Report, 1869, pp. 98–99; AAAG George Baldey to Frank M. Coxe, April 27, 1869, in Dept Gulf, vol. 266, Coxe to Baldey, May 9, 10, June 28, 1869, all in Dept La, Letters Recd, all in RG 393, NA. See also *Senate Executive Documents*, 41st Cong., 3rd Sess., No. 16, Pt. 1, p. 15, Opelousas *Journal*, May 15, July 10, 1869.

14. Warmoth to Mower, April 30, 1869, Richard Vance to Baldey, August 6, 1869, both in Dept La, Letters Recd, Baldey to CO, detachment of the 19th Infantry, May 3, 1869, in Dept Gulf, vol. 266, Mower to Townsend, May 4, 1869, Townsend to Mower, May 5, 1869, both filed with 5 MD, Telegrams Recd, all in RG 393, NA. See also *Senate Executive Documents*, 41st Cong., 3rd Sess., No. 16, Pt. 1, p. 16.

days before returning to Jackson Barracks. As he had done before, Mower asked for and received approval of his conduct from the War Department. However, the New Orleans *Times* condemned the interference in civil affairs by the "hireling soldiery."[15]

But no sooner was one fire dampened than another broke out. Former Union army officer Ross Wilkinson, a prominent Republican in Caddo Parish, reported a threat had been made against his life by unnamed "desperadoes." Subsequently Mower received Warmoth's familiar plea for troops. Cooperating with Mower, General Joseph Reynolds, commander of Texas, temporarily provided F Troop, 6th Cavalry, to patrol Caddo and protect Wilkinson. The use of troops for such domestic duties displeased General Sherman in Washington. Nevertheless, the post at Shreveport, so carefully dismantled only a few weeks before, was temporarily reestablished.[16]

Meanwhile, the embers flamed again in Jefferson. Warmoth wanted Mower to reassign a detachment to the town because a local judge had created a crisis by issuing an injunction against the Metropolitan Police, prohibiting "them from performing their duty in Jefferson City and parish." Mower sent two companies of the 25th Infantry and two Gatling guns to the town, stationing them near the courthouse. When Secretary of War John A. Rawlins learned that troops had returned to Jefferson, he admonished Mower to use his forces "only to preserve the peace" in time of dire need. Upon receiving the secretary's comment, Mower withdrew the soldiers, whose presence had possibly prevented another riot. Following up on Rawlins' admonition, General Sherman emphatically told Mower that "troops must not be used to do the work of Police . . . and . . . soldiers should only be called on when unlawful assemblages occur too large to be controlled by the civil powers of the State."[17]

The remainder of the summer passed quietly, and Warmoth advised Mower in September that the troops could be withdrawn from Ope-

15. Mower, Annual Report, 1869, p. 98; New Orleans *Times*, May 20, 1869; Warmoth to Mower, May 18, 1869, in Dept La, Letters Recd, Mower to Sherman, May 19, 1869, in Dept Gulf, vol. 266, Townsend to Mower, May 19, 1869, filed with 5 MD, Telegrams Recd, all in RG 393, NA.

16. Warmoth to Mower, May 22, 1869, in Dept La, Letters Recd, Townsend to Mower, May 31, 1869, Sherman to Mower, May 24, 1869, both filed with 5 MD, Telegrams Recd, Mower to Warmoth, June 5, 1869, in Dept Gulf, vol. 266, all in RG 393, NA; Mower, Annual Report, 1869, p. 99.

17. Mower to Townsend, June 14, 17, 1869, Mower to Warmoth, June 14, 1869, all in Dept Gulf, vol. 266, Warmoth to Mower, June 15, 1869, Townsend to Mower, June 22, 1869, both in Dept La, Letters Recd, Townsend to Mower, June 17, 1869, filed with 5 MD, Telegrams Recd, all in RG 393, NA.

lousas and Winnsboro. Although Captain Coxe reckoned that "loyal citizens" wanted the army to remain in Opelousas indefinitely, the soldiers
were probably pleased to leave the town. They had been living in leaky
tents for five months and looked forward to the security and warmth of
their barracks. Certainly, most of the town's white citizens expressed "a
sense of relief" when the troops marched away. Following the final session of the district court at Winnsboro, Lieutenant Vance and his detachment returned to Baton Rouge. Warmoth told Mower that using the soldiers had been necessary to quiet Franklin Parish and protect the court.[18]

However, Warmoth's requests for military assistance had not ended.
He soon asked for troops to protect prisoners in the Ouachita Parish jail
in Monroe. Remembering Sherman's past warnings, Mower doubted the
advisability of dispatching soldiers before violence had occurred. His reluctance represented quite a change in attitude by the general who, next
to Sheridan, was most closely associated with the Radical Republicans.
Under these circumstances, Mower requested orders from Washington.
Replying through Adjutant General Townsend, General Sherman left to
Mower's "discretion the power to aid, or withhold aid from, the civil
power," but reminded him "that the State authorities should exhaust their
power *first*." Evidently, Mower decided not to send any troops to Monroe at that time.[19]

Mower thankfully welcomed the quietude of December, when, after
studying inspection reports, he recommended closing the distant and uncomfortable post on Ship Island in the Gulf of Mexico. Toward the end
of the month, the secretary of war approved Mower's recommendation.
Undoubtedly, Mower would have liked personally to supervise the closing of Ship Island, the post where he had spent several months separated
from the mainland and the mainstream of military and political affairs.[20]

However, in early January, 1870, Mower contracted a severe case of
pneumonia. Army and civilian doctors tried but could not effect a cure.
On the night of January 6 Mower died at the age of forty-seven. Quite in
contrast to the outpouring of grief for Rousseau the year before, Louisiana newspapers and citizens took only perfunctory notice of Mower's

18. Coxe to Baldey, September 23, 1869, Warmoth to Mower, September 27, October
26, 1869, all in Dept La, Letters Recd, *ibid.*; Mower, Annual Report, 1869, p. 99; Opelousas
Journal, October 23, 1869; Baton Rouge *Tri-Weekly Advocate*, October 29, 1869.

19. Warmoth to Mower, October 15, 1869, Townsend to Mower (emphasis in the original), November 9, 1869, both in Dept La, Letters Recd, RG 393, NA.

20. Townsend to Mower, December 29, 1869, *ibid.*

death. Adjutant General Townsend appointed Colonel Charles H. Smith, then commanding troops at Little Rock, Arkansas, temporary commander of the Louisiana department.[21]

Mower's two periods of command in Louisiana differed from each other in several respects. In 1869 Mower served for a year, whereas, in 1867 he had commanded only for three months. In 1867 Mower had dominated Governor Benjamin Flanders, but the authority of an elected civilian governor was a significant brake on the general's actions in 1869. Warmoth was a capable and skillful executive who wielded many of the powers formerly held by the military commander and at the same time courted the army and knew its value to his Republican administration. Moreover, Mower had to abide by rules that had not existed in 1867. In 1869 Mower no longer had the power to remove or appoint officeholders on his own. Warmoth made any new appointments, and the army had little or no say in who was chosen. In 1867 Mower could (and did) send troops to any potential trouble spot in the state on his own orders. In 1869 Mower acted judiciously, mostly in response to Warmoth's requests for military assistance, and usually the general sought retroactive approval of his actions from the War Department.

General Sherman's attitude was another restraining influence on Mower. Sherman shared the opinion of many white Louisianians who believed that frequent military assistance to local Republicans was uncalled for and more dangerous than helpful. Mower, who had not completely shed his Radical heritage, soon realized that the tone of Reconstruction had changed militarily and politically. The Republicans in Louisiana expected the army's aid at any time, but officials in Washington were more reluctant to condone the use of soldiers as local policemen. The sharp edge of the Reconstruction crusade had worn dull. Mower, the acolyte who had served at Sheridan's Radical altar, could no longer count on the unstinting support of higher command.

Under the altering conditions of Reconstruction, Louisiana Democrats wondered about the future of their state and their party. In January, 1870, the Monroe *Ouachita Telegraph* ran an editorial that reflected the hopes of many Democrats. "The reconstruction of the South is nearly finished up,

---

21. Baldey to John Ludeling, January 7, 1870, in Taliaferro Papers; New Orleans *Daily Picayune*, New Orleans *Times*, both dated January 7, 1870; New Orleans *Bee*, Baton Rouge *Tri-Weekly Advocate*, both dated January 8, 1870; Monroe *Ouachita Telegraph*, January 15, 1870; Charles H. Smith to Baldey, January 8, 1870, filed with 5 MD, Telegrams Recd, RG 393, NA; *Army and Navy Journal*, January 15, 1870, vol. VII, No. 22, p. 333.

and so too is the Radical party. The two have been fast friends and will expire together." [22] At this time only one southern state, Tennessee, had shaken off Radical control, but Virginia and North Carolina Democrats were consolidating their power and would elect Conservative governors and legislative majorities later in 1870. Looking at these positive signs, Louisiana Democrats hoped that the time of redemption was near at hand for the Pelican State. Louisiana Republicans were on the verge of an open split in their party, and the army in the state appeared to be moribund. However, obituaries in either case would have been premature.

On March 31, 1870, the Adjutant General's Office in Washington issued an order reshuffling the military commands in the South and separating Arkansas and Louisiana. The orders shifted Arkansas to the Department of Missouri and placed Louisiana and Texas in the newly designated Department of Texas. General Joseph J. Reynolds, commander of troops in Texas since 1868, officially took command of the new department on April 16. Reynolds had served with garrison forces in Texas after his graduation from West Point in 1843. He taught history and geography at the Military Academy from 1846 until 1857 when he resigned from the service with the rank of first lieutenant. His army career apparently finished, Reynolds became a professor at Washington University in St. Louis, Missouri. When southern forces fired on Fort Sumter, Reynolds left St. Louis, went to Indiana, and raised two volunteer regiments. During the war he fought in the battles of Chickamauga and Chattanooga, and in 1864 he supervised the defenses of New Orleans. In the postwar years he had commanded troops in Arkansas and served along the Rio Grande. His pale eyes, stringy beard, and narrow lips made for a less than authoritative presence. Rather than move to New Orleans, Reynolds, who was deeply involved in Texas politics, decided to keep his headquarters in Austin. [23]

Accompanying the change in departmental structure, another order directed the 25th Infantry to move from Louisiana to the Texas frontier. The 19th regiment was to garrison Louisiana by itself. By June all of the soldiers of the black regiment had been transferred to Texas. During April and May, Colonel Charles Smith redistributed the companies of the 19th Infantry from Arkansas to posts at Jackson Barracks, Baton Rouge, Shreveport, and Forts Jackson, St. Philip, and Pike. [24]

22. Monroe, *Ouachita Telegraph*, January 22, 1870.
23. Cullum, *Register of West Point*, II, 78–79; Warner, *Generals in Blue*, 397–98.
24. Smith to Joseph J. Reynolds, April 22, 1869, Smith to AAG, Dept Texas, May 25,

Joseph J. Reynolds

The decreasing strength of the army in Louisiana probably made Governor Warmoth feel somewhat uneasy, but he had already taken steps to provide his administration with its own armed support. In April the Louisiana legislature had passed a bill, sponsored by the governor, to create the state's first postwar militia. As governor, Warmoth commanded the state troops, and he chose as adjutant general James Longstreet, an important Confederate general who had become a Republican. Longstreet had resided in Louisiana since March, 1869, when President Grant had appointed him surveyor of customs for the port of New Orleans. During the summer of 1870, Longstreet organized and trained the militia, which was composed almost entirely of blacks.[25]

Warmoth realized that his unproven militia would be inadequate to protect the polls in the state's November elections, and he wanted the army to strengthen Louisiana's garrisons. The governor and other Republican officials asked General Reynolds to send additional troops to aid the 19th Infantry before the polls opened. However, no reinforcements were sent. President Grant believed that Louisiana was safe enough, but Florida was not. Therefore, he directed Reynolds to send two companies of the 19th regiment to Tallahassee for election duty there.[26]

By election day, November 7, six infantry companies were assigned to New Orleans. According to Warmoth, the Crescent City and Shreveport were the most likely spots for disturbances during the voting, and the soldiers in those towns were especially watchful for anything unusual. Lieutenant Colonel Romeyn B. Ayres commanded the companies in New Orleans in the absence of Colonel Smith, who had been called to serve on a special army board in Washington. Republicans did very well in the election, which was quiet and orderly. Warmoth's handpicked man, former governor Benjamin F. Flanders, won the race for mayor of New Orleans. Republicans captured all of Louisiana's congressional seats and elected a majority of the next state legislature.[27]

Although November 7 passed quietly in New Orleans and Shreveport,

26, 1870, all in Dept Texas, Letters Recd, RG 393, NA; Annual Report, Dept Texas, 1870 (Microcopy M-619, reel 828), RG 94, NA.

25. William L. Richter, "Longstreet: From Rebel to Scalawag," *Louisiana History*, XI (Summer, 1970), 215–30.

26. Warmoth to Reynolds, November 3, 1870, AG James Fry to Reynolds, November 6, 1870, both in Dept Texas, Letters Recd, RG 393, NA.

27. Fry to Romeyn B. Ayres, November 2, 1870, Ayres to Fry, November 25, 1870, both *ibid.*; Reynolds to CO, Shreveport, November 3, 1870, Reynolds to Warmoth, November 4, 1870, both in Dept Texas, Letters Sent, RG 393, NA. Taylor, *Louisiana Reconstructed*, 185–86.

a riot unexpectedly erupted in Baton Rouge after the polls had closed. The reasons for the fighting are unknown, but clashes between armed groups left four blacks dead and about twenty blacks and whites wounded. Soldiers from the local garrison went quickly to the scene and arrested one Negro and fifty-nine whites, many of whom were among the town's most prominent citizens. After the army restored order, Captain Edward S. Meyer placed Baton Rouge under martial law, and soldiers patrolled the town's streets for several days. Because of "insufficient evidence," the charges were dropped, and all of the accused men were released.[28]

Despite the postelection violence in Baton Rouge and a disturbance in Donaldsonville, Governor Warmoth viewed the results of the canvass favorably. He later called it "the quietest and fairest election ever held in the State of Louisiana up to that time." The New Orleans *Republican* defended the use of the army to guard the polls, claiming that "no honest man can have any objection to the presence of United States troops." In contrast, the New Orleans *Times* denounced the army after the election with the blazoned headline "Have We a Military Government?" The *Times* claimed that Warmoth deserved "grave censure for inflicting upon this city the insult and disgrace of such employment, in a time of profound peace, of the military forces of the Federal Government." The *Times* concluded with the forlorn hope that this display of military power for partisan political purposes would be "the last exhibition of the sort ever made in this city."[29]

Colonel Smith did not return from his official business in Washington until January, 1871, and therefore missed the exciting activities after the election. To reacquaint himself with his command, he inspected the posts and soldiers in Louisiana during February. A few weeks later he made use of the information gained on the inspection when he conferred with General Sherman in New Orleans.[30]

After questioning Smith and reviewing his own notes, Sherman recommended several changes in troop dispositions and posts in Louisiana.

28. Baton Rouge *Weekly Advocate*, November 12, 1870; New Orleans *Daily Picayune*, November 11, 1870; Report of CO, Baton Rouge, November 14, 1870, in *Senate Executive Documents*, 41st Cong., 3rd Sess., No. 16, Pt. 1, p. 17; Baton Rouge *Tri-Weekly Advocate*, December 5, 1870.

29. Warmoth, *War, Politics, and Reconstruction*, 101; New Orleans *Daily Picayune*, November 10, 11, 12, 1870; New Orleans *Republican*, November 10, 1870; New Orleans *Times*, November 8, 1870.

30. AAG Henry C. Wood to Ayres, January 3, 1871, SO No. 30, Dept Texas, February 13, 1871, both in Dept Texas, Letters Recd, RG 393, NA.

First of all, for reasons that are not clear, Sherman wanted the main post in the state located at Baton Rouge instead of Jackson Barracks near New Orleans, the capital city, where political confrontations were common. Furthermore, Sherman recommended closing all posts in Louisiana except Baton Rouge and Jackson Barracks. Forts Jackson and St. Philip (which Sherman called "unfit for the habitations of man") and Fort Pike (which he called "utterly useless") deserved to be manned by only small caretaker squads. Subsequently, Sherman convinced General Reynolds of the economy of his plan. During the summer Reynolds closed the post at Shreveport—once again leaving northern Louisiana without an army garrison. The soldiers in the twin forts were ordered to Baton Rouge. Thus consolidated by the late summer of 1871, the army in Louisiana prepared to face the state's next political crisis.[31]

In 1871 Henry Clay Warmoth still held substantial power in Louisiana, but he was losing his domination over the state's Republican party. Various men had opposed Warmoth from the beginning of his term as governor in 1868. Since then the anti-Warmoth forces had coalesced into a formidable group that included some of Louisiana's most important black politicians, who had been angered by Warmoth's veto in 1868 of a state civil rights bill. Warmoth had vetoed the bill because he believed that its promises of additional rights were unrealizable at that time. Some black leaders insisted that the law be on the books whether or not a majority of whites would abide by it. Moreover, James F. Casey, the Republican collector of customs for New Orleans who was married to the sister of Julia Dent Grant, the president's wife, led a biracial personal following of his own against the governor. The ultimate split came in 1871 when Warmoth opposed Casey's elevation to the U.S. Senate and persuaded the legislature to elect one of his own supporters, Joseph R. West, a former Union army officer from Louisiana. After this victory Warmoth tried to oust Casey from power and called for his resignation as collector of customs. Casey refused to resign and thereafter was titular leader of the anti-Warmoth Republicans, called the Custom House Ring. Grant and Warmoth had disliked each other for years; there had been a personal argument between the two men near Vicksburg during the war. The

---

31. Sherman to Townsend, April 21, 1871, *ibid.*; Reynolds to Warmoth, May 3, 1871, Reynolds to C. H. Smith, May 8, 1871, both in Dept Texas, Letters Sent, RG 393, NA; SW, "Annual Report, 1871–1872," in *House Executive Documents*, 42nd Cong., 2nd Sess., No. 1, pp. 96–97; Baton Rouge *Tri-Weekly Advocate*, July 12, 1871.

Casey-Warmoth feud simply added to the enmity between the president and the governor. Other anti-Warmoth leaders included U.S. Marshal Stephen B. Packard, a former Union army officer from Maine who displaced Casey as the actual boss of the ring; Oscar J. Dunn, black lieutenant governor who wanted increased powers for himself and disdained Warmoth's lack of support for Negro rights and education; and U.S. Senator William Pitt Kellogg, a former Vermont lawyer and Warmoth supporter who had decided his future was with the pro-Grant Custom House Ring.[32]

Warmoth's high-handed operation of the state government and personal control of the state voting supervisors, the Metropolitan Police, and the state militia created many enemies. No doubt Warmoth and his cronies were corrupt, but Louisianians needed no lessons in political pettifoggery from a young Missouri lawyer or anyone else. Indeed, many of his opponents, whether Democrats or Republicans, wanted him out so that their own factions could have more influence in filling state jobs, getting state public works contracts, and grabbing other spoils of office. Warmoth described the situation accurately in his oft-quoted statement: "Why damn it, everybody is demoralized down here. Corruption is the fashion."[33]

In July, 1871, Packard, Casey, and Dunn decided to force a test of strength at the party's state convention, scheduled to begin on August 9. At stake was the election of the new Republican state central committee, which Packard was determined to control. However, the Custom House leaders knew that Warmoth controlled a majority of the convention delegates. Therefore, Packard appointed several extra deputy marshals and pulled from his sleeve the trump card in any game of Reconstruction politics—the army.[34]

Hoping to prevent violence between the Republican factions, Colonel Smith ordered two companies of soldiers from Jackson Barracks into New Orleans one week before the convention began. Observers specu-

---

32. Taylor, *Louisiana Reconstructed*, 201, 209–214, 250–51; Binning, "Henry Clay Warmoth," 171–72, 180–83, 196–98.
33. Roger W. Shugg, *Origins of Class Struggle in Louisiana* (Baton Rouge, 1939), 227.
34. Stephen B. Packard to James F. Casey, July 28, 1871, William P. Kellogg to A. T. Ackerman, July 29, 1871, Oscar J. Dunn to Grant, July 29, 1871, all in Letters Recd by the U.S. Justice Dept from Louisiana, 1871–1884 (Microcopy M-940, reel 1), RG 60, NA; hereinafter cited as Justice Dept Letters. For an excellent discussion of the convention see Binning, "Henry Clay Warmoth," 238–53.

lated openly about which Republican faction the troops would support. The New Orleans *Times* predicted that in the event of a showdown the army would aid the Custom House Ring.[35]

Marshal Packard used his official position to bring pressure on General Reynolds to send in troops. In a telegram, Packard charged that "thugs and bruisers" would try to disrupt the convention and requested "a guard of soldiers . . . to protect the custom-house and other public property." This was simply a pretense on Packard's part to obtain the army's support and deny Warmoth his rightful role in the convention. As U.S. marshal, Packard asked Reynolds for the soldiers without explaining that the anticipated "thugs and bruisers" were other Republicans and that the Custom House, rather than the state capitol or some other building, was the location of the convention. Reynolds, probably prompted by his own pro-Grant Republicanism, ordered Colonel Alfred Sully, commanding troops in New Orleans, to place guards at the Custom House, leaving Sully to decide how many companies to send. Astutely displaying his understanding of the peculiar situation, Sully acknowledged Reynolds' order, but added that "the trouble is between two factions of the republican party and is not the act of persons enemies [*sic*] of the Gov't but of those who profess to be its friends. It is entirely a political row among republican politicians." Nevertheless, Sully was prepared to send in his soldiers.[36]

A special detachment of three companies of the 19th Infantry, supported by two Gatling guns, under the command of Captain Jacob H. Smith marched up to the Custom House at about 8:30 A.M. on August 9. Smith later said that he occupied the building on orders from Colonel Sully only "to protect United States property" and disclaimed any intention of assisting one side or the other at the convention. Although the Gatlings were not used, their presence gave the name "Gatling Gun Convention" to the meeting that was about to take place.[37]

About 11:00 A.M. Warmoth entered the building, followed by thirty delegates and well-wishers. Once inside, the governor recognized several

35. New Orleans *Times*, August 5, 1871.
36. Packard to Reynolds, August 8, 1871, in *House Miscellaneous Documents*, 42nd Cong., 2nd Sess., No. 211, p. 127; AAG Wood to Alfred Sully, August 8, 1871, in Dept Texas, Letters Sent, RG 393, Sully to Wood, August 8, 1871, in AGO File 2747 of 1871 (Microcopy M-666, reel 27), RG 94, both in NA; Taylor, *Louisiana Reconstructed*, 216.
37. Sully to Jacob H. Smith, August 9, 1871, in *House Reports*, 42nd Cong., 2nd Sess., No. 92, p. 10; New Orleans *Times*, August 10, 12, 1871; New Orleans *Daily Picayune*, August 10, 1871; *House Miscellaneous Documents*, 42nd Cong., 2nd Sess., No. 211, pp. 100–101.

of the special deputy marshals, all of whom were armed. Warmoth then happened to glance through a door that was temporarily ajar and saw Custom House leaders and delegates holding a caucus in an obvious attempt to organize the convention and elect the state central committee while the Warmoth faction was absent. According to Captain Smith, Warmoth summoned his followers, and standing on a chair so he could see over the crowd, he gave an impromptu speech in which he "made some remarks not very complimentary to the Army." Apparently some of his remarks were also not very complimentary to Packard. Fearing an altercation between the marshals and Warmoth's men, Captain Smith told the governor that he would have to stop his speech and leave the building. Without dissenting, Warmoth and his friends walked out of the Custom House and across the street to Turner's Hall and waited for the rest of their delegates. Subsequently the Warmoth faction held their own ineffectual meeting, but the national Republican party recognized the Custom House's state central committee.[38]

Packard had successfully maneuvered the army into a position where soldiers forced Warmoth out of the convention on the grounds of preventing a disturbance that would damage government property. Warmoth claimed that the army had disrupted the legal activities of the convention and prevented his delegates from participating in the meeting. However, Mayor Flanders believed that the presence of the soldiers at the Custom House had "prevented a scene of bloodshed which would again have disgraced this city."[39]

New Orleans newspapers roundly condemned Packard and his minions. Warmoth's *Republican*, for example, flatly accused Packard of obtaining military assistance "under false representations" and concluded that the ultimate responsibility of the party's split rested with President Grant himself for condoning the Custom House Ring. The New Orleans *Bee* commented, "Who, a year ago, could have imagined that Gov. Warmoth would be prevented by an officer of the United States army . . . from making in public a speech to his friends and followers?" Only the *Picayune* dissented from the chorus of criticism, saying that it would pre-

38. New Orleans *Times*, August 10, 1871; New Orleans *Republican*, August 10, 1871; Ella Lonn, *Reconstruction in Louisiana after 1868* (New York, 1918), 102–104; Warmoth, testimony, Jacob H. Smith, testimony, both in *House Miscellaneous Documents*, 42nd Cong., 2nd Sess., No. 211, pp. 300, 305, 100.

39. Taylor, *Louisiana Reconstructed*, 217–18; Warmoth, testimony, Flanders to Packard, November 27, 1871, both in *House Miscellaneous Documents*, 42nd Cong., 2nd Sess., No. 211, pp. 357, 200.

fer military government to "the corrupt, degraded, meretricious, ignorant, rapacious, remorseless, and wholly unscrupulous rule" of the Republicans.[40]

Despite his recent difficulties, Warmoth still nurtured hopes for a second term. Lieutenant Governor Dunn died unexpectedly in November, and Warmoth's political fortunes seemed brighter when he persuaded the state senate to elect as Dunn's replacement P. B. S. Pinchback, an important black leader and a Warmoth supporter. Naturally, the governor looked ahead with some optimism to the next test of political strength, the meeting of the state legislature in January, 1872.[41]

Meanwhile, the War Department made yet another series of alterations in the Military Division of the South. On November 1 Louisiana was joined with Arkansas, Mississippi, and three forts in Florida—Fort Barrancas in Pensacola, Fort Jefferson in the Dry Tortugas, and Key West—to form the new Department of the Gulf under the command of Brevet Major General William H. Emory, who established his headquarters in New Orleans on November 28. During Emory's tenure, the army participated in some of the most dangerous events during Reconstruction—events so disturbing that General Sheridan eventually had to return to Louisiana.[42]

40. New Orleans *Republican* and New Orleans *Bee*, both dated August 10, 1871; New Orleans *Daily Picayune*, August 17, 1871.

41. Taylor, *Louisiana Reconstructed*, 218–21.

42. William H. Emory to Henry W. Halleck, November 29, 1871, in Dept Gulf, vol. 139/DSL, RG 393, NA; SW, "Annual Report, 1871–1872," 82.

CHAPTER VI

Send Me Another Regiment

Brevet Major General William Hemsley Emory chose as his headquarters a house at the corner of Camp and St. Joseph Streets, some ten blocks distant from the Custom House and prepared to fulfill his new assignment as commander of the Department of the Gulf, just as he had capably fulfilled a variety of duties during his thirty-eight-year army career. In 1871 Emory celebrated his sixtieth birthday, making him the oldest officer to command Louisiana during Reconstruction. He had been appointed to West Point from his home state of Maryland and was graduated in 1831, ranked in the middle of his class. He had then served as a second lieutenant in the artillery for five years and resigned from the army in 1836.

After working as a civil engineer for two years, he was reinstated in the Topographical Engineers with the rank of first lieutenant and was second in command of the army survey detachment that completed marking the boundary between the United States and Canada. At the outbreak of hostilities with Mexico, Emory was appointed chief engineer in General Stephen W. Kearny's Army of the West, winning brevets of captain and major in the California fighting. Following the Mexican War, Emory spent most of his time commanding survey parties, making maps, and writing reports.[1]

At the start of the Civil War, Lieutenant Colonel Emory commanded all U.S. soldiers in the Indian Territory. Threatened by Texas state troops, Emory managed to extricate himself and his soldiers, taking them to Fort Leavenworth without losing a man. Ordered to report to the East, Emory took over a brigade in the Army of the Potomac and served in the Peninsula campaign, receiving a brevet of colonel for gallantry at the battle of Hanover Court House in May, 1862. Transferring

1. Donaldsonville *Chief*, December 6, 1871; *Dictionary of American Biography*, VI, 153–54.

to the Department of the Gulf, Emory commanded a division in the Port Hudson and Red River campaigns and for a time supervised the defenses of New Orleans. In 1864 he took command of the XIX Army Corps and returned to the eastern theater.

In Phil Sheridan's Shenandoah Valley campaign, Emory and the XIX Corps fumbled their opportunity to acquit themselves well, and instead were handled roughly by General Jubal Early's Confederate forces. Sheridan and Emory got along well enough, despite the older man's lack of flair and his difficulties on the battlefield. In fact, Sheridan recommended Emory for a brevet of major general of volunteers for meritorious action at the decisive battle of Cedar Creek.[2] The two men remained on cordial terms after the war, but they did not serve together in the same department. The results of years of desert sun and campaign bivouac showed plainly on his pouchy, creased, and bewhiskered face, giving Emory the proper effect of a soldier who had served his country well. He had applied his skills, experience, and dedication to assignments mean and grand, dangerous and routine. Failure was not in his record. Now the army had sent him to Louisiana with its barely believable politics and its scarcely credible circumstances.

Upon his arrival in New Orleans, Emory learned about the unsettling events of the past few months, especially the intraparty struggle at the Republican convention in August. Emory's senior officers probably warned him about the possibility of trouble at the upcoming session of the legislature, scheduled to open on January 1, 1872. However, Emory ordered no extraordinary military preparations for the new year.

Unsure of exactly what the army's role was if the political parties in Louisiana did turn to violence, Emory applied for some operational guidelines from General Henry W. Halleck, commander of the Military Division of the South at Louisville. Halleck's adjutant sent the following reply: "You will use the troops of your command to preserve order as in your judgment may be proper *without referring to these headquarters . . .* but reporting such action [as you take]. No further instructions [are] deemed necessary."[3]

Halleck's noncommittal orders typified the ones sent out by division headquarters and the War Department to southern commanders desper-

---

2. T. Harry Williams, *Hayes of the Twenty-third: The Civil War Volunteer Officer* (New York, 1965), 233, 256–57, 297, 299–300; Philip H. Sheridan to Edwin M. Stanton, April 18, 1866, in Sheridan Papers.

3. Robert N. Scott to Emory, December 2, 1871 (my italics), in *House Miscellaneous Documents*, 42nd Cong., 2nd Sess., No. 211, p. 93.

William H. Emory

ate for some concrete instructions to direct them through the unusual situations of Reconstruction.[4] The military hierarchy left as many of the difficult decisions as possible to the commanders on the spot, letting them take the credit (or the blame) for whatever happened. Such nebulous orders hurt Emory more than any other southern commander because Louisiana was consistently the most troublesome southern state to the national administration in Washington.

On January 1, 1872, the Louisiana legislature opened amid conditions designed to prevent the assembling of a quorum in the senate—conditions that led to tension-filled days for the remainder of the month. Stephen Packard had schemed with the aid of most of the Democrats in the legislature to impeach Governor Warmoth. Once impeached, Warmoth would be suspended from office while awaiting trial in the senate. Packard, however, knew that he could not muster two-thirds of the senators to vote for conviction. Therefore, he arranged for eleven Republican senators and three of their Democratic colleagues to leave New Orleans aboard the U.S. revenue cutter *Wilderness*. Their absence would prevent obtaining a quorum in the senate, and when the house impeached the governor, he would be effectively, if temporarily, removed from office. This part of Packard's plan was successful; the senate did not have a quorum for the first nineteen days of the legislative session. Moreover, the Packard forces succeeded in obtaining the necessary cooperation of the House speaker, George W. Carter, a former crony of Warmoth's. However, Carter was not acting solely out of any spirit of revenge or simple antagonism to an old political ally: if Packard's scheme worked completely, Carter might become acting governor of the state. The Custom House faction challenged the legality of Lieutenant Governor Pinchback's election by the state senate the month before. If Packard's men nullified Pinchback's election and then impeached Warmoth, Carter, as speaker of the house, would assume the governorship.[5]

The legislature met as scheduled, and the plot began to unfold. On January 2, after perfunctory activities on opening day, the house voted narrowly (forty-nine to forty-five) to continue Speaker Carter in his influential position. However, the next day the Warmoth forces called for an election of a new speaker, and when Carter declined to acknowledge the motion, the Warmothites moved toward the podium, threatening to

4. Sefton, *Army and Reconstruction*, 213–14, 216–17.
5. See Taylor's excellent discussion of Packard's machinations in *Louisiana Reconstructed*, 222–23. See also Binning, "Henry Clay Warmoth," 217–20.

force Carter to relinquish his seat. Carter had prepared for such a threat, and several well-armed hired thugs surrounded the speaker and prevented the coup. The house adjourned in disarray.[6]

On the evening of January 3, after being apprised of the situation at the capitol, Emory decided to use his troops to prevent civil disorder. He ordered Colonel Charles Smith in Baton Rouge to prepare four of his six companies to move to New Orleans. All four companies from Jackson Barracks marched into the city, taking up positions downtown to prevent a collision between Packard's men and Warmoth's militia, which the governor had mobilized under the field (or street) command of James Longstreet.[7]

The next morning, Packard attempted to regain control of the legislature and remove the opposition's leadership. Producing some trumped-up charges, Packard dispatched deputy U.S. marshals with orders to arrest Warmoth, Lieutenant Governor Pinchback, twenty-two legislators, and Algernon S. Badger, chief of the Metropolitan Police. With the arrest of the legislators, the Custom House-Democratic coalition would have a working majority in the house, and with Warmoth, Pinchback, and Badger behind bars, what was left of the governor's faction would be leaderless. The deputies arrested everyone on Packard's list, but the marshal's gambit to control the house was foiled when several other pro-Warmoth representatives walked out of the capitol, leaving the house without a quorum. Warmoth's supporters soon posted bail for the governor and his friends, and by 1:00 P.M. the kings and the pawns were back on their original squares. It was Warmoth's move.[8]

The governor called for the legislature to meet in the capitol at 4:30 P.M., but few Democrats or Custom House Republicans were notified of the meeting. Upon calling the house to order, the Warmoth men elected their own house speaker, O. H. Brewster. The militia guarded the state house, and by nightfall Warmoth held the advantage after the day's turmoil.[9]

General Emory was now more convinced than ever that the army must keep the peace between the political factions. He ordered two of the

6. Taylor, *Louisiana Reconstructed*, 223; New Orleans *Daily Picayune*, January 2, 3, 4, 1872.

7. AAAG William T. Gentry to Charles H. Smith, January 3, 1872, in Dept Gulf, vol. 114/DSL, RG 393, NA; Donald B. Sanger and Thomas R. Hay, *James Longstreet* (Baton Rouge, 1952), 356.

8. Taylor, *Louisiana Reconstructed*, 223–24.

9. *Ibid.*

companies in Baton Rouge to rush to New Orleans. Despite the earlier advice from Halleck to use his own judgment in such matters, Emory telegraphed Washington, described the circumstances, and asked for official authorization to intervene in the political struggle. Secretary of War William W. Belknap approved Emory's request to use his troops to maintain order in Louisiana.[10]

Meanwhile, the authorities in Washington fretted over the arrest of Warmoth and the other state officials. Emory specified that no soldiers had assisted the deputies in their duties, but he left Packard's role in the affair undescribed. However, Governor Warmoth condemned the meddling marshal and pressed Senator Joseph West to tell President Grant that the Packard-Carter alliance would bring about "the *destruction* of the state government, unless the President takes immediate action and stops his officials." Upon hearing of the day's events, Grant proclaimed that the behavior of the "United States marshal is of such an extraordinary character that I will have the matter investigated at once." Nevertheless, Grant's actions seemed anything but impartial to Warmoth.[11]

Short of armed revolt, the most disturbing eventuality in Louisiana politics would have been the establishment of a second state government laying claim to rightful recognition over Warmouth, and George Carter set out to establish just such a government. He called for Custom House and Democratic members of the legislature to convene as a rival legislature at the meeting room over the Gem Saloon on Royal Street just off Canal. The Gem was known as one of "the oldest drinking Saloons in New Orleans," boasting "excellent liquor, and cozy places for confidential chat, dominoes, and chess." Carter quickly realized that he did not have a quorum and sent out some of his sergeants-at-arms to escort to the Gem any legislators they could find. A few days later some of Carter's sergeants-at-arms shot and killed Representative Walter Wheyland of Sabine Parish for refusing to accompany them to the Gem.[12]

It appeared that a riot as bad as the one of July 30, 1866, might break

---

10. Gentry to C. H. Smith, January 4, 1872, in Dept Gulf, vol. 139/DSL, RG 393, NA; William W. Belknap to William T. Sherman, January 4, 1872, AG William D. Whipple to Emory, January 4, 1872, both in AGO File 4882 of 1872 (Microcopy M-666, reel 93), RG 94, NA.

11. Edward Townsend to Emory, January 4, 1872, Emory to Townsend, January 5, 1872, both in *House Executive Documents*, 42nd Cong., 2nd Sess., No. 209, p. 1; Warmoth to Joseph R. West, January 4, 1872 (emphasis in the original), Grant to West, January 4, 1872, both in *House Executive Documents*, 42nd Cong., 2nd Sess., No. 268, pp. 49–50.

12. Gem description in New Orleans *Republican*, March 20, 1870; Taylor, *Louisiana Reconstructed*, 224–25.

out at any moment. Federal marshals, Metropolitan policemen, and black militiamen patrolled the streets, and many civilians probably were armed as they walked downtown. At the request of Longstreet and War-moth, Emory stationed soldiers at the state house, which rumor had pegged as the target of an attack by Conservatives. Infantrymen also guarded the Custom House.

On January 5, after the rivals held menacing demonstrations at the state house and the Gem Saloon, Emory decided to move the soldiers stationed near the Mechanics' Institute to billets on Magazine Street near his headquarters. The movement of the soldiers away from his capitol disturbed Warmoth, who thought that the general had sent the troops back to Jackson Barracks. The governor, anxious about his own safety and that of his administration, wanted a round-the-clock guard at the state house, but Emory reassured him that the soldiers were close enough to reach the scene quickly if violence occurred. Nevertheless, as a precaution Emory ordered Colonel Smith in Baton Rouge to bring three more companies to New Orleans, leaving only one company at regimental headquarters.[13]

At the end of their harrowing day, Emory and Warmoth separately addressed messages to officials in Washington. Emory told Adjutant General Townsend that only "the free display of the U.S. forces" had prevented violence in Louisiana's capital. Emory warned that "a very bloody riot" might occur, and he asked for reinforcements. "Send me another regiment," he implored. Warmoth predicted that "riot and tumult [were] imminent." He asked Grant to order Emory to work closely with state officials "in preserving the peace, and protecting the government from attack and overthrow." Secretary of War Belknap read Warmoth's plea, and he scribbled a postscript before forwarding it to the president: it was "best to let General Emory act in accordance with his own judgment."[14]

Meanwhile, the leaders of both Louisiana factions sought Emory's support. Carter wanted Emory to place a cordon of federal troops

13. New Orleans *Daily Picayune*, January 6, 1872; Warmoth to Emory, January 5, 1872 (two communications), in SW, "Annual Report, 1872–1873," in *House Executive Documents*, 42nd Cong., 3rd Sess., No. 1, p. 97; Emory to Warmoth, January 5, 1872, in Dept Gulf, vol. 114/DSL, Emory to C. H. Smith, January 5, 1872, in Dept Gulf, vol. 139/DSL, both in RG 393, NA.

14. Emory to Townsend, January 5, 1872, in *House Executive Documents*, 42nd Cong., 2nd Sess., No. 209, p. 2; Warmoth to Grant, January 5, 1872, in SW, "Annual Report, 1872–1873," 96; Belknap to Grant, January 5, 1872, in *House Executive Documents*, 42nd Cong., 2nd Sess., No. 268, p. 50.

around the Gem Saloon to protect the meeting hall and its occupants. Warmoth wanted soldiers to escort his sergeants-at-arms while they sought out and arrested members of the Carter legislature. But the general pointedly denied Carter's request for army protection, and he refused to provide a military escort for Warmoth's deputies, telling the governor not to let his officers initiate any violent acts, lest the whole situation "get beyond our joint efforts to control."[15]

Some of the New Orleans newspapers interpreted Emory's failure to move against the Carter legislature as an indication of his support for the Custom House–Conservative coalition, but in large measure, this was wishful thinking on their part. They were so entirely opposed to Warmoth that they wanted him out of office at almost any cost.[16] In fact, Emory had made every reasonable effort to remain impartial in the crisis, displaying his soldiers to overawe both sides. For all practical purposes, New Orleans was under martial law, although Emory had not officially declared it. The general desperately wanted the civilians to reach a satisfactory agreement among themselves, but the opposing forces were so evenly matched that he believed they could not settle the matter on their own and that eventually the army, acting on orders from Washington, would have to force them to accept a compromise. Neither Washington nor the Military Division of the South had given Emory much guidance. The division commander, General Henry Halleck, had been seriously ill, and when he died on January 9, Major General Alfred Terry assumed command. Emory then told Warmoth that he was going to ask Terry for additional troops.[17]

Both sides wanted the army or the president to declare martial law, but only if the declaration resulted in the military suppression of their rivals. Carter claimed that the absent senators (on board the *Wilderness* by his arrangement with Packard) feared for their lives and would return only if the army proclaimed martial law. Several state representatives appealed to Grant to oust Warmoth and institute martial law until the Carter legis-

15. George W. Carter to Emory, January 6, 1872, Emory to Carter, January 6, 1872 (two communications), Emory to Warmoth, January 6, 1872, all in *House Miscellaneous Documents*, 42nd Cong., 2nd Sess., No. 211, pp. 76, 86–87, 88.

16. Taylor, *Louisiana Reconstructed*, 222. See also New Orleans *Times*, January 6, 1872, New Orleans *Bee*, January 6, 7, 1872.

17. Emory to Warmoth, January 9, 1872, in *House Executive Documents*, 42nd Cong., 2nd Sess., No. 211, p. 89; Emory to AGO, January 9, 1872, in *House Executive Documents*, 42nd Cong., 2nd Sess., No. 209, p. 3; Emory to Warmoth, January 9, 1872, in Dept Gulf, vol. 114/DSL, RG 393, NA.

lature assumed its full powers. James Casey, Grant's brother-in-law, wanted an end to Warmoth's "usurpation," and Mayor Benjamin Flanders, who had switched his allegiance to the Custom House Ring, called for martial law as "the only solution of the difficulty." [18]

However, Emory preferred not to declare martial law just yet, believing that such action would be interpreted as "in the interest of the Governor's faction of the Legislature." Furthermore, the general had been approached by a special group of fifty-one New Orleans businessmen that had sent envoys to both political factions, pleading with them to end the crisis without martial law. Until these citizens had time to negotiate with the politicians, Emory planned to remain neutral. Despite Emory's decision, Collector Casey and Mayor Flanders reiterated their calls for military intervention, and Casey specifically requested that Emory order troops to guard the Gem Saloon. [19]

The reason for Casey's request was soon apparent, for Warmoth decided to break up the bogus legislature at the Gem and arrest Carter and some of his henchmen for the murder of Representative Wheyland. When he got wind of Warmoth's design, Carter informed Emory that his followers would resist any attacks. A short time later two companies of Metropolitan policemen "armed with Winchester rifles" marched to Royal Street. Warmoth asked Emory for soldiers "to assist me in suppressing any riotous demonstrations that may be made," meaning, naturally, any armed resistance by the Carter forces. Before Emory could act, the police moved in, but they met no resistance. Most of the legislators had abandoned the Gem. The police immediately instituted a citywide manhunt for Carter. Later in the day Carter asked Emory to help him regain possession of the Gem Saloon, but the general "positively refused." [20]

18. J. Henri Burch and others to Grant, January 9, 1872, in *House Executive Documents*, 42nd Cong., 2nd Sess., No. 268, pp. 54–55; Carter to Grant, James Casey to Grant, Flanders to Grant, all dated January 9, 1872, in Justice Dept Letters (Microcopy M-940, reel 6), RG 60, NA.

19. Emory to Townsend, January 9, 1872 (four communications), in *House Executive Documents*, 42nd Cong., 2nd Sess., No. 209, pp. 4–5; Casey to Grant, January 10, 1872, in Justice Dept Letters (Microcopy M-940, reel 6), RG 60, NA; Flanders to George H. Williams, January 10, 1872, in *House Executive Documents*, 42nd Cong., 2nd Sess., No. 268, p. 60.

20. New Orleans *Daily Picayune*, January 11, 1872; New Orleans *Bee*, January 11, 1872; Carter to Emory, January 10, 1872, and undated, 1872, in *House Executive Documents*, 42nd Cong., 2nd Sess., No. 211, pp. 74–75; Warmoth to Emory, January 10, 1872, in SW, "Annual Report, 1872–1873," 98; Emory to Townsend, January 10, 1872, in *House Executive Documents*, 42nd Cong., 2nd Sess., No. 209, p. 6.

The next day, January 11, a confident Governor Warmoth prematurely decided that "the danger of riot or tumult [had] about passed." He informed Emory that "by to-morrow at 12 o'clock you can safely withdraw your troops to the barracks." Thus assured, Emory ordered some of the soldiers to Jackson Barracks, and placed his hopes in the businessmen's "Committee of Fifty-one" to arbitrate the matters still unsettled between the political rivals. However, the businessmen failed in their effort. They told Emory that they had been unable "to make any compromise between the two factions" and recommended that the general declare martial law. Emory rejected their recommendation in the belief that the danger of riot was not imminent and returned all the soldiers to Jackson Barracks.[21]

In Washington, Grant sifted through the reports of the Louisiana situation and issued an unusually strong statement. The president informed Mayor Flanders, "Martial law will not be proclaimed in New Orleans, under existing circumstances, and no assistance will be given by Federal authorities to persons or parties unlawfully resisting the constitutional authorities of the State."[22] Grant's statement did not reduce the pressure against Warmoth as might have been expected. The Custom House bosses realized that it was difficult, if not impossible, for the president to give them overt assistance. But they thought that if he did not order Emory to give full military support to Warmoth, they might force the governor from office by threats, intimidation, or legal trickery. Throughout the crisis, Grant never gave his outright support to either faction.

Early on the morning of January 13, Warmoth learned that an armed mob intended to attack the Mechanics' Institute—the state house—and he called on Emory to order troops back into the city to prevent the overthrow of his government. "Threats are made," the governor wailed, "that not a stone of the State capitol shall be left upon another after they are through with their work." Emory immediately ordered Colonel Alfred Sully at Jackson Barracks to put his "troops under arms and move towards this city, with your Gatling guns of the largest size." Simul-

21. Warmoth to Emory, January 11, 1872, Emory, testimony before a congressional committee, both in *House Miscellaneous Documents*, 42nd Cong., 2nd Sess., No. 211, pp. 71–72, 61; Emory to AG/USA, January 11, 1872, in Justice Dept Letters (Microcopy M-940, reel 6), RG 60, NA; Emory to Townsend, January 12, 1872, in *House Executive Documents*, 42nd Cong., 2nd Sess., No. 209, p. 8.

22. Grant to Flanders, January 12, 1872, quoted in Warmoth, *War, Politics, and Reconstruction*, 138.

taneously, the general dispatched one of his aides to find the assembling mob and "to notify the ring leaders . . . that if any violence is used, it will be my duty to disperse them with grapeshot." [23]

A confrontation between members of the two factions appeared likely. The "Committee of Fifty-one," which at one time had seemed on the verge of negotiating a settlement between the political rivals, had broken up in despair. Now it was learned that the Carter legislature planned to resume separate meetings. Emory decided to ask again for reinforcements, addressing his request to General Townsend: "The hostility here is not against the United States, but against the State government, which is odious beyond expression, and I fear justly so, and to suppress a riot it is only necessary to make a show of United States forces, however small, which cannot be done by the use of infantry with that facility necessary to stay an impending riot." [24] Emory had described the formula he intended to use when a riot threatened: call out the troops, move them into public view, and remind the newspapers and civic leaders that the army was determined to enforce the peace. But Emory was finding it difficult to work with Warmoth and his administration. In most of his official correspondence and public statements, Emory maintained a façade of objectivity, but in this note to Townsend it was obvious what Emory thought about the governor of Louisiana.

By 11:00 A.M. the soldiers had been in positions near the state house for several hours. Carter assembled a mob of several thousand men, but they could not attack the legislative hall because Emory's troops blocked their way. Later the soldiers returned to their barracks, and another day in the crisis had passed. [25]

On the morning of January 14 Emory, tiring of the continuous pressure upon him and his soldiers, informed Warmoth, Carter, and Adjutant General Townsend that he would not send troops into the city again without direct orders from Washington. Apparently, Emory had changed his attitude about military intercession after reading a newspaper story in which U.S. Attorney General George H. Williams reportedly declared that troops should not be used unless martial law were pro-

23. AAG Gentry to Alfred Sully, January 13, 1872, in Dept Gulf, vol. 114/DSL, RG 393, NA; Warmoth to Emory and reply, both dated January 13, 1872, in *House Miscellaneous Documents*, 42nd Cong., 2nd Sess., No. 211, pp. 72, 90.

24. Emory to Townsend, January 13, 1872, in *House Executive Documents*, 42nd Cong., 2nd Sess., No. 209, pp. 9–10.

25. Lonn, *Reconstruction in Louisiana*, 128; Emory, testimony before a congressional committee, in *House Miscellaneous Documents*, 42nd Cong., 2nd Sess., No. 211, p. 62.

claimed. Undoubtedly, Emory was leery of continuously placing his soldiers in positions where they might be badly mauled if a riot did occur.[26]

Emory had made a bad error in notifying Carter and Warmoth of his decision. Carter immediately had handbills printed and distributed informing the populace of the general's decision to withhold the soldiers, and sure now of a free hand, he planned another attempt to capture the capitol. Warmoth, on the other hand, dispatched a frantic letter to Grant, describing Carter's preparations to overthrow the government and concluded that the city was "in imminent danger of riot . . . that may possibly be as fatal to New Orleans as was the late disaster in Chicago [i.e., the great Chicago fire of 1871]. The simple presence of troops will prevent domestic violence." Warmoth also informed Emory of Carter's plan and asked the general to provide military protection for his government.[27]

Emory promptly advised Carter that distribution of the handbills was, in the general's opinion, designed to inflame the populace. Therefore, despite what he had written earlier, he was sending soldiers into the city to prevent a riot, even though he had not received instructions from Washington. But the general was careful to remain neutral. Army protection for the Warmoth legislature, he said, was not to be interpreted as official recognition by the national government. Foiled once again, Carter called off his plans.[28]

Concerned that his display of troops had gone against the attorney general's reported statement on martial law, Emory wired Townsend pleading for advice. Townsend replied that, officially, the "Attorney General has given no opinion whatever." The adjutant general concluded his message with a sentence typical of instructions from higher headquarters to southern commanders: "Exercise your own discretion as to the course to be pursued, but do not bring the United States troops to the city without orders from here." Townsend's instructions reinforced Emory's notion about keeping his soldiers out of dangerous situations, but Emory's earlier decisions to intercede had kept the two factions from coming to

26. Emory to Warmoth, January 14, 1872, Emory to Carter, January 14, 1872, both in *House Miscellaneous Documents*, 42nd Cong., 2nd Sess., No. 211, pp. 91–92; Emory to Townsend, January 14, 1872 (two communications), in *House Executive Documents*, 42nd Cong., 2nd Sess., No. 209, pp. 10–11.

27. Warmoth to Grant, January 14, 1872, in *House Executive Documents*, 42nd Cong., 2nd Sess., No. 268, p. 76; Warmoth to Emory, January 14, 1872, in SW, "Annual Report, 1872–1873," 99.

28. Lonn, *Reconstruction in Louisiana*, 128; Emory to Warmoth, Emory to Carter, both January 14, 1872, in *House Miscellaneous Documents*, 42nd Cong., 2nd Sess., No. 211, pp. 90, 92.

blows over the control of the state government. Nevertheless, Emory informed Warmoth "that under instructions just received I cannot bring the U.S. troops into this city without orders from higher authority." [29]

Although he disliked Warmoth personally, Emory now realized that if the federal government did not make some show of support for the elected governor, opposition forces would topple the young carpetbagger's administration. Letting out all his fears and frustrations, Emory telegraphed Townsend again, warning that "if the troops are withdrawn [as, in effect, Townsend had just decided], an armed force of from four to eight thousand men with artillery, is ready to march against the capitol of the State, take possession, . . . and overthrow the governor." Emory concluded it was "essential that I be more positively instructed, with authority to show my instructions." Unmoved by Emory's emotion-charged telegram, Townsend calmly reiterated that there was no change in the instructions given earlier: the soldiers were to stay out of the city unless sent there "by orders from Washington." The ultimate decision to save Warmoth rested, as it always had, with President Grant. When the New Orleans *Bee* learned about the Townsend-Emory exchanges, it jubilantly printed a large headline: "The Federal Government Abandons Warmoth." [30]

Despite the *Bee*'s report, Warmoth continued tirelessly to plead his case to Washington but received little encouragement from the national administration. He also petitioned Emory to cooperate with the state police and militia but criticized the general's reluctance to provide aid to the beleaguered government. Attorney General Williams told Warmoth that the president was "unwilling to interfere in State matters with the military power of the Government, except in a clear case of legal right and overruling necessity." Warmoth must have felt insulted by this remark: after all, he was the legal governor of the state. President Grant tried to maintain an outwardly objective face toward the Louisiana muddle, but he supported his brother-in-law, James Casey, and favored Warmoth's eventual removal, so long as that step would not threaten to end Republican control of Louisiana. [31]

29. Emory to Townsend, January 14, 1872, Townsend to Emory, January 15, 1872, both in *House Executive Documents*, 42nd Cong., 2nd Sess., No. 209, pp. 11, 13; Emory to Warmoth, January 15, 1872, in Dept Gulf, vol. 114/DSL, RG 393, NA.

30. Emory to Townsend, January 15, 1872, in *House Executive Documents*, 42nd Cong., 2nd Sess., No. 209, p. 12; Townsend to Emory, January 15, 1872, in Dept Gulf, vol. 149/DSL, RG 393, NA; New Orleans *Bee*, January 16, 1872.

31. Warmoth to Joseph R. West, January 15, 1872, in *House Miscellaneous Documents*,

The situation in New Orleans remained quiet and calm for the next few days, but there was a noticeable increase in tension on Saturday, January 20. On that day the state senate finally met with a quorum present, and in an important test vote the members of the upper chamber confirmed the nomination of Warmoth's lieutenant governor, P. B. S. Pinchback. Carter had not expected Warmoth to have enough votes to confirm Pinchback, and the governor's victory on this issue frustrated Carter's hopes to control either house of the legislature, at least for the time being. In desperation, Carter issued a call for his followers to assemble on Monday, January 22, at 10:00 A.M. and to endeavor to carry the state house by force of arms.[32]

Emory, learning from informants that nine hundred well-armed men would answer Carter's call on Monday and that two artillery pieces might be brought out of hiding for the occasion, informed Townsend of the seriousness of this new situation. Townsend thereupon ordered Emory to place a guard around the U.S. Mint and to put all his soldiers on alert.[33]

On Monday morning the city girded for open warfare, and the army prepared to prevent it. Downtown store owners and French Quarter shopkeepers kept their businesses closed. Dozens of men began gathering near their assembly point, the statue of Henry Clay on Canal Street. Warmoth ordered his men to form a cordon around the Mechanics' Institute; seven hundred policemen and militiamen stood ready to defend the state government. Learning that more men were arriving at the Clay statue, Emory at 10:00 A.M. ordered Colonel Sully to bring all the companies and two Gatling guns from Jackson Barracks to Jackson Square. Next, Emory handed two identical dispatches to a waiting aide, telling him to deliver one to Warmoth and the other to Carter. The messages informed them that President Grant had directed Emory "to suppress a conflict of

---

42nd Cong., 2nd Sess., No. 211, p. 314; Warmoth, P. B. S. Pinchback, and O. H. Brewster to Grant, George H. Williams to Warmoth, Grant to William W. Belknap, all dated January 15, 1872, in *House Executive Documents*, 42nd Cong., 2nd Sess., No. 209, pp. 14–16. A summary of these messages was reported in the New Orleans *Bee*, January 17, 1872.

32. Emory to AGO, January 17, 19, 20 (two communications), 1872, all in *House Executive Documents*, 42nd Cong., 2nd Sess., No. 209, pp. 16–17; New Orleans *Daily Picayune*, January 21, 1872.

33. Emory to Townsend, January 21, 1872, in *House Executive Documents*, 42nd Cong., 2nd Sess., No. 209, p. 18; Townsend to Emory, January 21, 1872, in Dept Gulf, vol. 149/DSL, RG 393, NA.

armed bodies of men should such occur, and to guard public property from pillage and destruction."[34]

At 11:15 A.M., holding Emory's dispatch in his hand, Carter addressed the crowd of several hundred persons gathered around the Clay statue. He told the throng that Emory's soldiers were coming into the city to prevent the overthrow of the Warmoth regime. Therefore, Carter said, he would not attack the state house. Several men in the crowd remonstrated. Lead and they would follow, they shouted. But Carter was adamant and told everyone to disperse. At this time a lone mounted army officer rode toward the assemblage, trying to ascertain the mood of the crowd. The arrival of the officer convinced the doubters that Carter's appraisal of the situation was accurate, and the gathering began to break up. In a short time the troops marched through the downtown streets, and by 12:30 P.M. most of the shops and stores had opened for business.[35]

Emory had successfully averted a great catastrophe. Although his instructions had been phrased, rather ambiguously, "to suppress a conflict . . . *should such occur,*" Emory had interpreted the orders in such a way that he sent the soldiers *before* the fighting began. He thereby defused the worst threat to the peace and stability of Louisiana since the tragic riot of July, 1866, when Phil Sheridan was commanding the department. From his Chicago headquarters, General Sheridan wrote approvingly to Emory offering his "congratulations on getting through with the New Orleans . . . troubles so well."[36]

After the populace returned to their normal pursuits, Emory remarked that he believed "the presence of the United States troops would be sufficient" to prevent an insurrection—a confident comment, doubtless intended for the leaders and members of the political factions who had nearly plunged the state into civil disorder. But Emory had had no assurances that his six hundred soldiers could forestall bloodshed in the streets. Each day difficult and unfamiliar problems had plagued the gen-

34. Emory to Sully, January 22, 1872, in Dept Gulf, vol. 114/DSL, Sully to AAG Gentry, January 22, 1872, in Dept Gulf, vol. 149/DSL, both in RG 393, NA; Townsend to Emory, and reply, both dated January 22, 1872, in *House Executive Documents*, 42nd Cong., 2nd Sess., No. 209, p. 19.

35. New Orleans *Times*, New Orleans *Daily Picayune*, New Orleans *Bee*, all dated January 23, 1872; Emory to Townsend, January 22, 1872, in *House Executive Documents*, 42nd Cong., 2nd Sess., No. 209, pp. 19–20; Lonn, *Reconstruction in Louisiana*, 132.

36. Sheridan to Emory, January 25, 1872, in William H. Emory Papers, 1871–1876, Beinecke Rare Book and Manuscript Library, Yale University.

eral, who had commanded the department for only a month at the time the crisis began. A remarkable combination of luck and cool-headedness on Emory's part had resolved the crisis peacefully.[37]

The struggle over the control of the legislature permanently soured the relationship between Emory and Warmoth. In a letter to Adjutant General Townsend, Emory frankly gave his opinion of Warmoth and his followers, calling them "men of unparrallelled [sic] audacity and venality." But Emory had no warm words for Casey and the Custom House Ring, which the general believed was "so blinded by passion and revenge, as to be willing at any moment to sink Genl Grant and his administration, to gain an insignificant point in Louisiana." The Democrats stood little better in Emory's estimation, holding "all the wealth and intelligence of the State and most of the white muscle," but misusing these assets, pressing Warmoth and the ring "to acts of violence & folly." By implication the only stable, uncorrupt pillar in Louisiana politics was the army.[38]

In the aftermath of these events, the disappointed editor of the New Orleans *Bee* commented that "Warmoth's strength at Washington was evidently underrated by Carter and his followers."[39] On the contrary, Carter and Packward overestimated their own ability to carry off the legislative chicanery that they had planned so carefully. Emory's prudent use of troops and Warmoth's tenacity nullified the Packard-Carter scheme to gain control of the house, and therefore the governor was saved, temporarily, from impeachment. Warmoth might have prevented the confrontation by meekly resigning in early January, but it was not in his nature to give up easily, and he never once indicated that he considered this course. Instead, he used all of his authority as the elected chief executive to keep himself in power. Warmoth held a distinct advantage over Carter and the Custom House Ring—he did not have to mount an armed attack to take office. Ultimately this was the decisive factor in the entire affair. Packard and Carter never overcame Warmoth's claim to legitimacy.

In February, 1872, Governor Warmoth was beginning the final year of his term. The Custom House Ring refused to let him alone and redoubled its efforts to unhorse Warmoth by the time of the next election, if not before. In addition, the Democrats organized public protests against Warmoth's blemished authority.

37. Emory, testimony before a congressional committee, in *House Miscellaneous Documents*, 42nd Cong., 2nd Sess., No. 211, p. 64.
38. Emory to Townsend, January 29, 1872, in Emory Papers.
39. New Orleans *Bee*, January 23, 1872.

For their part, Republican party leaders alleged that the Democrats had committed several acts of violence against blacks in the hinterland parishes of Grant and Rapides, prompting General Emory to send Lieutenant William M. Bandy to investigate the charges. Bandy's report must have substantiated some of the Republican claims, for on March 30 Emory ordered a detachment of one officer and twenty enlisted men to Colfax in Grant Parish to safeguard the civil rights of citizens under the so-called Enforcement Acts. In 1870 and 1871 Congress passed three acts directed at organizations such as the Ku Klux Klan that conspired to prevent Republicans from voting, serving on juries, and holding office. Persons convicted in federal courts under these acts were subject to both fines and prison sentences. Moreover, federal judges and the president were authorized to order the army to help U.S. marshals arrest violators of the acts and to protect persons whose rights had been threatened or abused. In emergencies, the president could suspend *habeas corpus* and order the army and the navy to govern selected areas by martial law until proper civil officials were capable of resuming control. The detachment Emory sent to Colfax remained in the town about two weeks to investigate the Republicans' complaints and returned to its garrison at Baton Rouge in April.[40]

By May, 1872, Emory recognized that there were five political factions in Louisiana. The Custom House Ring, led by Marshal Stephen Packard, Collector James Casey, and Senator William Pitt Kellogg, remained staunchly loyal to Grant and contained Republicans who were, of course, diametrically opposed to Governor Warmoth. The governor assembled a variety of Republicans who supported him and, for one reason or another, opposed Grant. Following the lead of dozens of prominent Republicans in other states, they called themselves "liberals." In May Warmoth led a Louisiana delegation to a national convention at Cincinnati, where eccentric newspaper editor Horace Greeley was nominated for president on the Liberal Republican ticket. Lieutenant Governor P. B. S. Pinchback organized a third Republican faction in Louisiana, composed mostly of blacks. As an ultimate goal, Pinchback hoped to heal the divisions in his party, but his immediate goals were to secure more state offices for blacks and, not surprisingly, an important position for himself. A fourth group, the Reform faction, was a small collection of wealthy

40. AAAG Gentry to CO, Baton Rouge, March 30, 1872, in Dept Gulf, vol. 139/DSL, RG 393, NA; Everette Swinney, "Enforcing the Fifteenth Amendment, 1870–77," *Journal of Southern History*, XXVIII (May, 1962), 202–203.

whites, mostly former Whigs, who were dissatisfied with both Grant and the Custom House Ring. The Reformers wanted a more honest and efficient Louisiana government, but they soon realized that they were not strong enough to bring about such a drastic change by themselves. The divisions in the Republican party naturally nurtured Democratic hopes of winning control of the state government for the first time since the Civil War. But political necessities being what they were, each faction began seeking an alliance with one or more of the other groups to ensure victory in November.[41]

In early June the Democrats and Reformers held separate convocations in the Crescent City. For governor, the Democrats picked John McEnery, a rabid anti-Republican conservative from Ouachita Parish, and selected a full roster of candidates for the other state offices. The Reform party likewise chose its own candidates, but made overtures to the Democrats about a possible merger of their two slates. After some negotiations, the Democrats accepted two Reformers on their ticket and absorbed the smaller splinter group.

In Baton Rouge two groups of Republicans, Pinchback's blacks and the Custom House faction, assembled independently. Prior to these convocations, the Pinchback wing had surprisingly endorsed Warmoth for another term, but he was firmly committed to the Liberals and had declined the nomination. Vowing to unite the state's Republicans, Pinchback lobbied at the Custom House meeting, advocating an important office for Warmoth, but the ring bosses rejected this proposal. Instead, they selected Senator Kellogg and Caesar C. Antoine, a black leader from Caddo Parish, for governor and lieutenant governor, respectively. Naturally disappointed that his ideas for unification had been quashed, Pinchback nevertheless forlornly held onto his hopes for some sort of combined Republican ticket.

On August 5 the Louisiana Liberals convened their state convention in New Orleans. Some delegates talked about nominating Warmoth, but the governor shrewdly figured that the best chance of defeating the Custom House gang lay in choosing a candidate who was acceptable to some of the other factions. Persuaded by his reasoning, the delegates nominated former Confederate Colonel David B. Penn for governor. In an unusual twist, Penn's nomination presaged a direct alliance with Warmoth's bitter enemies of long-standing, the Conservative Democrats. In

41. Lonn, *Reconstruction in Louisiana*, 141–49; Taylor, *Louisiana Reconstructed*, 227–31.

fact, the national Democratic party blazed the pathway to such an alliance when it nominated the Liberal candidate, Horace Greeley, for president in July. It remained for Liberal Republicans and Democrats in the North and South to bury old and bloody political hatchets and fuse their state tickets in order to defeat Grantism.

The Liberals' choice of D. B. Penn facilitated the merger in Louisiana when, unexpectedly, Penn gained in popularity throughout the state. The Louisiana Democrats, who had thought that the Liberals would have to beg subserviently for alliance, realized that concessions on their own part were in order. Accordingly, the two groups arranged for the "fusion" of their slates. Warmoth wisely advised that Penn head the ticket, but a few Liberals and many Democrats favored McEnery, and he retained his nomination for governor. Penn became the Fusionists' choice for lieutenant governor, and several other Liberals found places on the combined ticket.

The Liberal-Democratic-Reform fusion made it natural for the Pinchback and Custom House Republicans to unite. Several of Warmoth's old allies, including James Longstreet, abandoned the governor's unholy alliance with the Democrats and scurried across town to the Kellogg camp, where preparations were already underway to merge the Pinchback–Custom House tickets. Kellogg and Antoine remained the party's nominees for governor and lieutenant governor, but Pinchback secured the slots of secretary of state and superintendent of education for two of his men, and the nomination of congressman-at-large for himself.[42]

Throughout these political developments, Emory waited patiently, watching the maneuvers and meetings of the different groups. Finally, he found the political battlelines drawn between two coalitions. On one side, Kellogg led the Custom House Ring, Pinchback's Republicans, plus Longstreet and a few disaffected Warmothites. On the other side, the Democrats, the Reformers, and Warmoth's Liberal Republicans supported McEnery. After considering the political situation in Louisiana and the rest of his department, Emory decided that consultation with his superiors was in order and requested permission to go to Washington. The War Department granted his request, and he spent most of the month of September in the East.[43]

42. For discussions of the foregoing political developments, see Lonn, *Reconstruction in Louisiana*, 152–64; and Taylor, *Louisiana Reconstructed*, 232–36.

43. AG Thomas Scott to Emory, August 31, 1872, in Dept Gulf, vol. 149/DSL, RG 393, NA.

Meanwhile, during September and October, the Louisiana registrar's office opened the registration books to prospective voters. Hundreds of Democrats, theretofore unregistered, came forward to sign the rolls. The large number of men registering to vote was an encouraging sign to the editor of the Alexandria *Democrat*, who wrote that Conservatives hoped this election would be different from those in the past when "they were perfectly certain that the Radical managers would cheat them out of the fruit of their labors."[44]

Despite whatever tricks the Republicans had used before, the Democrats knew that the army's role in the fall election was still important. The army was not supposed to interfere in the free, open, and honest democratic political process. However, the campaigns and elections of the 1870s were no more free, open, and honest than those of the 1860s had been, and Louisiana politicians of all factions were quite aware of this. Under the Enforcement Acts, the army could be just as influential as it had been in the 1860s. The Democrats harbored justifiable fears that the Custom House Ring might purposely involve the army in the election to aid the Republican party.

In fact, soon after returning from his conferences in Washington, and before either side issued a call for military assistance, Emory began a concerted program designed to put an army unit in every important Louisiana town by election day on November 4. General William T. Sherman's adjutant, Colonel William D. Whipple, authorized Emory to use his soldiers to protect the rights of voters under the Enforcement Acts. The general first ordered soldiers to Monroe, where the *Ouachita Telegraph* denounced the prospect of using soldiers in an election "to rescue the Radical ticket" from defeat. During the remainder of October, Emory sent detachments to eleven other Louisiana towns that normally did not have garrisons, including Alexandria, Colfax, Cheneyville, Opelousas, St. Martinville, Pointe a la Hache, Shreveport, Harrisonburg, Winnsboro, Vienna, and Homer.[45]

Nevertheless, Emory's main concern was to keep the peace in New

---

44. Alexandria *Democrat*, September 25, 1872; Lonn, *Reconstruction in Louisiana*, 167; James A. Rawley, "The General Amnesty Act of 1872: A Note," *Mississippi Valley Historical Review*, XLVII (December, 1960), 480–82.

45. William D. Whipple to Emory, October 23, 1872, in Dept Gulf, vol. 149/DSL, Gentry to CO, Jackson Barracks, October 24, 1872, in Dept Gulf, vol. 114/DSL, Emory to CO, Baton Rouge, October 24, 1872, Gentry to CO, Baton Rouge, October 25, 30, 1872, Gentry to Capt. W. H. Bartholomew, October 28, 1872, all in Dept Gulf, vol. 139/DSL, all in RG 393, NA; Monroe *Ouachita Telegraph*, October 26, 1872.

Orleans. He ordered Colonel Smith in Baton Rouge to bring two companies under his personal command to the Crescent City. On October 29 two batteries of the 3rd Artillery arrived in New Orleans from Fort Barrancas in Pensacola, bringing the city's garrison to 317 men present for duty.[46]

According to most contemporary accounts, the 1872 campaign was, by Louisiana standards, surprisingly calm. Some Democrats believed that they had a chance to win the election legitimately, but not content to rely solely on legitimate methods, they also resorted to using physical and economic threats against black voters. A favorite tactic of the Conservatives was threatening to fire blacks from their jobs if they voted for the Republican ticket. However, the Democrats perpetrated few incidents of outright violence against Republicans of either color, perhaps because of the wide distribution of soldiers across Louisiana. Although it was relatively peaceful, contemporary observers and historians agree that the election of 1872 was one of the most fraudulent in Louisiana history. Both sides freely stuffed ballot boxes and used such time honored ploys as relocating polling places or shortening the hours that the polls were open. Several parishes eventually submitted two sets of voting returns.[47]

According to Emory, the election on November 4 "passed quietly" in New Orleans, and nothing out of the ordinary had been "reported from the interior," but the Fusionists and Democrats began clamoring that soldiers in the interior parishes had interfered in the election. William Hunter, a supporter of the Fusion ticket in Concordia Parish, told Governor Warmoth that "many of our most quiet colored friends felt so hurt at such a wanton display of Military Despotism they quietly preferred staying Home and this is Doubtless one Great cause of our short vote." The *Ouachita Telegraph* editorialist criticized the army's effect in his parish, claiming that "whites were considerably intimidated by the presence of United States troops, and were prevented from using . . . energetic means to carry the Fusion ticket." Despite these protestations, the Democrats eventually conceded Ouachita Parish to the Republicans.[48]

46. Gentry to C. H. Smith, October 29, 1872, in Dept Gulf, vol. 114/DSL, Lt. J. B. Burbank to Gentry, October 28, 1872, in Dept Gulf, vol. 149/DSL, both in RG 393, NA; Post Returns, Jackson Barracks, October 1872, in Records of the AGO (Microcopy M-617, reel 524), RG 94, NA.

47. William E. Highsmith, "Louisiana During Reconstruction" (Ph.D. dissertation, Louisiana State University, 1953), 269–70; Binning, "Henry Clay Warmoth," 294–322; Taylor, *Louisiana Reconstructed*, 239–41.

48. Emory to Townsend, November 4, 1872, in Dept Gulf, vol. 139/DSL, RG 393, NA;

Although Emory sent some soldiers to guard the ballot boxes in Covington, within a few days he saw no need to leave the other detachments scattered at their temporary posts across the state. Therefore, most of the units that had been given special election duty had returned to their regular garrisons by the end of November. Meanwhile another political crisis had developed.[49]

The crisis centered around the Returning Board, a state agency that was responsible for deciding if voting returns were legal or fraudulent and validating the final tally. At Warmoth's insistence, the legislature had passed a law establishing the Returning Board in 1870, and by controlling this board the governor virtually had the power to declare who was elected. The divisions in the Republican party split the Returning Board into two parts, with Warmoth presiding over one and John Lynch, a Custom House Republican, the other. Each appointed different men to fill the vacancies on his board and procured different judges to swear in the new panel members. Both tried to obtain the parish returns and have their board declare the winners of seats in the legislature and the prize plum, the governorship.[50]

When the Returning Board split, throwing Kellogg's election into doubt, General Emory realized that either side might use violence to uphold the findings of its board, and he ordered the soldiers at Jackson Barracks to be prepared to move into New Orleans "at a moment's notice." Believing that Governor Warmoth was responsible for cooking up this latest political mishmash, Emory advised Adjutant General Townsend that the governor had "displaced the legally constituted Board of Election returns" and filled a new board with "his partisans." Obviously ready to believe the worst about Warmoth, Emory was unlikely to use his troops to benefit the young carpetbagger or his allies of convenience, McEnery and Penn. Consequently, when Marshal Stephen Packard asked Emory's assistance in obtaining the election returns for John Lynch, the general

---

William Hunter to Warmoth, November 9, 1872, in Henry Clay Warmoth Papers, #752, Southern Historical Collection, University of North Carolina, Chapel Hill (microfilm copy at Louisiana State University Library, Baton Rouge); Monroe *Ouachita Telegraph*, November 9, 1872.

49. Gentry to CO, Jackson Barracks, November 9, 1872, in Dept Gulf, vol. 139/DSL, RG 393, NA. For examples of troop orders, see Gentry to Capt. A. W. Allyn (Shreveport), November 15, 1872, Gentry to Capt. J. H. Bradford (St. Martinville), November 12, 1872, Gentry to Capt. Bartholomew (Monroe), November 16, 1872, all in Dept Gulf, vol. 139/DSL, RG 393, NA.

50. The best account of the incredibly complex web is Taylor, *Louisiana Reconstructed*, 241–44.

requested authority to procure the returns for the Custom House's board. At this early stage in the crisis, however, the authorities in Washington were not ready to grant Emory's request. After a conference with President Grant, General Sherman ordered Emory not to interfere, "except in case of riot," thus temporarily preventing him from acting on behalf of Lynch and Kellogg. Nevertheless, Emory anticipated trouble, and he decided to bring in reinforcements; two more batteries of artillery at Fort Barrancas were ordered to board a steamer bound for Louisiana.[51]

Meanwhile, William Kellogg was apprehensive about Grant's attitude toward the Louisiana imbroglio. He wrote to Republican leader William E. Chandler, begging him to learn "the *real feeling* of the Administration towards us, and towards our complications." Would the army support his claim to the governorship if a federal court requested such support? He claimed that "the destiny of the party as well as the well-being of the community may depend upon the action of the military department of the Government." In a strangely revealing passage, Kellogg added: "God knows I never have desired this office of Governor; I do not want it now. If I consulted my own feelings simply I would abandon this whole thing. . . . The whole thing is distasteful to me and if I can put the responsibility upon the Federal government you may be sure I shall do it." Kellogg did not reveal these self-doubts in his official correspondence. On the contrary, he assumed that he was the governor–elect and was prepared to call upon the federal government to take his side.[52]

While Kellogg expressed his misgivings, Collector James Casey went to the nation's capital and personally explained the political situation in Louisiana to President Grant. Soon thereafter the Washington authorities acted to support the candidate of the Custom House Ring. Attorney General Williams directed Marshal Packard "to enforce the decrees and mandates of the United States courts, no matter by whom resisted," adding that "General Emory will furnish you with all necessary troops for that purpose." Adjutant General Townsend sent these same orders to Emory and added that the orders came from the president. Acknowledging Townsend's telegram, Emory said that "no requisition has yet been made but the troops are in hand and ready to act promptly." All that re-

51. Gentry to CO, Jackson Barracks, November 13, 1872, Emory to AGO, November 15, 1872, in Dept Gulf, vol. 139/DSL; Sherman to Emory, November 16, 1872, Major J. M. Brannan to AAG/Dept Gulf, November 27, 1872, both in Dept Gulf, vol. 149/DSL, RG 393, NA.

52. Kellogg to William E. Chandler, November 23, 1872 (emphasis in the original), Justice Dept Letters (Microcopy M-940, reel 6), RG 60, NA.

mained was for a cooperative federal judge to issue a ruling favorable to Kellogg's candidacy.[53]

In the meantime, on December 4 Warmoth's board, now chaired by Gabriel DeFeriet, named McEnery Louisiana's next governor and announced that a majority of Fusionists had been elected to the legislature. DeFeriet awarded the state's electoral votes to Greeley.

On December 5 the Custom House bosses persuaded federal circuit Judge Edward H. Durell to declare that Warmoth's returning board had violated a court order restraining either board from announcing the election results. Durell authorized Marshal Packard to occupy the state house and prevent any "unlawful assemblage" there. In other words, federal authorities could stop the Fusionist legislature from meeting. Basing their actions on Durell's decree, the Custom House Republicans now prepared to capitalize on the orders issued two days before by Attorney General Williams and Adjutant General Townsend.[54]

At 2:00 A.M. on December 6, Packard executed Durell's mandate. Loosely interpreting the judge's order, Packard asked for and received soldiers from Emory under the Enforcement Acts. Batteries F and L of the 1st Artillery commanded by Captain Richard H. Jackson went with Packard and some of his deputies to occupy the capitol. Emory also ordered four companies of the 19th Infantry to come into the city from Jackson Barracks, quartering them near department headquarters on Magazine Street. Reinforcements were therefore close by in case Warmoth's forces resisted Packard's occupation of the Mechanics' Institute. The next morning the New Orleans *Times* lambasted Judge Durell for using "flimsy and audacious pretences" to bring the army into the dispute.[55]

On December 9 Lynch's returning board declared that Kellogg had been elected governor and gave the state's electoral votes to Grant. Ac-

53. Taylor, *Louisiana Reconstructed*, 244; Williams to Packard, December 3, 1872, in *House Executive Documents*, 42nd Cong., 3rd Sess., No. 91, p. 13; Townsend to Emory, December 3, 1872, in Dept Gulf, vol. 149/DSL, Emory to Townsend, December 3, 1872, in Dept Gulf, vol. 139/DSL, both in RG 393, NA.

54. Taylor, *Louisiana Reconstructed*, 244–45. See also William Gillette, *Retreat from Reconstruction, 1869–1879* (Baton Rouge, 1979), 111.

55. New Orleans *Times*, December 7, 1872; Althea D. Pitre, "The Collapse of the Warmoth Regime, 1870–1872," *Louisiana History*, VI (Spring, 1965), 182–85; Post Returns, New Orleans, December, 1872, in Records of the AGO (Microcopy M-617, reel 844), Post Returns, Jackson Barracks, December, 1872 (Microcopy M-617, reel 524), both in RG 94, NA.

cording to Lynch's count, Republicans would heavily dominate the next legislature: seventy-seven Republicans to thirty-two Fusionists in the house; twenty-eight Republicans to eight Fusionists in the senate. These results did not satisfy the Fusionists, who countered Lynch's announcements by establishing yet another returning board!

The Fusionist board upheld the election of sixty-six legislators approved by the Lynch board, but counted in many other candidates not acknowledged by Lynch. Consequently, in several cases two men claimed to have been elected to the same seat in the legislature, and during the next few months two legislatures existed, one composed predominantly of Republicans and the other consisting of men loyal to McEnery. From time to time, in the bizarre reality of Louisiana politics, men who had been endorsed by both returning boards attended sessions of each legislature.[56]

On December 9 the Kellogg legislature assembled, and the house promptly impeached Governor Warmoth by a vote of fifty-seven to six, suspending him from office until the senate could hold a trial and reach a verdict. Until then, Lieutenant Governor Pinchback was to be acting governor of Louisiana. Pinchback notified Grant of Warmoth's impeachment and requested the "protection of the United States government" for the new administration. Actually, Emory's troops continued to occupy the state house, thus effectively discouraging the Fusionists from attacking the capitol. Following Pinchback's suggestion, the legislature passed a resolution calling on the president to order federal troops to defend the state government from domestic violence, though the acting governor admitted that New Orleans was calm and quiet. Attorney General Williams replied to Pinchback on Grant's behalf: "Whenever it becomes necessary in the judgment of the President, the State will be protected from domestic violence."[57]

Warmoth never acknowledged Pinchback's authority. He told Grant that Pinchback, aided by some U.S. soldiers, had broken into the executive offices and usurped the governorship. During the next two months both men claimed to be governor of the state. Nevertheless, Warmoth no

56. Taylor, *Louisiana Reconstructed*, 246.
57. *Ibid.*, 247–48; P. B. S. Pinchback to Grant, December 9, 1872, Resolution of the Louisiana Legislature, December 9, 1872, both in *House Executive Documents*, 40th Cong., 3rd Sess., No. 91, p. 16; Williams to Pinchback, December 11, 1872, in *Senate Reports*, 42nd Cong., 3rd Sess., No. 457, p. 843.

doubt realized that he was effectively out of office. His term expired in January, 1873, and though the Republicans made a pretense of holding a trial in the senate, no verdict was ever reached.[58]

Finally on December 12, after persistent badgering by Pinchback and Casey, Attorney General Williams informed Pinchback that President Grant had officially recognized him "as the lawful executive of Louisiana, and that body assembled at Mechanics' Institute [as] the lawful legislature of the state." Williams added that the army had been ordered to give Pinchback and his government full protection "from disorder and violence." The Attorney General also informed McEnery of Grant's decision. Using blunt language, Williams told McEnery, who still claimed to be governor-elect, that Grant's resolve would "not be changed, and the sooner it [was] acquiesced in the sooner good order and peace will be restored."[59]

For General Emory, Grant's recognition of Pinchback had come none too soon. In Emory's opinion, a riot had been averted by having troops escort Packard's deputies to the state house on December 6. But helping the marshal occupy the capitol had only slightly improved a "deplorable" situation. The loyalty of the city's population was divided between two governors and two legislatures. Making the situation more tense, Pinchback had reappointed James Longstreet to his job of state militia commander.[60]

Longstreet's appointment tested Emory's support of the Pinchback regime. George G. Waggaman, one of Warmoth's old officers, refused to surrender the state arsenal on Carondelet Street to Pinchback's militia, and Emory feared that the two groups would fight over the building. Pinchback called on Emory to expel Waggaman and his men. The general responded by asking Pinchback not to take any "aggressive steps" against the arsenal until the national authorities had been told about the confrontation. Emory fired off a telegram to Adjutant General Townsend, informing him that the "parties are face to face with arms in their hands. I beg an immediate answer." Townsend replied succinctly, "You

58. Warmoth to Grant, December 11, 1872, in *House Executive Documents*, 42nd Cong., 3rd Sess., No. 91, p. 18.

59. Pinchback to Grant, December 12, 1872, Casey to Grant, December 11, 12, 1872, Williams to Pinchback, December 12, 1872, John McEnery to Grant, December 12, 1872, Williams to McEnery, December 13, 1872, all in *House Executive Documents*, 42nd Cong., 3rd Sess., No. 91, pp. 19–21, 23–24.

60. Emory to AGO, December 11, 12, 1872, both in Dept Gulf, vol. 114/DSL, RG 393, NA.

may use all necessary force to preserve the peace, and will recognize the authority of Governor Pinchback." Bolstered by these orders, Emory sent Colonel Charles Smith to the arsenal, relaying Townsend's orders to Waggaman, who immediately turned over the arsenal to the army. Within a short time, Colonel Smith allowed Pinchback's militia to occupy the building, and the latest confrontation had ended without bloodshed.[61]

However, all the signs pointed to future upheaval. McEnery claimed the title of governor-elect, despite the fact that Grant had unequivocally recognized Pinchback and obviously intended Kellogg to be Louisiana's next governor. White resentment against the Custom House and the army was smoldering. An editorial in the *Picayune* announced that it would be "folly" for Louisianians "to resist the military authority of the United States," but that a great force of men would assemble to support McEnery, if he called for them to muster. On Christmas Day, 1872, Troop L, 7th Cavalry, reinforced the New Orleans garrison.[62] Emory and his soldiers were preparing to guard against the "folly" of resistance to Kellogg's inauguration on January 13, 1873.

61. Emory to Pinchback, December 14, 1872, *ibid.*; Emory to AGO, December 13, 1872, Townsend to Emory, and reply, both December 14, 1872, in *House Executive Documents*, 42nd Cong., 3rd Sess., No. 91, pp. 25–26; New Orleans *Daily Picayune* (afternoon edition), December 14, 1872; Taylor, *Louisiana Reconstructed*, 249.

62. New Orleans *Daily Picayune*, December 14, 1872; Emory to AAG, MilDivSouth, December 25, 1872, in Dept Gulf, vol. 114/DSL, RG 393, NA.

CHAPTER VII

The Flashing of
Bayonets in Our Streets

In January, 1873, John McEnery and William Pitt Kellogg both prepared to take the oath as governor of Louisiana. President Grant had already indicated his support of Kellogg, but McEnery was determined to hold his own bogus inauguration in the hope that it might later enable him to assume the governorship. In the meantime, McEnery and the Democrats planned to organize a shadow government. The Fusionist legislature scheduled its opening ceremonies on January 6, the same day that the Republican legislature would meet and one week before the dual inaugurations of McEnery and Kellogg. General Emory felt trapped between the two contending political forces and feared that the simplest barroom brawl or street fight might incite open warfare in New Orleans. Although he believed that McEnery's claim to office was invalid, and President Grant and the army high command had ordered him to sustain the administration of Acting Governor P. B. S. Pinchback, Emory doubted his own authority to transfer this support to Kellogg.[1]

Grant and General William T. Sherman understood the gravity of the Louisiana situation. In an effort to strengthen Emory's hand, Sherman ordered Emory "to use your troops to preserve peace, should a contingency arise which in your judgement calls for it." Emory released this statement to the New Orleans newspapers, hoping that it might persuade McEnery to cancel his inauguration, but the latter was unmoved by the general's orders.[2]

McEnery's intractability pointed to the possibility of a confrontation between Democrats and Republicans, and therefore, on January 4 Emory decided to show that the army intended to preserve the peace. He placed the troops in the Crescent City on full alert. Following the pattern he had

1. Emory to AAG, MilDivSouth, January 1, 1873, Emory to P. B. S. Pinchback, January 3, 1873, both in Dept Gulf, vol. 114/DSL, RG 393, NA.
2. Sherman's orders, sent by AAG William Whipple to Emory, January 4, 1874, in *House Executive Documents*, 42nd Cong., 3rd Sess., No. 91, p. 31; New Orleans *Republican*, January 7, 1873.

adopted the previous year, Emory informed the newspapers of his orders, and they dutifully reported these military preparations.[3]

Meanwhile, Grant, Sherman, and Attorney General Williams made two important decisions concerning the Kellogg-McEnery rivalry. First, the Washington authorities ordered Emory not to interfere with the meeting of McEnery's legislature, so long as it did not obstruct or disrupt "the administration of the recognized government of the state." Furthermore, Emory was instructed not to prevent McEnery's inauguration. Grant and his advisors did not want to spark a riot between the army and McEnery's defenders. Perhaps once McEnery was inaugurated, he would realize his own ineffectiveness and "resign" gracefully, and his government would collapse of its own dead weight.[4]

On January 6, the day picked for the opening of the legislatures, businesses closed and crowds gathered in downtown New Orleans. A carnival atmosphere prevailed despite the military preparations openly displayed in the city. The Metropolitan Police, commanded by Algernon Badger, assembled near the arsenal on Carondelet Street. Each policeman was well armed, and four brass cannon, hitched to horse teams, were parked in the street. Emory had a substantial military force in the city: five companies of the 19th Infantry occupied quarters in the Magazine Street Barracks; Troop L, 7th Cavalry, dismounted and picketed their horses in Tivoli Circle; and two batteries of artillery waited nearby with two Gatling guns. The whole force totaled 438 men, which was only about 50 men less than the entire 19th regiment at that time.[5]

Across town, the political rivals prepared to open their legislatures. More than four thousand persons had gathered to watch the arrival of the Fusionists and perhaps catch a glimpse of McEnery himself. Knots of armed lookouts posted themselves around the Odd Fellows Hall, the designated meeting site of the shadow government. Following much fanfare and speech-making, McEnery's legislature adjourned without a quorum. At the state capitol, more than two thousand Kellogg support-

3. Emory to AGO, January 5, 1873, in Dept Gulf, vol. 139/DSL, Gentry to CO, New Orleans, January 5, 1873, in Dept Gulf, vol. 114/DSL, both in RG 393, NA; New Orleans *Republican*, January 5, 1873; New Orleans *Times*, January 5, 1873.

4. Sherman to Emory, January 5, 1873, Williams to Packard, January 4, 1873, both in *House Executive Documents*, 42nd Cong., 3rd Sess., No. 91, pp. 31–32. See also Gillette, *Retreat from Reconstruction*, 113.

5. New Orleans *Times*, January 7, 1873; SW, "Annual Report, 1872–1873," 118–19; Post Returns, Jackson Barracks, January, 1873, in Records of the AGO (Microcopy M-617, reel 524), Post Returns, New Orleans, December, 1872 (Microcopy M-617, reel 844), both in RG 94, NA.

ers applauded the opening of the *de jure* legislature, which had a quorum but transacted no important business. Much to Emory's relief, the afternoon passed with the air of a holiday; no violence occurred, and the troops were not sent to either legislature. Emory believed that the massive display of military force had prevented a riot.[6]

Within a week, however, Emory faced a similar peace-keeping test during the dual inaugurations. He specifically asked Sherman if Kellogg should be automatically recognized upon his inauguration simply because Pinchback had been acknowledged previously. Sherman did not immediately reply to Emory's question, and the Louisiana commander logically assumed that he should recognize Kellogg in the absence of orders to the contrary. Emory also considered, however, that "the situation is becoming more complicated, and in my opinion, the use of troops simply to keep the peace cannot lead to a satisfactory or permanent solution of the difficulties here."[7]

January 13 dawned a "fair and lovely" day in New Orleans, and the political factions prepared themselves for the spectacle of two inaugurations. Emory apparently believed that the previous week's show of force had been warning enough. He posted only one company of soldiers at the state house and did not bring in the Jackson Barracks garrison as he had the week before. McEnery and Kellogg were inaugurated separately at the seats of their respective governments amid loud ovations but without violence.[8]

After the unusual events of recent weeks, President Grant took it upon himself to issue a special executive message on the Louisiana situation. The president summarized the conflict between the contending factions and remarked that he was "anxious to avoid any appearance of undue interference in State affairs." Grant acknowledged that the army had been employed in the emergency, and he concluded that unless Congress offered a better solution, the administration would continue to recognize Kellogg's "*de facto* government."[9]

6. New Orleans *Times*, January 7, 1873; Emory to Sherman, January 6, 1873, in *House Executive Documents*, 42nd Cong., 3rd Sess., No. 91, p. 33; Emory to Sherman, January 8, 1873, in Dept Gulf, vol. 114/DSL, RG 393, NA; Lonn, *Reconstruction in Louisiana*, 222.

7. Emory to Sherman, January 9, 1873, in Dept Gulf, vol. 114/DSL, RG 393, NA; Emory to Whipple, January 11, 1873, in *House Executive Documents*, 42nd Cong., 3rd Sess., No. 91, p. 33.

8. Lonn, *Reconstruction in Louisiana*, 223; New Orleans *Times*, January 14, 1873; New Orleans *Republican*, January 14, 1873.

9. Grant Presidential Message to Congress, February 25, 1873, in James D. Richardson (comp.), *Messages and Papers*, VII, 212–13.

A week after Grant's message to Congress, there was a clash between the political factions in Louisiana. On February 27, acting in his capacity as "governor," John McEnery appointed a former Confederate officer, Fred N. Ogden, as brigadier general and commander of the Louisiana "militia." Ogden let it be known that he planned to take over all of the stations of the Metropolitan Police, which Kellogg recently had integrated into the official state militia, commanded by James Longstreet. Inevitably, rumors of Ogden's intentions circulated throughout New Orleans. On March 5 General Sherman ordered Emory "to prevent any violent interference with the State government of Louisiana." Emory moved three companies of soldiers from the Magazine Street barracks to the Custom House, but he made no effort to protect the police stations. That evening, members of Ogden's Democratic militia brandished their weapons as they walked through the streets of New Orleans, and at about 9:30 P.M. Ogden's pickets cordoned off a portion of the French Quarter. With five hundred men following him, Ogden led an attack against the Jackson Square police station.[10]

While the Conservatives fired their guns at the station house, Republican reinforcements marched to the rescue, and Kellogg requested the army's help in putting down the disorder. Algernon Badger, newly designated commander of the Metropolitan Brigade of former policemen, brought about 180 militiamen and an artillery piece to the scene of the skirmish. The sounds of fighting drifted over Jackson Square, and the boom of the Metropolitan's cannon added to the din. Meanwhile, Emory ordered Colonel Charles Smith and the entire Jackson Barracks garrison into the city, and telegraphed General Sherman, informing him of the situation.[11]

About an hour after the fighting began, the first army soldiers arrived near the besieged police station. An officer on Emory's staff, Captain Charles King, detached himself from the column and made his way cautiously to Ogden. At the same time Colonel Smith sought out "general" George Waggaman of the Democratic forces. The army officers brought orders from Emory telling the Democrats to abandon their attack on the police station and disperse. Faced with the possiblity of clashing with the

10. Sanger and Hay, *James Longstreet*, 366; Sherman to Emory, March 5, 1873, in AGO File 4882 of 1872 (Microcopy M-666, reel 93), RG 94, NA; New Orleans *Times*, March 6, 1873.

11. Gentry to CO, Jackson Barracks, March 5, 1873, in Dept Gulf, vol. 114/DSL, Emory to Sherman, March 5, 1873, in Dept Gulf, vol. 139/DSL, RG 393, NA; New Orleans *Times*, March 6, 1873.

19th Infantry, Ogden and Waggaman promptly complied with Emory's orders, and within an hour the streets of the French Quarter were quiet and empty, disturbed only by the sounds of an occasional squad of infantrymen on patrol.[12]

Knowing that he had Emory's support and that the Metropolitan Brigade controlled the city's streets, Governor Kellogg decided to act against the Democratic legislature. He ordered Longstreet and Badger to occupy Odd Fellows Hall and disperse the opposition legislators. However, Kellogg made his decision without notifying Emory. About noon on March 6 a force of 125 Metropolitans surrounded Odd Fellows Hall and occupied the building. Several Democratic legislators scampered out the rear door before the circle was closed. The Metropolitans had disrupted McEnery's legislature, but their action did not force it out of existence.[13]

In a note to Emory, McEnery protested Kellogg's actions against his legislature. The general replied that the Metropolitans had acted without his knowledge and that their orders had come from Kellogg, who was recognized as the legal governor of the state. Furthermore, Emory warned McEnery that he would "use the whole force of the United States" to block an attack on Kellogg's government. The outcome of the recent altercations pleased Kellogg and made him feel more secure in office. On the other hand, McEnery's claims to the governorship had received a temporary setback.[14]

The arrangement of troops devised by General Sherman in 1871 had made it necessary for soldiers to be frequently shifted about. Emory and Colonel Smith reconsidered the disposition of forces in Louisiana. Emory decided to transfer the headquarters of the 19th Infantry, which Sherman had placed in Baton Rouge, back to Jackson Barracks. He assigned eight companies there, doubling the size of the garrison.[15]

While Emory was shifting his soldiers to the southern part of the state, newspapers were publishing ominous reports about the chaotic situation in Grant Parish in central Louisiana.[16] Following his inauguration, Kellogg had ousted two Fusionists who claimed to have been elected parish

12. New Orleans *Times*, March 6, 1873; New Orleans *Republican*, March 6, 1873.

13. New Orleans *Times*, March 7, 1873; Taylor, *Louisiana Reconstructed*, 255.

14. Emory quoted in New Orleans *Times*, March 7, 1873; Lonn, *Reconstruction in Louisiana*, 228–29.

15. Charles Smith to Emory, February 3, 1873, in Dept Gulf, Letters Recd, SO No. 45, March 21, 1873, in SO, Dept Gulf, both in RG 393, NA.

16. New Orleans *Times*, April 2, 7, 1873; New Orleans *Republican*, April 8–12, 1873; Alexandria *Democrat*, April 9, 1873; New Orleans *Daily Picayune*, April 7, 8, 1873.

judge and sheriff and replaced them with two Republicans. Once in office, the Republicans formed a local black militia unit and ordered it to patrol the streets of Colfax, the parish seat. The militiamen dug earthworks in the courthouse yard and extended their patrols to include the main roads in the parish. After several altercations occurred, the local whites, outraged and insulted by the Republicans' behavior, planned to attack the courthouse and regain control of the parish. The reports from Colfax had disturbed Kellogg to such an extent that on April 10 he considered sending General Longstreet to investigate the situation. The governor invited Emory to order one of his staff officers to accompany Longstreet, but Emory declined the invitation, apparently believing that the situation was not serious enough to warrant sending an official observer.[17]

On Easter Sunday, April 13, the Fusionist sheriff, Christopher C. Nash, and several hundred men attacked the Colfax courthouse. The fighting lasted for several hours, but the black militia repulsed the attackers. Consequently, the sheriff and his posse set fire to the courthouse and shot several of the defenders as they tried to escape. Later, Nash and his followers arrested thirty-seven blacks, and that night the Conservatives killed most of them without the formality of a trial. The courthouse defenders had killed one white Democrat in the fighting and wounded nine others. It was impossible to determine the number of Negro casualties, but probably more than one hundred were killed and wounded. The New Orleans *Republican* described the Colfax riot as a "massacre," but the state's Democratic press praised the decisive action of Nash and his cohorts. New Orleans *Times* printed details of the battle under the headline "War at Last!!"[18]

Emory and Kellogg were stunned by the dimensions of the Colfax riot, and both men were determined to have order restored in Grant Parish. Kellogg told Emory that the parish was "in a State of insurrection." He wanted federal soldiers sent there immediately. Emory agreed with the governor's conclusion and ordered Company K, 19th Infantry, from Baton Rouge to Colfax "to preserve the peace." However, all of the steamship captains at Baton Rouge refused to allow the army to use their

17. Lonn, *Reconstruction in Louisiana*, 240–44; Emory to Kellogg, April 10, 1873, enclosed with Lt. E. M. Hayes to Emory, April 10, 1873, both in Dept Gulf, Letters Recd, RG 393, NA.

18. Taylor, *Louisiana Reconstructed*, 269–70; New Orleans *Republican*, April 16, 1873; New Orleans *Times*, April 16, 1873.

vessels, claiming that it would ruin their business relations with white citizens. Irritated at their recalcitrance, Emory ordered two infantry companies at Jackson Barracks to make the trip up river as soon as a boat could be chartered in New Orleans.[19]

Kellogg realized that it would take several days for the army to reach Colfax. He was afraid that, if his authority were not reestablished quickly, the whole of northern Louisiana might rise in a rebellion patterned after the Colfax riot. Therefore, he ordered some units of the Metropolitan Brigade to Colfax. Furthermore, he begged Emory to send army detachments to Caddo, Ouachita, Richland, and Jackson Parishes. Emory responded by ordering Captain Clayton Hale to take a company of the 16th Infantry from Jackson, Mississippi, to Monroe, but he temporarily withheld action on the other requests. Actually, Emory was very concerned about the situation in Colfax, and he wanted approval from his superiors before sending soldiers to all of the northern parishes.[20]

Before a reply came from Louisville or Washington, Emory located a steamer captain who agreed to take army units to Colfax. Two companies—ninety-seven officers and men—embarked on April 19 under the command of Captain Jacob H. Smith. He was ordered to learn all that he could about the riot and "to bury the dead and take care of the wounded." The soldiers arrived at Colfax on the evening of April 21, eight days after the riot ended. Captain Smith and his men inspected the area and spoke with a U.S. deputy marshal who had found a shallow grave in which sixty-nine blacks were buried. After a few days the soldiers moved to the vicinity of Pineville, where they established a temporary garrison in the old buildings formerly used by the Louisiana State University.[21]

Emory concluded that the "Colfax massacre would probably never have occurred if United States troops had been in the neighborhood." Emory lamely blamed their absence on "the unexpected recall of the

19. Kellogg to Emory, April 15, 1873, in Dept Gulf, Letters Recd, Gentry to CO, Baton Rouge, April 15, 1873, Emory to AAG, MilDivSouth, April 17, 1873, both in Dept Gulf, vol. 139/DSL, Gentry to CO, Jackson Barracks, April 17, 18, 1873, both in Dept Gulf, vol. 114/DSL, all in RG 393, NA.

20. Kellogg to Emory, April 18, 1873, in Dept Gulf, Letters Recd, Emory to AAG, MilDivSouth, April 18, 1873, Emory to William Whipple, April 18, 1873, both in Dept Gulf, vol. 139/DSL, SO No. 61, April 18, 1873, in SO, Dept Gulf, all in RG 393, NA.

21. Post Returns, Jackson Barracks, April 1873, in Records of the AGO (Microcopy M-617, reel 524), RG 94, NA; Gentry to Jacob H. Smith, April 19, 1873, in Dept Gulf, vol. 114/DSL, RG 393, NA; New Orleans Daily Picayune, April 25, 1873; Alexandria Democrat, May 14, 1873; Taylor, Louisiana Reconstructed, 270.

Cavalry in this Department to the frontier where sudden emergencies required their presence."[22] Emory was correct in his supposition that if troops had been near Alexandria or Colfax the battle might have not occurred. However, according to General Sherman's plan, there were no soldiers assigned to posts north of Baton Rouge, and it was unlikely that Emory would have sent any without extraordinary justification. In fact, Emory had refused even to order a staff officer to accompany General Longstreet to Grant Parish before the battle took place.

Evidently, Emory failed to fully comprehend the threat posed by that white resistance to Republican rule. At Colfax, the Democrats had fired a warning shot across the bows of Kellogg's ship of state. After the Colfax battle, the Democrats used violence against Republicans whenever and wherever possible, avoiding contact with U.S. soldiers and disdaining the power of Kellogg's militia.[23] The Democrats could jeopardize the existence of civil order throughout Louisiana unless Emory were reinforced and allowed to use his soldiers to guard some of Kellogg's parish officials, although it was impossible for the army to protect every Republican officeholder. If Democrats were allowed to terrorize the hinterland parishes, New Orleans and the state government itself were vulnerable.

But Emory was not alone in failing to recognize the full importance of the Colfax riot. The authorities in Washington had no intention of allowing the Democrats to overthrow the Republicans, but they had no clear idea of how to counteract the violence of the McEnery forces, nor could they decide how the army should aid Kellogg. Grant wanted the army to differentiate between "local disturbances" and "direct violent attacks on the central organization of the state government" without recognizing that the former provided fuel for the latter. Secretary of War George M. Robeson concluded that, "if the State government needs and desires the aid of United States troops to maintain the public peace or prevent rebellion, the Legislature, or the Governor, if it be not in session, should apply to the President directly . . . for such aid," rather than simply issuing requests to Emory. In fact, Emory already had reminded Kellogg of this legal procedure. Accordingly, Kellogg begged Grant to send soldiers to Shreveport, a center of Conservative strength in Caddo Parish.[24]

22. Emory, Departmental Report, September 25, 1873, in Records of the AGO, Annual Reports (Microcopy M-666, reel 138), RG 94, NA.

23. Taylor, *Louisiana Reconstructed*, 271–72.

24. George M. Robeson to Sherman, April 19, 1873, in New Orleans *Republican*, April 20, 1873; Emory to Kellogg, April 19, 1873, in Dept Gulf, vol. 114/DSL, RG 393, NA;

Replying for Grant, Secretary Robeson contradicted his earlier statement and informed Kellogg that Emory could move the soldiers in his department anywhere he wanted and that the governor should apply to Emory for military support. Therefore, Kellogg and Marshal Packard again petitioned Emory for military assistance. The general ordered Captain William J. Lyster to take two companies to Shreveport and preserve the "peace and order of the community" but to "refrain from entanglements in the [local] political discussions."[25]

Secretary Robeson's contradictory orders, President Grant's apparent lack of confidence, General Sherman's reluctant authorizations, Emory's prior unheeded warnings, and Kellogg's sheeplike bleatings pointed up the fact that federal Reconstruction was uncoordinated. The more the Democrats used violence, the more Grant worried and fretted, unsure of how to react. He received increasing criticism from Republican congressional leaders, who found grumbling easier than taking action. Neither critics nor policy makers could offer the president sound advice on how to dampen Louisiana's governmental tinderbox.

Meanwhile, a serious crisis was developing in St. Martin Parish. Former Confederate colonel Alcibiades DeBlanc had been encouraging local Democrats to refuse to pay their state taxes. Moreover, he had organized a local militia outfit, which had been intimidating Republicans and preventing them from exercising the duties of their elected offices. On May 4 Kellogg dispatched Algernon Badger and 125 state militiamen to St. Martinville to seat the Republicans and collect the taxes. Approaching the town, Badger's men exchanged gunshots with DeBlanc's forces. Assuming that the tardy taxpayers might have violated some federal laws, Marshal Packard asked Emory for a company of U.S. soldiers to assist him in making arrests in the rebellious parish. At first Emory was unwilling to send in his troops without permission from higher authority, but on second thought he ordered Colonel Charles Smith and Company H, 19th Infantry, to St. Martinville. Traveling by rail to Brashear City, the soldiers were stranded there by uncooperative steamboat captains who refused to take them on to "the seat of war."[26]

Kellogg to Grant, April 25, 1873, in AGO File 4882 of 1872 (Microcopy M-666, reel 93), RG 94, NA.

25. Robeson to Kellogg, May 5, 1873, Packard to Emory, May 1, 1873, Kellogg to Emory, May 13, 1873, all in Dept Gulf, Letters Recd, Emory to AG, MilDivSouth, May 12, 1873, in Dept Gulf, vol. 139/DSL, AG Edward R. Platt to William J. Lyster, May 13, 1873, in Dept Gulf, vol. 114/DSL, all in RG 393, NA.

26. Emory to AAG Joseph Taylor, MilDivSouth, May 6, 7, 1873, in Dept Gulf, vol.

Finally, on May 10 Colonel Smith hired a steamer to transport his soldiers up Bayou Teche, but they arrived too late to participate in the fighting, which actually had involved only occasional skirmishing. The white "militia" had dispersed, and Badger and his Metropolitans arrested the feisty DeBlanc, who later boasted that if the federals had not arrived he would have chased the Metropolitans out of St. Martin Parish. Under custody of a U.S. marshal, DeBlanc stepped off of the steamboat at New Orleans, and a sympathetic crowd, led by John McEnery, accorded him "a hero's welcome." [27]

Evidently the violence in St. Martin and the complaints of Republicans from several parts of the state finally convinced Emory that the whole Louisiana situation was more dangerous than he had realized before. He wrote a grim description of circumstances to General Sherman: "In my judgement a Regiment or half regiment of Infantry, and if possible a squadron of Cavalry, in addition to the present force is necessary to keep the peace in this city and state, and prevent actual violence . . . which is threatened in nearly every Parish of the state." Sherman simply recommended that Emory contact General McDowell in Louisville. On May 8 Emory had strengthened the Crescent City's garrison and warned General McDowell at Louisville that a "general insurrection" was possible in Louisiana, unless more troops were ordered to the Department of the Gulf. McDowell replied that he had no extra cavalry available, but that he would send additional infantry if Emory's need for it became evident. [28]

The restoration of order in St. Martin had pleased Kellogg, but he had little time to feel satisfied. Soon violence threatened to erupt in other parts of Louisiana, especially in the northern parishes. The governor admitted to President Grant that domestic violence existed in "several parishes of this state which the State authorities are unable to suppress." Fed-

---

139/DSL, Packard to Emory, May 6, 1873, in Dept Gulf, Letters Recd, AG Platt to Charles H. Smith, May 6, 1873, in Dept Gulf, vol. 114/DSL, all in RG 393, NA; New Iberia *Sugar Bowl*, May 8, 1873; New Orleans *Times*, May 5, 6, 8, 1873.

27. Emory to AAG, MilDivSouth, May 10, 1873, in Dept Gulf, vol. 139/DSL, RG 393, NA; Alcibiades DeBlanc to John McEnery, May 14, 1873, in Lafayette *Advertiser*, May 24, 1873; New Iberia *Sugar Bowl*, May 15, 1873; New Orleans *Daily Picayune*, May 17, 1873; Taylor, *Louisiana Reconstructed*, 274–75.

28. Emory to Sherman, May 8, 1873, Emory to AAG Taylor, MilDivSouth, May 8, 1873, both in Dept Gulf, vol. 139/DSL, RG 393, NA; Sherman to Emory, May 9, 1873, in HQ/USA, Letters Sent (Microcopy M-857, reel 8), RG 108, NA; Post Returns, Jackson Barracks, May 1873, in Records of the AGO (Microcopy M-617, reel 524), McDowell to Emory, May 9, 1873, in AGO File 4882 of 1872 (Microcopy M-666, reel 93), both in RG 94, NA.

eral soldiers were needed to protect Republican officeholders, he insisted. State Auditor Charles Clinton expressed the feelings of many Republicans when he exclaimed that it was "impossible to collect taxes or for any officer of the State to perform his duties." Two Republicans at Minden in Webster Parish begged Kellogg to obtain U.S. soldiers to unseat McEnery officials who had usurped some local offices. Dutifully, Kellogg asked Emory to send some infantrymen to Minden, and the general replied that they would be sent as soon as the U.S. marshal requested them through proper channels. Packard soon applied for military aid, and apparently the army reinstated Kellogg's officials.[29]

Kellogg also complained that Democrats had threatened or intimidated several state judges and that squads of soldiers might be needed to guard courtrooms across the state. Officials were having a particularly difficult time in Grant Parish. J. Ernest Breda, district attorney for the Ninth Judicial District, decided that the Colfax rioters would never be brought to trial unless the army guarded the courthouse. Breda based his conclusion on the fact that seventy-five armed men had ridden into Colfax and "openly & violently threatened to break up the court if any thing was done against" the accused rioters. These acts occurred while "U.S. troops were at Pineville 30 miles from Colfax." Obviously disappointed by the army's inadequate protection, Breda asked Attorney General Williams "what is to be done by those who have only a Kellogg Commission for authority & no U.S. troops to protect them." Breda's complaints highlighted the predicament facing many Republicans in the South during Reconstruction. Their governance depended upon the direct support of the army. Even with soldiers located only a few miles away, as Breda's examples effectively demonstrated, white Democrats could intimidate Republicans or violate their rights with impunity.[30]

On May 22, in response to the advice of Attorney General Williams and other advisors, President Grant issued an executive proclamation regarding Louisiana's troubled condition. Grant commanded the "tur-

29. Kellogg to Grant, May 13, 1873, R. B. Taylor to Kellogg, May 13, 1873, T. E. Heath to Kellogg, May [?], 1873, Packard to George Williams, May 31, 1873, all in Justice Dept Letters (Microcopy M-940, reel 6), RG 60, NA; Charles Clinton to Kellogg, May 16, 1873, in Justice Department Papers (Microcopy M-940, reel 1), RG 60, NA; Kellogg to Emory, May 22, 1873, in Dept Gulf, Letters Recd, Emory to Kellogg, May 22, 1873, in Dept Gulf, vol. 114/DSL, both in RG 393, NA.

30. Kellogg to Williams, May 20, 1873, in Justice Dept Letters (Microcopy M-940, reel 6), RG 60, NA; J. Ernest Breda to J. R. Beckwith, August 11, 1873, Breda to Williams, August 11, 1873, both in J. Ernest Breda Letters, Special Collections Division, Howard-Tilton Memorial Library, Tulane University, New Orleans.

bulent and disorderly persons" who were challenging Kellogg's government "to disperse and return peaceably to their respective abodes within twenty days from this date." Although it was hardly a drastic ultimatum, the president warned the "disorderly persons" that Kellogg had properly applied for the army's support under Article IV, section 4, of the Constitution and that in the event of further disorders and violence, the army would intervene.[31]

A few days later Emory reported that Grant's proclamation had produced the desired "tranquilizing effect" on New Orleans, and that he was probably going to return the soldiers to Jackson Barracks soon. However, he did not recommend moving the companies located in Shreveport, Alexandria, St. Martinville, or Monroe. Those soldiers were "having an excellent effect in giving peace and a feeling of security in the neighborhoods where [they were] stationed." However, Emory advised the Military Division of the South that, because a bad yellow fever season was predicted, he planned to move his department's headquarters and several companies of troops out of Louisiana sometime in July to more healthy locations in Mississippi.[32]

In July Emory began shifting some units out of Louisiana to the "summer encampment," moving some in Monroe that he had earlier recommended be left in place. The companies at Jackson Barracks took the train to the town of Mississippi City, located on the Gulf coast near Biloxi. Emory ordered a corporal's guard to stay behind at the barracks. Apparently anticipating that his withdrawal of these forces would be thought reckless, Emory saw to it that company-sized garrisons remained in New Orleans itself, St. Martinville, and Baton Rouge. Alexandria and Shreveport each had two companies on duty. Emory defended his arrangements to General McDowell, writing that the "chief agitators" who had inspired most of the "political disturbances in both city and state" had left Louisiana. Emory anticipated "no disturbances whatever either in city or country until along in the fall as the time approaches for the meeting of Congress, when . . . [agitators may try] to influence the action of that body." Emory relocated his department headquarters to the town of Holly Springs in northern Mississippi near the Tennessee border. He then left the South to visit his family in New York, promising to "re-

31. Grant, Presidential Proclamation, May 22, 1873, in Richardson (comp.), *Messages and Papers*, VII, 223–24.
32. Emory to AAG, MilDivSouth, June 9, 12, 1873, both in Dept Gulf, vol. 114/DSL, RG 393, NA.

turn at a moment's warning" if trouble developed in the department.[33]

While in the North, Emory consulted with his superiors in Washington. According to the New York *Herald*, Emory reportedly had recommended to the War Department that most of the troops in Louisiana be "removed to the more congenial fields of the [Western] border where they can attend to the red devils" who had been conducting raids along the frontier. The *Herald* concluded that Americans (and particularly southerners) were tired of being "blinded by the flashing of bayonets in our streets, startled by the rumble of Gatlin [*sic*] guns, and the trump, tramp, of the regulars." The editor of the Lafayette *Advertiser* printed the *Herald*'s editorial with a note of approval.[34]

On returning to Holly Springs from his leave on September 7, Emory learned that the yellow fever season was worse than usual. Eventually the number of deaths due to the disease exceeded the total reported in the epidemic of 1870. Consequently, Emory believed that his idea of a "summer encampment" on the healthier ground in Mississippi had saved the lives of some of his soldiers. However, once back in the Gulf Department, Emory had to put aside thoughts of the danger of disease and concentrate on the use of his troops.[35]

In October Packard requested the army's help. Two deputy marshals, T. W. DeKlyne and J. B. Stockton, had been assigned to the Colfax riot case, and they had drawn up a list of several men who allegedly had participated in the fight. Packard wanted a military posse to accompany DeKlyne and Stockton into Grant Parish. Previously, Emory had been fearful that if renewed violence occurred in Grant Parish, soldiers might be caught in the cross fire between local Democrats and the federal marshals. Nevertheless, Emory acceded to Packard's request, ordering a company to Colfax. Six of the accused men surrendered peaceably to the marshals and their military escorts.[36]

Reflecting on Packard's requisitions and Kellogg's calls, Emory knew that the soldiers under his command, particularly the 19th Infantry, had

33. AG Platt to CO, Monroe, July 2, 1873, Platt to CO, Jackson Barracks, July 5, 1873, Emory to AAG, MilDivSouth, July 11, 22, August 11, 1873, all in Dept Gulf, vol. 114/DSL, RG 393, NA.

34. Lafayette *Advertiser*, September 13, 1873.

35. Emory to AAG, MilDivSouth, September 7, 1873, in Dept Gulf, vol. 114/DSL, RG 393, NA; Shreveport *Times*, September 1–November 1, 1873; Taylor, *Louisiana Reconstructed*, 433.

36. Emory to AGO, September 17, 1873, in Dept Gulf, vol. 114/DSL, RG 393, NA; Shreveport *Times*, November 2, 1873. For an account of the trials connected with the Colfax riot, see Franklin, *Reconstruction After the Civil War*, 206–208.

been "actively used during the year," and he indicated that perhaps it was time for McDowell to consider exchanging the regiments in the Department of the Gulf with those stationed elsewhere. "The duty which the Army is called upon to perform in this Department is of such a character and so closely interwoven with political matters that it has been not only a very delicate one but embarrassing to those charged with its execution," wrote Emory with some disgust. He continued, "Without any power to correct abuses or originate measures . . . [the Army has been] called upon to sustain the law and keep the peace, against machinations skillfully devised by adroit men to perpetuate fraud and foment violence." Furthermore, Emory implied that service against the Plains Indians was better and more honorable than trying to prevent "conflicts between armed bodies of men, both claiming to be acting by authority of the Executive of Louisiana." While Emory reestablished his headquarters at New Orleans and brought the companies back from Mississippi to garrison Jackson Barracks, McDowell agreed to consider Emory's suggestion about transferring some of his troops.[37]

A few weeks after Emory and his soldiers had resettled in New Orleans and their other posts, the Democrats announced plans to hold a legislative session; the ritual was set for January 5, 1874. McEnery wrote to Emory, asking if he would prevent the meeting or aid the Metropolitans if they acted to disperse the Democrats. McEnery stressed that he and his followers wanted no conflict with federal authorities. Emory replied that the army would not interfere with the Democratic legislature, so long as its meeting was peaceful. However, Emory reminded McEnery that Kellogg was the recognized governor of Louisiana; and in the event of any violence, U.S. forces would support Kellogg. Keeping Emory's warning in mind, McEnery completed his plans for the meeting.[38]

On January 5 the two legislatures met as scheduled. The Republicans and a few maverick Democrats, recognized as officially elected by the Republican Returning Board, assembled at the capitol, and a quorum was present in each house. In contrast, the McEnery Democrats gathered in their leader's private offices at No. 35 Carondelet Street, but both houses lacked a quorum. McEnery tried to put a brave front on the meet-

37. Emory, Departmental Report, September 25, 1873, in Records of the AGO, Annual Reports (Microcopy M-666, reel 138), RG 94, NA; Emory to AGO, October 29, 1873, in Dept Gulf, vol. 114/DSL, RG 393, NA.

38. McEnery to Emory, December 25, 1873, in AGO File 4882 of 1872 (Microcopy M-666, reel 93), RG 94, NA; Emory to McEnery, December 26, 1873, in Dept Gulf, vol. 114/DSL, RG 393, NA.

ing, but he knew that it had been a failure. Consequently, the other Democrats and Fusionists who had been officially elected went to the state house and took their seats the next day. On January 9 the McEnery caucus passed a resolution excusing the remaining "legislators . . . until such time as the Legislature shall not be prevented by Federal authority from proceeding with its legitimate business." Thereupon the McEnery legislature adjourned, losing any claims it had to legitimacy.[39]

Outside of New Orleans, Louisiana was unusually calm, but Emory feared that any reduction in the number of troops in the state might encourage acts of violence by the Democrats. Emory advised General McDowell in Louisville that no garrisons in Louisiana could be "weakened or broken up without injury to the order and good government of the vicinity" in which the soldiers were located. In essence, Emory was expressing concern over Kellogg's capability to govern areas of the state that were not within easy reach of either the army or the Metropolitans. McDowell shared the same concern, and in giving testimony before a congressional committee, he indicated that Louisiana had been "in a very disturbed condition" and was "likely to remain so for some time to come." However, there were no major outbreaks of violence in the state during the early months of 1874. Emory's concern about weakening the army's posts seemed unjustified.[40]

Although Louisiana was unusually peaceful, an outbreak of violence between Republican factions in Arkansas tested Emory's leadership and judgment. For the most part, there had been little violence associated with Reconstruction in Arkansas, and therefore, garrisoning the state had not been a demanding task. However, in the 1872 state election two Republicans, Joseph Brooks and Elisha Baxter, both claimed to have been elected governor. Baxter and some of his supporters had occupied the Arkansas capitol in Little Rock and appeared to have established claim to the executive office, but in April, 1874, fighting broke out between the militias of the two governors, initiating the so-called Brooks-Baxter War.[41]

39. New Orleans *Times*, January 7, 10, 1874.

40. Emory to AAG, MilDivSouth, January 2, 1874, in Dept Gulf, vol. 115/DSL, RG 393, NA. See also Joe Gray Taylor, "New Orleans and Reconstruction," *Louisiana History*, IX (Summer, 1968), 204. McDowell, testimony, January 24, 1874, in *House Report*, 43rd Cong., 1st Sess., No. 384, p. 257.

41. Otis A. Singletary, *Negro Militia and Reconstruction* (Austin, 1957), 50–53; Earl F. Woodward, "The Brooks and Baxter War in Arkansas, 1872–1874," *Arkansas Historical Quarterly*, XXX (Winter, 1971), 315–36.

If past experience in Louisiana were any guide, it appeared logical that the army would intervene, prevent a battle between the factions, and either reinstate Baxter or keep the peace until the authorities in Washington decided whom to recognize. However, President Grant hesitated to choose sides immediately between the two contestants. He directed Secretary of War Belknap to order the commanding officer at Little Rock, Captain Thomas Rose, "to take no part in the political controversy . . . unless it should be necessary to prevent bloodshed or collision of armed bodies."[42]

No one—not the president, secretary of war, Adjutant General Townsend, or General McDowell—ordered Emory to go to Little Rock. Nor did Emory decide to go to Arkansas. Instead, he ordered Captain Rose "to observe the strictest neutrality in regard to the question of the State Government." However, Rose discovered that his two infantry companies were not adequate to prevent civil disorder. Clashes occurred between the rival Arkansas militias in late April and early May.[43]

On May 11 Captain Rose, disregarding the normal chain of command, bypassed Emory's headquarters and telegraphed the War Department directly to ask for reinforcements. General Sherman scribbled a note on the flap of the captain's telegram: "I have seen no orders of any kind relieving him [Rose] from the supervision of his Department Commander and until he recognizes him I have not one word to say, Except that in my judgment it is time for General Emory to go in person to Little Rock and exercise command in his own Department, or be relieved." This was the first official indication that Emory's military superiors were not satisfied with his conduct. Four days later, on May 15, President Grant resolved the Arkansas dispute by recognizing Baxter's claim to the governorship.[44]

What had kept Emory in New Orleans during the height of the Brooks-Baxter controversy? First of all, the rivalry between the Republican claimants in Arkansas had been going on since 1872 and previously had involved little more than verbal jousting. Apparently, Emory hoped that the Republican politicians would resolve the conflict themselves if they were left alone, but Brooks and Baxter did not reach an accommodation. Furthermore, during April heavy rains caused some of

42. Orville Babcock, Grant's personal secretary, to William W. Belknap, April 16, 1874, in Grant Papers.

43. Emory to AAG, MilDivSouth, April 16, 1874, in Dept Gulf, vol. 115/DSL, RG 393, NA; Singletary, Negro Militia, 54–65.

44. Sherman's comment written on Thomas Rose to Edward Townsend, May 11, 1874, quoted in Sefton, Army and Reconstruction, 238.

the worst flooding in Louisiana history, and the state's rivers and bayous were overflowing. The high water obstructed travel from New Orleans to Little Rock.[45] Moreover, Rose communicated only infrequently with Emory, who, as the crisis wore on, seemed satisfied to let Rose fend for himself. Fortunately, the president stepped in and resolved the matter. Judging from Sherman's displeasure, had Grant not acted, Emory might have been relieved of his command. Meanwhile, Louisiana Democrats began to organize forces that were definitely Emory's responsibility.

On April 27, 1874, several prominent St. Landry Parish Democrats met in Opelousas and formed Louisiana's first White League, an organization designed to intimidate blacks and Republicans and pledged to use force if necessary to remove Radical officials. Emboldened by the fact that only a few of the Colfax rioters had been arrested and prosecuted, Conservative leaders throughout Louisiana believed that the concerted use of violence against Republican parish officeholders would cripple Kellogg's state government. During 1874, Democrats in the neighboring state of Mississippi were successfully carrying out just such a campaign, and the example was not lost on McEnery's supporters. A newly founded Conservative newspaper, the Alexandria *Caucasian*, trumpeted a warning to Republicans: "we [the Democrats], having grown weary of the tame submission to this most desolating war of the negro upon us, propose to take a bold stand to assert the dignity of our manhood, to say in tones of thunder . . . STOP! THIS FAR SHALT THOU GO, AND NO FURTHER!"[46]

Emory, since his arrival in Louisiana, had often heard such Democratic remonstrances. He paid no attention to this warning. In fact, the initial stirrings of the White League failed even to disturb Emory's plans to transfer most of the troops in Louisiana to the healthy encampments in Mississippi during the upcoming yellow fever season, just as he had the year before. It is possible that the news of Emory's plan to remove the troops encouraged the growth of the White Leagues. In any case, General McDowell approved the plans.[47]

While Emory concerned himself with these routine matters, Conser-

---

45. Reports of flooding in New Orleans *Times*, April–May, 1874.
46. Alexandria *Caucasian*, May 23, 1874. An excellent summary of League activities is Taylor, *Louisiana Reconstructed*, 280–81.
47. Emory to AAG, MilDivSouth, May 23, 1874, in Dept Gulf, vol. 115/DSL, AAG Chauncey McKeever to Emory, June 3, 1874, in MilDivSouth, vol. 2/DSL, both in RG 393, NA.

vative leaders became more outspoken. On June 9, upon returning from a trip to Washington, D.C., John McEnery gave an impassioned speech to a crowd of about seven hundred persons in New Orleans, encouraging them to establish "an organization so strong that their votes will have to be counted, their candidates elected and seated. . . . You must fight for the white people now; the civilization of a thousand years is not to be swept away." After McEnery stepped aside, E. John Ellis, a staunch Democrat and one of the local White League organizers, addressed the throng. "Louisiana has suffered for all the Union, but in that suffering she has conquered. When the day of liberty comes, there will then be no blue coats to interfere with us." [48]

Ellis' prediction appeared to come true almost immediately. On June 9, the same day that McEnery and Ellis were inspiring the Canal Street crowd with their oratory, Emory's adjutant ordered Colonel Charles Smith to prepare his 19th Infantry to move to the Indian frontier in Kansas. These orders removed from Emory's command a regiment that had more than four years of Reconstruction experience in Louisiana and Arkansas and whose officers were familiar with state politics and problems. [49]

News of the 19th regiment's impending departure no doubt delighted the Democratic party's leaders, who had been busy recruiting White League forces throughout Louisiana. During May, June, and July, independent White League companies were organized in at least eighteen parishes, including Orleans, Caddo, Rapides, Grant, Red River, Natchitoches, and Terrebonne, all of which had been locations of anti-Republican violence of one kind or another in past months. Although the White League leaders communicated with one another, they lacked a unified "high command" or state headquarters. [50]

Despite the ominous activities of the White League, General Emory initially planned to close down most of the posts where units of the 19th Infantry had been stationed. Their replacements, the men of the 3rd Infantry from Indian Territory and Kansas, were not scheduled to arrive in the Department of the Gulf until the fall. A small detachment (only nineteen men) was stationed at Jackson Barracks outside New Orleans, where

48. New Orleans *Daily Picayune*, June 10, 1874.
49. AAAG William W. Sanders to Charles H. Smith, June 9, 1874, in Dept Gulf, vol. 115/DSL, RG 393, NA.
50. Taylor, *Louisiana Reconstructed*, 280–83.

Emory concluded that there was little chance "of the possible renewal of political disturbances" for the time being.[51]

McEnery and the Democrats must have observed these military maneuvers with hopeful interest. The New Orleans *Republican* and the *Times* provided them with reliable reports. The report in the *Republican* that "Seven companies of the Third Infantry, which will relieve the Nineteenth, will encamp at Holly Springs, Mississippi, for the summer" was particularly gratifying. The account was true—very few troops would be left in Louisiana during the summer.[52]

Following the departure of the 19th regiment, the White League increased its activities. The New Orleans White League completed its organization during June, and the *Picayune* openly advocated military training and drills for a white militia brigade. Accordingly, the New Orleans White League held public drills during the summer, but usually without weapons. Although the White League was becoming more active in New Orleans, Emory had no intention of preventing their drills and meetings, and he prepared to put his summer encampment policy into effect.[53]

On June 22 Emory and a few of his staff officers arrived at Holly Springs, Mississippi. While awaiting the arrival of the 3rd Infantry from Kansas, the general decided to leave garrisons at Baton Rouge and Colfax for the summer. Including the detachment of nineteen men at Jackson Barracks, there were 130 officers and soldiers in Louisiana. General Sherman ordered Emory to hold the 3rd regiment in Mississippi for several weeks, which coincided with Emory's summer encampment plan. This would allow the soldiers to acclimate themselves to the heat of the South and let the worst of the fever season pass.[54]

The threat of fever did not deter the White Leagues from mounting campaigns of intimidation against Republicans in several parishes. In late June and early July the Natchitoches League opened the campaign, threatening bodily injury to four members of the Natchitoches Parish police jury. Heeding the warning, the four men hastily resigned, and two state tax collectors packed up and left town along with them. In the fol-

51. Emory to AAG, MilDivSouth, June 4, 1874, in Dept Gulf, vol. 140/DSL, RG 393, NA.

52. New Orleans *Republican*, June 17, 1874; New Orleans *Times*, June 18, 1874.

53. New Orleans *Daily Picayune*, June 21, 1874; Taylor *Louisiana Reconstructed*, 283–84.

54. Post Returns, Baton Rouge, June 1874, in Records of the AGO (Microcopy M-617, reel 86), RG 94, NA; AAG Platt to Emory, June 22, 1874, in Dept Gulf, vol. 140/DSL, GO No. 18, June 22, 1874, in GO, Dept Gulf, Emory to AAG, MilDivSouth, June 27, 1874, in Dept Gulf, vol. 115/DSL, all in RG 393, NA.

lowing weeks, White Leagues in other parishes applied similar tech-
niques against both Republican officeholders and Negroes, forcing out
many officials and scaring blacks into a subservient role. The Opelousas
Courier expressed the opinion, widely held by Conservatives, that the
"object of the White League is to put the control of the state government
into the hands of the white people of the state." For example, Alcibiades
DeBlanc and his White League company, acting with impunity since the
removal in June of the army garrison from St. Martinville, forced several
Republicans to leave St. Martin Parish. White Leagues intimidated and
threatened the lives of Republicans in other parishes, including Bossier,
Avoyelles, Iberia, and Caddo. Armed riders disrupted a Republican
meeting at Homer in Claiborne Parish, and other Leaguers threatened to
kill Allen Green, an important Republican leader in Lincoln Parish.
Many white Republicans moved to New Orleans, and a few left the state.
The Conservative newspapers ominously reported that several blacks
had been lynched in the Red River parishes. In Shreveport, the *Times*
supported the White League, promising a war "to the death upon carpetbaggers and scalawags." In other places, such as Coushatta in Red River
Parish, the Conservatives held mass meetings and political candidates delivered fiery speeches. All of this activity demonstrated that outside of
New Orleans and the garrison towns of Baton Rouge and Colfax, Governor Kellogg's power was steadily eroding, and by the end of the summer the Republicans had no authority at all in some parishes.[55]

Cognizant that Kellogg's government was losing power almost daily,
the New Orleans *Republican* pleaded for calm and order and warned "violent and intolerant men of all parties, our own included, . . . that if
organized bodies of armed men shall confront each other . . . the armed
occupation of the State will be a very probable consequence. Let all unite
their counsels to avoid it." However, the New Orleans *Picayune* belittled
the *Republican*'s words of caution, crowning the Conservative point of
view with the claim that "the most abject spectacle we can imagine is that
of a regiment of able-bodied human beings crouching and whimpering
before the effigy of the United States Army."[56]

55. Taylor, *Louisiana Reconstructed*, 284–86; H. Oscar Lestage, "The White League in
Louisiana and its Participation in Reconstruction Riots," *Louisiana Historical Quarterly*,
XVIII (July, 1935), 652–56, 670; Singletary, *Negro Militia*, 135; Lonn, *Reconstruction in Louisiana*, 264; Allen Green to Packard, July 17, 1874 (forwarded by Packard to Emory, July 22,
1874), in *House Executive Documents*, 44th Cong., 2nd Sess., No. 30, p. 262; New Orleans
Daily Picayune, August 12, 21, 22, 26, 1874; Shreveport *Times*, July 9 and August 14, 1874.
56. New Orleans *Republican*, August 2, 1874; New Orleans *Daily Picayune*, August 27,
1874.

Under these disconcerting circumstances, Republican leaders realized that only the army was capable of restoring order, but the detachment of nineteen men at Jackson Barracks was an ineffective force, and the commanders at Baton Rouge and Colfax would not act without orders from department headquarters. Complicating matters further, General Emory had gone north (as he had the previous summer) to consult with his superiors in Washington and visit his family in New York. He did not intend to return until the fever season had ended.[57]

In Emory's absence, the senior officer at Holly Springs was Colonel DeLancey Floyd-Jones, commander of the 3rd Infantry which had recently arrived in Mississippi. A native of New York, Floyd-Jones was a West Point graduate (class of 1846) and a veteran of both the Mexican and Civil Wars. But he had no experience in dealing with Reconstruction, and he must have been horrified at the complexities of southern politics. In an effort to acquaint himself with the populace around Holly Springs, Floyd-Jones invited the residents of the area to the army camp to listen to the regiment's "magnificent brass band." However, as the New Orleans *Times* observed, Crescent City residents would have to wait to hear the band because Colonel Floyd-Jones was "acclimating the men" of his regiment at Holly Springs, "where they will in all probability remain for the next three months, when they will be assigned to the posts vacated by the Nineteenth Infantry." Therefore, until the 3rd regiment finished its acclimation, it was unavailable for duty in Louisiana.[58]

This arrangement was not helping the Republicans, and Kellogg and Packard both believed that several Louisiana parishes needed immediate military protection. They formally requested that more soldiers be sent to the state. From Holly Springs, Adjutant General Edward Platt forwarded the Republican requests for soldiers to Emory and informed the Republican leaders "that troops can be sent as [you have] requested . . . only by the orders of the President of the United States." Platt referred the Republicans' pleas "to the higher authorities."[59]

Without the army's support, Kellogg's government was precipitously close to collapse. In several parishes the Democrats had taken control of local offices. By the end of August, about fourteen thousand men,

57. Platt to Emory, July 10, 1874, in Dept Gulf, vol. 140/DSL, RG 393, NA.
58. Dept Gulf, Journal of Events kept by AAG, p. 28, RG 393, NA; Cullum, *Register of West Point*, II, 171–72; New Orleans *Times*, July 12, 14, 1874.
59. Platt to Packard, July 31, 1874, Platt to Kellogg, July 31, 1874, both in Dept Gulf, vol. 115/DSL, Platt to Emory, July 30, 1874, Platt to Kellogg, August 4, 1874, both in Dept Gulf, vol. 140/DSL, all in RG 393, NA.

many of them former Confederates, had been recruited into the various White League companies in Louisiana. White League leader John Ellis informed his brother that the Democrats would be "in control of the Gov't within six months." Ellis claimed to have reliable information that "5000 armed & equipped men from the Country [were ready to fight] at one weeks notice." Ellis concluded that "the days of that accursed [Republican] party in Louisiana are numbered."[60]

By then, Kellogg was desperate enough to make his case directly to the authorities in Washington. Having received no help from Captain Platt in Holly Springs, Kellogg petitioned U.S. Attorney General George Williams and President Grant for federal aid. Kellogg reminded Attorney General Williams that Louisiana was "the only Southern State that is practically without the presence of U.S. troops." The governor claimed that his administration had "enforced and executed the laws and maintained order in this City and in all but the remote border Parishes of the State," but that now it was necessary for the stability of his government to have the 3rd Infantry occupy the various posts in Louisiana vacated by the 19th Infantry.[61]

Kellogg began his letter to Grant by saying "I regret to trouble you again about our affairs," and he went on to describe some of the White League activities in Louisiana. Kellogg "respectfully and earnestly" asked the president to order the 3rd Infantry into Louisiana's vacant posts and suggested other locations where military force was needed to end "the outrages and violence now prevailing" across the state. Kellogg assured Grant that "the heated term here has apparently passed and the state is healthier than it has been for many years." In other words, there had been no yellow fever epidemic in 1874, and the fresh troops of the 3rd Infantry were not in danger of infection if they moved into the Bayou State. Finally, Kellogg told the president that if the troops came into Louisiana now, they would assure a "quiet and fair election" in the fall and might prevent "a formal call" for them at a later date. Neither Kellogg's logic nor the desperate tone of his letter were able to persuade the president to act at that time. After the White League's subsequent murderous acts in Red River Parish, though, the president changed his mind.[62]

60. Lonn, *Reconstruction in Louisiana*, 257–58; E. John Ellis to Tom Ellis, August 3, 1874, in E. John Ellis Papers, Department of Archives and Manuscripts, Louisiana State University Library, Baton Rouge.

61. Kellogg to Williams, August 26, 1874, in Justice Dept Letters (Microcopy M-940, reel 2), RG 60, NA.

62. Kellogg to Grant, August 19, 1874, *ibid.*

One of the strongest White League units was in Red River Parish, near Shreveport. The Conservatives opposed the parish's Republican bosses, the brothers Marshall and Homer Twitchell, two Vermont carpetbaggers who controlled local offices in the town of Coushatta, the parish seat. Following the familiar example of their confederates in other parishes, the Red River White League threatened, shot, wounded, and killed several Republicans. On August 28 a thousand armed White Leaguers assembled in Coushatta and arrested Homer Twitchell and several other prominent Republicans, including U.S. Marshal Henry A. Scott. On August 29 Homer Twitchell and five other officials agreed to resign from office. The next day, after releasing Scott, a few League members escorted the Republicans out of the parish, supposedly taking them to Shreveport for their own safety. About forty miles outside of Coushatta a group of armed riders stopped the travelers. Immediately gunshots rang out and within a few moments all of the defenseless Republican officials had been killed. The "Coushatta Massacre" rocked the foundations of Republicanism in Louisiana. The killings conclusively proved the power of the White Leagues and demonstrated its intentions.[63]

Following the Coushatta murders, both Marshal Packard and Governor Kellogg begged Attorney General Williams to convince President Grant that the army was needed in Louisiana. Kellogg told Williams that only the arrival of the 3rd Infantry would calm the unrest in the state. Supporting the requests by Kellogg and Packard, Louisiana's Attorney General, A. P. Field, concluded that "Unless protected by Military force every white republican in Louisiana will be either murdered or driven from the state before November."[64]

The Conservative press exulted in their victory. The rabid Shreveport *Times* explained that the "white people of this State have been driven to desperation" to throw off the "damnable bondage" of the Radical Republicans, a few of whom had received "justice" near Coushatta. "The eagles have struck down their foe and swept away," concluded the frenzied *Times* editorialist. "Now let the buzzards of Radicalism squat upon the carcasses and scream." The New Orleans *Bulletin* joined the Conservative chorus, warning that in the future "If the soldiers choose to

---

63. Taylor, *Louisiana Reconstructed*, 287–91.
64. Packard to Williams, August 30, 1874, Kellogg to Williams, August 30, 1874, both in *Senate Executive Documents*, 43rd Cong., 2nd Sess., No. 13, pp. 10–11; A. P. Field to Williams, September 1, 1874, in Justice Dept Letters (Microcopy M-940, reel 2), RG 60, NA.

get mixed up in broils with which they have no concern, they must expect to come out with punched heads and torn uniforms. The time has passed when a blue coat stuck up on a pole can make us bow in abject submission." [65]

Another newspaper supporting the White League, the Rayville *Richland Beacon*, had previously proclaimed that the "day of deliverance is drawing nigh, when Louisiana will be freed from the manacles of military despots, and her people allowed to enjoy liberty and the pursuit of happiness." [66] If the president or the army did not act soon, the White Leagues were ready to strike the deciding blow against the Republicans: the removal of Governor Kellogg himself.

65. Shreveport *Times*, September 3, 1874; New Orleans *Bulletin*, August 28, 1874.
66. Rayville *Richland Beacon*, February 1, 1873.

CHAPTER VIII

Emory and the
Insurrection of 1874

On September 5, 1874, in Washington, D.C., a messenger handed General Emory a letter from General of the Army William T. Sherman. Emory scanned the brief note: "Matters of importance in your Department demand your presence at your Headquarters and I regret the necessity which compels me to ask you to proceed thither at once, stopping in Louisville to confer with Genl. McDowell." Sherman gave no details about the "matters of importance," but Emory could imagine that the Democrats and Republicans were at each other's throats again. Emory immediately packed his trunks and took the next train to Louisville, where he met with McDowell on September 8. His superior ordered Emory to distribute the 3rd Infantry among several towns in Louisiana in the hope that the reappearance of the soldiers would neutralize the White League's activities in the state. Following the conference with McDowell, Emory proceeded to Holly Springs, Mississippi. Neither Sherman nor McDowell directly ordered him to go to Louisiana, although Emory gave McDowell reason to believe that he would be going on to New Orleans. Apparently Governor Kellogg and his Custom House Republicans were facing their gravest crisis, and the climactic confrontation between Louisiana's political rivals was at hand.[1]

Prompted by the Coushatta massacre and other "recent atrocities in the South," President Grant and Attorney General Williams had made important announcements. On September 2 Grant had ordered Secretary of War William Belknap to have "troops available in cases of emergency." But the president failed to give the war secretary any specific instructions

1. Sherman to Emory, September 5, 1874, in Emory Papers; Irvin McDowell to Sherman, September 8, 1874, in AGO File 3579 of 1874 (Microcopy M-666, reel 169), RG 94, NA. An indication that McDowell expected Emory to travel to New Orleans is in AAG Chauncey McKeever to Emory, September 15, 1874, in MilDivSouth, vol. 2/DSL, RG 393, NA.

regarding the dispatch of reinforcements to Louisiana, one of the states Grant condemned for showing "a disregard for the law . . . that ought not to be tolerated in any civilized government." On September 3 Attorney General Williams had sent a circular to all U.S. marshals and attorneys in the South ordering them to "detect, expose, arrest, and punish the perpetrators" of the recent violent acts in the southern states. Williams indicated that federal troops would give the marshals and attorneys "all needful aid" in making these investigations and arrests, but like the president, the attorney general failed to supply any details about the promised military aid.

Several Louisiana newspapers printed Grant's letter to Belknap and Williams' circular to his subordinates, and the Conservative press chose to interpret the absence of any specific military orders as a sign that the national administration was not going to support Kellogg. The Shreveport *Times* mistakenly reported that the 3rd Infantry had not been ordered to Louisiana but that, if it were, the day had passed when Louisianians could be intimidated "by the phantom of the Federal army in the person of a regiment or so of soldiers." The *Times* warned that Kellogg's "infamous government cannot longer misgovern here, *and in the next sixty days Louisiana must be a free State or a military camp.*" But on September 5 Grant finally publicized the orders sending the 3rd Infantry to Louisiana. The army intended to establish or reinforce posts at New Orleans, Baton Rouge, Shreveport, Alexandria, Monroe, Harrisonburg, and St. Martinville. Apparently the Kellogg government had been saved—or so it seemed. The Shreveport *Times*, undoubtedly speaking for most white Louisianians, insisted again that the state's citizens were not cowed by these military preparations. "*Trumpets are sounding in the gloom,*" but not, the *Times* clearly implied, the trumpets of the U.S. Army.[2]

The Conservatives waited expectantly for the delivery of weapons purchased by their agents outside Louisiana, while Kellogg's Metropolitans made every effort to intercept the arms shipments. On September 8 the police impounded "a furniture wagon" loaded with cases containing seventy-two rifles. Acting on an informant's tip, the Metropolitans boarded the steamship *City of Dallas* on September 11 and seized six cases of rifles. On September 12 Republican constables confiscated ten

2. New Orleans *Times* and New Orleans *Daily Picayune*, both dated September 4, 1874; Shreveport *Times* (emphasis in the original), September 5, 8, 1874.

cases of Belgian rifles with bayonets from a train that had just arrived in the Crescent City from Jackson, Mississippi. The New York *Times* reported that almost three hundred rifles had been seized by the police since the beginning of the month.[3]

Meanwhile, outside New Orleans, Republicans reported that the White League had stepped up its activities. For example, state Senator Marshall H. Twitchell, brother of one of the men slain near Coushatta, described a "reign of terror" in Red River Parish, claiming that it had turned into an armed camp of the White League. Sheriff B. F. O'Neal of Bossier Parish called conditions in his jurisdiction "horrible" and said that it was "impossible to execute a criminal proceeding against a white man." The New Orleans *Republican* reported that the White League in St. Martin Parish was "on a war footing" and that the Democrats were casting solid shot at a local foundry for two brass Napoleons. In view of the success of these actions, the White League had reason to believe that it could overthrow Kellogg before army troops occupied their posts throughout the state.[4]

On September 11 General Emory finally arrived at his headquarters in Holly Springs to find his staff preparing to transport the 3rd Infantry to Louisiana. But the staff had not arranged for trains to take the soldiers to New Orleans until September 14 or 15. The officers had neither attempted to assemble a special train nor commandeered the necessary locomotive and coaches. Furthermore, the unit selected to garrison Monroe had been needlessly detained because no medical officer was available to accompany it. Although the staff had been working for several days to effect the 3rd regiment's change of station, there was no sense of urgency at department headquarters. McDowell had not given him a deadline for relocating the troops, and Emory saw no reason to change or improve upon the existing arrangements. However, he did order the commanding officer at Fort Barrancas in Pensacola to send two batteries of artillery to Baton Rouge as soon as possible.[5]

3. New Orleans *Bulletin*, September 9, 1874; New Orleans *Republican*, September 11, 13, 1874; New York *Times*, September 12, 1874; Taylor, *Louisiana Reconstructed*, 291–92.

4. Marshall H. Twitchell and E. W. Dewees to George H. Williams, September 10, 1874, in *Senate Executive Documents*, 43rd Cong., 2nd Sess., No. 13, p. 12; B. F. O'Neal to Packard, September 10, 1874, in *House Executive Documents*, 44th Cong., 2nd Sess., No. 30, p. 395; New Orleans *Republican*, September 10, 1874.

5. SW, "Annual Report, 1874–1875," in *House Executive Documents*, 43rd Cong., 2nd Sess., No. 1, p. 51; AAG Edward R. Platt to Packard, September 10, 1874, Platt to CO, Fort Barrancas, September 11, 1874, both in Dept Gulf, vol. 140/DSL, RG 393, NA;

Emory's initial lack of urgency can be attributed to his ignorance of the situation in Louisiana. Captain Edward Platt of Emory's staff conferred with the general and gave him a stack of letters and telegrams pertaining to recent events in Louisiana. After reading them, Emory became aware that he faced the possibility of an insurrection on a scale unknown since the Civil War. In one of the letters, Captain Arthur Allyn, commanding the company at Colfax, described in detail the Coushatta massacre and the activities of the White League in central Louisiana. Emory later claimed, "At that time the name of the White League was not familiar [to] me," and apparently Platt had to apprise him of the facts concerning the organization. Thus informed, Emory wrote Marshal Stephen Packard, telling him that he feared the army's forces were "inadequate" to suppress the League, a comment that surely did not cheer Packard. Nevertheless, Emory ordered Platt to send instructions, in accordance with the attorney general's circular of September 3, to all detachment commanders of the 3rd Infantry reminding them to furnish assistance to U.S. marshals in Louisiana. Excluding his orders to the Barrancas garrison, the orders Emory had given since his arrival at headquarters were routine, and he had done nothing to hasten the departure of any of the units from Holly Springs.[6]

Emory finally became alarmed on Sunday, September 13, when a telegram arrived from Packard. The urgency—almost panic—of the message was unmistakable. According to the marshal, a violent encounter between the White League and the state militia was likely to occur in New Orleans within the next few hours unless the army intervened. The crisis had been precipitated over the arrival of a substantial arms shipment aboard the steamer *Mississippi*. State authorities meant to block delivery of the rifles to the White League, which was just as determined to receive the consignment. David B. Penn, McEnery's "lieutenant governor," and "Colonel" Fred Ogden, McEnery's "militia commander," issued a summons for citizens to assemble at the Clay statue, at the in-

---

Emory to McDowell, September 11, 1874, forwarded by McDowell to Sherman, September 11, 1874, in AGO File 3579 of 1874 (Microcopy M-666, reel 169), RG 94, NA.

6. Arthur Allyn to Platt, September 3, 1874, endorsed by Emory, September 12, 1874, in *Senate Executive Documents*, 43rd Cong., 2nd Sess., No. 17, pp. 16–17; Emory's remark about the White League in New Orleans *Times*, January 1, 1875; Emory to Packard, September 11, 1874, Platt to COs of St. Martinville, Baton Rouge, Jackson Barracks, Harrisonburg, Monroe, Shreveport, September 13, 1874, all in Dept Gulf, vol. 115/DSL, RG 393, NA.

tersection of Canal and St. Charles streets at 11:00 A.M. on Monday, September 14. Broadsides and posters announcing the assembly had been distributed throughout New Orleans. Packard begged Emory to send troops to New Orleans immediately.[7]

The crisis generated by the arrival of the *Mississippi* conveniently coincided with Democratic plans. The New Orleans *Times* later reported that Penn had met with White League officers on Friday, September 11, and outlined a plan to overthrow the Kellogg government on Monday, September 14. Penn called for all available White League units to gather on Monday, when they would attempt to entice Longstreet's state militia into a general engagement. Once victorious, the White League would place Penn in the state house. McEnery, who was purposely out of the city to avoid being arrested if the plan failed, would then return and assume the governorship. If there was such a plan, Packard obviously did not know about it. He would surely have told Emory about it in his telegram, for the information would have shown, even more clearly, the need for the army's help.[8]

"From ordinary sources this [Packard's] telegram would not have received much attention," Emory later wrote, but Packard's desperate tone was authoritative coming from a U.S. marshal, and it spurred Emory to action. He planned to hire a special train to take four companies of soldiers to New Orleans. He expected that the train would arrive between 11:00 A.M. and noon. As if not quite convinced of the impending clash, Emory warned Packard that it was very important "the emergency should not have been overstated." Packard immediately replied that the emergency was genuine and to hurry the troops on their way.[9]

Now convinced, Emory decided to order two additional detachments, the company of troops on duty at Jackson, Mississippi, and the caretaker squad at Jackson Barracks, to guard the New Orleans Custom House. He also considered sending Lieutenant Colonel John R. Brooke, second in command of the 3rd Infantry and a distinguished combat officer in the Civil War, with a special detachment on an express train, but he had to discard this idea, apparently because no trains were available. Instead, he

7. Packard to Emory, September 13, 1874, in Dept Gulf, vol. 115/DSL, RG 393, NA; Taylor, *Louisiana Reconstructed*, 292; SW, "Annual Report, 1874–1876," 55–56; Lonn, *Reconstruction in Louisiana*, 269.

8. New Orleans *Times*, September 23, 1874.

9. SW, "Annual Report, 1874–1875," 55–56; Emory to Packard, and reply, both dated September 13, 1874, in Dept Gulf, vol. 115/DSL, RG 393, NA.

placed Brooke in command of the main force of four companies, which finally left Holly Springs at 9:00 P.M. on Sunday. Emory gave no indication that he would take command himself at New Orleans.[10]

Emory notified McDowell of Brooke's departure and requested that the division commander send reinforcements to Louisiana from Alabama. McDowell, however, doubted that the emergency was genuine. He reminded Emory of General Sherman's advice "not to call for force from without unless in case of manifest necessity" and temporarily withheld the Alabama troops.[11]

Early on the morning of September 14 dozens of armed men made their way through the streets of New Orleans, moving to designated locations according to Penn's and Ogden's plans. White League officers assembled at 58 Camp Street, the headquarters of the Democratic forces. Several businessmen and shopkeepers opened their stores temporarily, but by noon all had bolted their doors. Responding to Penn's summons, more than five thousand men had gathered at the Clay statue before noon.[12]

At the meeting several speakers criticized the Kellogg government and demanded the governor's "abdication." The assembled men promptly adopted a resolution to that effect, and at one o'clock a delegation went to the state house to demand Kellogg's resignation. Kellogg refused to meet with the "delegates." One of his aides told them that the governor declined to consider their proposal while armed mobs roamed the streets of the city. The delegates returned to the Clay statue and reported Kellogg's response, which was met by a derisive roar from the crowd. The leaders then instructed the men to return to their homes, collect their weapons, and return at 2:30 P.M. By 3:00 hundreds of armed men had returned to the streets. In the interim White League units had been busy building street barricades composed of street cars, boxes, mattresses, iron gates, and other handy objects. There was no longer any pretense of simply ob-

10. Platt to CO, Jackson Barracks, Emory to CO, Jackson, Mississippi, Platt to Packard, all dated September 13, 1874, in Dept Gulf, vol. 140/DSL, RG 393, NA; Platt to Col. DeLancey Floyd-Jones, and Platt to John R. Brooke, both dated September 13, 1874, in Dept Gulf, vol. 115/DSL, RG 393, NA.

11. Emory to AAG, MilDivSouth, September 13, 1874, in Dept Gulf, vol. 140/DSL, McKeever to Emory, September 13, 1874, in MilDivSouth, vol. 2/DSL, both in RG 393, NA; McDowell to Sherman, September 13, 1874, in AGO File 3579 of 1874 (Microcopy M-666, reel 169), RG 94, NA.

12. New Orleans Daily Picayune, September 15, 1874; Taylor, Louisiana Reconstructed, 292–93.

taining the arms aboard the steamer *Mississippi*; the objective now was to overthrow the Kellogg government.[13]

Meanwhile, the Republicans were nervously wondering how to protect themselves. The train bearing the company of soldiers from Jackson arrived, and Packard directed them to the Custom House, where Governor Kellogg had gone for self-protection. The other troop train from Holly Springs had been expected around noon, but it had been unaccountably detained. (Later it was reported that the railroad company, cooperating with the Democrats, had delayed the train en route to New Orleans.) Unable to explain the train's tardiness, Emory admitted that "conflict seems inevitable now."[14]

The White League moved to its task with the confident step of campaign veterans. Methodically they "occupied the city hall and . . . cut the wires of the fire alarm and police telegraph" just after Kellogg sent out a final desperate plea for troops "to put down the domestic violence and insurrection now prevailing." The soldiers in the Custom House, outnumbered, outgunned, and lacking the direction of a senior officer, could only stand and protect federal property.[15]

Kellogg's state forces were also outnumbered. James Longstreet and Algernon Badger led a total of about 3,500 men, most of them blacks, including more than five hundred Metropolitans, Badger's former policemen. Supporting the militia were two small cannon and a Gatling gun. Opposing the state forces were more than five thousand White Leaguers and associated hangers-on, commanded by Fred Ogden. Most of the Leaguers were from the New Orleans area, but some of them were from outlying parishes.[16]

The rival forces clashed around four o'clock on the afternoon of September 14 in an encounter that became known as the "Battle of Liberty Place." For a while the Metropolitans matched the White League shot for shot, but the numbers, experience, and enthusiasm of the Leaguers proved overpowering. Badger fell, seriously wounded, and his men re-

13. Singletary, *Negro Militia*, 75–77; New Orleans *Daily Picayune*, September 22, 1874.
14. Packard to Williams, September 14, 1874, in *Senate Executive Documents*, 43rd Cong., 2nd Sess., No. 13, pp. 13–14. On the delay of the train, see Stuart O. Landry, *The Battle of Liberty Place* (New Orleans, 1955), 162. Emory to AAG, MilDivSouth, September 14, 1874, in Dept Gulf, vol. 140/DSL, RG 393, NA.
15. Packard to Williams, and Kellogg to Grant, both dated September 14, 1874, in *Senate Executive Documents*, 43rd Cong., 2nd Sess., No. 13, p. 13.
16. Taylor, *Louisiana Reconstructed*, 293.

treated. Longstreet reportedly blanched when he heard the familiar rebel yell issuing from the throats of his opponents, who only a few years before had worn Confederate gray. Longstreet's militia broke ranks after exchanging volleys with the White League, leaving the streets, littered with their dead and wounded, in the hands of the Democratic forces. In less than sixty minutes the Kellogg government had fallen. Total casualties on both sides amounted to more than one hundred wounded and twenty-five killed. The insurgents made no attempt to attack the Custom House. In fact, they scrupulously avoided coming into contact with the army or any federal authorities. However, the victorious Leaguers systematically plundered the state arsenals and picked up dozens of rifles discarded by the state militia.[17]

"Adjutant General" John Ellis of the White League posted a "General Order" of the McEnery-Penn government congratulating "the troops in the field" for their accomplishments. "Lieutenant Governor" Penn issued a call for the "militia of the State"—meaning the White Leagues—"*to arm and assemble under their respective officers for the purpose of driving the usurpers from power.*" Seeking to justify the League's action to the national government, Penn wrote to President Grant to explain that Louisianians had acted "to maintain the legal authority of the persons elected by them to the government of the State against . . . usurpers." He added that the citizens maintained "their unswerving loyalty and respect for the United States Government and its officers."[18]

About the time that Penn issued his proclamation, Lieutenant Colonel John Brooke and four companies of the 3rd Infantry arrived in New Orleans. Some spectators cheered and applauded the troops as they marched through the city. It was impossible to determine whether the cheers came from Republicans who were glad to see the soldiers or from Democrats who were pleased at the soldiers' tardiness. Brooke found a telegram containing orders from Emory awaiting him. The secretary of war and Emory ordered Brooke "to protect at its seat the Government . . . of the State of Louisiana as represented by Governor Kellogg and protect it

17. Singletary, *Negro Militia*, 78; Taylor, *Louisiana Reconstructed*, 294; Lonn, *Reconstruction in Louisiana*, 271n; Landry, *Liberty Place*, 99.
18. Ellis, order, and Penn, Proclamation (emphasis in the original), both dated September 14, 1874, in *House Reports*, 43rd Cong., 2nd Sess., No. 261, Pt. 2, p. 281; Penn to Grant, September 14, 1874, in *Senate Executive Documents*, 67th Cong., 2nd Sess., No. 263, p. 131.

from being overthrown . . . by violence." Obviously, Brooke had arrived too late to obey these orders, which would have taken him into
battle against the White League.[19]

Additional orders from Emory soon arrived, advising Brooke to consolidate his forces with those already in the city, to retain all troops passing through the city, and to learn the intentions of the insurgent forces. If
he concluded that the insurgents intended to engage the army, Brooke
was to bring in the Gatling guns from Jackson Barracks and defend all
federal property, but was not to fire unless fired upon. Brooke hastened
to carry out these orders, hoping that the civilians were prudent enough
not to challenge the U.S. Army. It is unclear whether Brooke met personally with any of the Democratic leaders, but the colonel described the
situation as "very critical" and estimated that the White League intended
"to fight even U.S. troops if necessary to gain their ends." The colonel
requested that Emory send massive reinforcements at once.[20]

Emory relayed Brooke's ominous message to General McDowell, end-
ing with a warning that the forces in New Orleans were "utterly inadequate to quell a city in arms." Shocked by the news of the battle, Emory
had hoped "that the display of United States forces" would be enough to
reestablish order, but now he believed that it was impossible to sustain
Kellogg "without a bloody conflict except by ordering a larger force than
I have at my command in the City of New Orleans." Despite his use of
the phrase "at my command," Emory gave no indication that he intended
to assume personal command in New Orleans.[21]

In the meantime, the Conservatives acted quickly to consolidate their
position. On September 15 Longstreet abandoned the state house, which
was immediately occupied by the White League. By the end of the day
the Conservative forces had occupied all of the city's police stations and
state arsenals, confiscating more than 1,600 rifles, 46,000 rounds of am-
munition, and four cannon. They controlled all state facilities. Accordingly, Penn sent word to McEnery, asking him to come to New Orleans
and assume the governorship.[22]

The national authorities, when they realized what had happened in

19. Packard to Williams, September 14, 1874, in *Senate Executive Documents*, 43rd
Cong., 2nd Sess., No. 13, p. 14; Platt to Brooke, September 1, 1874, in Dept Gulf, vol.
140/DSL, RG 393, NA; New Orleans *Daily Picayune*, September 15, 1874.

20. Platt to Brooke, Emory to Brooke, Emory to AAG, MilDivSouth, all dated September 14, 1874, in Dept Gulf, vol. 140/DSL, RG 393, NA.

21. Emory to AAG, MilDivSouth, September 14, 1874, *ibid.*

22. Fred Ogden to Penn, and reply, both dated September 15, 1874, in *House Reports*,

New Orleans, took steps to help Kellogg, who was still besieged in the Custom House. Responding to the governor's official request for assistance, President Grant issued a special proclamation on September 15 ordering all "turbulent and disorderly persons [who] have combined together with force and arms to overthrow the State government of Louisiana . . . to disperse and retire peaceably to their respective abodes within five days from this date," or face the military power of the United States. General Sherman ordered McDowell to move his troops as his judgment dictated, "so as to best sustain the proclamation." [23]

For some reason Emory failed to learn of Kellogg's official request for the federal government's help, and he was unaware that the Grant administration was planning to support Kellogg. In fact, during the early hours of September 15 Emory seemed reluctant to help Kellogg at all. Perhaps this reluctance signified his complete disgust with Reconstruction, or perhaps Emory realized that no matter how favorably he concluded the dreadful situation in Louisiana, he could be held responsible for the tardy arrival of the troops to New Orleans. Indeed, at this point (the morning of September 15), he exhibited no desire to take command of the soldiers in New Orleans. On the contrary, he remained closeted in Holly Springs, making plans to send more soldiers to Louisiana and preparing for the arrival of reinforcements from outside his department, although these tasks could have been handled capably by one of his subordinates.

Now that Kellogg had been turned out of office, Emory suspected that the war secretary's orders of the previous day—protecting the Kellogg government—were invalid. Consequently, Emory asked McDowell and Adjutant General Townsend if the army should "aid in suppressing [the] insurrection or in keeping Governor Kellogg in his seat." Emory emphasized that he had heard "no call on the President for troops by the Governor." [24]

Brooke informed Emory that Kellogg had petitioned for troop support, but Emory reminded the colonel that such a request was not "an

---

43rd Cong., 2nd Sess., No. 261, Pt. 2, pp. 821–22; Emory to AAG, MilDivSouth, in Dept Gulf, vol. 140/DSL, RG 393, NA; Kellogg, testimony before a congressional committee, in *House Reports*, 43rd Cong., 2nd Sess., No. 100, Pt. 2, p. 199.

23. Kellogg to Grant, September 15, 1874, in William Pitt Kellogg Papers, Department of Archives and Manuscripts, Louisiana State University Library, Baton Rouge; Grant, Proclamation, September 15, 1874, in Richardson (comp.), *Messages and Papers*, VII, 276–77; Sherman's aide-de-camp Joseph C. Audenried to McDowell, September 15, 1874, in Letters Sent, HQ/USA (Microcopy M-857, reel 8), RG 108, NA.

24. Emory to AGO, and Emory to AAG, MilDivSouth, both dated September 15, 1874, in Dept Gulf, vol. 140/DSL, RG 393, NA.

application for troops within the meaning of the Constitution." Kellogg had to make his request directly to the president before it was valid. Technically, Emory was correct, but it was hardly a time to be technical. With obvious reluctance the general relayed Kellogg's request to McDowell.[25]

General McDowell and Adjutant General Townsend were determined to end the insurrection, and finally, on the afternoon of September 15, they directed Emory to take charge of the troops in New Orleans. Furthermore, Townsend ordered Emory to "use all the means at your command to give protection [to Kellogg] until you receive final instructions." Responding to these directions, Emory reminded Townsend that the state forces had been "utterly routed" and that the "insurgents" held the "state Capitol and state arsenal and all of the city except public buildings occupied by United States force[s]." Emory doubted his "ability to put the thing down," especially if the White League planned to defy the army. He added, "If they do resist, my force is so dispro-portionate that the fight must go against us." He ended with a forlorn promise to "do the best we can."[26]

Until Emory arrived, the responsibility for preventing open warfare in Louisiana rested with Colonel Brooke. Bypassing Emory, General Townsend directed Brooke to "preserve the peace and order to the best of your ability." However, he added a proviso—Broke must submit all "orders for the suppression of violence . . . to the Secretary of War for approval." These orders restricted Brooke's initiative in the event of an emergency. Considering the speed with which the White League had defeated the state militia, orders from Washington might arrive too late to benefit Brooke. The colonel was caught in the classic dilemma of the army officer in Reconstruction: do not act unless you must and then only on directions from higher authority.[27]

In this case, however, the massive reinforcements that Brooke had requested earlier were on their way to Louisiana. McDowell ordered six infantry companies to New Orleans from posts in Alabama, Tennessee, Georgia, and South Carolina. It would take several days for these units to

25. Emory to Brooke, and Emory to AAG, MilDivSouth, both dated September 15, 1874, *ibid.*

26. Townsend to Emory, September 15, 1874, in AGO File 3579 of 1874 (Microcopy M-666, reel 169), RG 94, NA; Emory to AGO, September 15, 1874, *ibid.* (reel 172); McKeever to Emory, September 15, 1874, in MilDivSouth, vol. 2/DSL, RG 393, NA.

27. Townsend to Brooke, September 15, 1874, in AGO File 3579 of 1874 (Microcopy M-666, reel 169), RG 94, NA.

arrive, but once on the scene there would be more soldiers in New Orleans than at any other location in the United States. The New Orleans *Republican* gratefully reported the news about these reinforcements.[28]

Disregarding the meaning of these reinforcements and the president's proclamation, an enthusiastic crowd of more than 10,000 persons cheered the "inauguration" of D. B. Penn on September 16. Penn assumed the duties of "acting governor" in McEnery's absence. He appointed a new police chief and drew funds from the state treasury. The Shreveport *Times* hoped that, with Penn now in office, Grant would not attempt to reinstate Kellogg. In contrast, the New Orleans *Republican* promised, "As soon as the boys in blue shall have arrived bloody work may be expected, unless the Pennites throw down their arms. The result is awaited with confidence and without fear."[29]

The army's actions justified the *Republican's* confidence. McDowell personally relayed the substance of Grant's proclamation to Emory and informed him to expect reinforcements soon. Townsend ordered Emory to prevent Penn from withdrawing any more money from the Louisiana treasury. Moreover, Townsend emphatically stressed, "Under no circumstances can the insurgent gov't of Louisiana be recognized. Within [the] five days given by [Grant's] proclamation for the dispersal of the insurgents, such action will be taken as the emergency may require."[30]

Apparently inspired by Townsend and McDowell's decisiveness, Emory prepared to take charge in Louisiana. He ordered a company of infantry, initially bound for Shreveport but delayed in Jackson, Mississippi, to head for New Orleans. Amending a previous order, he instructed the commanding officer at Fort Barrancas to send all available soldiers to the Crescent City as soon as transportation was available. Before leaving for New Orleans himself, Emory wired ahead to Brooke and Colonel Floyd-Jones, directing them to meet him at the St. Charles Hotel that night. Finally, Emory boarded the evening train in Holly Springs.[31]

At a stop along the way, probably in Vicksburg, John McEnery and a

28. McDowell to AGO, September 15, 1874, *ibid.*; New Orleans *Republican*, September 17, 1874.

29. Shreveport *Times*, and New Orleans *Republican*, both dated September 17, 1874; Taylor, *Louisiana Reconstruction*, 295.

30. Townsend to Emory, September 16, 1874 (two communications), in AGO File 3579 of 1874 (Microcopy M-666, reel 169), RG 94, NA.

31. Emory's aide-de-camp Luke O'Reilly to Major Samuel A. Wainwright, O'Reilly to Major J. B. Brannan, O'Reilly to Brooke, all dated September 16, 1874, in Dept Gulf, vol. 140/DSL, RG 393, NA.

small retinue coincidentally boarded the same coach in which Emory rode. It is not known if the two men spoke to one another. The train arrived at the New Orleans depot at 10:00 P.M. on September 16. According to the reporter for the New Orleans *Republican*, McEnery stepped "majestically out of the car," greeted by a blaring brass band and the huzzahs and whoops of friends and supporters. Only a few feet away on the same platform, "there stepped from the other end of the same car a quiet elderly gentleman." General William H. Emory had at last arrived to take command.[32]

Brooke and Floyd-Jones briefed their commander, who then arranged a conference with McEnery and Penn. Emory read Grant's proclamation to the two politicians, who acknowledged their familiarity with the document. Then the general bluntly told them to abide by the president's directions, end the insurgency, and order the dispersal of their forces. In reply, the Democrats denied that there had been an "insurrection," and claimed that they were the legal state executives. However, McEnery and Penn both said that they had neither "the power nor the inclination to resist" the federal army. They made no immediate concessions to Emory's demands, but the general gave them till morning to think over the situation.[33]

They responded just as Emory wanted. On September 17 McEnery and Penn issued a joint proclamation announcing that General Emory "was not permitted to recognize our government in any way, and that immediate submission and a surrender of the property of the State to the United States would be the only means of avoiding the employment of the military and naval force of the United States to compel obedience." Protesting that federal forces were improperly intervening in state affairs, the Democrats ordered their "state troops" to turn in all "captured arms" and return to their homes. However, the Democrats plainly stated that they would surrender the occupied state buildings only to the army and not to Kellogg's representatives. Accordingly, Emory designated Colonel Brooke acting military governor of New Orleans and officer in charge of the detachment that would receive the surrender of the state house from the White League.[34]

32. New Orleans *Republican*, September 18, 1874.

33. McEnery to Emory, September 17, 1874, in *House Reports*, 43rd Cong., 2nd Sess., No. 261, Pt. 2, p. 825.

34. McEnery and Penn, Proclamation, "GO No. 4" [McEnery forces], both dated September 17, 1874, *ibid.*, 824, 827; New Orleans *Daily Picayune*, September 18, 1874; Special Circular, Dept Gulf, September 17, 1874, in GO, Dept Gulf, RG 393, NA.

In preparation for the unusual ceremony, a company of soldiers "marched down Canal Street to the lively music of their fifes and drums," turned into the French Quarter and stopped near the St. Louis Hotel, which had been serving as the state capitol since June. Thousands of persons quietly watched the soldiers form ranks outside the building. At about four o'clock McEnery officially relinquished control of the state house. John Ellis, adjutant general of the White League, described the "very sad scene": "McEnery & his officers clustered about him all in civilian garb; Gen. Brooke and staff [were] brilliantly uniformed; then came the formal demand [for surrender] in the name of the U.S. Govt: McEnery with husky broken voice all trembling with emotion read his reply. . . . The soldier [Brooke] was then seated in the Governor's chair and we all quietly withdrew and proceeded up Royal Street to Canal. Men stood by with stern faces & Women wept—the decline of our brief day of liberty." Ellis was afraid that he, McEnery, Penn, and Ogden would be arrested by the army or, worse, by Kellogg's police. Emory, however, opposed such arrests. He advised Grant that it would be best to avoid civil prosecution of these leaders mainly because they had peaceably and promptly yielded to Grant's proclamation.[35]

Certainly it was unusual—if not unique—in American history for an army officer to reseat a state governor who had been removed from office by an armed *coup*. Taking Townsend's advice, on September 18 Emory sent an official dispatch to Kellogg informing him of McEnery's surrender and offering "the necessary military support to re-establish the State Government." Kellogg was unenthusiastic about resuming office immediately and seemed quite content to let the army maintain control. Nevertheless, he agreed to take office again the next day.[36]

Kellogg's lack of enthusiasm was understandable. He had less power or authority outside of New Orleans than he had before September 14, which had been little enough. Emory acknowledged that "Nearly every parish in the State, following the example of New Orleans, is more or less in a State of insurrection." A riot had occurred in the town of Bayou Sara, near Baton Rouge, for example, and Emory had immediately or-

35. John Ellis to Tom Ellis, September 21, 1874, in Ellis Papers; New York *Times*, September 18, 1874; McEnery to Brooke [September 17, 1874], in *Senate Executive Documents*, 67th Cong., 2nd Sess., No. 263, p. 133, Emory to Grant, September 17, 1874, in Dept Gulf, vol. 115/DSL, RG 393, NA.

36. Emory to AGO, September 18, 1874, in Dept Gulf, vol. 140/DSL, Emory to Kellogg, September 18, 1874, in Dept Gulf, vol. 115/DSL, Kellogg to Emory, September 18, 1874, in Dept Gulf, Letters Recd, all in RG 393, NA.

dered a detachment of troops from the nearby barracks to put down the disturbance and protect Kellogg's officials. Elsewhere, Captain Arthur Allyn at Alexandria reported that "the country was on fire," and it appeared that his "little force" (about fifty men) was a "tempting morsel" for the White League. The Leaguers wisely refrained from attacking the soldiers, but they repeatedly threatened Kellogg's officials.[37]

The army's assistance gratified Governor Kellogg, who resumed the duties of his office on September 19, "relieving Brooke of responsibilities which he was glad to be rid of," according to the New Orleans *Republican*. To his relief Kellogg learned that in several parishes where Republicans "had been ousted the old Incumbents [were] going back peaceably." He wrote Attorney General Williams that, according to recent reports, the country was "quieter than expected" and that New Orleans had settled down remarkably well. However, Kellogg added a note of caution: "No reports yet received from Red River country." General Emory was prepared to send reinforcements to the garrisons in the Red River parishes as soon as he consolidated his forces in New Orleans and determined how many soldiers he wanted to station outside the city.[38]

Additional military detachments began to arrive in Louisiana from several states. Advance units of the 2nd Infantry from Alabama arrived at Jackson Barracks on September 18. The remainder of the 3rd Infantry from Mississippi joined Brooke's four companies in New Orleans. On September 20 four companies of the 22nd Infantry came in from Michigan and were posted at the state house. Three batteries of the 1st Artillery from Fort Barrancas were quartered in the city by September 21. Three other companies of the 22nd regiment detrained at the city depot on September 22 and moved into makeshift quarters in a rented warehouse.[39]

Louisiana newspapers devoted considerable space to the arrival of the massive reinforcements, while simultaneously interjecting stinging criticisms of Grant and Kellogg. For example, the Shreveport *Times* re-

37. Emory to AAG, MilDivSouth, September 18, 20, 1874, both in Dept Gulf, vol. 140/DSL, RG 393, NA; Arthur Allyn, testimony before a congressional committee, in *House Reports*, 43rd Cong., 2nd Sess., No. 261, Pt. 3, p. 156; Allyn to Platt, October 2, 1874, in *House Reports*, 43rd Cong., 2nd Sess., No. 101, Pt. 2, p. 63; Taylor, *Louisiana Reconstructed*, 295.

38. Kellogg to Williams, September 22, 1874, in Justice Dept Letters (Microcopy M-940, reel 2), RG 60, NA; New Orleans *Republican*, September 20, 1874.

39. Emory to AAG, MilDivSouth, September 19, 1874, Emory to AGO, September 20, 1874, both in Dept Gulf, vol. 140/DSL, Dept Gulf Journal of Events, pp. 30–31, RG 393, NA; Post Returns, Jackson Barracks, September 1874, in Records of the AGO (Microcopy M-617, reel 524), RG 94, NA.

marked that Grant "could have as well set a toad in the gubernatorial chair, surrounded it with soldiers and proclaimed it Governor; it would have received the same obedience that Mr. Kellogg will receive." The New Orleans *Times* listed the men who had served as governor during 1874—Kellogg, Penn, McEnery, and Brooke—and concluded that "These [were] all the Acting Governors we have had this year—but it's not our fault that we haven't had more. Times are hard, and we can't afford as much style as Costa Rica." The New Orleans *Bulletin* warned that "it will take a regiment of Federal soldiers in each parish to sustain . . . the officials and appointees of the Kellogg usurpation. . . . Is the Government prepared to quarter that number of soldiers in Louisiana to maintain in power a fraudulent and infamous government?"[40]

Newspaper commentary aside, in Emory's opinion New Orleans was secure, guarded by nineteen companies of infantry and artillery, but the reports of continuing White League activity in north Louisiana worried him. He informed McDowell that the "Red River Parishes west of Alexandria are in such a condition that I do not think order can be maintained without the use of Cavalry." Therefore, Emory requested that McDowell arrange for a squadron of cavalry to be sent from Texas, one of the states and territories in the Military Division of the Missouri, commanded by Philip H. Sheridan. Initially, Secretary of War Belknap had asked Sheridan to consider annexing Louisiana into his division, which extended from Canada to the Rio Grande and from the Mississippi River to the Rocky Mountains, or simply to take personal command of the troublesome state. Sheridan replied that he had "no desire to ever have any control over Louisiana," but that he was always "ready to do anything within [his] power to help . . . the President in his embarrassing duties, . . . [no matter] how unpleasant it may be."[41]

Subsequently General Townsend asked Sheridan if he could spare an entire cavalry regiment for service in Louisiana. Sheridan responded that six troops of the 7th Cavalry and a full regiment of infantry were available to assist Emory. After consulting with the president, Belknap directed Sheridan to send only the cavalry, without its flamboyant field

40. Shreveport *Times*, September 22, 1874; New Orleans *Times*, September 20, 1874; New Orleans *Bulletin*, September 22, 1874. See also similar comments in Thibodeaux *Sentinel*, Natchitoches *People's Vindicator*, and Alexandria *Caucasian*, all dated September 26, 1874, New Orleans *Daily Picayune*, September 19, 1874, Monroe *Ouachita Telegraph*, September 25, 1874, Alexandria *Democrat*, September 30, 1874.

41. McDowell to Col. Whipple, September 25, 1874, in Justice Dept Letters (Microcopy M-940, reel 6), RG 60, NA; Sheridan to Belknap, September 22, 1874, in Sheridan Papers.

commander, Lieutenant Colonel George A. Custer, whose Democratic proclivities were well known. On September 28, following his inspection of troops in and around New Orleans, Emory returned to his headquarters to find Townsend's telegram informing him that the 7th Cavalry was on its way to Louisiana.[42]

By the end of September Emory was in command of twenty-six companies belonging to six regiments. Nineteen companies (846 men) were in New Orleans or at nearby barracks. The seven other companies (less than fifty men each) were stationed in Baton Rouge, Colfax, St. Martinville, Pineville, Monroe, Shreveport, and Coushatta. Emory had a total of 1,182 men in Louisiana and an additional 172 soldiers in Arkansas and Mississippi, about one-third of all the troops stationed in the South, excluding Texas. He also had the aid of seven U.S. Navy ships, carrying fifty-one guns, docked along the New Orleans waterfront or anchored in the Mississippi River.[43]

Emory now had to look ahead to the midterm elections scheduled for November 2. Republican politicians would, undoubtedly, call for the army to protect voters, guard polling places, and uphold the Kellogg government. The specific limits of the army's authority were really less clear in 1874 than they had been under the Military Reconstruction Acts seven years before—and even then the range of military authority had been difficult to define. At least Sheridan and his lieutenants had operated under the legal umbrella of laws passed by Congress, and for the most part, the officers who enforced those laws expected (and received) the support of the War Department and Congress. Emory asked McDowell to give him exact military duties along with guidelines on military power that could be used effectively and with assurance during the political campaign. Emory wanted these guidelines so that the soldiers "performing such duties [would be] protected by law in the execution of them." Without saying so specifically, he probably was hoping for the same sort of protection that Sheridan's men had enjoyed under the Military Reconstruction Acts. Emory believed that this protection was essential if the

42. Townsend to Sheridan, September 25 and 27, 1874, Townsend to Belknap, September 26, 1874, in Justice Dept Letters (Microcopy M-940, reel 6), RG 60, NA; Sheridan to Townsend, Whipple to Sheridan, Townsend to Emory, all dated September 28, 1874, in AGO File 3579 of 1874 (Microcopy M-666, reel 169), Belknap to Townsend, September 28, 1874, in AGO File 3579 of 1874 (Microcopy M-666, reel 170), both in RG 94, NA.

43. SW, "Annual Report, 1874–1875," 84–85; New Orleans Republican, September 29, 1874; Sefton, Army and Reconstruction, 262.

army was to be used to ensure the integrity of Kellogg's government. In reply, McDowell told Emory "to aid the U.S. civil officers" without acting on his own. Then McDowell perceptively asked Sherman, "If more than this is lawful and is desired, I beg to be informed what it is." By 1874 nothing more was lawful or desired by most Americans.[44]

The army had only limited choices, and its influence in southern Reconstruction had declined. Only a politically dedicated or a foolhardy commander would do more than higher authorities specifically allowed. Under these circumstances, Emory did not see any "prospect of these [southern] governments improving or becoming more stable so long as they are based upon universal suffrage or until the suffragists become better educated."[45] Emory's reference was obviously to black voters, and his opinion was probably shared by most of the army officers in the southern states. The army's top command was split on the matter of how (or even whether) to continue enforcing a policy of equal rights for blacks. For several years General Sherman had wanted the army to divest itself of its police duties in the South. General Sheridan, however, still believed that old rebels had no place in government. Furthermore, Sheridan contended that southern Republicans, if they were to survive in office, had to rely on the votes of unintimidated Negroes, who depended upon the army to protect them.

By 1874 the national government did not have enough soldiers in the South to protect all Republicans, black or white, or even to ensure the existence of their state governments. By the end of 1874 the Democrats had carefully used a skillful combination of court suits (as in the case of the Colfax rioters), intimidation, voter registration, measured applications of violence, and ballot box stuffing to regain control of Tennessee, Virginia, North Carolina, Georgia, Alabama, Arkansas, and Texas. Only Mississippi, South Carolina, Florida, and Louisiana had Republican governments at the end of the year.

General Emory faced the prospect that the Democrats would continue to use all of these tactics to regain control of Louisiana and Mississippi as well. John McEnery had not "resigned," and the White Leagues had not

44. Emory to AGO, September 30, 1874, in *Senate Executive Documents*, 43rd Cong., 2nd Sess., No. 17, p. 60; Emory, "Report on the Condition of Affairs in Louisiana" (complete version in Dept Gulf, vol. 115/DSL, RG 393, NA, partial version in SW, "Annual Report, 1874–1875," 56); McDowell to Sherman, September 28, 1874, in AGO File 3579 of 1874 (Microcopy M-666, reel 170), RG 94, NA.
45. Emory, "Report on the Condition of Affairs in Louisiana."

disbanded. In fact, they remained watchful and hopeful, prepared to rise to the call again if the opportunity presented itself. The dispirited Republicans looked ahead to the fall elections with trepidation, while the Democrats viewed their own prospects with anticipation. Emory and the army regarded both factions with apprehension.

CHAPTER IX

Beneath a Soldier's Vocation

If General Emory reached the midterm election of November 2 without renewed outbreaks of violence in his department, he would count himself a lucky man. The Democrats were full of confidence, and according to Emory, they expected "to carry enough of the legislature to be masters of the situation. Should they do so, order may rule; but if they are defeated, conflict and violence will be the inevitable consequences, unless suppressed by the presence of a strong military force." Clearly Emory's respect for the Louisiana Republican party had reached such a low point that he did not seem to care if any of their candidates won. On the contrary, he indicated that it might be best for all concerned if the Democrats won most of the offices.[1]

Emory had no desire to plunge the army deeper into Louisiana's political morass, but regardless of his personal feelings, he planned to do everything in his power to ensure that the election was peaceful. The only way to guarantee a quiet election was for the army to station a detachment near every polling place. This was impossible, but Governor Kellogg wanted soldiers distributed throughout the state. The Grant administration—especially Attorney General Williams—supported Kellogg's wishes, and during October the Washington authorities encouraged Emory to comply with most of Kellogg's requests for soldiers.

Having received no orders to the contrary, Emory took steps to implement the old orders McDowell had given him on September 8 concerning the distribution of soldiers in Louisiana. To comply with these old orders, which had originally been drafted by Attorney General Williams, Emory had to reduce the number of soldiers serving in and around the Crescent City, but he considered New Orleans pacified, and he expected that the reductions would be offset by additional reinforcements. Conse-

1. Emory to AGO, October 1, 1874, in *Senate Executive Documents*, 43rd Cong., 2nd Sess., No. 17, p. 61.

quently, Emory sent out three companies of the 3rd Infantry to garrison Alexandria, Coushatta, St. Martinville, and Breaux Bridge. He thereby protected six of the nine towns in the Department of the Gulf that Williams and McDowell had earmarked for occupation.[2]

Based on his understanding of orders issued by the War Department in September, Emory expected at least six troops of the 7th Cavalry to arrive in New Orleans soon, and he planned to use some of these soldiers to garrison two of the remaining towns on Williams' list. He was disappointed to learn that McDowell had diverted two cavalry troops to posts in Alabama. When the other four troops arrived in Louisiana, Emory sent two of them to Shreveport and held the other two in New Orleans.[3]

When President Grant learned that Emory had sent some companies out of New Orleans, he directed Adjutant General Townsend to learn the reasons for the transfers. Emory explained that he was trying to abide by orders he had been given earlier and concluded that "the peace and quiet of the state demanded the action." But Grant had become concerned about the troop strength in the Division of the South, and reflecting the president's concern, Secretary of War Belknap ordered General Sheridan to send a regiment of infantry to McDowell. Sheridan picked the 13th Infantry, under the command of Lieutenant Colonel Henry A. Morrow, and McDowell ordered the regiment to report to Emory in New Orleans.[4]

Although more infantry was on its way to Louisiana, the Republicans there wanted cavalry reinforcements. Marshal Packard and U.S. Attorney James Beckwith requested that Emory station a cavalry troop at Colfax to help the U.S. deputy marshal to serve his warrants. Emory replied that he had tried to garrison the state according to the directions of Williams and McDowell, and that if McDowell had not reduced the number of cavalry units sent to Louisiana, a troop would have been available for duty at Colfax. Undeterred by Emory's refusal, Packard and Beckwith petitioned Attorney General Williams to use his influence on their behalf, and he conferred with Secretary of War Belknap. Eventually,

---

2. Dept Gulf, Journal of Events, p. 33, AAG E. R. Platt to CO, St. Martinville, October 7, 1874, both in Dept Gulf, vol. 115/DSL, all in RG 393, NA; McDowell to Sherman, September 8, 1874, in AGO File 3579 of 1874 (Microcopy M-666, reel 169), RG 94, NA.

3. Emory to AAG, MilDivSouth, October 5, 1874, Emory to AGO, October 6, 1874, both in Dept Gulf, vol. 140/DSL, Dept Gulf, Journal of Events, p. 33, RG 393, NA.

4. Townsend to McDowell, Emory to AAG, MilDivSouth, Belknap to Sherman, Sheridan to Belknap, all dated October 7, 1874, in AGO File 3579 of 1874 (Microcopy M-666, reel 170), RG 94, NA; New Orleans *Republican*, October 9, 1874.

the War Department ordered Emory to assign some cavalry for duty at
Colfax. Troop K, 7th Cavalry, joined two other companies of the 7th
regiment operating as a squadron along the Red River.[5]

To command this cavalry contingent and all of the other soldiers in
north Louisiana, Emory chose Major Lewis Merrill of the 7th Cavalry.
His command was designated "the District of the Upper Red River," and
he established his headquarters at Shreveport. Merrill was graduated
from West Point in 1855, and he had a competent record in the Civil War.
Unlike Colonel Floyd-Jones and most of the officers in the 3rd Infantry,
Merrill was an experienced Reconstruction commander, having served in
South Carolina in 1871 when President Grant had declared martial law in
several counties in that state. Merrill, who was a staunch Republican, had
strictly interpreted the Enforcement Acts and supervised the arrest of
several members of the Ku Klux Klan. Consequently, South Carolina's
Democratic newspapers had commonly referred to the major as "Dog
Merrill." Although the army's usefulness as a police force apparently was
declining in the South, Merrill still believed that the army should play an
important supervisory role in state politics, aiding Republicans whenever
possible by protecting black voters, arresting troublesome Democrats,
and reseating ousted Republican officeholders.[6]

Meanwhile, even before Merrill arrived in the Red River District,
General Emory grudgingly had ordered the post commanders at Shreveport and Coushatta to reinstate elected Republican officials who had been
removed by the White League in Caddo and Red River parishes. Furthermore, Governor Kellogg wanted soldiers to reseat judges, clerks of
court, court recorders, and sheriffs in Avoyelles and Rapides parishes.
Rather than acceding wholeheartedly to Kellogg's request, Emory informed General Townsend that he feared Kellogg's appeal would be "followed by many requisitions of the same kind . . . of very doubtful pro-
priety." Townsend's reply was apparently just what Emory wanted to
hear. "Appropriations are so small," Townsend wrote, that "movements
of troops must necessarily be curtailed." Emory promptly utilized

5. Packard and Beckwith to Emory, October 8, 1874, Emory to Packard, October 9,
1874, Packard and Beckwith to Williams, October 10, 1874, Williams to Belknap, October
10, 1874, Townsend to McDowell, October 12, 1874, all in AGO File 3579 of 1874 (Microcopy M-666, reel 170), RG 94, NA; Dept Gulf, Journal of Events, p. 33, in RG 393, NA.

6. Emory to AGO, October 8, 1874, in AGO File 3579 of 1874 (Microcopy M-666, reel
173), RG 94, NA; Platt to Lewis Merrill, October 15, 1874, in Dept Gulf, vol. 115/DSL,
RG 393, NA; Pfanz, "Soldiering in the South," 593; Cullum, Register of West Point, II,
406–407.

Townsend's new instructions, ordering Major Merrill and Captain George E. Head at Monroe to reinstate "in their offices such [Republican] officials as may have been deposed," but not to take their soldiers outside their present posts "for that purpose" without specific approval from department headquarters.[7]

Just as Emory had predicted, on October 16 Kellogg asked for more military assistance. The governor wanted the army to install officials in Natchitoches, Bossier, DeSoto, and Lincoln parishes. Emory informed Townsend that he had "troops enough in position to seat most of the Kellogg officials" if Townsend issued the necessary orders. When Townsend appeared reluctant to issue the orders, Kellogg and his Custom House cohorts again sought the help of Attorney General Williams, claiming that the soldiers were also needed to protect the voters in those parishes on election day. Williams dutifully informed Secretary of War Belknap of Kellogg's request, urging him to order Emory to send soldiers into several parishes.[8]

Emory was under pressure from the White League and the Democrats, and the Kellogg administration and the Republicans, and suddenly higher authorities seemed to believe that Emory had too many soldiers in his department. As units of the 13th Infantry arrived in Louisiana, Secretary of War Belknap ordered Emory to transfer some companies of the 2nd and 18th regiments to Alabama. Consequently, while fresh troops were arriving in New Orleans, needing quarters and food, other soldiers were traveling to potential danger spots in the interior or leaving the state. Emory's staff was equal to the task, and during the last two weeks of October, New Orleans bustled with the activity of troop trains and marching soldiers. By the end of the month all ten companies of the 13th Infantry had arrived in New Orleans from the Department of the Platte, replacing companies of other regiments that were transferred to Alabama.[9]

7. Platt to COs, Shreveport and Coushatta, both dated October 12, 1874, in Dept Gulf, vol. 115/DSL, RG 393, NA; Kellogg to Emory, and Emory to AGO, both dated October 14, 1874, Townsend to Emory, and Platt to CO, Upper Red River Dist, both dated October 15, 1874, all in AGO File 3579 of 1874 (Microcopy M-666, reel 170), RG 94, NA; Platt to George E. Head, October 16, 1874, in *House Reports*, 44th Cong., 1st Sess., No. 816, p. 233.

8. Kellogg to Emory, October 15, 1874, Emory to AGO, October 16, 1874, Williams to Belknap, October 20, 1874, in AGO File 3579 of 1874 (Microcopy M-666, reel 170), RG 94, NA; Kellogg, Packard, and others to Williams, and Kellogg to Williams, both dated October 19, 1874, in Justice Dept Letters (Microcopy M-940, reel 2), RG 60, NA.

9. Belknap to Townsend, October 15, 1874, in AGO File 3579 of 1874 (Microcopy

While this repositioning of forces took place, Major Merrill had been having a difficult time in his new command. Merrill had arrived in Shreveport on October 19, and immediately begun a personal campaign to control the "fools and unreasoning hot heads" who had been creating "considerable bad feeling & excitement" throughout northern Louisiana. He opened his campaign by ordering an army detachment to assist U.S. Deputy Marshal J. B. Stockton in arresting James H. Cosgrove, the Conservative editor of the Natchitoches *People's Vindicator*, a leading White League publication. After taking Cosgrove into custody, Stockton and his escort arrested thirteen prominent citizens in Coushatta, charging them with either violating the Enforcement Acts or participating in the "Coushatta Massacre." During the next few days, Merrill's troopers assisted in the arrest of five other men who had signed a proclamation announcing that they would not renew work contracts with blacks who voted for the Republicans in November. Merrill informed Emory that "it would be certain death to any native here to initiate proceedings" against these men, and therefore, he had issued the warrants for their arrest. Merrill concluded that the arrest of these men would have a beneficial effect on other Conservatives in his district.[10]

Louisiana's Democratic press bitterly denounced Merrill's "scurvy actions." The New Orleans *Bulletin* dubbed Merrill a "political bummer with shoulder straps" who did the bidding of "political blacklegs." The Shreveport *Times* accused the major of "bedraggling his uniform in the filth of partisan politics and using the troops under his command to persecute . . . a peaceable community." Furthermore, the *Times* reminded its readers of Merrill's experiences in South Carolina, and likened Merrill and the army to vultures feeding off of the "defenseless" states of South Carolina and Louisiana. The New Orleans *Picayune* added its voice to the chorus of criticism, saying that Merrill's actions deserved "the reproach of the nation and the wrath of his superiors."[11]

Because his actions were "exciting much discussion and comment,"

M-666, reel 170), Post Returns, Jackson Barracks, October 1874, in Records of the AGO (Microcopy M-617, reel 524), both in RG 94, NA; AAG Chauncey McKeever to Emory, October 20, 1874, in Dept Gulf, vol. 151/DSL, Emory to AAG, MilDivSouth, October 23, 1874 (two communications), in Dept Gulf, vol. 140/DSL, all in RG 393, NA.

10. Merrill to AG, Dept Gulf, October 24, 1874, in Dept Gulf, vol. 151/DSL, RG 393, NA; Merrill to AAG, Dept Gulf, October 25, 1874, in *Senate Executive Documents*, 43rd Cong., 2nd Sess., No. 17, p. 407; Natchitoches *People's Vindicator*, October 24, 1874; Shreveport *Times*, October 22, 25, 1874.

11. New Orleans *Bulletin*, October 27, 1874, Shreveport *Times*, October 27, 1874, New Orleans *Daily Picayune*, October 25, 1874.

Emory demanded a full explanation of the unusual occurrences from Merrill, although the general had no intention of removing him. Reporting as Emory ordered, Merrill explained that by the time he had arrived in the "disturbed country" along the Red River, Kellogg's officeholders had been "violently ousted" and McEnery's supporters had replaced them. Merrill began reseating Republican officials and arresting men who, in his opinion, had violated the Enforcement Acts. He believed that such arrests were absolutely necessary if the army was to maintain order. Merrill concluded that the district was becoming quiet and orderly.[12]

Merrill's explanations satisfied Emory, who then turned his attention to specific plans for the election. Adjutant General Townsend, writing for President Grant, asked Emory his "views as to stationing troops in New Orleans on [the] day of [the] election." Townsend reminded Emory that the army's objective was "to confirm every individual in his legal right to vote." However, Townsend cautioned Emory to avoid "all appearance of military interference." Emory replied that the "whole city and [the] river front [were] completely commanded" by eleven infantry companies and several navy warships. Three other companies were guarding the state capitol, and ten companies were at Jackson Barracks. Moreover, during the last several days different units had been "taking exercise" in the streets of the city, parading to demonstrate the army's intention to keep the peace on election day. However, there were more than one hundred polling places in New Orleans, and it would be difficult to supervise every one. Moreover, the Democrats had not been idle. Emory pointed out that many Conservatives had registered and were legally entitled to vote. This could lead to a close election, but Emory did not expect an armed "conflict" unless one side challenged the other for "the custody of the ballot boxes" or disputed the election results after they were tabulated. To discourage either of these eventualities, Emory informed Townsend that he planned to bring more soldiers into the city on election day.[13]

By election day Emory had stationed his soldiers at twenty towns in

12. Emory to AGO, October 25, 1874, in AGO File 3579 of 1874 (Microcopy M-666, reel 171), RG 94, NA; Emory to AGO, October 26, 27, 1874, Merrill to AAG, Dept Gulf, October 27, 1874, Emory to McDowell, October 29, 1874, all in *Senate Executive Documents*, 43rd Cong., 2nd Sess., No. 17, pp. 2–4, 7–11.

13. Townsend to Emory, October 27, 1874, Emory to AGO, October 28 and 31, 1874, in *Senate Executive Documents*, 43rd Cong., 2nd Sess., No. 17, pp. 62–63; Monthly Returns, Dept Gulf, October 1874, RG 393, NA; New Orleans *Republican*, October 24, 27, 1874.

thirteen parishes and ordered detachments to several important locations in New Orleans, including five police stations. Other soldiers, who had not been given specific guard duties, paraded through the city's streets. The parade and the evidence of soldiers near public buildings were correctly judged by the Democrats as a reminder that the army would not tolerate any violent demonstrations. In New Orleans itself Emory termed November 2 "Perfectly quiet." The reports from post and detachment commanders around the state generally echoed Emory's own—there was little violence on election day.[14]

However, peace and quiet did not necessarily mean an open election. Considerable evidence indicates that many blacks were unable to freely cast their ballots. Methodical intimidation by the Democrats had convinced blacks that voting Republican was not worth their jobs or perhaps their lives. Captain Arthur Allyn, commanding Company B, 16th Infantry, at Colfax, said that by November 2 the blacks in Grant Parish were so fearful that no "colored man could vote as he wished in the larger portion of the parish." Agreeing with Allyn's conclusions, Major Lewis Merrill related that Conservatives in Caddo and DeSoto parishes often threatened to discharge their black employees if they supported the Republican party. Merrill said that these threats "had the effect to a very great extent to deter the negroes from voting, or to make them vote the democratic ticket." Lieutenant William Gerlach, leading a detachment of the 7th Cavalry to the Campo Bello precinct in Caddo Parish, looked on aghast at blacks who "threw themselves on the ground shouting with joy" as he and his troopers rode through the village. After guarding the polls during the election, Gerlach said he was "fully convinced that the colored population in Caddo Parish . . . [was] terror stricken." Captain James H. Gageby, commanding at St. Martinville, testified that "armed parties" had terrorized blacks in St. Martin Parish before the election, but that November 2 had passed quietly. From this kind of testimony by army officers, it appears that the Conservatives successfully intimidated many blacks, who consequently either decided not to vote or voted Democratic.[15]

14. New Orleans *Times*, January 1, 1875; New Orleans *Daily Picayune*, November 1, 1874; Emory, testimony before a congressional committee, in *House Reports*, 43rd Cong., 2nd Sess., No. 101, Pt. 2, p. 60.

15. Arthur Allyn, testimony before a congressional committee, in *House Reports*, 43rd Cong., 2nd Sess., No. 261, Pt. 3, pp. 157, 159; Merrill, testimony, William Gerlach to AAG, Red River Dist, November 4, 1874, James H. Gageby, testimony, all in *House Reports*, 43rd Cong., 2nd Sess., No. 261, Pt. 2, pp. 183, 952, 705, 707, 711; Taylor, *Louisiana Reconstructed*, 299.

Nevertheless, the army influenced the outcome of the election in favor of the Republicans. In some cases, the mere presence of army detachments probably encouraged some blacks to vote who otherwise would not have tried. These votes meant victory in some parishes, or at least they helped the Returning Board to substantiate a Republican victory. Four of the thirteen parishes where soldiers had been stationed went Democratic, but the results might have been worse—even catastrophic—for the Republicans had the army not been present. The army ultimately saved the election for the Republicans by protecting the state Returning Board during its deliberations. The board, the final arbiter of Louisiana's elections, was composed of four Republicans and only one Democrat. The chairman of the board was none other than former governor James Madison Wells, who called himself a "conservative," but who usually cooperated with the Republicans.[16]

While the Returning Board deliberated, it became commonplace for company commanders in Louisiana to assist Marshal Packard and his deputies when they served arrest warrants. Usually, the assistance involved nothing more than traveling a few miles and arresting some fugitives whom the deputy did not want to confront alone. Sometimes the soldiers helped to escort the accused individuals to a local jail. The longer the deputies relied on the army to provide their posses, the more bitter Louisianians became. The Conservatives regularly avoided any confrontation with marshals who had army escorts. But in late 1874 an extraordinary series of incidents occurred in northern Louisiana demonstrating the Democrats' audacity and disrespect for the representatives of the federal government.

On October 25, 1874, Lieutenant Benjamin H. Hodgson led a detachment of fourteen soldiers of the 7th Cavalry to assist U.S. Deputy Marshal Edgar Selye, who held arrest warrants for three men in the town of Homer in Claiborne Parish and one man in the town of Vienna in Lincoln Parish. All of the men were charged with violating the Enforcement Acts. Hodgson and Selye proceeded to Homer, where they arrested Mayor S. R. Richardson and two other local officials. Several townspeople gathered around the wagon carrying the arrested men, shouting threats and curses at the soldiers and promising to free the prisoners. Making their way out of Homer, Hodgson, Selye, and their entourage

16. Lowrey, "Political Career of Wells," 1,094; Taylor, *Louisiana Reconstructed*, 302.

went to Vienna and arrested the fourth man on the marshal's wanted list. Rumors abounded in Vienna that armed riders were planning to intercept the detachment and free the prisoners. The lieutenant and the marshal muscled their prisoners out of town. About a mile outside of Vienna, Selye told Hodgson that he should cut the telegraph wires, thus preventing White Leaguers from learning their whereabouts and movements. Believing that he and his soldiers "were in imminent danger," the lieutenant clipped the cables. The party then proceeded to Monroe without incident.[17]

Within a few days, Judge J. E. Trimble at Vienna issued arrest warrants for Selye and Hodgson. The Lincoln Parish sheriff assembled a posse of twenty men and went to Monroe, planning to arrest the marshal and the lieutenant. Following the sheriff and his official posse were more than 150 well-armed "volunteers." On November 6 this mounted force rode into Monroe and apprehended the two federal officers. Hodgson and Selye were hustled onto horseback and surrounded by the sheriff's posse and the volunteers. The group then galloped out of Monroe, heading towards Vienna. Captain George Head hastily assembled a dozen soldiers and sent them chasing pell-mell after the posse.[18]

Learning of the arrests propelled Major Merrill into action. He wired Hodgson in Vienna, directing him to find out what specific charges the sheriff's warrant contained. Next, Merrill informed department headquarters of Hodgson's arrest, adding that he was ordering Lieutenant James M. Bell to take a troop of cavalry to Vienna. Merrill considered going to Vienna himself, but he realized that he was widely disliked in north Louisiana and that his presence might be "regarded as an attempt . . . [to secure Hodgson's] forcible release and cause the whole white league force to go there." Merrill wisely decided to remain in Shreveport, hoping ultimately to beat the Conservatives at their own legal game by winning the case in court.[19]

Accordingly, Merrill telegraphed Captain Head in Monroe, ordering

17. New Orleans *Daily Picayune*, October 29, 1874; Edgar Selye, statement, enclosed with Henry A. Morrow to AAG, Dept Gulf, November 17, 1874, Benjamin H. Hodgson to Morrow, November 14, 1874, both in AGO File 3579 of 1874 (Microcopy M-666, reel 171), RG 94, NA.

18. Hodgson to Merrill, November 6, 1874, in *Senate Executive Documents*, 43rd Cong., 2nd Sess., No. 17, p. 31. See also Shreveport *Times*, November 7, 1874.

19. Merrill to Hodgson, Merrill to AG, Dept Gulf, both dated November 6, 1874, in *Senate Executive Documents*, 43rd Cong., 2nd Sess., No. 17, pp. 32–33.

him to take "every disposable man" of his command and go "at once" to Vienna. But Captain Head was not cooperative perhaps because he held pro-Democratic sympathies. Head informed Merrill that all available men had followed the sheriff's posse at the time of Hodgson's arrest. Furthermore, most of the garrison's infantrymen had just returned from an eighteen-mile march and were in no condition to leave Monroe for at least two days. Displeased by Head's attitude, Merrill ordered him to proceed to Vienna "with all the men you can take" regardless of their condition.[20]

Meanwhile, the adjutant general of the Department of the Gulf, on orders from Emory, cautioned Merrill to "instruct [his] officers to be very guarded, in aiding to enforce one law, not to violate another." In conclusion, the adjutant general advised Merrill to have Hodgson's case transferred from Trimble's state court to the nearest federal circuit court. Merrill acknowledged the adjutant general's telegram and notified Hodgson of these instructions from headquarters. Simultaneously, the major sought to hire an attorney to defend the unfortunate lieutenant and learned that Hodgson and Selye were charged with contempt of court for not obeying a writ of *habeas corpus*, namely for failing to produce in Trimble's court the four prisoners the army detachment had arrested.[21]

On November 7, before Hodgson's attorney (a local lawyer named W. R. Hardy) could apply to have Hodgons's case transferred to a U.S. court, Judge Trimble arraigned the lieutenant and Marshal Selye on charges of contempt of court. Trimble found the pair guilty, sentenced them to ten days in jail, and fined them one hundred dollars each. The speedy trial destroyed Merrill's plans to conduct a slow, methodical defense in a federal court.[22]

General Emory was kept abreast of the situation in Vienna by Merrill's frequent telegrams. When he learned that Hodgson and Selye had been convicted, he sent a special message to General Townsend, giving him the salient facts in the unusual case. Emory added that he was sending Colonel Henry Morrow of the 13th Infantry to investigate the entire matter. Before Morrow arrived, Frank Morey, a local Republican, filed a

---

20. Merrill to George Head, Head to Merrill, both dated November 6, 1874, *ibid.*, 33.
21. AAG, Dept Gulf to Merrill, Merrill to AAG, Dept Gulf, Merrill to Frank Morey, Merrill to Hodgson, Morey to Merrill, all dated November 6, 1874, *ibid.*, 33–34.
22. Hodgson to Merrill, Merrill to Hodgson, Merrill to AAG, Dept Gulf, all dated November 7, 1874, *ibid.*, 36.

complaint against Captain Head for "unofficer-like and disgraceful" conduct, public drunkenness, and fraternizing with the White League. Obviously, Morey had recognized Head's Democratic sympathies.[23]

Suddenly, Judge Trimble announced some decisions that astonished everyone connected with the case. He nullified Hodgson's sentence, rescinded his fine, and discharged the lieutenant from custody. By all appearances the case had ended, but on November 10 Judge Trimble filed new charges against Hodgson for cutting the telegraph wires. Considering these new circumstances, W. R. Hardy advised Merrill that Head was "invaluable" to the conduct of the case because he had "formed and now controls public opinion [in Vienna]." Merrill had disliked Hardy from the beginning of the case, and now his patience with the annoying attorney had worn thin. Dismissing Hardy by calling him "an obstinate ignoramous," Merrill again ordered Head to have Hodgson's case transferred to a federal court. Piqued by Merrill's language, Hardy responded in kind. "There is a wide difference between a gentleman and a Blackguard," Hardy boomed. "You furnish an illustration." Colonel Morrow's arrival in Vienna on November 10 finally made Hardy's services unnecessary and placed Captain Head in a subordinate position. After questioning the principals in the case, Morrow suggested to Merrill that Hodgson be placed under military arrest and tried at court-martial for cutting the telegraph wires. While awaiting court-martial, Lieutenant Hodgson was placed in protective custody in Monroe.[24]

North Louisiana newspapers relished the controversy caused by the Hodgson case, using it as an opportunity to criticize the army and its officers. For example, the Shreveport *Times* referred to the lieutenant as a "reckless and lawless subaltern," whose guilt was a foregone conclusion. The *Times* delightedly pointed out that Major Merrill was making "an ass . . . of himself in keeping up all this military display and excitement."[25]

When it convened, the military court found Hodgson guilty on two

23. Emory to AGO, November 7, 8, 1874, in AGO File 3579 of 1874 (Microcopy M-666, reel 171); Morey to Merrill, November 9, 1874, in AGO File 3579 of 1874 (Microcopy M-666, reel 172).

24. Head to Merrill, November 9, 10, 1874, W. R. Hardy to Merrill, November 10, 13, 1874, Morrow to Merrill, November 10, 11, 1874, Head to AAAG, Red River Dist, November 16, 1874, all in *Senate Executive Documents*, 43rd Cong., 2nd Sess., No. 17, pp. 43–47, 30.

25. Shreveport *Times*, November 8, 1874. See also Monroe *Ouachita Telegraph*, November 13, 20, 27, 1874.

counts: conduct unbecoming an officer and a gentleman during the arrest of the Caliborne Parish prisoners and destroying a telegraph wire belonging to Western Union. The court handed down an unofficial reprimand as the only punishment for these infractions, citing the "very novel circumstances under which Lieutenant Hodgson was suddenly placed" as the reason for the light penalty. Hodgson was restored to duty with his company.[26]

The Hodgson case was unique during the Reconstruction years in Louisiana. A Conservative judge issued a warrant for the lieutenant's arrest without consulting Major Merrill, who commanded the Red River District, Captain Head, who was temporarily Hodgson's immediate superior, or the state's attorney general. Some satisfactory accommodation could have been worked out with one or more of these officers in relation to the charges against Hodgson. Instead, the judge and his sheriff demonstrated their insolence and disrespect for the army, and coincidentally for U.S. Marshal Edgar Selye. The sheriff risked bringing on a general engagement with the army when he boldly led his posse and volunteers into Monroe and abducted Hodgson and Selye. However, the sheriff might have been counting on the cooperation (or at least inaction) of Captain Head. Once Hodgson and Selye had been arrested, Emory and Merrill elected to press for their release in court, rather than sending a large armed force to Vienna and demanding that they be set free. Such an action likely would have been viewed as a military assault on the courts and would not have earned any friends for either the army or the Grant administration. Even so, the Hodgson case embarrassed Major Merrill, General Emory, and the army. By the time the lieutenant's court-martial ended in December, the whole affair had placed another black mark beside Emory's name. Once again, he had failed to ensure law and order in Louisiana.

In the weeks following the Hodgson incident, it was evident that the Republicans' hold on northern Louisiana was deteriorating, despite Major Merrill's conscientious command of the Upper Red River District. In Merrill's opinion, most Republicans needed to maintain their "actual residence in the military camp" for self-protection if they tried to exercise the duties of elected or appointed office during the day. Furthermore, Merrill claimed that "the entire black population of this section is absolutely terror-struck," standing "in almost hourly apprehension of the visits of

26. GO No. 29, Dept Gulf, December 30, 1874, containing results of the court-martial of B. H. Hodgson, in *House Reports*, 43rd Cong., 2nd Sess., No. 261, Pt. 2, pp. 950–52.

White Leaguers." Major Henry L. Chipman, serving with the 3rd Infantry in Shreveport, corroborated Merrill's claims and advised that it would be unwise "to withdraw any of the troops stationed" in the northern parishes. Subsequently, Merrill asked Emory to send additional soldiers to the Upper Red River District. Emory doubted the necessity of more troops in North Louisiana. Merrill was already commanding three troops of cavalry and five companies of infantry—only two companies shy of a complete regiment. Therefore, Emory ordered Colonel Morrow to investigate "the condition of the troops, [and] the character of the locality in which they are placed" throughout north Louisiana.[27]

Morrow's reports contrasted starkly with Merrill's and Chipman's opinions. First of all, Morrow recommended that in the future federal soldiers should no longer provide posses for the U.S. marshals. With the Hodgson case fresh on everyone's mind, Morrow thought that if Emory could be persuaded to adopt this recommendation, "the Army will be relieved from a most unpleasant and onerous duty, and a great cause of local irritation will be removed." Moreover, Morrow believed that no additional soldiers were needed in the Upper Red River District. In fact, the colonel advised Emory to withdraw most of the soldiers from northern Louisiana. Morrow emphasized that while there was "*not the slightest disposition to oppose the General Government,*" there was considerable opposition to Kellogg's administration. Only "the presence and force of Federal soldiers" was restraining the "open defiance" of most whites against the Kellogg regime, which could not "maintain itself in power a single hour without the protection of Federal troops." In Morrow's opinion, if the Returning Board declared Republicans elected in Caddo and DeSoto parishes, "Nearly all influential and responsible citizens concur fully and entirely in the view that violence to any extent will be justified" to take the Republicans out and put Democrats into office. By supporting Kellogg, the army was going against "the personal and political feeling in the breasts of nineteen-twentieths of the white inhabitants of the State."[28]

Meanwhile, the situation in New Orleans appeared to be quite dangerous. The soldiers had been withdrawn from the capitol on November

27. Merrill to AAG, Dept Gulf, November 18, 1874, Merrill to AG, Dept Gulf, November 26, 1874, Emory to AGO, November 28, 1874, Platt to Morrow, November 28, 1874, all in *Senate Executive Documents*, 43rd Cong., 2nd Sess., No. 17, pp. 19, 50–53; Henry L. Chipman to AAG, Dept Gulf, November 23, 1874, in Dept Gulf, Letters Recd, RG 393, NA.

28. Morrow to AAG, Dept Gulf, December 3, 11, 24, 1874, all in *Senate Executive Documents*, 43rd Cong., 2nd Sess., No. 17, pp. 67–68, 70–74.

24 at General Townsend's direction in order to reduce the military expenses of the New Orleans garrison. On December 9 Governor Kellogg warned President Grant that the White League might attack the state house at any time. He asked the president to permit Emory to station soldiers in and around the capitol to protect James M. Wells and the other members of the Returning Board, who were meeting there. Supporting the governor's request, Wells informed Grant that the "members of the board are being publicly and privately threatened with violence." U.S. District Attorney James R. Beckwith wrote Attorney General Williams that loyal Republicans in New Orleans were "surrounded by an armed camp with a force exceeding by far the federal land forces now in the city. . . . There is no respect for Law either State or federal. The condition is Volcanic and may culminate in bloodshed at any moment." [29]

All of these "rumors of intended violence" had not escaped Emory's attention, and he decided to forestall any repetition of the events of September 14. He put the troops at Jackson Barracks on a round-the-clock alert and informed local political leaders of his plans to keep the peace. Privately, however, Emory revealed his doubts about continuing the present Reconstruction policy in Louisiana, asking both General Townsend and General McDowell if, in the event of an attack on Kellogg, the army should defend the governor or wait for him officially to apply to the president for help. [30]

General Townsend promptly replied that the "President directs that you make arrangements to be in readiness to suppress violence, and have it understood that you will do it." Emory gratefully accepted those firm orders, and borrowing Townsend's words, he sent Major Merrill what was virtually a duplicate message. Democratic leaders soon learned about Emory's orders. Suddenly, the potential for violence decreased, and Emory wired the adjutant general, telling him that it appeared "armed conflict will not be used by contending parties to settle the pending political troubles in this city." Now that a measure of calm had been restored

29. Kellogg to Grant, December 9, 1874, Wells to Grant, December 10, 1874, both in *Appleton's Annual Cyclopedia and Register of Important Events for 1874* (New York, 1875), 502; Post Returns, New Orleans, November 1874, in Records of the AGO (Microcopy M-617, reel 844), RG 94, NA; Beckwith to Williams, December 11, 1874, in Justice Dept Letters (Microcopy M-940, reel 2), RG 60, NA.

30. Emory to AAG, MilDivSouth, December 13, 1874, in Dept Gulf, vol. 140/DSL, RG 393, NA; Platt to CO, Jackson Barracks, December 13, 1874, and Emory's endorsement, Emory to AGO, December 15, 1874, both in *Senate Executive Documents*, 43rd Cong., 2nd Sess., No. 17, pp. 65–66; Emory to AG, MilDivSouth, December 15, 1874, in AGO File 3579 of 1874 (Microcopy M-666, reel 172), RG 94, NA.

to politics, the politicians and the soldiers all waited for the Returning Board to announce the election results.[31]

On December 22 and 24 James Wells and his board released the official returns, after selectively voiding the returns from several precincts. The board was dominated by Republicans, and consequently many observers believed that it would declare Republican candidates elected in a majority of the contests. Surprisingly, Wells and his cronies declared only fifty-three Republicans elected to the state house of representatives, as against fifty-three Democrats. In a move sure to cause future trouble, the board announced that it was impossible to determine the winners of five legislative seats, leaving the final decision up to the new house itself. Furthermore, Democrats had won two of Louisiana's six congressional seats. The Conservatives dominated the local elections in Orleans Parish and were victorious in many other municipal and parish elections across the state. The Republicans were horrified by these results, but they still had a majority in the state senate.[32]

Even before the Returning Board announced the election results, President Grant and his advisors had considered sending a special envoy to Louisiana.[33] This was not a decision made on the spur of the moment. The events that had taken place during recent months in Louisiana had eroded the administration's confidence in General Emory, and therefore, Grant had decided to send to Louisiana a senior officer in whom he had the utmost confidence. That officer was General Philip H. Sheridan. When it came to carrying out Reconstruction policy, Grant probably had more confidence in Sheridan than in any other army officer, not excepting General William T. Sherman. Sherman's position on Reconstruction was well known. Had he been assigned to New Orleans, he might have recommended that the time had come for the army to withdraw from Louisiana, leaving Kellogg to his fate. The general wrote his brother, Senator John Sherman, that he thought it was the army's duty to "keep the peace always; but not [to] act as bailiff constables and catch thieves. That should be beneath a soldier's vocation." Even under the most trying circumstances Grant had refused to abandon Kellogg, and he would never have wanted any kind of open rift on his southern policy with

31. Townsend to Emory, and reply, both dated December 16, 1874, in *Senate Executive Documents*, 43rd Cong., 2nd Sess., No. 17, pp. 65–66; Platt to Merrill, December 17, 1874, in Dept Gulf, vol. 140/DSL, RG 393, NA.

32. New Orleans *Republican*, December 23, 25, 1874; Taylor, *Louisiana Reconstructed*, 303–304.

33. New York *Times*, December 28, 1874.

Sherman. Perhaps, then, it was not so surprising that the president picked "Little Phil" to go to Louisiana.[34]

On Christmas Eve, Secretary of War William Belknap sent a telegram to Sheridan at his Chicago headquarters, explaining that Grant wanted him "to visit" Louisiana and Mississippi to "ascertain the true condition of affairs" in those states. In fact, Belknap gave Sheridan virtual carte blanche, permitting him to take command of all or any state within the Military Division of the South, and leaving to his discretion how much, if anything, to tell McDowell about the special mission. Belknap added it was "best that the trip should appear to be one as much of pleasure as of business." After concluding his investigations, Sheridan was to give the president a complete personal report in Washington. Until then, Grant expected Sheridan to keep him informed "from time to time." Sheridan acknowledged Belknap's message and prepared for his trip to the Bayou State.[35]

Initially, Sheridan did not divulge the full implications of his orders to either the press or the public. He followed Belknap's suggestion and gave the impression he was on a pleasure trip. Some observers believed that he simply planned to pass through Louisiana on his way to Cuba. Sheridan's fiance, Miss Irene Rucker, bolstered this notion by announcing that she intended to go along on the trip. Sheridan notified his subordinate commanders, Generals John Pope and C. C. Augur, that he simply wanted "to take a little trip to the south for two or three weeks & may possibly go as far as Havana."[36]

But most of the reports in the newspapers indicated that Sheridan had not fooled the journalists by pretending he was on a trip to Cuba. The New York *Times* reported on December 28 that Sheridan was going to New Orleans to "take command." The *Times* hastened to add that Sheridan's mission "implies no dissatisfaction with, or want of confidence in Gen. Emory." In New Orleans the local newspapers quickly picked up the story. The New Orleans *Times* claimed that Sheridan was carrying orders giving him "immediate sway" over Louisiana. The *Republican*

34. Sefton, *Army and Reconstruction*, 240; O'Connor, *Sheridan*, 328–29; Sherman to John Sherman, January 7, 1875, in Rachel S. Thorndike (ed.), *The Sherman Letters: Correspondence Between General and Senator Sherman from 1837 to 1891* (New York, 1894), 342.

35. Belknap to Sheridan, December 24, 1874, Sheridan to Belknap, December 26, 1874, in *Senate Executive Documents*, 43rd Cong., 2nd Sess., No. 13, pp. 19–20. See also Sefton, *Army and Reconstruction*, 240.

36. William H. Dixon, *White Conquest* (2 vols.; London, 1876), II, 40, 42; Sheridan to John Pope, Sheridan to C. C. Augur, both dated December 28, 1874, in Sheridan Papers.

predicted that Sheridan would assume command of the Department of the Gulf, attaching it to his grand Military Division of the Missouri. At first, the *Picayune* doubted that Sheridan was coming to Louisiana, but by December 29 it was resigned to the fact.[37]

Meanwhile, no one in Washington or Chicago had informed General Emory about Sheridan's mission or its objectives. In a widely circulated interview, Emory said that he had "received no official intelligence concerning the reports alluded to, nor of any measures looking to my removal." Using an interesting phrase, Emory accused "the banditti in Washington who are writing for the newspapers" of trying to turn public opinion against him. To Emory, it may have seemed that everyone was against him, but it was more than just the press coverage of Louisiana's problems that had brought him to the brink of losing his command. Even Emory acknowledged that "the state of things is daily growing worse." Evidently, Grant wanted someone in New Orleans, as the New York *Times* reported, "of such rank that in case of an emergency he can act without special orders from Washington." Emory had apparently lost his committment to his unusual mission—protecting the Kellogg government. Consequently, Grant had lost confidence in Emory, and he wanted someone in Louisiana who was dedicated to Reconstruction.[38]

Late on the night of December 30, Phil Sheridan stepped off the train at New Orleans. Accompanying him was his brother, Captain Michael V. Sheridan, his trusted aide-de-camp Major George A. Forsyth, and his fiance, Miss Irene Rucker. The New Orleans *Republican* reported that Sheridan's staff officers appeared to be "out for a holiday and intending to visit Havana before their return to Chicago." Sheridan was trying to keep up the pretense of a pleasure trip. Unfortunately, his mission to New Orleans was going to be anything but a holiday.[39]

37. New York *Times*, December 28, 1874; New Orleans *Times*, December 28, 1874; New Orleans *Republican*, December 30, 1874; New Orleans *Daily Picayune*, December 27–30, 1874.

38. New York *Times*, December 30, 1874; Emory's endorsement (December 27, 1874) on letter, Morrow to AAG, Dept Gulf, December 24, 1874, in *Senate Executive Documents*, 43rd Cong., 2nd Sess., No. 17, p. 74.

39. New Orleans *Republican*, December 31, 1874.

CHAPTER X

The Return of the Little Villain

Phil Sheridan was more despised by white Louisianians than any other northern general with the possible exception of Ben Butler. No other general had done more to change the structure of their society and their politics. Sheridan's first command in Louisiana had been marked by contention, and his second Reconstruction assignment followed the same pattern. Indeed, controversy seemed to attend the little general. Since Sheridan was last in Louisiana, eastern do-gooders had condemned him for his harsh warfare against the Indians, diplomats had shuddered when he offended the French while serving as an official observer during the Franco-Prussian War, and politicians had criticized him for his administration of Chicago after the catastrophic fire of 1871. The possibility that Sheridan would assume command in Louisiana had aroused speculation in the press, and the White League took his assignment to the state as an "ominous token." Mincing no words, the New Iberia *Sugar Bowl* branded Sheridan the "little villain" soon after his arrival.[1]

White Louisianians were antagonized by Sheridan's presence because they knew him too well. They knew that his stern reputation was well deserved, and moreover, they knew that they could not bluff him. Obviously, the resentment many white Louisianians felt toward him made Sheridan's assignment more difficult. Such ill will might have been shown toward General Alfred Terry or any other new commander who was given the mission to pacify the rebellious Louisianians. But Sheridan's past reputation should have made it clear to Grant that, as Claude Bowers wrote, "A microscopic search of the army could not have discovered a single officer . . . more provocative of the people of New Orleans." Similarly, James Sefton wrote that "Sheridan's mere presence in Louisiana was enough to antagonize people." Sheridan's biographer, Richard O'Connor, concluded, "If there was one man in the North com-

1. O'Connor, *Sheridan*, 305–15. New Iberia *Sugar Bowl*, February 11, 1875.

pletely ineligible to effect a cooling off of political passions at New Orleans, that man was Phil Sheridan."[2]

Sheridan was not in New Orleans to cool off passions. He was there to
quash the rebellion that had been obvious since the Battle of Liberty
Place. In fact, Sheridan was one of the few Radicals left. Stevens, Sum-
ner, and Mower were dead; other Radicals had defected to the Liberal
Republicans or had retired from politics; General Pope had been posted
to the West to fight Indians; General Dan Sickles left the service to become minister to Spain. Their passing from the political scene reflected a
decline in the popularity of Grant's Reconstruction policy, which had
consistently involved using the army to support Republican regimes in
the South. By 1875 most northerners displayed a noticeable lack of concern about the ideals of Reconstruction, civil rights for blacks, and
punishment of lawless or traitorous former Confederates. Although
Grant's policy was essentially obsolete, he wanted Louisiana to remain in
Republican hands. To achieve this end the federal government would
have to take firm control again. Sheridan's arrival, therefore, was a signal
to the Democrats—cease and desist, or face the consequences of military
suppression.

On January 1 Sheridan met with Emory, his old comrade in arms from
the Shenandoah Valley campaign. At first they may have talked briefly
about the war, the battles in which they fought together: Opequon,
Fisher's Hill, and Cedar Creek. After the last battle Sheridan had recommended that Emory be breveted major general of volunteers. Sheridan
usually dealt brusquely with subordinates, but he may have shown some
consideration for Emory, who had entered the army the same year that
Sheridan was born. They finally turned their conversation to Louisiana
politics. The legislature was scheduled to open in three days, and the Returning Board had left five house seats unfilled. The state House of Representatives had to choose five new members to fill those seats. By then
Emory recognized the potential for violence whenever the Louisiana legislature convened. He showed Sheridan the orders that had been sent by
Adjutant General Townsend and the president in December—"suppress
violence and have it understood that you will do it." Simultaneously, he
handed Sheridan his draft of orders for the disposition of troops on January 4. After reading the documents, Sheridan replied that the president's
orders were "explicit and unambiguous." Sheridan remarked that it was

2. Claude G. Bowers, *The Tragic Era: The Revolution after Lincoln* (Cambridge, Mass.,
1929), 443; Sefton, *Army and Reconstruction*, 244; O'Connor, *Sheridan*, 328.

his "duty as a military officer . . . to prevent riot and bloodshed." Sheridan then showed Emory the orders from Belknap, authorizing him to assume command of the Department of the Gulf. According to Emory, "from that moment" he took no action without consulting Sheridan or without the senior general's specific orders. For all practical purposes Sheridan was in command.[3]

On January 2 Sheridan telegraphed Belknap, informing him that the mood in New Orleans was "feverish" but that he did not anticipate "any serious trouble." Responding to Governor Kellog's warning that the White League might instigate a disturbance on January 4, and perhaps even attempt to occupy the capitol, Emory ordered Colonel Philippe Regis de Trobriand of the 13th Infantry and Colonel DeLancey Floyd-Jones of the 3rd Infantry to protect the legislature. Sheridan left Emory's orders unchanged. Without telling Emory of his purpose, Sheridan had definitely decided "to annex this department to my Military Division and eventually change the department commander," for he had come to doubt Emory's "ability to keep things steady and inspire confidence." To replace Emory, Sheridan recommended Colonel Ranald Slidell Mackenzie, one of his favorite cavalry officers. But Sheridan indicated that he would not displace Emory immediately.[4]

The Democrats and Republicans caucused separately on January 3. Each party planned to have its nominee elected speaker of the house. The Democrats picked former New Orleans mayor Louis Wiltz, and the Republicans chose former governor Michael Hahn. The details of these meetings remained secret, leading to frantic speculation that the Republicans would use the militia, the police, or the army to secure the election of their nominee, or that the Democrats would use the White League to obtain the election for their candidate. The political atmosphere in New Orleans was more emotionally charged than at any time since the arms-laden steamer *Mississippi* had arrived the previous September.[5]

As stipulated in Emory's orders, between 7:00 and 8:00 A.M. on January 4, army units occupied positions near the Custom House and the old St. Louis Hotel, which was serving as the state capitol. Colonel John

---

3. The description of the conversation is based on Sheridan's testimony in the case of *Vaughn v. Sheridan, Emory, and de Trobriand*, undated, in Sheridan Papers; Emory to AGO, March 27, 1875, in AGO File 3579 of 1874 (Microcopy M-666, reel 173), RG 94, NA.

4. Kellogg to Emory, January 2, 1875, in AGO File 3579 of 1874 (Microcopy M-666, reel 173), RG 94, NA; AAG Platt to Floyd-Jones, January 2, 1875, in Dept Gulf, vol. 115/DSL, RG 393, NA; Sheridan to Belknap, January 2, 1875, in Sheridan Papers.

5. Lonn, *Reconstruction in Louisiana*, 293–95.

Brooke commanded five companies of the 22nd Infantry and three companies of the 13th Infantry in a line from the corner of Chartres and St. Louis streets, along St. Louis Street to the levee. Colonel Henry Morrow commanded seven companies of the 13th regiment stationed at the Importer's Bonded Warehouse on Chartres Street. Colonel Floyd-Jones was in charge of the reserve, comprising four companies of the 13th Infantry and two companies of the 22nd Infantry positioned underneath the sugar storage sheds on the levee. One battery of the 1st Artillery, with a Gatling gun and a twelve-pound Napoleon, supported Floyd-Jones' reserve. Colonel de Trobriand, wearing a civilian suit, personally commanded a company of the 13th Infantry outside the state house on St. Louis Street. The force totalled more than seven hundred officers and enlisted men.[6]

By 9:00 A.M. the senior commanders were ready to inspect the troops. Emory toured the lines, returning immediately to his temporary headquarters in the Custom House, which was guarded by Captain Frederick W. Benteen's Troop H, 7th Cavalry. At ten o'clock Sheridan and his staff (all in civilian attire) left their rooms at the St. Charles Hotel and inspected the battle-ready soldiers. Sheridan neither offered any comments nor directed that any changes be made in the disposition of the soldiers.[7]

Outside the capitol, a large and boisterous crowd, including members of all political factions, policemen, and state militiamen, assembled. Undoubtedly, many of the civilians in the throng were armed. State senators and legislators slowly made their way through the crowd, identifying themselves to the policemen guarding the doors. Kellogg had ordered his constables to admit only legislators, newspaper correspondents with approved credentials, and other persons who were on state business. By one means or another, however, dozens of ineligible persons entered the building, clogging the halls, filling the chairs set aside for spectators, and occupying several rooms of the onetime hotel.[8]

At noon the clerk, shouting over the hubbub, called the house to order and began checking off the names of the legislators. Fifty-two Repub-

6. Philippe Regis de Trobriand to AAG, Dept Gulf, January 6, 1875, in AGO File 3579 of 1874 (Microcopy M-666, reel 173), RG 94, NA; Marie Caroline Post [ed.], *The Life and Memoirs of Comte Regis de Trobriand* (New York, 1910), 444–46. The 13th Infantry was a mere skeleton of a regiment, mustering only 338 officers and men, which accounts for the seeming disparity in the number of companies (twenty-three) present and the small total of soldiers. See Post Returns, Post of New Orleans, January 1875, in Records of the AGO (Microcopy M-617, reel 844), RG 94, NA.

7. De Trobriand to AAG, Dept Gulf, January 6, 1875, in AGO File 3579 of 1874 (Microcopy M-666, reel 173), RG 94, NA; Post [ed.], *Memoirs of de Trobriand*, 444–46.

8. See Lonn's vivid description in *Reconstruction in Louisiana*, 295.

licans and fifty Democrats answered the roll call. Acting on a cue, a Democrat nominated Louis Wiltz for speaker of the house. A nightmare of confusion that reminded Republicans of the eventful opening of the legislature in 1872 ensued as different men called for order, requested recognition from the chair, and shouted threats at opponents across the room. Wiltz sprang out of his seat and stepped to the podium, grabbing the gavel from the hand of the frightened clerk, who was fruitlessly trying to declare Wiltz's nomination out of order. Suddenly one of the spectators, who identified himself as a justice of the peace, came forward and quickly administered the oath to Wiltz, who assumed the speakership. Without missing a beat, Wiltz "administered the oath to the members *en masse*," accepted the nomination of a Conservative for permanent clerk, declared him elected, and to complete his *coup*, appointed dozens of sergeants-at-arms. These men instantly identified themselves, turning "down the lapels of their coats, upon which were pinned blue ribbon badges, on which were printed, in gold letters, the words 'assistant sergeant-at-arms.'" Under the protection of his sergeants-at-arms, Wiltz forced the election of Democrats to the five contested house seats left vacant by the Returning Board.[9]

During all of this activity the Republicans had been protesting vociferously, shouting epithets at Wiltz and other Democrats, and calling for points of order, which Wiltz studiously ignored. Sensing that they had lost this round of the contest, the Republicans attempted to leave the chamber and thereby destroy the quorum of the house. Brandishing knives and pistols, the sergeants-at-arms blocked some of the exits, forcing several Republicans to remain in the room, but others, aided by Kellogg's police, escaped to the dubious safety of the hallway.[10]

The Republicans notified General Hugh J. Campbell, Kellogg's militia commander, of the extraordinary proceedings in the house chamber, calling on him to restore order. Unwilling to take this responsibility, Campbell located Colonel de Trobriand and asked him to pacify the unruly legislators. Simultaneously, a messenger from Wiltz approached de Trobriand, presenting a similar request from the Democratic speaker, who said that the noise from the "idlers" in the hallways was disrupting the decorum of the house. Under any circumstances it was unusual for the Democrats to request the army's help. Accompanied by two junior

9. *Ibid.*, 296; Sheridan to Belknap, January 8, 1875, in *Senate Executive Documents*, 43rd Cong., 2nd Sess., No. 13, p. 28.

10. Lonn, *Reconstruction in Louisiana*, 296.

officers, de Trobriand followed the Republican and Democratic politicians into the house, where his "entrance was saluted by general applause." At Wiltz's urging, de Trobriand ordered the lobby cleared of everyone who had no official business in the capitol, but he made no attempt to unseat the speaker. Acknowledging another round of applause, de Trobriand left the chamber. Pleased with their handiwork, the Democrats proceeded to consider other legislative business.[11]

Meanwhile, Governor Kellogg asked de Trobriand to remove the Democrats who, he claimed, had been illegally seated. De Trobriand replied that he could only consider such a request in "written and explicit orders." Pulling pen and paper from his desk, Kellogg wrote two similar notes, one to de Trobriand and the other to General Emory. The governor requested that the army "clear the hall and State-house of all persons not returned as legal members of the house of representatives by the returning-board of the State." De Trobriand decided to wait until Emory gave him corroborating orders before he went to the legislature again.[12]

At the Custom House, Emory considered Kellogg's note for a moment, then crossed the room and asked Sheridan to advise him on a course of action. Sheridan read Kellogg's note and replied "were I the Department commander I would not hesitate to comply with the requisition of the Governor." Furthermore, Sheridan pointedly "suggested" that Emory should warn de Trobriand "that no member of the State Legislature returned as such by the returning board" should be removed from his seat. Emory incorporated Sheridan's suggestion into his orders.[13]

Armed with written orders from Emory and Kellogg, de Trobriand, after changing from civilian dress into his army uniform, reentered the house chamber. Supporting the colonel was a lieutenant who commanded a squad of soldiers carrying bayoneted rifles. De Trobriand's subaltern read the orders of both the governor and General Emory to the house. Wiltz protested against de Trobriand's mission and warned him that the Louisiana legislature was a legally constituted civil body and that the army would have to employ force if it wanted to remove any of the legislators. De Trobriand replied that he had his orders and his "only

11. Post [ed.], *Memoirs of de Trobriand*, 446–47; de Trobriand to AAG, Dept Gulf, January 6, 1875, in AGO File 3579 of 1874 (Microcopy M-666, reel 173), RG 94, NA.

12. Post [ed.], *Memoirs of de Trobriand*, 448; Kellogg to de Trobriand, January 4, 1875, in *House Reports*, 43rd Cong., 2nd Sess., No. 101, Pt. 2, p. 306.

13. The description of the conversation is based on Sheridan's testimony in the case of *Vaughn v. Sheridan, Emory, and de Trobriand*, undated, in Sheridan Papers; Emory to de Trobriand, January 4, 1875, in Post [ed.], *Memoirs of de Trobriand*, 448.

duty was to obey [them]." Accordingly, de Trobriand located each of the
five Democrats whose place had been challenged and asked them if their
election had been approved by the Returning Board. Each man replied
that he was a legal representative, but acknowledged that the Returning
Board had not authenticated his election. After giving a short speech de-
crying their removal, the five Conservatives were individually escorted
from the chamber by armed soldiers. In protest, the rest of the Democrats angrily stalked out of the legislature, leaving the house to the Republicans, who promptly elected Michael Hahn speaker and selected Republicans to fill the five vacant seats. The army had thwarted another
attempt by the Democrats to gain power in Louisiana.[14]

The Democratic press was predictably incensed by the army's actions
at the legislature. The New Orleans *Bulletin* called the expulsion of the
Conservatives "another outrage, planned and perpetrated against the
people of Louisiana" by the "outlaws of civilization"—the carpetbaggers.
The New Orleans *Times* observed that Louisiana had been ruled by
"musket and sword and central authority, and everybody knows it." The
Picayune judged that de Trobriand's action was "the most violent, the
most illegal, the most shameless act yet permitted by an administration
whose history is one of violence, illegality and shamelessness un-
paralleled in the history of any free government." However, the *Republican* chided the Democrats for calling the same soldiers "military des-
pot[s]" who had been so helpful to them earlier in the day.[15]

Obviously the Democrats had not been satisfied with holding one-half
of the seats in the house of representatives and had shown that they too
would use the army to their own advantage if the opportunity presented
itself. The Democrats could have bargained with the Republicans for two
of the five seats left vacant by the Returning Board. Had the bargaining
been successful, it would have given the Republicans an unsteady majority of one in the house. Instead of trying this or some similar negotiated
settlement, the Conservatives chose to attempt another *coup*. Predictably,
the attempt failed, but the rest of the nation viewed the Democrats as the
injured party in the fracas. Soon General Sheridan provided more fuel for
his critics, inciting their wrath anew against himself, Louisiana Republicans, and the Grant administration.

At 9:00 P.M. on January 4 Sheridan "assumed control over the Depart-

14. Sefton, *Army and Reconstruction*, 241; Post [ed.], *Memoirs of de Trobriand*, 449–50.
15. New Orleans *Bulletin*, New Orleans *Times*, New Orleans *Daily Picayune*, all dated
January 5, 1875; New Orleans *Republican*, January 7, 1875.

ment of the Gulf." (The *Picayune* wryly commented that this announcement meant "Sheridan's Cuba excursion has been temporarily post-
poned.") He informed Belknap that there was "in this State . . . a spirit of
defiance to all lawful authority, and an insecurity of life which is hardly
realized by the General Government or the country at large. The lives of
citizens have become so jeopardized, that, unless something is done to
give protection to the people, all security usually afforded by law will be
overridden."[16]

Sheridan's solution to Louisiana's "spirit of defiance" was a stiff dose of
his own bravado, tempered with his own certain logic, which was completely lost on most people of the day. Sheridan sent Belknap two telegrams recommending that stern measures by taken in Louisiana. The
telegrams immediately caused consternation throughout the country.
Sheridan claimed "that the terrorism now existing in Louisiana, Mississippi, and Arkansas could be entirely removed and confidence and fair
dealing established by the arrest and trial of the ringleaders of the armed
White Leagues." The little general recommended that if Congress or the
president declared the Leaguers "banditti, they could be tried by a military commission" and removed from politics.[17]

Sheridan made his intentions quite clear in these telegrams, which the
Democratic press immediately branded the "banditti" messages. He
would not act without authorization from Grant or Congress, but he was
recommending the same treatment for the White League's leaders as he
had recommended for the Indian chiefs of the warring southwestern
tribes.[18] The idea in each case was to supersede or bypass any form of
civilian courts. This could not be done without declaring martial law or
reinstituting military government, and President Grant was opposed to
both of these alternatives. Therefore, as harsh as his proposal may have
seemed, Sheridan actually had very few options left open to him. The use
of massive military reinforcements was out of the question. The time for
that way of dealing with the problem had passed, for the army was too
small and spread too thin. Moreover, the Grant administration did not

16. Sheridan to Belknap, January 4, 1875, in *Senate Executive Documents*, 43rd Cong.,
2nd Sess., No. 13, p. 21. At the same time, Sheridan informed McDowell that he was taking command of the Gulf Department: Sheridan to McDowell, January 4, 1875, in Sheridan
Papers.

17. Sheridan to Belknap, January 5, 1875 (two communications), in *Senate Executive
Documents*, 43rd Cong., 2nd Sess., No. 13, p. 23. See also Sefton, *Army and Reconstruction*,
242.

18. O'Connor, *Sheridan*, 327–28.

have enough support in Congress or throughout the nation to insist on an entirely military solution. On the other hand, Grant did not want to acknowledge defeat and simply allow the Democrats to overthrow the Kellogg government by the use of violence and intimidation. As Joe Gray Taylor has pointed out, Sheridan recognized that the civilian courts often had proven ineffective in trying cases under the Enforcement Acts, and the use of a military commission seemed to be the only practical alternative available. Some sort of continued military support was imperative if Kellogg was to remain in office.[19]

Sheridan's proposal for military trials, his banditti messages, and de Trobriand's interference in the legislature were condemned by most newspapers in the North and South and by many important men of affairs, both in and out of Congress. Louisiana's Democrats sent a resolution to Congress denouncing Sheridan, and many other legislatures followed suit. Similar legislative resolutions and memorials were prepared in Ohio, Tennessee, Arkansas, New York, Pennsylvania, New Jersey, Texas, and by the Rochester, New York, Board of Aldermen; the Baltimore, Maryland, City Council; and the governors of Ohio, Wisconsin, and Georgia. These resolutions were widely applauded across the country, indicating a great decrease in popular support for Grant's Reconstruction policies. A special public meeting was called at New York City's Cooper Institute, where such speakers as William Cullen Bryant, E. L. Godkin, William M. Evarts, Whitelaw Reid, and Charles A. Dana denounced Sheridan and the army. The New York *Times* compared Sheridan's actions to those of Oliver Cromwell during the Protectorate and called the banditti dispatch an unwarranted "blood-and-iron message." The *Times* was disappointed "that a very able graduate of West Point, and a soldier who has so gallantly and faithfully fought for the supremacy of the Constitution, should know so little of its requirements."[20]

But the criticisms of the New York *Times* were mild compared to the diatribes from the Louisiana press. The Shreveport *Times* said that Sheridan exhibited all the "brush instincts of the lowest class of Irish" and branded him with the epithet "Piegan H. Sheridan," a reference to the army campaign against the Piegans in Montana that nearly wiped out the

19. Taylor, *Louisiana Reconstructed*, 307.

20. Memorial of the Louisiana legislature, January 20, 1875, in *Senate Miscellaneous Documents*, 43rd Cong., 2nd Sess., No. 45, pp. 1–5; New York *Times*, January 6, 7, 8, 12, 14, 15, 16, 1875. See also Lonn's description of the nationwide reaction to the events in *Reconstruction in Louisiana*, 301–307, and Gillette's descriptions in *Retreat from Reconstruction*, 124–30.

tribe. Denying that there were any bandits or murderers in the White Leagues, the New Orleans *Bulletin* ironically predicted that the banditti messages might earn Sheridan a place as an "unsurpassed writer of fiction." The *Picayune* blasted Sheridan unmercifully, calling him a "mailed and booted ruffian" who failed to understand the "principles of American republicanism" and "whose only notion of power [was] the power of the sword."[21]

Despite these bitter tirades, Sheridan had his supporters, though it was difficult to find any in Louisiana outside of Kellogg, Packard, and their cronies. Demonstrating unusual boldness, the Republican editor of the Donaldsonville *Chief* defended Sheridan in an editorial. He had formed, wrote the editor, the "correct opinion of the state of society existing in Louisiana." Many persons in the North sent letters to Sheridan endorsing his policies. These missives undoubtedly bolstered his ego, and they indicate that he was still very popular outside the South. Secretary Belknap assured him that the "President and all of us have full confidence and thoroughly approve your course."[22]

However, in a special message to the U.S. Senate, Grant displayed less than complete confidence in his old compatriot. Grant tried to excuse Sheridan's and de Trobriand's actions, saying that there were unusual "circumstances connected with the late legislative imbroglio in Louisiana which seem to exempt the military from any intentional wrong in that matter." The president emphasized that the army had acted on Governor Kellogg's lawful request to remove "a body of unauthorized persons" from the house. Grant said that Sheridan had "suggested summary modes of procedure against them [the White Leaguers], which, though they can not be adopted, would, if legal, soon put an end to the troubles and disorders in that State." These were hardly words of unstinting support, but the president concluded that "If error has been committed by the Army in these matters it has always been on the side of the preservation of good order." The New York *Times* seemed to speak for most people in the country, however, concluding that, "if Federal troops are henceforth to play this important part in Louisiana politics, the least we can ask is that they should be placed under a commander who is able to

21. Shreveport *Times*, January 6, 9, 1875; New Orleans *Bulletin*, January 7, 10, 1875; New Orleans *Daily Picayune*, January 6, 8, 1875. See also New Orleans *Times*, January 6, 1875, Alexandria *Democrat*, January 6, 13, 1875.

22. Donaldsonville *Chief*, January 9, 1875. Many letters of support sent to Sheridan during January are filed in Sheridan Papers. Belknap to Sheridan, January 6, 1875, in *Senate Executive Documents*, 43rd Cong., 2nd Sess., No. 13, p. 25.

keep his head and his temper under control." Obviously, the events in Louisiana had greatly damaged the standing of the Grant administration in the public eye.[23]

Sheridan's actions and pronouncements continued to infuriate the Democratic press. Sheridan erroneously reported that the White League was "trying to make arrangements to surrender to the civil authorities, fearing to come under my jurisdiction." On the contrary, the White League was recalcitrant and unrepentant. The New Orleans *Times* indicated that Louisiana Democrats were just biding their time, waiting until the army was put back into "its proper subordinate relation toward civil authority." Furthermore, Sheridan reported to Secretary Belknap that since 1866 White Leaguers and other lawless individuals in Louisiana had committed thousands of murders—perhaps as many as 3,500—and that the perpetrators had gone unpunished in almost every case. The New Orleans *Times* concluded that Sheridan was unqualified to describe incidents that "he never saw, and to pronounce on questions with which he is wholly incompetent to deal." The *Picayune* derisively called Sheridan the "eminent author and statistician." The *Picayune* concluded that the puffy pronouncements Sheridan had made since his return to Louisiana had "shown . . . exactly what sort of a man Grant wanted in New Orleans, [and] we understand why Gen. Emory failed to give satisfaction." Subsequently Sheridan revised his estimate of the number of murders, setting the figure specifically at 2,141. He made this revision after receiving reports from some of his subordinate commanders, including Major Lewis Merrill.[24]

To no one's surprise, many of the murders listed in Sheridan's report had allegedly occurred in the Red River parishes, the district commanded by Major Merrill. Moreover, according to Merrill's latest information, several prominent north Louisiana Democrats had discharged many of their black employees who had voted for Republicans in the November election. Furthermore, Conservative leaders publicly announced that they planned to refuse to employ or sell goods to blacks who remained

23. Grant, message to the Senate, January 13, 1875, in Richardson (comp.), *Messages and Papers*, VII, 305–14. See also the excellent analysis of the president's message by Sefton, *Army and Reconstruction*, 245. New York *Times*, January 10, 1875.

24. Sheridan to Belknap, January 6, 1875, in Sheridan Papers; New Orleans *Times*, January 7, 11, 1875; Sheridan to Belknap, January 7, 10, 1875, in *Senate Executive Documents*, 43rd Cong., 2nd Sess., No. 13, pp. 25, 29–31; New Orleans *Daily Picayune*, February 16, January 16, 1875; Sheridan to George F. Hoar, February 8, 1875, in *House Executive Documents*, 44th Cong., 2nd Sess., No. 30, p. 298.

loyal to the Republican party. The Conservatives also pledged not to deal with planters or merchants who hired or traded with Republicans. Sheridan expressed his concern over Merrill's reports to Belknap and ordered the major to come to New Orleans for consultations.[25]

Merrill arrived in the Crescent City on January 26, and the next day he was seated before a congressional committee that had been sent to investigate the condition of affairs in the southern states and to deduce if there had been any improprieties in the Louisiana election of the previous November. The committee was composed of three Republicans, George F. Hoar of Massachusetts, chairman, William A. Wheeler of New York, William P. Frye of Maine, and one Democrat, Samuel S. Marshall of Illinois. The committee called on several civilians and army officers to relate their opinions and observations on conditions in Louisiana. Testifying before the visiting congressmen, Merrill reiterated his comments concerning the deplorable situation in northern Louisiana and contradicted Sheridan's statement that the White League had been cowed. Merrill said that the "State government has no power outside the United States Army, which is here to sustain it. . . . The White League is the only power in the State." As might be expected, the Shreveport *Times* condemned "Dog" Merrill's testimony, accusing him of lying in all particulars, except the fact that the army was protecting Kellogg's government.[26]

In contrast, the Shreveport *Times* complimented Colonel Henry Morrow on his testimony before Hoar's committee. Morrow told the congressmen (as he had reported previously to General Emory) that it was unnecessary for the army to station troops in northern Louisiana. Furthermore, Morrow believed the assurances of the "better class of people," who promised him that if the Democrats controlled the state, blacks would not lose any of their political rights. According to Morrow, the "universal sentiment" among the "better class" indicated that they would prefer to have a military government replace Kellogg, thus assuring that the state would be "fairly and honestly administered." But it was certainly debatable whether most Louisianians or most army officers

---

25. A list of the alleged murders is in *House Executive Documents*, 44th Cong., 2nd Sess., No. 30, pp. 458–544; Merrill to AG, Dept Gulf, January 11, 1875, in *Senate Executive Documents*, 43rd Cong., 2nd Sess., No. 17, p. 58; Sheridan to Belknap, January 16, 1875, in New Orleans *Republican*, January 19, 1875; Merrill to AG, Dept Gulf, January 22, 1875, in Dept Gulf, vol. 151/DSL, RG 393, NA.

26. Merrill, testimony, in *House Reports*, 43rd Cong., 2nd Sess., No. 261, Pt. 2, pp. 175–76, 179–81, 189–90; Shreveport *Times*, January 29, 30, 1875.

really wanted to have the Grant administration reinstitute a military government.[27]

Some of the officers, such as Morrow and Head, opposed military aid for Kellogg because they were Democrats, but others were simply tired of the thankless duty in Louisiana. For example, Lieutenant Lorenzo Cook of the 3rd Infantry told the congressional committee that he gladly would pay his own expenses if he were transferred to the Great Plains. "You would rather be among the Indians?" one of the congressmen asked. "I would rather be among the Comanches than among these igno- rant . . . priest ridden people," Cook replied, with some evident anti- Catholic bias. Frances Roe, wife of Lieutenant Fayette W. Roe of the 3rd Infantry, recorded in her memoirs that "the service for the officers has often been most distasteful. Many times they have been called upon to escort and protect carpetbag politicians of a very low type of manhood." In fact, the longer Reconstruction lasted in Louisiana, the more uncom- fortable most soldiers became. General Sherman told President David Boyd of Louisiana State University that he was glad Grant had "sent Sheridan to New Orleans instead of me."[28]

Uppermost in Sheridan's thoughts was the matter of deciding who should replace Emory as commander of the Department of the Gulf. Al- though he had annexed the department to his military division, Sheridan did not want to exercise command over the troublesome region any longer than was absolutely necessary. Sheridan had previously recom- mended Ranald Mackenzie for the position, perhaps as a compliment to the young colonel. However, several senior officers would have had to be bypassed in order to give him the assignment. Ultimately Sheridan real- ized that Mackenzie was too high-strung and impetuous to handle the Louisiana assignment effectively.[29]

Although he conceded that it was unwise to elevate Mackenzie to the command, Sheridan had definitely decided that Emory must be replaced. His was no "hasty and unsupportable appraisal of Emory's abilities." In- stead, Sheridan had correctly deduced that the secretary of war and the president were dissatisfied with Emory's performance. In 1866 Sheridan had recommended to Grant that Emory be retained on active duty. In

27. Morrow, testimony, in *House Reports*, 43rd Cong., 2nd Sess., No. 261, Pt. 2, pp. 197–98, 202–205; Shreveport *Times*, February 3, 1875.
28. Lorenzo Cook, testimony, in *House Reports*, 43rd Cong., 2nd Sess., No. 261, Pt. 2, p. 344; Frances M. A. Roe, *Army Letters from an Officer's Wife* (New York, 1909), 157; Sher- man to Boyd, February 18, 1875, in Sherman Letters/Boyd Papers.
29. Sefton, *Army and Reconstruction*, 244.

contrast, in 1875 Sheridan described Emory to Secretary Belknap as "a very weak old man, entirely unfitted for this place and [he] should be retired or relieved, and some good man sent here in his place." In Sheridan's opinion, Emory had become "uncertain and unsteady"—meaning that Emory no longer supported the Louisiana Republicans. Forcing the old officer to retire was "the best way to make the change," Sheridan decided. To replace him Sheridan considered Alfred H. Terry, but finally recommended Brigadier General Christopher C. Augur, commander of the Department of Texas.[30]

The importance of selecting a new departmental commander and the need to discuss "other matters," including the campaign against the Indians in the Southwest, prompted Sheridan to ask Belknap if he could come to Washington to confer with him and the president. Belknap approved the trip. Before leaving New Orleans on March 6, Sheridan cancelled the Mardi Gras carnival (scheduled for March 9), apparently fearing that the large and boisterous crowds might become violent.[31]

Four days later Sheridan met with President Grant at the White House. Grant concurred with Sheridan's choice of General Augur to replace Emory. Consequently, on March 11 Adjutant General Townsend notified Emory that he was relieved of his command. General Sherman suggested that Sheridan should divest himself of the Department of the Gulf, but Grant allowed him to retain control over the department indefinitely. Before returning to New Orleans, Sheridan planned to spend several days in New York City and Chicago.[32]

Meanwhile, on March 25 Augur arrived in New Orleans, and in a brief ceremony held at noon the next day, he assumed command. General Emory delivered a short speech to the assembled soldiers, officers, civilians, and reporters. The band of the 13th Infantry played martial airs while Emory personally introduced each officer to General Augur. Under what must have been emotional circumstances, Emory kept his composure. Bidding adieu to a few close acquaintances and Congressman William Wheeler, Emory left New Orleans on March 27. Colonel de

30. *Ibid.*; Sheridan to Grant, May 4, 1866, Sheridan to Belknap, February 9, 24, 1875, all in Sheridan Papers.

31. Sheridan to Belknap, March 4, 1875, Belknap to Sheridan, March 5, 1875, in AGO File 3579 of 1874 (Microcopy M-666, reel 173), RG 94, NA; E. Merton Coulter, *The South During Reconstruction, 1865–1877* (Baton Rouge, 1947), 299.

32. New Orleans *Republican*, March 11, 1875; Townsend to Emory, March 11, 1875, in Dept Gulf, vol. 151/DSL, RG 393, NA; Sherman's adjutant William D. Whipple to Townsend, March 11, 1875, Townsend to Sherman, March 13, 1875, both in AGO File 3579 of 1874 (Microcopy M-666, reel 173), RG 94, NA.

Trobriand and Captain Edward R. Platt (Emory's trusted adjutant for more than three years) were among the small party of officers who bade him good-bye at the depot.[33]

The press reaction to Emory's removal was mixed. The Democrats could not overlook the way that Emory's objective handling of numerous crises since 1872 had thwarted their grabs for power. On the other hand, the Conservatives commiserated with Emory because his removal came at the hands of the detested Sheridan. The Natchitoches *People's Vindicator* wrote that "Poor old Gen. Emory" had been "grossly and flagrantly maltreated" by his superiors. The New Orleans *Bulletin* pictured Emory as having been "snubbed by the President, insulted by Gen. Sherman, overslaughed by Sheridan, and doomed to attend the whistle-call of [Kellogg,] the most abject human being in Christendom." The *Bulletin* generously concluded that Emory had "left a favorable impression on all who bear in mind the stern will by which the army is ruled and the stringent orders which he, as a soldier, felt bound to obey." However, three other important Democratic newspapers (the Shreveport *Times*, Monroe *Ouachita Telegraph*, and Alexandria *Democrat*) did not print any messages of forgiveness or farewell.[34]

Strangely enough, the New Orleans *Republican* found itself agreeing with most of what the Democratic newspapers had written about Emory. Surprisingly, the *Republican* stated that if Emory "were a politician he might be a Conservative; being a soldier, he . . . [has done] his duty as a soldier, recognizing only the power of federal and State laws, and the wishes of superior officers." Above all, the *Republican* called Emory a "good soldier" and "a true gentleman" who had "been considerate of the opinions and desires of all."[35]

In Emory's opinion, Sheridan had abruptly and unjustly—even ruthlessly—terminated his command of the Department of the Gulf. Emory later told his lawyer that he had been "deprived of command for the mistakes of another," obviously meaning Sheridan. During the legislative crisis, Sheridan himself said that he was "willing to be held responsible for the acts of the military as conservators of the public peace upon that day." In any case, most observers placed the responsibility for the army's

33. New Orleans *Times*, March 26, 27, 1875; New Orleans *Daily Picayune*, March 28, 1875.
34. Natchitoches *People's Vindicator*, January 23, 1875; New Orleans *Bulletin*, January 29, March 13, 1875. See also New Orleans *Times*, March 26, 1875, New Orleans *Daily Picayune*, March 13, 1875.
35. New Orleans *Republican*, March 26, 1875.

action on Sheridan because he was the senior officer present.[36] Emory did not—perhaps he could not—admit that he was removed not for his part in the legislative wrangle, but for his failure to prevent the insurrection of September, 1874. Grant and Belknap were probably both sorry that the crisis reached the point on September 15 when Adjutant General Townsend virtually had to order Emory to take command of the soldiers in New Orleans. Once he arrived in New Orleans, Emory handled the dangerous situation satisfactorily. Although he remained in charge of the soldiers in Louisiana for three months following the insurrection, when Sheridan arrived it was almost a foregone conclusion that there would be a change in commanders.

Emory had persevered under intense pressure during more than three years of Reconstruction duty in the state with the most recalcitrant populace in the South. Prior to the September insurrection, he had done an adept job, skillfully maneuvering his troops and using his resources, maintaining Kellogg in office without persecuting McEnery. Although he maintained the peace after the insurrection, Emory was not as effective a commander as he had been before. The unusual exigencies of postwar Louisiana politics literally exhausted him, undoubtedly left him embittered toward Reconstruction, and unfortunately ruined any feelings of comradeship he had shared with Phil Sheridan during the Civil War. Eventually, Congress approved Emory's promotion to brigadier general. On July 1, 1876, after more than forty-three years of service, General Emory retired from the army.

36. Emory to James Emott, April 15, 1875, in Emory Papers; Sheridan to Belknap, January 8, 1875, in *Senate Executive Documents*, 43rd Cong., 2nd Sess., No. 13, p. 27. See also Sefton, *Army and Reconstruction*, 243.

CHAPTER XI

Augur and the 1876 Election

Christopher Columbus Augur and William Emory had seen service together in Louisiana under Banks during the Civil War. Consequently, Augur was no stranger to the state, though he had not been there since 1863. Augur began his military career in 1839, entering West Point as a cadet from Michigan, where his family had moved after his birth in New York in 1821. His class, which was graduated in 1843, produced thirteen generals, three for the South and ten for the North, including Ulysses S. Grant. After serving in the Mexican War and at various frontier posts, Augur was promoted to the rank of major in 1861 and appointed commandant of cadets at West Point. He spent most of the early months of the war at the Military Academy, impatiently waiting for field service. In 1862 Augur commanded a division under Banks in the Shenandoah Valley and was wounded at the Battle of Cedar Mountain. He recovered from his wound and accompanied Banks to Louisiana, where he directed the left wing of Banks's army at the siege of Port Hudson. In late 1863 Augur returned to the East, serving there as commander of the XXII Army Corps and the Department of Washington. By the end of the war Augur had attained the rank of major general of volunteers. After the war Augur successively commanded the Department of the Platte and the Department of Texas. Self-conscious about his balding head, Augur combed his hair to cover it and ostentatiously groomed his flaring and flourishing whiskers into one of the grandest hirsute displays in the officer corps. Sheridan, who had been his superior while Augur commanded the Department of Texas, considered him politically reliable. But by 1875 Augur was one of a growing number of senior officers who no longer supported the bygone Radical views on Reconstruction that had once dominated the thinking of the commanders of the five Military Districts. On April 4, 1875, a few days after Augur had assumed com-

Christopher C. Augur

mand of the Department of the Gulf, Sheridan returned to New Orleans to be on hand for a special session of the legislature.[1]

Governor Kellogg had called the special session to enable the legislature to consider the so-called Wheeler Compromise. Republican Congressman William A. Wheeler of New York had been serving with George F. Hoar's House subcommittee which was investigating the Louisiana election of 1874. In early February, Wheeler suggested an "adjustment" that would effectively establish a truce between Louisiana's antagonistic Republicans and Democrats by allowing the Democrats to regain all of the disputed seats in the legislature—and more besides—if they ceased trying to overthrow Governor Kellogg and permitted him to serve the remainder of his term. Before General Emory had left Louisiana, even he had talked to Wheeler about devising some sort of truce for Louisiana's warlike politics, urging the congressman to find a solution beneficial to all concerned, including the Grant administration. As Wheeler devised it, George Hoar's congressional investigating committee would determine the number of new Democrats in the house, based upon a reexamination of the election returns. Wheeler's adjustment implied from the outset that the Democrats would be given a majority in the house and the right to pick the speaker, which had been their twin objectives in January when Colonel de Trobriand had intervened on behalf of the Republicans.[2]

Sizable blocks in each party continued to oppose a political settlement, but eventually the Democrats saw advantages in Wheeler's proposal. The compromise might remove Louisiana from the national spotlight and thus reduce the consistent support that the Grant administration had given to Kellogg. Some Conservatives had been on the fringes of political power for too long: the obvious fact that they would hold office and control the house encouraged the Democrats to accept adjustment. Moreover, some Democrats realized that the house had the power to initiate impeachment proceedings against a governor. Although such an action would violate the compromise, some farsighted Conservatives probably anticipated the likelihood of impeachment occurring several months after they were comfortably in control of the house. Despite the

---

1. Warner, *Generals in Blue*, 12; New Orleans *Bulletin*, April 6, 1875.
2. Emory to James Emott, April 15, 1875, in Emory Papers; Lonn, *Reconstruction in Louisiana*, 361–79. See also James T. Otten, "The Wheeler Adjustment in Louisiana: National Republicans Begin to Reappraise Their Reconstruction Policy," *Louisiana History*, XIII (Fall, 1972), 356–66.

logic of these arguments, John McEnery and former New Orleans mayor Louis Wiltz opposed Wheeler's arbitration, and the Shreveport *Times* and the New Orleans *Bulletin* both disapproved of the plan. On the other hand, the *Picayune* favored compromise because it would redress "the violent interference of Gen. Sheridan" in Louisiana politics. Many Republicans were reluctant to endorse any compromise, believing that it was unnecessary to give anything to the Conservatives. Overcoming P. B. S. Pinchback's resolute opposition, Kellogg persuaded a majority of Republicans to support adjustment as a way to ensure the stability of the government for the remaining two years of his term.[3]

In mid-March Hoar's committee met in New York to examine the returns of the Louisiana election of 1874 and specify the terms of the settlement. The committee certified the election of sixty-three Democrats and forty-seven Republicans in the house, but it did not tamper with the composition of the senate, where twenty-seven Republicans outvoted nine Democrats. Governor Kellogg may have been surprised by the size of the majority awarded to the Democrats in the house, but he supported the compromise nonetheless. General Sheridan, feigning disinterest, waited expectantly, suspicious of the practicality and advisability of the unusual arrangement. On April 15 the house overwhelmingly approved the Wheeler Compromise by a vote of eighty-nine to eighteen. The senate followed suit two days later, by a vote of thirty-three to three. The Democrats sealed the adjustment but refused to renominate Louis Wiltz as speaker of the house. Instead, they chose E. C. Estilette, a Democrat who received Governor Kellogg's support.[4]

Shortly after the senate approved the compromise, General Sheridan left New Orleans, and the Democratic press chorused "good riddance" at his departure. The "Shenandoah rough-rider" (as the New Orleans *Bulletin* called him) had left more bitterness in the wake of his second tour of duty in Louisiana than he had after the first. Sheridan had expressed his low opinion of Louisianians in his banditti despatches, and the state's white Democrats viewed him with a combination of hatred and fear, for the general was a man who had no sympathy for their goals.[5] Acceding to the wishes of President Grant, Sheridan had gone to New Orleans,

3. Shreveport *Times*, January 29, 1875; New Orleans *Bulletin*, February 6, March 23, 1875; New Orleans *Daily Picayune*, February 24, April 10, 1875.

4. New Orleans *Bulletin*, April 13, 1875; Taylor, *Louisiana Reconstructed*, 308–309.

5. Sheridan to Kellogg, Sheridan to E. O. C. Ord, both dated April 16, 1875, in Sheridan Papers; New Orleans *Daily Picayune*, March 13, May 22, 1875; New Orleans *Bulletin*, April 2, 1875.

although he disliked the idea of a second tour of duty in the Bayou State. Subsequently, he had handled the situation there according to his own views on Reconstruction, which had remained essentially unchanged since 1867, but he had been unable to bend the political forces in Louisiana to his will. By 1875 the Democrats in Louisiana were much stronger than they had been in the 1860s. There were many Conservative city councilmen, mayors, police jurors, sheriffs, legislators, and many more registered Democratic voters. Sheridan found that it was very difficult to carry out a governmental policy when a substantial portion of the state's population was opposed to that policy, no matter how just it might be. Sheridan, Emory, and Augur did not have enough soldiers to police the entire state, and the army could no longer provide adequate protection for Louisiana's Republicans. The president was finding it impossible to continue the old interventionist Reconstruction policy in the South without the support of the majority of the elected officials, newspapers, citizens of the northern states, and the army officers responsible for enforcing the policy.

Following the Wheeler Compromise and Sheridan's departure, an unnatural calm, lasting several months, settled over Louisiana. Adding to this quietude was the resignation of George Williams as U.S. Attorney General. Williams had been one of Kellogg's primary supporters in the national government, frequently advocating the use of the army to sustain the Republicans in Louisiana. His successor, Edwards Pierrepont, was disinclined to act as "Secretary of State for Southern affairs" and mainly devoted his attention to the increasing number of cases of corruption involving members of the Grant administration. Williams' retirement, coupled with the Wheeler adjustment, afforded General Augur a leisurely introduction to his duties as commander of the Department of the Gulf, which remained attached to Sheridan's Military Division of the Missouri.[6]

The apparent settlement of the "Louisiana question" prompted the reduction of troop strength in the state. In early May, acting on Sheridan's orders, Captain Frederick Benteen's troop of the 7th Cavalry returned to frontier duty in Dakota Territory. Two weeks later the seven companies of the 22nd Infantry that had been sent to Louisiana following the insur-

---

6. The phrase "Secretary of State for Southern affairs" cited in William B. Hesseltine, *Ulysses S. Grant, Politician* (New York, 1935), 374.

Louisiana, 1876

rection of September, 1874, were returned to their regular duty stations in New York and Michigan.[7]

Augur saw this as an opportune time to take some trips. First, he made a tour of his department, inspecting soldiers and barracks at Jackson, Mississippi; Little Rock, Arkansas; and Shreveport. He later traveled to San Antonio to visit his family, which had not moved to Louisiana, and to Chicago, where he attended the wedding of General Sheridan and Irene Rucker. (The Shreveport *Times* said that it wished the newlyweds "many little banditti.")[8]

By June the summer fever season was close at hand, and Augur prepared to send the soldiers out of New Orleans. Augur had no trepidations about moving his troops to Mississippi in the summer of 1875. He must have known that the year before Emory had left New Orleans virtually without military protection, but the political situation was different one year later. The White League had been inactive, and the Democratic politicians appeared to be satisfied with the provisions of the Wheeler Compromise. Consequently, in July Sheridan permitted Augur to send the Crescent City garrison to Holly Springs for the summer encampment. Augur decided that it was unnecessary to move the soldiers from the other posts in Louisiana. After seeing the troops off, Augur went on leave to visit his family in San Antonio. He was reluctant to send his family to New Orleans since there was an outbreak of yellow fever. Therefore, he decided to take them to his home in Ogdensburg, New York.[9]

On November 6 Augur returned to Louisiana and ordered the soldiers at Holly Springs to occupy their regular positions at New Orleans. The year before, Emory's command had comprised 1,998 soldiers distributed at nine posts, but by November, 1875, Augur had only 921 officers and men under his command at eight posts (counting New Orleans and Jackson Barracks as one garrison). By comparison, there were 575 soldiers in South Carolina, 480 in Virginia, 311 in Georgia, 293 in Florida, 247 in North Carolina, 210 in Tennessee, 178 in Mississippi, and 89 in Arkansas. Augur's soldiers were inactive during the early weeks of 1876. The

7. AAG Richard C. Drum to CG, Dept Gulf, April 28, 1875, in Dept Gulf, vol. 151/DSL, RG 393, NA; SW, "Annual Report, 1874–1875," pp. 84–85.

8. Augur to AAG, MilDivMo, April 29, May 7, 1875, in Dept Gulf, vol. 141/DSL, RG 393, NA; Shreveport *Times*, June 20, 1875.

9. Sheridan, endorsements, July 8, 1875, on the medical report by Dr. V. B. Hubbard to Augur, in Dept Gulf, Letters Recd, Augur to Lt. Jacob A. Augur, August 1, 1875, in Dept Gulf, vol. 141/DSL, both in RG 393, NA; Augur, report, September 9, 1875, in SW, "Annual Report, 1875–1876," *House Executive Documents*, 44th Cong., 1st Sess., No. 1, p. 115.

state legislature convened on January 3 with none of the forebodings of violence that had been common in previous years.[10]

On February 28, near the end of the legislative session, Democrats in the house of representatives shattered the existing political tranquility. They succeeded, by a vote of sixty-one to forty-five, in impeaching Governor Kellogg and thus violated one of the cardinal provisions of the Wheeler Compromise. When it came, the move caught the Republicans off guard. If the senate failed to act on the impeachment before the legislature adjourned, the Democrats planned to claim that Kellogg was technically out of office, thus making Lieutenant Governor C. C. Antoine "acting governor"—duplicating the peculiar arrangement of Warmoth and Pinchback a few years before. Accordingly, the Republicans in the state senate demanded specific impeachment charges from the house. On the evening of February 28 the senate acquitted Kellogg on all charges by a vote of twenty-five to nine, allowing him to retain his precarious seat. The impeachment episode convinced Kellogg that he would not be a candidate for governor in the 1876 election.[11]

Within a few hours, however, everyone seemed to put aside the ill will created by the impeachment to celebrate the Mardi Gras. General Sheridan had canceled the Shrove Tuesday celebrations the previous year, and perhaps for that reason Mardi Gras day, February 29, 1876, was a particularly festive occasion. A few army units marched in the parades, and it was traditional for a squad of soldiers, disguised in cheerful costumes, to act as guards for Rex, the king of carnival. The make-believe royalty of Mardi Gras invited selected officers and their wives to attend the Rex and Comus balls. Since this was one of the most important social events in New Orleans, the invitations indicate that the hostility of some of Louisiana's prominent citizens toward the army had mellowed somewhat.[12]

For several weeks following Mardi Gras, Louisiana politics remained remarkably peaceful, and consequently, in April General Sheridan ordered the three remaining troops of the 7th Cavalry from the Department of the Gulf to Dakota Territory, where they were needed for a sum-

10. Post Returns, Post of New Orleans, November, 1875, in Records of the AGO (Microcopy M-617, reel 844), RG 94, NA; Post Returns, Jackson Barracks, November, 1875, in Records of the AGO (Microcopy M-617, reel 524), RG 94, NA; Monthly Returns, Dept Gulf, November 1874, November 1875, RG 393, NA; New Orleans *Daily Picayune*, January 4, 1876; SW, "Annual Report, 1875–1876," pp. 146–57.
11. Taylor, *Louisiana Reconstructed*, 310.
12. Edward King, *The Great South* (Hartford, Conn., 1879), 43; Roe, *Army Letters*, 154; New Orleans *Daily Picayune*, February 29, March 1, 1876.

mer campaign against the Sioux. With the departure of the cavalry, Augur gave orders discontinuing the District of the Upper Red River, which had been in existence since October, 1874. The exit of Lewis Merrill and his cavalry left Augur without any mounted troops serving in his department, a deficiency that Augur keenly felt in the 1876 election campaign.[13]

The first violent incidents associated with that campaign occurred in May near Coushatta. An unidentified gunman severely wounded Republican state Senator Marshall H. Twitchell and killed his traveling companion, George King, former Republican tax collector for Red River Parish. Twitchell's brother had been killed by unknown assailants in the same area two years earlier.[14]

A second incident frightened Republicans throughout the state and demonstrated that the army was unable (or unwilling) to protect Republicans at all times and in all places. Democrats in the little town of Bayou Sara, in West Feliciana Parish, had been threatening Republican officials for several weeks, hoping to force them out of office. In late February, responding to Republicans' request for help, General Augur had sent Company B, 13th Infantry, Captain Gustavus M. Bascom commanding, from Baton Rouge to Bayou Sara to ensure the safety of the officials. On May 11 a group of angry blacks killed Marx Aaronson, a white farmer who had whipped several Negroes responsible for butchering cattle on his land. Four days later white vigilantes from West Feliciana, cooperating with an armed posse of Mississippians led by the sheriff of Wilkinson County, hunted down Aaronson's killers, hanging two of them and killing several others in a shoot-out. Captain Bascom made no effort to stop the vigilantes or arrest the Mississippians. The white "bulldozers" took advantage of Bascom's apathy to ride through the parish threatening black voters and generally intimidating Republicans.[15]

Democrats justified the actions of the vigilantes, citing the violent acts that blacks supposedly had committed in the parish. However, Lieutenant Governor C. C. Antoine, himself a black, took exception to the Democrats' evidence and called upon General Augur to restore order.

13. Post Returns, Post of Shreveport, March–April–May, 1876, in Records of the AGO (Microcopy M-617, reel 1169), RG 94, NA; Dept Gulf, Journal of Events, pp. 82, 85, RG 393, NA.

14. New Orleans *Daily Picayune*, May 3, 4, 1876.

15. D. A. Weber to Kellogg, March 6, 1876, in Kellogg Papers; Lt. Colon Augur to CO, Bayou Sara, March 7, 1876, in Dept Gulf, vol. 115/DSL, RG 393, NA; New Orleans *Daily Picayune*, May 15, 16, 19, 1876.

Acting on Antoine's plea, Augur ordered Bascom to have patrols march through the parish and prevent any disturbances. Furthermore, Augur wanted Bascom to write a complete report on the situation in the Felicianas.[16]

Reporting as ordered, Bascom informed the departmental adjutant that perhaps as many as thirty blacks had been killed in the recent fighting. Bascom tried to excuse his own inaction with the claim that most of the disturbances actually had taken place in Wilkinson County, Mississippi, which he mistakenly assumed was outside his jurisdiction. Within a few days the New Orleans *Picayune* reported that the area around Bayou Sara was quiet for the moment. Augur believed these reports and decided that no additional military action was necessary, but he had been forewarned. The "bulldozing" at Bayou Sara indicated that the political campaign could become a violent one. The general had missed an opportunity to deal sternly with lawless vigilantes intent on violating the civil and political rights of Republicans.[17]

On June 1 Augur left for Chicago, where he planned to confer with General Sheridan concerning Louisiana matters. The evening before Augur departed, Governor Kellogg wrote Sheridan, informing him that President Grant and U.S. Attorney General Pierrepont had pledged to "enforce the laws and secure a fair election" for Republicans. Kellogg asked Sheridan to provide Augur with "all the assistance" he could and reminded Sheridan that "the Republicans of this state depend greatly upon you." Kellogg would have been pleased to know that Sheridan had anticipated his request. He had already ordered Augur "to prevent bloodshed and lawless violence."[18]

Upon returning from Chicago, Augur initiated his usual summer plans for the New Orleans garrison, relocating it as a precaution against yellow fever. The Crescent City had been quiet and free of any major disturbances, and Augur believed that it would remain peaceful during the campaign. General Sherman had given Augur permission to relocate his troops to safer ground if disease appeared to endanger their health. Au-

16. New Orleans *Daily Picayune*, May 17, 1876; Augur to C. C. Antoine, May 16, 1876, in Dept Gulf, vol. 115/DSL, RG 393, NA; Augur to Gustavus M. Bascom, May 16, 1876, in *House Reports*, 44th Cong., 1st Sess., No. 816, p. 738.

17. Bascom to AAG, Dept Gulf, May 16, 1876 (two communications), in *House Reports*, 44th Cong., 1st Sess., No. 816, pp. 738–39; Augur to Sheridan, May 17, 1876, in Dept Gulf, vol. 142/DSL, RG 393, NA.

18. Kellogg to Sheridan, May 31, 1876, in Sheridan Papers; Sheridan to Augur, May 16, 1876, in MilDivMo, vol. 4, RG 393, NA. These orders initially came from Sherman and Grant.

gur made no plans to move any garrisons other than the one at New Orleans.[19]

The wisdom of not relocating any of the other garrisons became evident when a riot occurred on June 17 at the Mount Pleasant Plantation, situated about two miles south of Port Hudson in East Baton Rouge Parish. The disturbance involved more than two hundred white vigilantes and most of the plantation's blacks. Soldiers were sent to restore order but only after the trouble was over. The bulldozers lynched five blacks and left them hanging from trees as a warning to other Republicans in the area. Augur ordered Colonel John Brooke to investigate the incidents, and Brooke sent Captain Bascom to Mount Pleasant. Bascom's pro-Democratic feelings were evident in his report. He blamed the violence on a militant black organization called the "Union Right Step Republican Club." Bascom, who admitted being on friendly terms with several Democrats in the Baton Rouge vicinity, tried to exonerate the bulldozers. The New Orleans *Times* naturally agreed with Bascom's findings, and the *Picayune* printed an editorial filled with compliments for the captain. In contrast, the New Orleans *Republican* complained about "the one-sided conduct of this officer [Bascom], who does not comprehend his duty," and advised the army to transfer him. Disregarding the *Republican*'s sound advice, Augur left Bascom in command of the company at Bayou Sara.[20]

As a result of the Mount Pleasant disturbances, Augur established a new military district in central Louisiana and Mississippi. He created the District of Baton Rouge, comprising six Louisiana parishes (East and West Feliciana, East Baton Rouge, St. Helena, Livingston, and Tangipahoa) and three Mississippi counties (Wilkinson, Amite, and Pike). He placed Colonel Brooke in command of the district. The Thibodaux *Sentinel* remarked that Brooke, "clad in a once honorable, but now prostituted uniform," would fulfill the Republicans' "design of terrorizing the State." Providing its usual counterpoint to these Democratic comments,

19. Sherman to Augur, April 21, 1876, in Christopher C. Augur Papers, Illinois State Historical Library, Springfield; Post Returns, Jackson Barracks, July, 1876, in Records of the AGO (Microcopy M-617, reel 524), RG 94, NA; Post Returns, Post of New Orleans, July, 1876, in Records of the AGO (Microcopy M-617, reel 844), RG 94, NA.

20. New Orleans *Daily Picayune*, June 20, 21, 26, 1876; New York *Times*, June 20, 1876; Bascom to AAG, Dept Gulf, June 19, 1876, in *Senate Reports*, 44th Cong., 2nd Sess., No. 701, vol. 3, pp. 2,114–115; Bascom, testimony before a congressional committee, in *House Reports*, 44th Cong., 1st Sess., No. 816, pp. 735–36; New Orleans *Republican*, June 25, 1876.

the New Orleans *Republican* concluded that, under Brooke's protection, "the Republicans of the disturbed region were to be afforded something like justice at last."[21]

Soon after Brooke took command of the Baton Rouge District, another violent incident occurred. On July 11 a group of armed white vigilantes tried to arrest Gilbert Carter, a Negro who, the whites claimed, had been plotting to kill several prominent Democrats in the vicinity of Bayou Sara. They shot and killed him when, supposedly, he tried to escape. Colonel Brooke decided to investigate the matter personally and found that there was no clear evidence implicating Carter in any conspiracy. Moreover, Brooke determined that the whites had scornfully refused to take their charges to the local sheriff or district attorney. Brooke ordered Captain Bascom to "prevent bloodshed" in the future and stationed Company C, 13th Infantry, in Clinton, Louisiana, to provide more protection for blacks in the district. But taken together, the Mount Pleasant riot and Carter's murder were the opening salvos in a campaign of terror, demonstrating the Conservatives' determination to win the election of 1876.[22]

Officially opening the electoral contest, the delegates to the Republican state nominating convention had gathered on June 28 in New Orleans. Confirming everyone's expectations, Governor Kellogg declined renomination. U.S. Marshal Stephen B. Packard and former Lieutenant Governor P. B. S. Pinchback were left as the chief contenders. The convention nominated Packard, who, as leader of the Custom House faction, was the Republicans' logical choice. A native of Maine, Packard was thirty-seven years old in 1876 and had served without distinction as a captain in the 12th Maine Volunteer Infantry during the Civil War. In 1864 he came to Louisiana with his regiment. He married a local woman, and after the war ended he opened a law office in the Crescent City. Packard quickly became influential in the Republican party and was appointed U.S. marshal for Louisiana in 1869, subsequently exercising power beyond the limits of his job. In 1876 Packard decided to secure the governorship and the official powers that went with the office. Caesar C. An-

21. Dept Gulf, Journal of Events, pp. 90–91, RG 393, NA; Thibodaux *Sentinel*, July 1, 1876; New Orleans *Republican*, June 25, 1876.

22. Bascom to AAAG, Dist of Baton Rouge, July 13, 1876, in *Senate Reports*, 44th Cong., 2nd Sess., No. 701, vol. 3, p. 2,619; Brooke to Bascom, July 11, 1876, in Dist of Baton Rouge, vol. 162/DSL, Dept Gulf, Journal of Events, p. 93, RG 393, NA.

toine, Kellogg's lieutenant governor, was renominated to balance the Republican ticket. In a move to assure the support of black voters, the convention also nominated black politicians for secretary of state and superintendent of education.[23]

On July 24 the Conservatives met in Baton Rouge to nominate a standard bearer. The most likely candidates were "Governor" John McEnery; David B. Penn, hero of Liberty Place and one-time "acting governor"; former New Orleans mayor Louis Wiltz; and former Confederate General Francis T. Nicholls. Wiltz led on the early ballots, but McEnery broke the deadlock by withdrawing his name and announcing his support for Nicholls. The convention delegates followed McEnery's lead and overwhelmingly nominated "all that was left" of General Nicholls, who had lost his left arm at the battle of Winchester and his left foot at Chancellorsville. The convention completed its business, nominating Wiltz for lieutenant governor and filling the lesser spots on the all-white ticket with other stalwart Democrats. Running on his glorious blood-stained war record, Nicholls proved to be an excellent candidate.[24]

After the political conventions and following the accustomed practice that General Emory previously had adopted, Augur left Louisiana on a combined business-pleasure trip to Washington, D.C., and New York. He met with his superiors at the War Department for a few days and subsequently spent the remainder of July and most of August in Ogdensburg, New York, visiting his family. While on leave, Augur's adjutants kept him informed of the situation in the department.[25]

In the next few weeks, there were no major disturbances, riots, or violent incidents, but the Democrats probably derived a psychological boost from Augur's absence. Although Augur gave the Republicans only lukewarm support, his presence in Louisiana during the summer and his close attention to the details of the campaign might have discouraged some of the Democratic intimidation. Meanwhile, the Democrats were girding themselves for the final push of the campaign during September and October. In fact, the Democratic "bulldozers" in East and West Feliciana, East Baton Rouge, Morehouse, and Ouachita parishes set to their

23. Taylor, *Louisiana Reconstructed*, 481–82. On Packard's life, see New Orleans *Times*, July 4, 1876.
24. Taylor, *Louisiana Reconstructed*, 482–83. Ezra J. Warner, *Generals in Gray: Lives of the Confederate Commanders* (Baton Rouge, 1959), 224–25.
25. Dept Gulf, Journal of Events, p. 92, RG 393, NA.

work with unaccustomed ferocity, making it plain that they planned to deliver the votes of their parishes to the Democratic column. White employers fired several of their black employees who refused to pledge their support for the Democratic ticket. Several minor incidents in his district prompted Colonel Brooke to ask for reinforcements, but the departmental adjutant replied that Brooke had to make do with what soldiers he had. Time was running out for most local Republican officeholders, and without strong reinforcements, the army was unable to stop the final sands from dropping to the bottom of the hourglass.[26]

Officially, at least, national policy regarding the protection of Republican voters and officeholders in the South remained unchanged. In fact, the U.S. House of Representatives buoyed President Grant's hopes when it passed a resolution confirming his authority to use any army troops "not engaged in subduing the savages on the Western frontier . . . for protecting all citizens without distinction to race, color, or political opinion in the exercise of the right to vote." Moreover, the newly appointed U.S. attorney general, Alphonso Taft, informed General Sherman that he expected the army to aid any U.S. marshals who were trying to protect voters in the South.[27]

Louisiana's Democratic newspapers bitterly attacked the national administration's plans to use the army in the election. For example, the Shreveport *Times* criticized the planned cooperation between Attorney General Taft and General Sherman, and suggested, as it had in the past, that the soldiers were supposed to be serving on the frontier, rather than in the South. Disregarding the "bulldozing" that had already occurred and purposely distorting the role the army was intended to play, the *Picayune* asserted that "the presence of the army is itself calculated to exercise an undue and unlawful influence upon the colored voter, and is practical, effective intimidation." Counterattacking the *Picayune*, the New Orleans *Republican* defended Grant's policy, concluding that "The presence of the entire army of the United States in Louisiana would not deprive any Democrat of voting just as he thought best." Obviously, the majority of white Louisianians were intent upon electing General Nicholls. Turning the *Republican's* statement on its head, it actually might have taken the

26. *Senate Executive Documents*, 44th Cong., 2nd Sess., No. 2, pp. 11–12, 22, 26, 28–29; AAG, Dept Gulf to CO, Baton Rouge, August 17, 1876, in Dept Gulf, vol. 116/DSL, RG 393, NA; Taylor, *Louisiana Reconstructed*, 486–87.

27. J. Donald Cameron to Sherman, August 16, 1876, in New Orleans *Daily Picayune*, August 17, 1876.

entire U.S. army to guarantee any Republican the privilege of voting as he thought best.[28]

Meanwhile, Sheridan ordered Augur to come to Chicago for a conference. General Sherman had authorized Sheridan to send several extra infantry companies to Louisiana, and Sheridan agreed to use the proffered soldiers. Meeting in the commodious rooms of Sheridan's headquarters, "Little Phil" and Augur formulated a plan intended to stop the Democrats from riding roughshod over the Republicans during the last few weeks before the election. Augur returned to New Orleans on August 31 and gradually implemented the plan, issuing orders that eventually sent army detachments to more Louisiana towns and precincts than had ever been garrisoned before a single election.[29]

The need for such a plan was evident. Augur had been back in New Orleans only a matter of hours when he received a report that a bushwhacker had murdered B. F. Dinkgrave, the former Republican sheriff and tax collector of Ouachita Parish. Although the Democrats claimed that Dinkgrave's murder was the result of a personal feud unrelated to politics, Dinkgrave had a reputation as a political organizer among Ouachita blacks, and his murder was probably politically motivated. Consequently, General Augur ordered Captain James T. McGinnis, acting commander of the post at Monroe, "to prevent collisions between opposing factions." Remembering Captain George Head's previous associations with Ouachita Democrats, Augur also instructed McGinnis to maintain "friendly relations with all parties, but be intimate with none." McGinnis subsequently reported that Monroe was temporarily tranquil.[30]

Discounting McGinnis' assurances, Governor Kellogg believed that the Democrats would commit additional murders, unless the army protected Republicans throughout northern Louisiana. The governor suggested that Augur station troops in DeSoto, Morehouse, and Catahoula parishes. The general agreed to Kellogg's suggestion, planned to locate detachments in Mansfield and Bastrop, and ordered a reliable officer

28. Shreveport *Times*, July 7, August 24, September 10, 1876; New Orleans *Daily Picayune*, August 25, 1876; New Orleans *Republican*, September 5, 1876.

29. Sheridan to Augur, August 28, 1876, Sheridan to Sherman, August 28, 1876, both in MilDivMo, vol. 4, RG 393, NA.

30. Lonn, *Reconstruction in Louisiana*, 432; Augur to Lt. Jacob Augur, September 4, 1876, in Dept Gulf, vol. 116/DSL, James T. McGinnis to AAG, Dept Gulf, September 10, 1876, in Dept Gulf, vol. 154/DSL, both in RG 393, NA.

(Captain Clayton Hale) to investigate the situation in Harrisonburg.[31]

Augur took steps to strengthen several other posts in Louisiana. More than one hundred recruits, who had recently arrived in New Orleans, were distributed among the garrisons at Baton Rouge, Natchitoches, Coushatta, and Pineville. Furthermore, Augur dispatched Company G, 16th Infantry, from Mount Vernon Barracks, Alabama, to Baton Rouge. During October, Augur arranged for Republicans in other towns to receive military protection. Detachments consisting of one officer and ten or fifteen enlisted men marched into the towns of Colfax in Grant Parish, Minden in Webster Parish, Franklin in St. Mary's Parish, Evergreen in Avoyelles Parish, and St. Martinville in St. Martin Parish. In each case, the detachment commanders understood that they were to remain in the towns until the balloting was finished on November 7.[32]

On top of these precautions, Governor Kellogg raised Republican spirits, announcing that Phil Sheridan planned to come to New Orleans. The little general had been ordered to supervise the protection of the state Returning Board after the election had been held. Kellogg urged Secretary of War J. Donald Cameron to send Sheridan to Louisiana as soon as possible. Kellogg believed that "the moral effect of his presence in the city will go very far towards preserving the public peace." However, General Sherman informed Augur that "Sheridan will not come to New Orleans unless it is a case of extreme urgency." Answering a question from a reporter for the New Orleans *Times* on the likelihood of Sheridan's assuming command, Augur said that there was "no probable truth in the rumor of General Sheridan's visit to New Orleans." In view of these conflicting reports, Republicans did not know what to expect, but considering Kellogg's assurances, they hoped that Sheridan would be sent soon. Perhaps the effect of his presence would be equal to that of a regiment of soldiers.[33]

31. Augur to Kellogg, September 21, 1876, in Dept Gulf, vol. 116/DSL, AAG, Dept Gulf to CO, Jackson, Mississippi, September 21, 1876, in Dept Gulf, vol. 142/DSL, both in RG 393, NA.

32. AAG, Dept Gulf to COs, Baton Rouge (September 27, 1876), Natchitoches, Coushatta, and Pineville (all dated September 28, 1876), in Dept Gulf, vol. 154/DSL, Augur to Kellogg, October 24, 1876, AAG, Dept Gulf to CO, St. Martinville, October 27, 1876, both in Dept Gulf, vol. 116/DSL, Augur to Brooke, October 27, 1876, in Dept Gulf, vol. 142/DSL, Dept Gulf, Journal of Events, pp. 98, 100, all in RG 393, NA.

33. New Orleans *Daily Picayune*, October 23, 1876; Kellogg to Cameron, November 1, 1876, Sherman to Augur, November 6, 1876, both in AGO File 4788 of 1876 (Microcopy M-666, reel 298), RG 94, NA; New Orleans *Times*, November 7, 1876.

Until "Little Phil" arrived, Augur was charged with the responsibility of ensuring a peaceful election campaign. Although post commanders had been ordered to prevent violence, they hesitated to challenge armed groups of Democrats who used violence and intimidation on a broad scale, especially in the parishes of East Baton Rouge, East and West Feliciana (all in the District of Baton Rouge), Morehouse, and Ouachita. Despite the fact that army garrisons had been established in each of these parishes, white vigilantes, or "bulldozers" as they were commonly called, terrorized local Republicans almost at will. By election day on November 7 many Republicans had been threatened, bullied, shot at, roughed up, or had had their property damaged or destroyed by Conservatives who believed that the election of Francis Nicholls would rescue their state from Republican misrule.[34]

Preelection violence was particularly fierce in the District of Baton Rouge. In fact, Colonel Brooke recorded more than fifty occurrences of politically inspired violence in East Feliciana alone between June and November. Following the election, Lieutenant William S. Davis, who had once been ambushed by vigilantes, testified that the parish was "overwhelmingly republican," but that most Republicans had been intimidated to such an extent that they were afraid to vote. If Republicans voted in East Feliciana, their ballots were not counted. Although East Feliciana had 2,127 registered black voters, not a single vote was recorded for Rutherford B. Hayes, the Republican presidential candidate, or for Stephen Packard, the Republican gubernatorial candidate. The murder of Ike Mitchell, one of Bayou Sara's most prominent black businessmen, undoubtedly had a petrifying effect on his friends and neighbors in West Feliciana. In an effort to dissuade the Democrats from using violence, Colonel Brooke provided pickets for Republican rallies and sent soldiers with federal marshals to arrest accused "bulldozers." Despite Brooke's efforts, the Democrats dominated the District of Baton Rouge in the election.[35]

The situation was just as chaotic in the northeastern part of the state, where Captain Clayton Hale tried to protect the Republicans in Ouachita

34. Taylor, *Louisiana Reconstructed*, 485–89, contrasts with the noticeably pro-Democratic view of the campaign in Lonn, *Reconstruction in Louisiana*, 431–37.

35. Brooke, testimony before a congressional committee, in *Senate Reports*, 44th Cong., 2nd Sess., No. 701, vol. 2, pp. 1,694–695, vol. 1, pp. iii–iv; Davis, testimony, in *Senate Executive Documents*, 44th Cong., 2nd Sess., No. 2, pp. 227–28; Bascom to AAG, Dist of Baton Rouge, October 3, 1876, Brooke to AAG, Dept Gulf, October 28, 1876, both in Dist of Baton Rouge, RG 393, NA.

and Morehouse parishes. Several different "mounted and armed organizations of white men" rode through the parishes, whipping blacks, breaking into and ransacking their homes, and disrupting Republican political rallies. The vigilantes told blacks to vote Democratic or not to vote at all. On at least six separate occasions during October and November, Hale dispatched army detachments to guard Republican campaign meetings. Hale usually designated his most dependable officer, Lieutenant Henry M. McCawley, to command the detachments. On one occasion twenty armed Democrats boldly rode into a Republican rally, and it was clear to McCawley that they "meant mischief." When the Conservatives tried to disrupt the convocation, McCawley personally challenged the most vocal Democrat to a fight, and subsequently the noise subsided. Hale himself attended a similar meeting just prior to the election. The visiting Democrats ummercifully heckled the Republican speakers. Drawing his sword, Hale threatened to order his soldiers to disperse the hecklers unless they remained quiet. The Democrats stopped their harassment and, when the rally ended, rode away, two abreast in a cavalry-style column under good discipline, openly displaying their weapons.[36]

Among the numerous forms of intimidation the Democrats used in Ouachita, murder was the most terrifying. On October 11 two masked white men killed Primus Johnson and wounded Eaton Logwood at the latter's farm located six miles north of Monroe. Both Johnson and Logwood were Negroes. Johnson had been an important Republican leader in the parish and had built a school for black children near Monroe. Lieutenant McCawley investigated the incident. Under the lieutenant's questioning, Logwood named the captain of a local vigilante group as one of the murderers. Hale severely criticized all of the local civil authorities in Ouachita for not taking charge of the case, especially indicating his lack of respect for the district judge ("a time-serving man, desirous of adapting his course to the changing political condition of the State") and the federal deputy marshal, whom the captain branded as "a Coward" who was "utterly worthless." The Donaldsonville *Chief*, a Republican newspaper, advised Republicans to take heed: Johnson's murder was proof that the Democrats were using every available means to win the election.[37]

---

36. Clayton Hale, testimony before a congressional committee, Henry M. McCawley, testimony, both in *Senate Executive Documents*, 44th Cong., 2nd Sess., No. 2, pp. 331, 333, 337; Hale, testimony, McCawley, testimony, both in *Senate Reports*, 44th Cong., 2nd Sess., No. 701, vol. 1, pp. 629–30, 247–48.

37. Hale to AAG, Dept Gulf, October 12, 1876, in Monroe *Ouachita Telegraph*, November 3, 1876; Donaldsonville *Chief*, November 4, 1876.

Although the intentions and tactics of the Democrats were obvious, General Augur had not ordered the soldiers at the summer encampment to return to New Orleans. The big city had been quiet, and therefore, Augur could have used these troops at other locations in the state. Eventually, toward the end of October, Augur decided to reestablish the garrison in the Crescent City to ensure that it would remain quiet during the election.[38]

Acting on the personal request of Governor Kellogg, Augur dispatched soldiers to several towns, including Delta and Tallulah in Madison Parish, Houma in Terrebonne Parish, and the West Baton Rouge Landing. On his own initiative Augur stationed soldiers in the towns of Port Hudson and Breaux Bridge. He attempted to show the flag in as many different locations as possible. By election eve on November 6, almost eight hundred officers and enlisted men had been sent to twenty-one towns and forty separate parish precincts outside of New Orleans, but by then the bulldozers had done their work.[39]

Reports from army officers across the state indicated that November 7, 1876, was one of the quietest election days in Louisiana history. Although there was virtually no violence at the ballot boxes, Democrats patrolled the roads in some parishes, especially near Baton Rouge and Monroe. Captain Hale said "that the town of Monroe . . . was encircled and picketed by armed men," who discouraged blacks from coming in to cast their ballots. Colonel John Brooke emphasized that most blacks in the Baton Rouge area had been so intimidated before the election that they were too scared to vote. Lieutenant William Gerlach, an army officer who had come to sympathize with the Democrats, claimed that he had not witnessed any intimidation of blacks by whites, but he acknowledged that some Conservatives had used various means to "coax" Negroes into voting for the Democratic ticket. Despite General Augur's effusive congratulations to his soldiers for their "good conduct and courtesy" on election day, the army obviously had been unable to prevent the Democrats from striking fear into black voters in several parts of Louisiana.[40]

38. SO No. 207, Dept Gulf, October 28, 1876, in SO, Dept Gulf, RG 393, NA.
39. Kellogg to Augur, November 4, 1876 (two communications), in Dept Gulf, Letters Recd, Augur to Kellogg, November 4, 1876, in Dept Gulf, vol. 116/DSL, all in RG 393, NA; SW, "Annual Report, 1876–1877," in *House Executive Documents*, 44th Cong., 2nd Sess., No. 1, pp. 99–100.
40. Augur to AAG, MilDivMo, November 7, 1876, in Dept Gulf, vol. 142/DSL, RG 393, NA; Hale, testimony before a congressional committee, in *Senate Executive Documents*, 44th Cong., 2nd Sess., No. 2, p. 336; Brooke, testimony, in *Senate Reports*, 44th Cong., 2nd Sess.,

It appeared that the Democrats had won a signal victory in the election of 1876. "The Carnival of Thieves, State and National, [was] at an End," trumpeted the Shreveport *Times*. Francis Nicholls' election seemed assured, and the New Orleans *Picayune* believed that Samuel J. Tilden, the Democratic presidential candidate, had undoubtedly carried Louisiana and the nation. But the New Orleans *Times* was reluctant to award the laurels of victory just yet and predicted that Tilden's winning margin would be very narrow. In contrast to the gloom of the *Times*, the New Orleans *Republican* was hopeful about Hayes's chances, encouraging all Republicans in the state to "Hold the Fort" and remain "Steady." The *Republican* warned that it was going to be "A Very Close Vote."[41]

So many conflicting and confusing elements attended the election of 1876 that a winner could not be named for almost four months. Even in an era without the benefit of computers and electronic mass communications, the results of a national election were usually known within a week's time. The initial results in 1876 indicated that Tilden undoubtedly had carried sixteen states, including his home state of New York, giving him a total of 184 electoral votes, only one shy of the amount needed for victory. On the other hand, Hayes had won in seventeen states, and he unquestionably deserved two of Oregon's three electoral votes, giving him a total of 165 electoral votes, twenty less than the number needed to win the presidency. But there were twenty disputed electoral votes. In addition to one disputed electoral vote in Oregon, all of the votes from Florida (four), South Carolina (seven), and Louisiana (eight) were contested. The election therefore hinged on the results in three southern states (which still had Republican governments), where each party was claiming to have won. In Oregon the Democrats forced one of Hayes's electors to resign when he admitted that he was a Post Office employee since persons holding federal jobs were ineligible to serve as electors. The man who had finished second was a Democrat, but Oregon's voters had overwhelmingly supported Hayes, and within a short time some of Tilden's supporters and several Democratic newspapers conceded that Hayes deserved the contested electoral vote in Oregon. If Hayes could obtain the remaining nineteen votes from the southern states, he would be elected.

No. 701, vol. 2, p. 1696; William Gerlach to Mayor of Baton Rouge Leon Pastremski, November 16, 1876, in *House Reports*, 44th Cong., 2nd Sess., No. 156, Pt. 1, p. 75.

41. Shreveport *Times*, November 8, 1876; New Orleans *Daily Picayune* and New Orleans *Times*, both dated November 10, 1876; New Orleans *Republican*, November 9, 1876.

In the first hours following the election even Hayes believed that Tilden had won, but in a matter of days he saw that victory was possible. Republican leaders, especially Zachariah Chandler, Grant's secretary of the interior, encouraged the governors of Florida, South Carolina, and Louisiana to hold their states for Hayes. The Republicans wanted authenticated election returns for their candidate sent to Washington as soon as possible. Meanwhile, northern and southern Democrats maintained their claim that Tilden had carried the unredeemed southern states.[42]

The furor over the electoral votes in the three former Confederate states made Grant realize that the army must protect the ballots against damage, tampering, or abduction. Consequently, on November 10 he directed General Sherman to order Augur "to preserve peace and good order and to see that the proper & legal boards of canvassers are unmolested in the performance of their duties." Furthermore, if Augur had any "suspicion of fraud . . . on either side it should be reported & denounced at once." Sherman promptly telegraphed the president's instructions to Sheridan, who relayed them verbatim to Augur. Moreover, Sheridan suggested that, under the unusual circumstances attending the contested election, Augur should gather most of his soldiers into New Orleans. Sheridan told Augur simply to ask for reinforcements if he needed them.[43]

Responding to Grant's orders, and acting on Sheridan's suggestion, Augur planned to assemble most of the troops in Louisiana in the Crescent City. As soon as the ballots were safe, Augur ordered Colonel Brooke to bring most of his soldiers from Baton Rouge to New Orleans, leaving only a small detachment at Clinton and one infantry company at Baton Rouge. Augur directed the commanders at Coushatta and Natchitoches to dismantle their posts "at once" and transport their garrisons to the Crescent City. The commander at Pineville was ordered to send one of his two companies to the capital. When completed, these movements left only two companies on duty in central Louisiana. During the next few days the army abandoned Alexandria, Shreveport, and

42. Keith I. Polakoff, *The Politics of Inertia: The Election of 1876 and the End of Reconstruction* (Baton Rouge, 1973), 201–210; T. Harry Williams (ed.), *Hayes: The Diary of a President, 1875–1881, Covering the Disputed Election, the End of Reconstruction, and the Beginning of Civil Service* (New York, 1964), 47.

43. Grant to Sherman, November 10, 1876, in AGO File 4788 of 1876 (Microcopy M-666, reel 298), RG 94, NA; Sheridan to Augur, November 10, 11, 1876, both in Dept Gulf, vol. 154/DSL, RG 393, NA.

Morgan City, and the garrison at Monroe was reduced to Captain Hale's lone company, the last one left in north Louisiana.[44]

To further ensure the safety of the Returning Board and to preclude the possibility of an insurrection in New Orleans, Augur drew on the resources of other states in his department. He ordered nine companies of the 16th Infantry to assemble in the Crescent City under Colonel Galusha Pennypacker, the regiment's commander. Infantrymen at Vicksburg, Columbus, Holly Springs, Jackson, and McComb, Mississippi; Mount Vernon Barracks, Livingston, Huntsville, and Mobile, Alabama; and Little Rock, Arkansas, boarded trains or steamers and rendezvoused in New Orleans. A reporter for the *Picayune* asked Augur if he believed that his force would be strong enough to maintain the peace. Stroking his whiskers and considering the question for a moment, the general "answered that it depended upon 'how belligerent the people were.'"[45]

By November 19 twenty-five companies of infantry from the 3rd, 13th, and 16th regiments (totaling 1,118 soldiers) had assembled in the New Orleans vicinity. The *Picayune* kept close tabs on the military arrivals, reporting to its readers that "New Orleans is beginning to assume a truly warlike appearance." Troops marched through the streets, mounted messengers maneuvered their horses in and out of the civilian traffic on Canal Street, groups of officers conferred in hotel lobbies, a detachment of U.S. Marines patrolled the riverfront, and "lumbering baggage wagons" transported military supplies to soldiers bivouacked in the city's parks. The *Picayune* concluded that the "very atmosphere breathed of the military."[46]

In spite of the thorough precautions Augur had taken, President Grant wanted Sheridan to command the troops in New Orleans. The president ordered his favorite general "to keep the peace and to protect the legal canvassing board in the performance of its duties," virtually the same orders he had given to Augur only a few days before. Reluctantly, even unwillingly, Sheridan bowed to the orders of his chief and prepared once

44. Augur to Brooke, November 9, 10, 1876, AAG, Dept Gulf to COs, Coushatta, Natchitoches, and Pineville, November 11, 1876, all in Dept Gulf, vol. 142/DSL, Dept Gulf, Journal of Events, pp. 107–110, RG 393, NA. See also Sefton, *Army and Reconstruction*, 248.

45. Dept Gulf, Journal of Events, pp. 108–110, in RG 393, NA; New Orleans *Daily Picayune*, November 11, 1876.

46. Monthly Returns, Dept Gulf, November 1876, in Dept Gulf, RG 393, NA; New Orleans *Daily Picayune*, November 12, 13, 1876.

again to enter the perilous labyrinth of Louisiana politics. Sheridan left his Chicago headquarters on November 13 and detrained in New Orleans two days later. The little general was now forty-five years old, and since the slashing Shenandoah Valley campaign, he had gained considerable weight, making him appear shorter than his five feet, five inches. A correspondent for the *Picayune*, who had met Sheridan the previous year, described him as "a smiling red-faced man, of a short cut Herculean style of architecture, and very . . . stout. . . . He would make a severe trial of any Fairbanks scale in the city." Remembering Sheridan's past adherence to Radical Reconstruction policies, the newspaperman believed that the general's cranium was "just the sort of a head calculated to hold an idea very tenaciously, and which would require an Archimedian battering ram to reduce into submission." The Shreveport *Times* disdainfully greeted the news of Sheridan's arrival. The *Times* accused Sheridan of using "the Army to Assist in the Infamous Work" of the Republican Returning Board. In a biting editorial, the *Times* claimed that the Radical Republicans had been doing the devil's work in Louisiana for many years and that the army had been acting as the agents of the Fallen Angel, protecting a Republican governor, who, like his Radical compatriots in the North, "dared not show all of . . . [his] cloven foot." [47]

According to the *Picayune*, Sheridan's presence "Phil-ed" Louisiana Republicans with courage, and outwardly the general indicated no dissatisfaction with the administration's Reconstruction policy. Actually, Sheridan was quite uncomfortable about having been asked to play the role of savior (or devil) in Louisiana politics. Augur had skillfully marshaled most of three infantry regiments in New Orleans, and he appeared to have the situation under control. On November 16, the day after he arrived, Sheridan wired Adjutant General Edward Townsend that there was "very little excitement [and] no appearance of any trouble." A few days later, Sheridan informed Sherman that there was no need for him to remain in Louisiana, and he asked to leave before the Returning Board ruled on the outcome of the election. (The only Democrat on the board had resigned. He was not replaced, and no one doubted that the board would eventually declare the Republicans victorious in Louisiana.) However, Sherman replied that both the president and Secretary of War Cameron would "feel more comfortable" if Sheridan remained until "the canvass

---

47. Grant to Sheridan, November 11, 1876, in AGO File 4788 of 1876 (Microcopy M-666, reel 298), RG 94, NA; New Orleans *Daily Picayune*, January 1, 1875; Shreveport *Times*, November 17, 1876.

[was] completed." Disgruntled, Sheridan nevertheless abided by his superiors' wishes and waited for another opportunity to ask to leave Louisiana.[48]

Since Sheridan's arrival, James Madison Wells had held several meetings of the Returning Board without interference from the Democrats. At Grant's urging, more than thirty "gentlemen of both political parties" had arrived in the city to "observe the conduct of the canvass." These so-called visiting statesmen included Republicans John Sherman, James Garfield, and Lew Wallace. Sometimes a few of the "visiting statesmen" attended the meetings of the Returning Board, which had called witnesses to testify concerning alleged Democratic bulldozing, and the witnesses' testimony appalled the northern politicians. Senator John Sherman wrote his wife, "We have already heard enough to show in some of the Parishes the most extraordinary system of intimidation & violence" in use by the Democrats. Sherman concluded that "the whole tone and elements of society are so different here and in Ohio that no one can realize the truth of what is here plain and palpable." Sherman's colleague, Ohio Congressman James A. Garfield, wrote Rutherford Hayes that he had "no doubt" about the "justice of our claim" to Louisiana's electoral votes.[49]

The Natchitoches *People's Vindicator* stridently protested the army's continuing protection of Kellogg and Grant's orders that had "nationalized" Louisiana, and menacingly asked, "Shall it be war or Tilden?" In fact, many politicians and newspaper editors of both parties were concerned about the possibility of a second civil war in late 1876 and early 1877. Angry Democrats, dismayed over the disputed election, were threatening to force Tilden's inauguration by sending thousands of armed men to Washington. Demonstrating his concern over this threat, President Grant ordered several additional army units into the nation's capital.[50]

48. New Orleans *Daily Picayune*, November 15, 1876; Sheridan to AGO, November 16, 1876, Sheridan to Sherman, and reply, November 22, 1876, in AGO File 4788 of 1876 (Microcopy M-666, reel 299), RG 94, NA.

49. Grant to Sheridan, November 11, 1876, in AGO File 4788 of 1876 (Microcopy M-666, reel 298), RG 94, NA; John Sherman to Cecilia Sherman, November 20, 1876, in John Sherman Papers, Manuscript Division, Library of Congress; James A. Garfield to Rutherford B. Hayes, November 23, 1876, in Rutherford B. Hayes Papers, 1876–1877, Manuscript Division, Library of Congress (microfilm copy, in Rutherford B. Hayes Library, Fremont, Ohio). See also Ralph J. Roske, "Visiting Statesmen in Louisiana, 1876," *Mid-America*, XXXIII (April, 1951), 89–102.

50. Natchitoches *People's Vindicator*, November 18, 1876; William A. Russ, Jr., "Was There a Danger of a Second Civil War During Reconstruction?" *Mississippi Valley Historical Review*, XXV (June, 1938), 39–58.

Political tensions were evident in Louisiana's capital as well, and violence was more likely to occur in New Orleans than Washington. Notwithstanding this possibility, Sheridan wired Sherman, "There is no military necessity for my presence here. It is not fair to Augur and I doubt if it is fair to me." Plainly, Sheridan wanted to leave Louisiana. After meeting with Secretary of War Cameron, Sherman gave Sheridan permission to return to Chicago. Sheridan thankfully made his plans to leave New Orleans within twenty-four hours and soothingly informed Adjutant General Townsend that the "canvass will give Louisiana to Hayes."[51]

Sheridan's last assignment in Louisiana during Reconstruction had been unproductive. There was little reason for his presence since Augur had blanketed New Orleans with soldiers, and Sheridan had waited impatiently for permission to leave virtually from the day he had arrived. After his departure on November 26, Augur once again was accountable for keeping the peace.[52]

A correspondent for the *Picayune* reported that Augur had "no apprehension of any disturbance" in Louisiana. Nevertheless, Augur ordered his regimental commanders to keep their soldiers under arms and prepared for any eventuality. Specifically, Augur directed Colonel de Trobriand and Colonel Brooke to maintain a close guard over the members of the Returning Board. Meanwhile, the soldiers and politicians waited for Wells to announce the results of the canvass.[53]

The Returning Board reached its decision in early December. Wells and his associates (dubbed the "Overturning Board" by the *Picayune*) nullified or discarded the returns from selected precincts in twenty-four parishes, throwing the election to Packard and Hayes. John Sherman and other visiting Republican politicians concurred in the Board's decision, stressing the evidence of widespread intimidation before the election that had prevented many blacks from voting or had persuaded some blacks to vote for the Democratic ticket. T. B. Tunnell, Jr. has argued that thousands of the state's blacks voluntarily abandoned the party of Lincoln because the Republicans had been corrupt and had failed to deliver on all of their political promises. He rejects most of the charges that the Democrats used fraud and intimidation against Republicans in the 1876 cam-

51. Sheridan to Sherman, November 24, 1876, Sherman to Sheridan, and Sheridan to AGO, both dated November 25, 1876, all in AGO File 4788 of 1876 (Microcopy M-666, reel 299), RG 94, NA.

52. New Orleans *Daily Picayune*, November 27, 1876.

53. *Ibid.*; Lt. Frank Baker to Brooke, November 27, 1876, in Records of HQ, 3rd Infantry, RG 391, NA.

paign. However, although conflicting in many particulars, the overwhelming weight of the military correspondence and the testimony given by men of both parties to congressional committees indicated conditions of unrest and violence in several parishes. Undoubtedly, Louisiana Republicans had found it difficult to organize an effective campaign—several of their black leaders had been killed, and members of the rank and file had been threatened with loss of their jobs or their lives.[54]

Answering the Returning Board, the Democrats cried "foul" and "fraud," and refused to abide by the Board's decision. Francis Nicholls, following the example of John McEnery in 1872, claimed to have been elected and planned to be inaugurated in January. Rejecting Nicholls' claims, Kellogg declared that Packard was the state's next governor and certified the Hayes electors. Reviving his dormant governorship, John McEnery proclaimed that Nicholls had carried Louisiana and forwarded to Washington a separate set of certificates giving the state's electoral votes to Tilden.

To the dismay of historians, the results of the election of 1876 will never be known to everyone's complete satisfaction. Contested elections and dual governments were familiar to Louisianians, but they could not be tolerated by the nation. Regardless of who certified the election returns or how they had been obtained, Congress had the responsibility to count the electoral votes of the individual states. Under the unique conditions which existed after the 1876 election, Congress would have to determine which set of returns to accept not only from Louisiana but from South Carolina and Florida as well, for rival officials in each of those states had sent multiple sets of electoral certificates to Washington.

In the meantime, Augur had to contend with a more immediate threat to civil order, one that was familiar to his subordinates, Colonels de Trobriand, Floyd-Jones, and Brooke. The state legislature was scheduled to convene in January, and it appeared that the Democrats would either challenge the Republicans for control of both houses or establish a rival legislature of their own. Augur telegraphed Sheridan, asking what to do when the legislature met. At this point even Sheridan hesitated to issue

54. New Orleans *Daily Picayune*, November 23, 1876; Taylor, *Louisiana Reconstructed*, 493; John Sherman and others to Grant, December 6, 1876, in *Senate Executive Documents*, 44th Cong., 2nd Sess., No. 2, pp. 7–8. See also Harry Barnard, *Rutherford B. Hayes and His America* (Indianapolis, 1954), 316–17. T. B. Tunnell, Jr., "The Negro, the Republican Party, and the Election of 1876 in Louisiana," *Louisiana History*, VII (Spring, 1966), 101–116. Polakoff accepts Tunnell's argument in *Politics of Inertia*, 183. See also William A. Dunning, *Reconstruction, Political and Economic, 1865–1877* (New York, 1907), 320–21, who claims that Louisiana properly belonged in the Democratic column.

orders on his own, and he passed Augur's question on to Sherman, who placed the matter before Secretary of War Cameron. Mindful that Governor Kellogg had not yet asked for assistance, Grant, Cameron, and Sherman reiterated their standing orders, directing Sheridan to tell Augur to "prevent violence, and keep the peace." Sheridan dutifully forwarded the orders to Augur, who then faced his greatest challenge as commander of the Department of the Gulf.[55]

55. Augur to Sheridan, December 30, 1876, Sherman to Cameron, December 31, 1876, Sherman to Sheridan, December 31, 1876, Sheridan to Augur, January 1, 1877, all in Justice Dept Letters (Microcopy M-940, reel 3), RG 60, NA; Sheridan to Sherman, December 30, 1876, in AGO File 4788 of 1876 (Microcopy M-666, reel 299), RG 94, NA.

CHAPTER XII

The Troops Are Not
a Political Engine

On New Years' Day, 1877, Louisiana's Democratic and Republican legislators convened separately and organized two different legislatures. Taking a necessary precaution, General Augur stationed several companies of infantry in the Orleans Hotel, which was adjacent to the state house, but he assigned no units to occupy the capitol itself. In addition, the general had posted soldiers at several locations throughout the city and had alerted them to be on guard against violence. Representatives of each party were prepared to continue the spectacle of dual governments. Cheering partisans surrounded St. Patrick's Hall, which temporarily housed the Democratic legislature. Several blocks away, meeting under the protection of the police and U.S. infantrymen, the Republican legislature passed an appeal for continued military protection, and Governor Kellogg sent it to President Grant.[1]

A few days later Kellogg addressed the president again, asking him to recognize Packard as the legitimate governor upon his inauguration and requesting that Augur be instructed to guard the new Republican administration, which was to take office on January 8. Grant's reply must have sent a shiver down the collective spines of all Louisiana Republicans. The president wrote that he felt "constrained to decline your request for the aid of troops to inaugurate the new State Gov't." Grant's caution was partly due to the fact that the outcome of the national election remained in doubt. Grant reminded Kellogg that Congress was investigating the Louisiana situation, and that in the meantime federal troops would "suppress violence if any should take place." But for the first time during Reconstruction, the president overtly and promptly had refused to recognize the Republican claimant to the governorship in Louisiana. Actually, Grant had been less inclined to order troops to intervene in southern poli-

1. Augur to Sheridan, January 4, 1877, in Dept Gulf, vol. 116/DSL, RG 393, NA; New Orleans *Times*, January 2, 1877; Kellogg to Grant, January 1, 1877, in Justice Dept Letters (Microcopy M-940, reel 3), RG 60, NA.

tics after the incident at the Louisiana legislature in January, 1875. Recently he had tended to take the advice of his secretary of state, Hamilton Fish, who opposed any help to Kellogg or Packard and preferred to have the army in Louisiana maintain the peace between rival parties. On the other hand, Secretary of War Donald Cameron and Secretary of the Interior Zachariah Chandler strongly urged Grant to recognize Packard and provide him with federal protection before the results of the presidential election were known.[2]

Meanwhile, in keeping with Grant's intentions and with the dual inaugurations of Packard and Nicholls forthcoming, General Augur kept up his guard. He had marshaled a strong force within the city: twenty-one infantry companies totaling more than one thousand soldiers camped in public parks or occupied makeshift barracks. On January 8 the rival governors took their oaths of office, Nicholls standing on a balcony of St. Patrick's Hall before an audience of several thousand well-wishers, Packard choosing to remain within the protective confines of the state house. There was no violence at either location.[3]

On the evening of his inauguration Francis Nicholls boldly decided that he would attempt to seat his state supreme court appointees and supplant the Metropolitan Police with a police force of his own. Nicholls later wrote that he had "resolved to take all risks *essential* to *our* success but to attempt nothing which . . . would be or might be considered by the federal government as essential to the National Republican Party." In other words, Nicholls decided not to attempt to overthrow Packard, as Penn, Ogden, and the White League had tried to overthrow Kellogg in 1874. Instead, he aimed to take control of some important government functions, leaving the state house and his Republican rival unmolested. Nicholls could not be sure of Augur's reaction—or of Packard's either. But the crippled general's scheme paid dividends during the remaining months of Reconstruction in Louisiana.[4]

In December President Grant had specifically ordered Augur to restore the peace if a riot occurred. Augur had no intentions of overstepping his

2. Kellogg to Grant, January 5, 1877, Grant to Kellogg, January 7, 1877, in Justice Dept Letters (Microcopy M-940, reel 3), RG 60, NA; Polakoff, *Politics of Inertia*, 269–79.

3. Post Returns, Post of New Orleans, January 1877, in Records of the AGO (Microcopy M-617, reel 844), RG 94, NA; New Orleans *Times*, January 9, 1877.

4. Barnes F. Lathrop (ed.), "An Autobiography of Francis T. Nicholls, 1834–1881," *Louisiana Historical Quarterly*, XVII (April, 1934), 255 (emphasis in the original). See also Garnie W. McGinty, *Louisiana Redeemed: The Overthrow of Carpetbag Rule, 1876–1880* (New Orleans, 1941), 94–95.

orders: he would not send in his soldiers until fighting actually had taken place. If no violence took place, the army, instead of protecting the Republicans, would remain strictly uninvolved. Consequently, Augur's strategy actually worked to the advantage of the Democrats.

Beginning at dawn on January 9, Fred Ogden's White Leaguers, serving as Nicholls' militia, started assembling in Lafayette Square. David Penn served as Ogden's adjutant. Word of the White League assembly reached the Republican leaders, who desperately dashed off telegrams to Grant, telling him that an insurrection was impending and calling on the federal government for protection. Marshal John Pitkin wired U.S. Attorney General Alphonso Taft, informing him that the White League was mustering, businesses were closing their doors, and everyone was expecting "bloodshed . . . within an hour."[5]

Moving with military discipline, the Leaguers left their assembly point and, joined by other Nicholls supporters, soon made up a force of about three thousand men. As a first step, they demanded the surrender of several police stations, and Packard's men withdrew without any show of resistance. Ogden then marched on the Cabildo, where the supreme court chambers were located. Learning what was afoot, Chief Justice John T. Ludeling vacated his office, and the Leaguers installed the Democratic justices without any opposition. By noon the Nicholls militia had occupied most of the city police stations and the state arsenal. Packard's militia and police fell back on the state house, and the windows of the building bristled with the rifles of the beleaguered Republicans. Without firing a shot, Nicholls had taken control of all of the important state government buildings, with the exception of the capitol.[6]

Messengers immediately brought word to Augur that the White League was marching. He alerted Colonels Pennypacker and Brooke, commanding companies located near the state house and in the Orleans Hotel, but Augur rejected any notions of placing his soldiers in the streets or forming a cordon around the Cabildo and the Jackson Square police station. Specially chosen U.S. Marine signal officers, perched atop the cupola of the state house, used signal flags to keep Augur and his staff at the Custom House informed as to the advance of the Leaguers and the

5. Packard to Grant, January 9, 1877, C. C. Antoine and Michael Hahn to Grant, January 9, 1877, both in Justice Dept Letters (Microcopy M-940, reel 3), RG 60, NA; John Pitkin to Alonzo Taft, January 9, 1877, in AGO File 4788 of 1876 (Microcopy M-666, reel 300), RG 94, NA.
6. New Orleans *Daily Picayune*, January 10, 1877; Taylor, *Louisiana Reconstructed*, 496.

retreat of the Metropolitans. Army officers, holding binoculars to their eyes, lined the balcony of the Orleans Hotel and watched the *coup* taking place. Kellogg and Packard met with Colonel de Triobriand, who promised that his soldiers would be deployed if violence occurred, but since there had been no engagements or collisions, the infantry remained uncommitted.[7]

Learning of the unsettled conditions in New Orleans, Secretary of War Cameron demanded that Augur send a complete report on the situation in the city. Furthermore, Cameron ordered Augur to warn all unauthorized armed groups to disperse or come into "conflict with United States authority sustained by the military power of the Government." Reporting as ordered, Augur explained that the unauthorized armed groups were the "new police and armed posse acting under orders of the Nicholls government." The Nicholls militia had "possession of the city except for the State House." Obviously, it was too late for Augur to prevent a *coup*. Augur advised Cameron that he had "declined to interfere on either side until there was a violent breach of the peace. My orders simply authorize me to prevent bloodshed. None has yet occurred." The next morning the White League still occupied all of the buildings captured the previous day. Responding to questions from reporters, Augur declared that he "would not furnish troops [to support] the State authorities on either side."[8]

Undeterred by Augur's statement, Marshal Pitkin pressed Attorney General Taft to use his influence on Packard's behalf. Pitkin asked Taft: "should not [the] commanding General be instructed to assist [the Republican] Supreme Judges to reoccupy their seats?" Momentarily disregarding Pitkin's plea, Taft and Cameron became concerned when they learned that a mob was threatening the capitol. Cameron ordered Augur not to let the mob molest the Republican legislature—in fact, Augur was to disperse the mob if one had gathered outside the state house. Augur replied that no "mob" threatened the legislature, but that a "larger crowd than usual" had congregated near the capitol. Augur saw no reason to disperse the crowd because members of both parties were allowed to enter and leave the building, and "Packard's police [were] on duty in front

7. AAG, Dept Gulf, to Galusha Pennypacker, January 9, 1877, in Dept Gulf, vol. 116/ DSL, George B. Russell to Augur, January 9, 1877, in Dept Gulf, Letters Recd, RG 393, NA.

8. J. Donald Cameron to Augur, and reply, both dated January 9, 1877, in AGO File 4788 of 1876 (Microcopy M-666, reel 300), RG 94, NA; New Orleans *Daily Picayune*, January 11, 1877. See also Sefton, *Army and Reconstruction*, 248–49.

of it." Regarding the Cabildo, Augur told Cameron that "Packard [had] applied for troops to assist . . . in regaining possession of [the] Supreme Court room," but Augur continued, he had declined to provide soldiers for that purpose, saying it was not a legitimate duty for the army. Cameron concurred with Augur's view of the situation; the federal authorities allowed the Democrats to remain in control of the Cabildo, and the army failed to disperse the crowds.[9]

Nevertheless, a minor disturbance on the afternoon of January 10 provided Packard with another opportunity to receive federal help. Captain George Russell, Augur's observer at the state house, reported that there was "Great excitement" in the streets near the capitol. Unknown persons had fired some shots at the state house, and vandals were breaking windows in buildings near Jackson Square. Under similar circumstances, certainly Sheridan and probably Emory would have sent troops to clear the streets of the French Quarter, or at least sent military messengers to the White League's officers to demand that they order their men to disperse. Lacking orders to march, the colonels held their troops in check. Captain Russell concluded that "the Republican leaders will determine to bring on a row—that is I am afraid they see it as their only resort to bring us [the Army] in." However, only a few shots were fired, and the White Leaguers, demonstrating their discipline, refused to bring on a general engagement. Thus passed the last logical opportunity for Augur to commit his troops in direct support of Packard's government.[10]

Still hopeful that he might persuade the army to act on his behalf, Packard arranged a meeting with Captain Russell. The governor asked Russell to help the Republicans reclaim the office of the recorder of mortgages, located in the Cabildo. Russell replied that Augur's orders specified "that if there was a fight" the army would "leave the 'ins' in & the 'outs' out." Toward the end of the meeting Packard informed Russell that he had telegraphed President Grant asking him to order the army to "protect officers holding Kellogg commissions."[11]

While Grant considered Packard's latest request for help, the governor's authority continued to erode. Nicholls' appointees, or Democrats

9. Pitkin to Taft, January 10, 1877, in Justice Dept Letters (Microcopy M-940, reel 3), RG 60, NA; Cameron to Augur, and reply, both dated January 10, 1877, in AGO File 4788 of 1876 (Microcopy M-666, reel 300), RG 94, NA; Packard to Augur, Janury 10, 1877, in Dept of the South and South Carolina, Letters Recd, RG 393, NA.

10. Russell to Augur, January 10, 1877, in Dept Gulf, Letters Recd, RG 393, NA. See also Taylor, *Louisiana Reconstructed*, 497.

11. Russell to Augur, January 12, 1877, in Dept Gulf, Letters Recd, RG 393, NA.

who claimed to have been elected in November, had taken office in several outlying parishes. Packard was becoming isolated in the capital. Then, suddenly, Packard's claim to office temporarily took on new life.[12]

On January 14 President Grant sent an important telegram to Augur, telling him that until now the administration had tried to remain neutral in the Louisiana dispute, "but it is not proper to sit quietly by and see the State government gradually taken possession of by one of the claimants for gubernatorial honors by illegal means." Grant admonished Augur that "the Supreme Court set up by Mr. Nicholls can receive no more recognition than any other equal number of lawyers convened on the call of any other citizen of the State," but the president stopped well short of directing the general to disperse the court. The president concluded his message with a surprisingly firm declaration: the Returning Board had "declared Mr. Packard Governor. . . . Should there be a necessity for the recognition of either, it must be Packard." The New Orleans newspapers obtained and printed Grant's telegram, which naturally disconcerted Louisiana's Democrats.[13]

Believing that his administration was now official, Packard issued a proclamation, "To the White Leaguers and their attendant Usurpers, The Supreme Court Cabal," ordering them to disperse. The Nicholls forces ignored the proclamation. Augur again refused to order his soldiers to clear the offending Democrats from the Cabildo. At this rebuff, Packard's optimism began to evaporate.[14]

On January 16 Secretary Cameron, acting on behalf of the president, attempted to clarify Grant's position. Cameron directed Augur to preserve "the present status throughout the state . . . until the Congressional committees now in Louisiana return [to Washington]." Therefore, Augur was to maintain the *status quo*, and considering the fact that the Democrats already held most of the state buildings and offices, the order favored the Democrats. In the coming weeks Augur adhered strictly to this order and was loathe to extend even the slightest help to the Republicans.[15]

12. Lonn, *Reconstruction in Louisiana*, 488–92.

13. Grant to Augur, in Justice Dept Letters (Microcopy M-940, reel 3), RG 60, NA; New Orleans *Republican*, January 16, 1877.

14. Packard to Grant, January 15, 1877, in Justice Dept Letters (Microcopy M-940, reel 3), RG 60, NA; Augur to Packard, January 15, 1877, in AGO File 4788 of 1876 (Microcopy M-666, reel 300), RG 94, NA.

15. Cameron to Augur, January 16, 1877, in AGO File 4788 of 1876 (Microcopy M-666, reel 300), RG 94, NA. This letter was featured in the New Orleans *Times* and the *Daily Picayune*, both dated January 17, 1877.

For example, Augur categorically denied Packard's request "to secure the surrender" of "state arms and munitions of War," which the Nicholls' forces had obtained when they captured the state arsenals. Lecturing the governor as if he were a schoolboy, the general explained that Secretary Cameron's order required that the *status quo* be maintained. "The surrender, without resistence [*sic*] of the Supreme Court room, the Arsenal, and all of the police stations" had taken place before the secretary's order, and therefore the army was not going to make the Democrats give them (or their contents) back to the Republicans. Augur stipulated that no changes would be made in the existing political situation until the president decided to recognize one of the two claimants. Augur's strict interpretation of his orders pleased the Democratic press. "'Oh, that Phil Sheridan were here!' was Packard's agonized cry when he discovered that Gen. Augur combined the qualities of an army officer with those of a gentleman," wrote the gleeful editor of the Shreveport *Times*.[16]

On the Republican side, the New York *Times* alertly pointed out that Augur "seems a little disposed . . . to give the Democratic claimant, Nicholls, the benefit of the doubt." Going further, the *Times* accused Augur of showing favoritism toward Nicholls by allowing him to maintain possession of the state offices. The newspaper concluded that the fiction of two governors in Louisiana must be ended soon, and implied that Packard should be recognized.[17]

To the obvious disappointment of many northern Republicans, dual governments continued to exist in Louisiana. In fact, Nicholls took every opportunity to improve his position. For example, on January 19 Nicholls appointed a Democrat to the position of state librarian. A party of White Leaguers escorted the appointee to his office, where he displaced the Republican librarian. Packard complained about this usurpation to both Augur and Grant. Caught red-handed, Nicholls recalled his librarian and "staff," permitting the Republican to resume his position.[18]

The controversy over officeholders broke out afresh when Packard accused Nicholls of seating judges and other local officials in Natchitoches and Ouachita parishes. An investigation revealed that the Democrats had

16. Packard to Augur, January 17, 1877, in Dept Gulf, Letters Recd, Augur to Packard, January 17, 1877, in Dept Gulf, vol. 116/DSL, RG 393, NA; Shreveport *Times*, January 19, 1877.

17. New York *Times*, January 18, 1877.

18. Packard to Grant, January 19, 1877, in Justice Dept Letters (Microcopy M-940, reel 3), RG 60, NA; Packard to Augur, Francis T. Nicholls to Augur, both dated January 19, 1877, in Dept Gulf, Letters Recd, RG 393, NA.

indeed taken office after Cameron's *status quo* order on January 16. Augur refused to remove the Conservatives, although it was well within his powers and responsibilities. Instead, he described the circumstances to the authorities in Washington and left the decisions to them. Eventually President Grant demanded that the Democratic judge in Natchitoches step down from the bench and surrender his position to a Republican, but he allowed all of the Democrats in Ouachita to remain in office. Patiently biding his time, Nicholls saw to it that the president's rulings were obeyed.[19]

Packard found Augur's inaction during these negotiations intolerable, and he wanted the general replaced. By remaining aloof and studiously avoiding any involvement, Augur was indirectly helping Nicholls, who counted on the fact that Augur would refuse to remove Democrats from office even if they had violated the *status quo*. Consequently, Packard and Marshal Pitkin wanted a new commander who would take a pro-Republican viewpoint. Packard and Pitkin failed in their efforts to have Augur removed in large measure because General William T. Sherman supported Augur and endorsed his posture of noninvolvement. Writing to a friend, Sherman described Augur with such glowing adjectives as "brave, intelligent, just and conscientious." Furthermore, Sherman complimented Augur on the way he had interpreted Secretary Cameron's orders. Suspecting that Augur might still have some dangerous times ahead, Sherman gave him some advice and support: "Keep perfectly cool and always depend on me as far as my influence goes to Sustain You in the Right." Turning his attention to the disputed presidential election, Sherman hoped that the leaders in Congress would formulate a plan resulting "in a general understanding."[20]

On January 29 Grant signed into law the bill passed by Congress creating a commission of eight Republicans and seven Democrats to pass judgment on the disputed electoral votes from the contested states. Two days later the Congress and the Electoral Commission began opening, examining, and counting the electoral votes of the 1876 election.[21]

On February 9 the Electoral Commission accepted the Republican cer-

---

19. Packard to Grant, January 25, 1877, Augur to AGO, Cameron to Augur, both dated January 26, 1877, all in Justice Dept Letters (Microcopy M-940, reel 3), RG 60, NA.

20. New Orleans *Daily Picayune*, January 21, 22, 1877; New Orleans *Times*, January 24, 1877; Sherman to David Boyd, January 23, 1877, in Sherman Letters/Boyd Papers; Sherman to Augur, January 22, 1877, in Augur Papers.

21. See James G. Randall and David H. Donald, *The Civil War and Reconstruction* (2nd ed., rev.; Lexington, Mass., 1969), 697–98.

tificates from Florida as legitimate and counted the first contested state for Hayes. Democrats feared that this decision by the commission foretold the outcome of the election. Consequently, Nicholls' official and unofficial emissaries in Washington began meeting with important Republicans. Representing Nicholls were Edward A. Burke, railroad entrepreneur and the general's former campaign manager, and John Ellis, former White League adjutant who was serving as a U.S. congressman from Louisiana. The Bayou State Democrats busily conferred with officials of the Grant administration, friends of Rutherford Hayes, and with President Grant himself, stressing that although Louisiana's electoral votes might be given to Hayes, the new president could still recognize the Nicholls government. Simultaneously, other Democrats and railroad executives were in almost daily contact with the Hayes camp, trying to reach a compromise that would give Hayes the presidency in exchange for federal favors to the railroad companies.[22]

Proceeding alphabetically, the electoral count in Congress had reached Louisiana, and the state's multiple sets of returns had been given to the Electoral Commission. Although many Louisianians were concerned whether the state would be decided for Hayes or for Tilden, Augur learned that most of the political discussions in the Crescent City concentrated on the governorship, not the presidency. Augur reported that "Packard's opponents are numerous," and significantly, Augur added, "I do not understand that they care so much who is President."[23]

On February 16 the Electoral Commission awarded Louisiana's electoral votes to Hayes, prompting Adjutant General Townsend to warn Augur about rumors that had been circulating in Washington predicting violence in New Orleans. He advised Augur to take all necessary precautions to prevent disturbances in the Gulf Department. Augur acknowledged Townsend's telegram, replying that there had been "a great deal of excitement here." Part of the excitement was due to the fact that the day before someone had slightly wounded Packard in a murder attempt on the streets of New Orleans. Otherwise, some Louisiana Republicans, overjoyed because Hayes had received the state's electoral votes, believed (or hoped) that the crisis was nearly over and that Packard's ultimate rec-

22. Taylor, *Louisiana Reconstructed*, 485, 495, 502; C. Vann Woodward, *Reunion and Reaction: The Compromise of 1877 and the End of Reconstruction* (Boston, 1966), *passim*.
23. Augur to AGO, February 15, 1877, in AGO File 4788 of 1876 (Microcopy M-666, reel 300), RG 94, NA. David Boyd expressed the same sentiment to John Sherman, February 16, 1877, in John Sherman Papers.

ognition was assured. Believing that the outcome was uncertain, Augur closely watched the rival governments and reported that New Orleans remained peaceful.[24]

Meanwhile, in Washington Nicholls' representatives had continued to meet with members of Grant's cabinet and friends of Hayes, who by all odds soon would be president-elect if the electoral count proceeded on schedule. The Louisiana press printed articles about these meetings, keeping army officers and politicians informed about the negotiations, which were only imperfectly understood. Unconfirmed press accounts claimed General Sherman had said that within a short time the army would be glad to let southerners take care of their own political affairs. Other news articles indicated that Grant had decided not to disturb Louisiana's precarious political balance, leaving the decision to recognize either Nicholls or Packard to his successor. By now Augur was aware of Grant's reluctance to make such a decision, and he continued to hold the army in its neutral position.[25]

On February 23 the Electoral Commission officially assigned Oregon's disputed electoral vote to Hayes, making it more important than ever for the Democrats to reach some accommodation with him. Several disgruntled northern Democrats, supported by some southerners, began filibustering in an attempt to block the electoral count. But the New Orleans Times, apparently fed on a steady diet of information from Nicholls, reported that Hayes was willing to let the South handle its own affairs and complimented him on his "New Departure" policy. After all, during the campaign Hayes had hinted that eventually the federal government would support "the efforts of the people of those states [Florida, South Carolina, and Louisiana] to obtain for themselves the blessings of honest and capable local government." In fact, he had promised that, if elected, he would work on behalf of that goal himself.[26]

After a meeting with Grant on February 26, Edward Burke informed Nicholls that the president believed northern public opinion was "clearly opposed to the further use of troops in upholding a State government." That night Burke, John Ellis, and several other Democrats met with James Garfield, John Sherman, and other Hayes Republicans at the old

24. Townsend to Augur, February 16, 1877, Augur to AGO, February 16, 17, 1877, all in AGO File 4788 of 1876 (Microcopy M-666, reel 300), RG 94, NA; New Orleans Times, February 16, 1877.
25. New Orleans Times, February 19, 20, 22, 1877; Sefton, Army and Reconstruction, 250.
26. Woodward, Reunion and Reaction, 194. Hayes's speech quoted in Polakoff, Politics of Inertia, 105.

Wormley Hotel in Washington. The Wormley conference capped weeks of negotiations between southern Democrats, railroad executives, newspapermen, and representatives of the Hayes camp. Burke obtained the Republicans' assurances that if Nicholls promised to protect the rights of Louisiana's Republicans, Hayes would recognize Nicholls and withdraw the troops, "thus allowing the Packard government to melt away," as the New Orleans *Times* cleverly described the arrangement. (A similar arrangement was made in regard to the government of South Carolina; in Florida, a Democratic governor had already taken office.) Furthermore, the *Times* reported that Nicholls intended to have the state legislature elect a moderate Republican to one of Louisiana's two vacant seats in the U.S. Senate. In exchange, the Democrats promised not to obstruct the electoral count, meaning that Hayes was the next president. Given the fact that Republicans controlled the presidency, the Supreme Court, the army, and the Senate (the Democrats held a majority in the House), Burke and his fellows apparently believed that they had made a good bargain. Louisiana Republicans were unable to refute the reports of the "Wormley bargain," and on March 1 the New Orleans *Times* jubilantly predicted that Packard would be out of the state house "within 48 hours." [27]

Undoubtedly the hoary tale of the Wormley conference cannot stand alone as the only factor in the Compromise of 1877. C. Vann Woodward has authoritatively presented the complex machinations of speculators, railroad entrepreneurs, and state and national politicians, showing that economic considerations, particularly federal aid to railroads and other internal improvements, played an important part in eventually reaching a compromise. However, if Nicholls and Ellis serve as examples, many Louisianians were primarily concerned about the recognition of Nicholls and the withdrawal of the troops. Such matters as a proposed southern railway, the appointment of a southerner to Hayes's cabinet, and the arrangement to make Garfield Speaker of the House were of secondary importance. Furthermore, Woodward perhaps depreciated the symbolic importance of Hayes's promise to withdraw the troops, even though Congress tried to limit his choices in the matter. In February, 1877, the House and the Senate failed to reach a compromise on an army appropriations bill for fiscal year 1877–1878. The Democrats seemed to believe

27. Edward A. Burke to Nicholls, February 26, 1877, in *House Miscellaneous Documents*, 45th Cong., 3rd Sess., No. 31, vol. III, p. 618; Woodward, *Reunion and Reaction*, 195–97. Reports in the New Orleans *Times* (February 28, 1877) and the *Picayune* (February 27, 1877), revealed the important aspects of the Wormley conference.

that if the army went unpaid, Hayes would not be able to use soldiers to prop up Republican regimes in South Carolina and Louisiana. Considering this to be a valid argument, historian Joe Gray Taylor asserted that this "would have forced the removal of the military anyway." Furthermore, Woodward claimed that this tactic "had been devised to insure the removal of the troops in case Hayes forgot his promises or was unable to carry them out." However, military appropriations were available for the first four months of Hayes's administration (through June, 1877), and as historians Randall and Donald have cogently pointed out, Woodward's "line of reasoning ignores the fact that failure to pay the troops did not mean disbanding the army; Hayes used unpaid troops to break [labor] strikes in the summer of 1877." There were no mass desertions from the army while it went unpaid, and the regiments obeyed the president's orders.[28]

Perhaps the arguments over appropriations and soldiers were merely academic, but in the early days of March, 1877, before Hayes was inaugurated, there was still some uncertainty about the presidential succession. A few Democrats threatened to block the final tabulation of the electoral votes, but they abandoned the filibuster, the count proceeded, and Hayes was elected by one electoral vote. Earlier, the president had told Edward Burke that when Hayes was inaugurated, the soldiers would be withdrawn. This information gave Louisiana Democrats reason to believe that all of their patient negotiations were about to pay off, but General Augur avoided any sort of recognition of his own.[29]

From his office in the state house, Stephen Packard made a desperate attempt to salvage his governorship, which apparently had been negotiated away in the Compromise of 1877. Begging Grant to recognize him as Louisiana's governor, Packard predicted that if the soldiers were withdrawn the Nicholls forces would attack the capitol and carry the last remaining Republican stronghold by main force. Packard's desperate tone and menacing prediction had no effect on Grant. Disdaining a personal reply, Grant directed one of his secretaries, Culver C. Sniffen, to draft a telegram to Packard. "In answer to your dispatch," Sniffen began, ". . .

---

28. Burke to Nicholls, February 20, 26, 28, March 2, 1877, all in *House Miscellaneous Documents*, 45th Cong., 3rd Sess., No. 31, vol. I, pp. 972, 980, 990–91, 1,041; Woodward, *Reunion and Reaction*, 8, 203; Taylor, *Louisiana Reconstructed*, 502; Randall and Donald, *Civil War and Reconstruction*, 969 n.

29. New Orleans *Times* and New Orleans *Democrat*, both dated March 2, 1877; Woodward, *Reunion and Reaction*, 200–201.

the President directs me to say that he feels it his duty to state frankly that he does not believe public opinion will longer support the maintenance of State government in Louisiana by the use of the military and that he must concur in this manifest feeling." Thrusting the knife home, Sniffen concluded that during the last few days of his administration, Grant wanted the army to continue to "protect life and property," but that it was not the president's "purpose to recognize either claimant" for the governorship. The Sniffen telegram devastated Packard's hopes. His only chance to continue his political career lay in convincing Hayes to recognize his claim to the governorship.[30]

General Sherman sent a copy of the Sniffen telegram to Augur for his information. After reading the message, Augur replied that he understood that the army was no longer needed to maintain the *status quo*, but simply needed "to protect property & life." It appeared to Sherman that Augur might have misunderstood the president's intentions. The commanding general tried to clarify matters for Augur, writing that he expected Augur to "prevent any material changes in the attitude of the contending parties till the new [national] administration can be fairly installed, and give the subject mature reflection."[31]

On March 5 Hayes was formally inaugurated, after surreptitiously taking the oath of office two days before. Some officials had feared that hotheaded Democrats might attempt to stop the inauguration, but no disruptions marred the ceremony. Speaking in conciliatory tones in his inaugural address, Hayes said that some southern states were not enjoying "wise, honest, and peaceful self-government." He encouraged southerners to be patient, indicating that important announcements regarding the status of the unredeemed state governments would be forthcoming "when the administration gets fairly to work."[32]

The language of Hayes's inaugural speech prompted the New Orleans *Times* to predict that the president would "issue general orders to all commanding officers in the South to withdraw their troops to government reservations." The *Times* and other Democratic newspapers undoubtedly were disappointed when Hayes announced that he was not going to decide between Nicholls and Packard immediately. Instead, the

30. Packard to Grant, Culver C. Sniffen to Packard, both dated March 1, 1877, in Grant Papers. See also Lonn, *Reconstruction in Louisiana*, 514–16.

31. Sherman to Augur, March 2, 3, 1877, Augur to Sherman, March 2, 1877, all in AGO File 4788 of 1876 (Microcopy M-666, reel 300), RG 94, NA.

32. New Orleans *Times*, March 5, 1877; Barnard, *Hayes*, 404, 408.

president planned to send a special committee to investigate the political situation in Louisiana, and he would not recognize either man until after the committee had made its report. In the meantime, Sherman informed Sheridan that Augur must hold to his old orders: "keep the peace."[33]

The prospect of having to endure the *status quo* was distasteful to Louisiana's Democratic newspaper editors, who were impatient with Hayes's policy. Clutching at straws, the Conservatives printed every rumor pertaining to the possibility of troop withdrawal. One rumor, which was widely believed, predicted that Hayes definitely would remove the soldiers from the Crescent City on March 19, but that day passed without any military movements. The New Orleans *Times* angrily asked, "Is the New Departure a Fraud?"[34]

In contrast to the Democrats, Packard was encouraged by Hayes's policy. Displaying a never-say-die attitude, Packard informed the president that the Louisiana legislature had adopted a resolution calling "for aid in suppressing domestic violence," making it plain that the state's Republicans were still hoping for federal aid and protection. Hayes replied that Secretary of War George W. McCrary had ordered Augur to maintain current political conditions until the special presidential commission arrived. Additionally, Augur was to report any changes that had taken place in the state governments since March 5. To assure himself that Augur's report would be complete, Packard provided him with a list of the large number of changes and appointments Nicholls had made since Hayes's inauguration.[35]

Basing his report partly on Packard's list, Augur stated that since March 5 each claimant for the governorship had attempted "to strengthen his government as best he could." Although Augur specifically acknowledged that Nicholls had "removed certain officers and appointed others," he tried to soften the impact of this information, saying that the new appointees had "entered upon their duties . . . without violence." Secretary

33. New Orleans *Times*, March 7, 8, 1877. See also New Orleans *Daily Picayune*, March 7, 8, 1877, Shreveport *Times*, March 8, 1877. Sherman to Sheridan, March 7, 1877, in AGO File 4788 of 1876 (Microcopy M-666, reel 300), RG 94, NA.

34. New Orleans *Democrat*, New Iberia *Sugar Bowl*, both dated March 15, 1877; New Orleans *Times*, March 22, 1877.

35. Packard to Hayes, March 21, 1877, in Justice Dept Letters (Microcopy M-940, reel 3), RG 60, NA; Hayes to Packard, March 26, 1877, in New Orleans *Times*, March 27, 1877; George W. McCrary to Augur, March 26, 1877, in AGO File 4788 of 1876 (Microcopy M-666, reel 300), RG 94, NA; Packard to Augur, March 26, 1877, in Dept Gulf, Letters Recd, RG 393, NA.

of War McCrary passed a copy of Augur's report to Hayes, noting that no reply was necessary. The army would not be ordered to oust Nicholls' officials and replace them with Republicans.[36]

Nevertheless, the implications of McCrary's inquiries about changes in the *status quo* disturbed Nicholls. He wrote to Louisiana Congressman Randall L. Gibson in Washington, explaining that McCrary's questions had "alarmed the community [and] elated our opponents." Nicholls wanted Gibson, who had been present during some of the negotiations leading to the Compromise of 1877, to learn Hayes's intentions. "If confidence is lost here either in me or the President, the consequences may be most serious," Nicholls concluded.[37]

But Nicholls was worrying needlessly, for on April 5 the special presidential commission arrived in New Orleans, and soon it was evident that its members intended to help the Democrat confirm his claim to office. Apparently Hayes had decided that the smoothest way to establish Nicholls' legitimacy was to encourage representatives and senators to leave the Packard legislature, thus giving the Democrats control of the official state legislature. The state Returning Board had authenticated the election of a large number of Democrats, but several seats were still disputed. If the Republicans who transferred to the Nicholls legislature cooperated with the Conservatives, they could elect Democrats to the vacant seats and subsequently control the legislature. During the next two weeks several of Packard's legislators deserted the state house, apparently bribed by the Democrats using funds provided by the Louisiana Lottery Company. However, the Republicans also had practical political and economic motives for shifting their loyalties. Packard was running out of money to pay their salaries, and if they did not join Nicholls' legislature, Democrats might claim their seats. Consequently, Packard lost most of his legislators, and each day he counted fewer adherents who supported his crumbling administration.[38]

In mid-April Packard's last flickers of hope died. Hayes ordered that on April 10 the troops protecting the capitol in Columbia, South Carolina,

36. Augur to McCrary, March 27, 1877, in Dept Gulf, vol. 116/DSL, RG 393, NA; McCrary to Hayes, March 27, 1877, in Hayes Papers.
37. Nicholls to Randall L. Gibson, March 26, 1877, in Francis T. Nicholls Letterbook, 1877, Department of Archives and Manuscripts, Louisiana State University Library, Baton Rouge.
38. Taylor, *Louisiana Reconstructed*, 504; Barnard, *Hayes*, 428–30.

be withdrawn to their barracks outside the city. Desperately, Packard sent Hayes one last plea for recognition, but it fell on deaf ears. The president declined even to send a reply.[39]

Obeying Hayes's orders, Secretary of State William M. Evarts informed the members of the presidential commission that the president intended "to remove the soldiers from the State-house [in New Orleans] to their barracks, and he desires that the time, circumstances, and preparation for such removal should give every reasonable security against its becoming the occasion or opportunity of any outbreak of violence." Evarts explained that Hayes wanted "to put an end to even an apparent military interference in the domestic controversies in the State of Louisiana."[40]

After Evart's message became public, the New Orleans *Times* reported that "The Troops May Now be Withdrawn Shortly." Subsequently, in an editorial, the *Times* described the "feeling of relief" in New Orleans now that Packard was literally a governor without a government. The editorial concluded: "So long as it is known that the troops are not to be used as a political engine, it will make no difference whether they remain in garrison . . . or whether they are removed entirely."[41]

On April 20 Hayes directed Secretary of War McCrary to order the infantrymen near the state capitol in New Orleans to be relocated on April 24 to Jackson Barracks outside the city. Only the soldiers stationed in the Orleans Hotel adjacent to the state house were being shifted; several hundred other soldiers would remain in the city. It was, therefore, a symbolic "withdrawal." McCrary issued the necessary orders to the military commanders, and Augur prepared to carry them out. Several important Louisiana newspapers printed stories about the planned withdrawal, and some included verbatim copies of the military telegrams revealing the army's plans. No delay or postponement was expected. The New Orleans *Democrat* reported that Packard had announced he planned "to gracefully retire."[42]

---

39. Packard to Hayes, April 16, 1877, in New Orleans *Daily Picayune*, April 17, 1877; Barnard, *Hayes*, 430.
40. William M. Evarts to Charles B. Lawrence *et al.*, April 13, 1877, in *House Executive Documents*, 45th Cong., 2nd Sess., No. 97, p. 9.
41. New Orleans *Daily Picayune*, April 17, 21, 1877.
42. Hayes to McCrary, McCrary to Sherman, Augur to Sherman, all dated April 20, 1877, in AGO File 4788 of 1876 (Microcopy M-666, reel 300), RG 94, NA; New Orleans *Times*, New Orleans *Daily Picayune*, Shreveport *Times*, New Orleans *Democrat*, all dated April 22, 1877.

During the next two days, Augur and his subordinates worked busily, preparing for the ceremony that would signal the end of the army's involvement in Louisiana politics. Enlisted men packed trunks and lashed them to wagons. The musicians of the 3rd Infantry band polished their instruments and uniform brass for the occasion. Colonels Brooke, Floyd-Jones, and de Trobriand closely supervised the last details of the transfer, while the quartermaster and his assistants arranged for the arrival of the additional soldiers at Jackson Barracks. On orders from General Augur, the troops dusted off their best uniforms and buffed their shoes, bringing out lustrous shines. Fittingly, it was to be a full dress parade.[43]

April 24 dawned gloomy, and a light drizzle fell throughout most of the morning. The Orleans Hotel, which had been serving as a barracks for five companies of the 3rd Infantry, bustled with activity. At 11:30 A.M. the band gathered at its assigned assembly point within the building, lining up to lead the day's momentous event. Twenty minutes later, responding to the shouts of their sergeants, five companies of infantrymen formed ranks on the stairways and in the hallways of the old hotel. Disregarding the rain, hundreds of persons turned out to watch the ceremony. According to the *Picayune*, "Royal and Chartres streets were absolutely jammed with a living mass of humanity, surging toward the point where the troops . . . were stationed." The *Democrat* reported that St. Louis Street was "lined with spectators" and the "throng was dense." The crowd waited expectantly.

Precisely at noon the band struck up a marching tune and began filing out of the Orleans Hotel. Led by Colonel Brooke, the troops came into the street. Catching the cadence provided by the drummers, the soldiers marched down St. Louis Street toward the levee. Scattered applause broke out from the crowd, a rebel yell split the air, then as the soldiers passed by there were many cheers, and finally the throng was "cheering continually." The roar of hundreds of voices drowned out individual expressions of delight. A *Picayune* reporter noticed that "the balconies of the houses on St. Louis Street were crowded with ladies, who manifested their joy by waving their handkerchiefs and smiling" at the troops passing beneath them.[44]

43. AAG, Dept Gulf to de Trobriand, April 22, 1877, in Dept Gulf, vol. 116/DSL, RG 393, NA.
44. New Orleans *Daily Picayune*, New Orleans *Democrat*, both dated April 25, 1877.

Black smoke curling from its funnels, the steamer *Palace* waited at the levee to take the soldiers to Jackson Barracks. The infantry companies halted and then, on orders from their officers, filed aboard the steamer. The lines were cast off, and the boat "left the moorings amid deafening cheers" from hundreds of spectators. The *Palace* moved out into the river, catching the current and getting up steam. The boat made its way down the Mississippi, and eventually it was lost to the sight of the onlookers.[45]

The army's long ordeal in Louisiana Reconstruction had ended.

---

45. New Orleans *Daily Picayune*, and New Orleans *Democrat*, both dated April 25, 1877.

Epilogue

Actually, as Clarence Clendenen has pointed out, the soldiers were not "withdrawn" from Louisiana. For that matter, the *Picayune* reminded its readers that "the order issued by the president referred only to those troops stationed in the Orleans Hotel, as they were considered the guard of Packard." More than 330 officers and men remained quartered in New Orleans until the end of May, and detachments occupied posts near four other towns. But practically, the result was the same as if they had left the city and the state. The army had ceased to be a factor in politics. Francis Nicholls took office as undisputed governor on April 26. The next day General Augur and his staff acknowledged the fact, making a formal call on the governor at the state house.[1]

Within the next three months the War Department virtually dismantled the Department of the Gulf. By the end of May, Augur had closed the army posts at Monroe, Clinton, St. Martinville, and Pineville, leaving only a detachment at Lake Charles. Responding to the need for more troops on the frontier, the 16th Infantry left Augur's department for duty at Fort Leavenworth, Kansas. During May and June the 3rd Infantry was reassigned to posts in Alabama. In July, acting on the orders of President Hayes, Secretary of War McCrary directed that army units from all over the nation be sent to the East and Midwest to put down the massive labor strikes that occurred in the summer of 1877. At the end of 1877 only thirty-five soldiers were serving in the New Orleans vicinity.[2]

---

1. Clarence C. Clendenen, "President Hayes' 'Withdrawal' of the Troops—An Enduring Myth," *South Carolina Historical Magazine*, LXX (October, 1969), 240–50; New Orleans *Daily Picayune*, April 25, 1877; Post Returns, Post of New Orleans, May, 1877, in Records of the AGO (Microcopy M-617, reel 844), RG 94, NA; AAG, Dept Gulf to Nicholls, April 27, 1877, in Dept Gulf, vol. 116/DSL, RG 393, NA.

2. Clendenen, "Hayes' 'Withdrawal' of the Troops," 248–50; Dept Gulf, Journal of Events, pp. 121–27, RG 393, NA; SW, "Annual Report, 1877–1878," in *House Executive Documents*, 45th Cong., 2nd Sess., No. 1, pp. 24–25.

It had not been the army's responsibility to guarantee the success of Reconstruction, only to carry out the policy, which changed from year to year, with the tools and men at its disposal. Despite their lack of experience in military government, most of the army's officers carefully administered the military Reconstruction Acts; and a few of them, notably Sheridan and Mower, took a genuine interest in enforcing the requirements of the Acts. Actually the army did a remarkable job, despite its inexperience, in administering an essentially hostile state. Subsequently, under Emory, the army offered some protection to what probably was, despite its faults, the most democratic government Louisiana had had until that time. The army—that most ungainly "political engine"—had helped to establish the groundwork of rights in the First Reconstruction that would form the basis of the Second Reconstruction a century later.

Phil Sheridan became commanding general of the U.S. Army late in his career, in 1884 upon the retirement of his friend William T. Sherman.

Following his retirement from the army in 1876, William H. Emory resided in Washington, D.C., observing politics, both civil and military, well into Grover Cleveland's first administration.

After leaving the governor's office, William Pitt Kellogg was elected U.S. Senator by the Packard legislature. There was some dispute over the legitimacy of his election, but the Senate finally approved his credentials over those of a Democrat who had been elected by the Nicholls legislature. Kellogg was one of the last Republicans to serve in Congress from Louisiana until the election of David Treen to the House of Representatives in 1972.

Nominated by the Democrats, Winfield Scott Hancock ran for the presidency in 1880. He was narrowly defeated by James A. Garfield. (Voting with the rest of the "Solid South," Louisiana gave its electoral votes to Hancock.) General Hancock remained in the army until 1886.

After failing to secure the Louisiana governorship, Stephen B. Packard applied to the Hayes administration for a job. The president appointed him U.S. consul in Liverpool, England.

Following Reconstruction, Christopher C. Augur served as commander of the Department of the South, comprising eight southern states, including Louisiana. Subsequently, he commanded the Department of Texas, and later he was in charge of the Department of the Missouri. Augur retired from the army in 1885.

John R. Brooke, Lieutenant Colonel, 3rd Infantry, was promoted successively to colonel, brigadier general, and finally, major general in 1897. During the Spanish American War he participated in the Puerto Rican campaign under General Nelson A. Miles. After the war, Brooke served as military governor of Cuba. He retired from the army in 1902.

After Reconstruction, Henry Clay Warmoth settled in Louisiana and purchased a sugar plantation in Plaquemines Parish. He ran for governor again in 1888, losing to Francis T. Nicholls. Many years later a modern power artist named Huey P. Long studied how Warmoth had governed the state during the postwar years. Warmoth was still living in Louisiana when Long was elected governor in 1928.

Departmental Changes Pertaining to Louisiana During Reconstruction, 1862–1877

DATE ESTABLISHED	DEPARTMENTAL DESIGNATION AND AREA
May 1, 1862	Department of the Gulf (parts of Louisiana, Texas, Florida, Mississippi)
May 7, 1864	Military Division of West Mississippi (occupied parts of Arkansas, Texas, Louisiana, Mississippi)
May 17, 1865	Department of the Gulf (Louisiana, Mississippi, Alabama, Florida)
May 29, 1865	Military Division of the Southwest (parts of Louisiana, and Arkansas, Texas, Indian Territory)
July 17, 1865	Military Division of the Gulf (Louisiana, Mississippi, Florida, Texas, Arkansas, Indian Territory)
August 6, 1866	Department of the Gulf (Louisiana, Texas, Florida)
March 2, 1867	5th Military District (Louisiana, Texas)
July 28, 1868	Department of Louisiana (Louisiana, Arkansas)
March 31, 1870	Department of Texas (Louisiana, Texas)
November 1, 1871	Department of the Gulf (Louisiana, Arkansas, Mississippi, some forts in Florida)
January 4, 1875	Department of the Gulf added to Military Division of the Missouri
June 26, 1876	Alabama and part of Tennessee added to Department of the Gulf
May 1, 1877	Department of the Gulf transferred from Military Division of the Missouri to Military Division of the Atlantic

Reconstruction Commanders of Louisiana, 1862–1877

DEPARTMENT COMMANDER *subordinate state commander*	DATES OF COMMAND
Benjamin F. Butler	May 1, 1862–December 17, 1862
Nathaniel P. Banks	December 17, 1862–June 9, 1864
Edward R. S. Canby	June 9, 1864–July 17, 1865
Stephen A. Hurlbut	September 23, 1864–April 22, 1865
Nathaniel P. Banks	April 22, 1865–May 17, 1865
Philip H. Sheridan	May 17, 1865–September 5, 1867
E. R. S. Canby	July 17, 1865–May 28, 1866
Charles Griffin	September 6, 1867–September 13, 1867
Joseph A. Mower	September 16, 1867–November 29, 1867
Winfield S. Hancock	November 29, 1867–March 18, 1868
Joseph J. Reynolds	March 18, 1868–March 25, 1868
Robert C. Buchanan	March 25, 1868–September 15, 1868
Lovell H. Rousseau	September 15, 1868–January 7, 1869
Robert C. Buchanan	January 11, 1869–March 31, 1869
Joseph A. Mower	March 31, 1869–January 6, 1870
Charles H. Smith	January 7, 1870–April 16, 1870
Joseph J. Reynolds	April 16, 1870–November 28, 1871
Charles H. Smith	April 16, 1870–November 28, 1871
William H. Emory	November 28, 1871–March 27, 1875
Christopher C. Augur	March 27, 1875–June 21, 1878

Approximate Troop Totals in Louisiana
During Reconstruction, 1865–1877

MONTH	YEAR	NUMBER OF TROOPS	NUMBER OF POSTS
June	1865	25,800	–
September	1865	23,747	–
January	1866	9,772	11
October	1866	5,124	10
October	1867	2,434	6
October	1868	2,254	12
October	1869	953	6
October	1870	598	5
October	1871	616	2
October	1872	427	14
November	1873	643	5
August	1874	130	3
September	1874	1,182	8
November	1874	1,998	9
November	1875	921	8
October	1876	529	9
November*	1876	800	21
November†	1876	1,390	4
April	1877	731	4

*Before election
†After election

Bibliography

PRIMARY SOURCES

Manuscripts

Augur, Christopher C., Papers, 1875–1877. Illinois State Historical Library, Springfield.

Breda, J. Ernest, Letters, 1873. Special Collections Division, Tulane University Library, New Orleans.

Buchanan, Robert C., Papers, 1867–1869. Maryland Historical Society, Baltimore.

Ellis, E. John, Papers. Department of Archives and Manuscripts, Louisiana State University Library, Baton Rouge.

Emory, W. H. / Battle of Liberty Place Papers, 1874. Special Collections Division, Tulane University Library, New Orleans.

Emory, William H., Papers, 1871–1876. Western Americana Collection, Beinecke Rare Book and Manuscript Library, Yale University, New Haven, Conn.

Fifth Military District Papers. U.S. Army Letterbook, 1867–1868. Duke University Library, Durham, N.C.

Flanders, Benjamin F., Papers, 1865–1870. Department of Archives and Manuscripts, Louisiana State University Library, Baton Rouge.

Grant, Ulysses S., Papers, 1865–1877. Manuscript Division, Library of Congress (microfilm copy in Louisiana State University Library, Baton Rouge).

Hayes, Rutherford B., Papers, 1876–1877. Manuscript Division, Library of Congress (microfilm copy in Rutherford B. Hayes Library, Fremont, O.).

Hornor, Joseph P., Collection, 1867. Department of Archives and Manuscripts, Louisiana State University Library, Baton Rouge.

Johnson, Andrew, Papers, 1865–1869. Manuscript Division, Library of Congress (microfilm copy in Louisiana State University Library, Baton Rouge).

Kellogg, William Pitt, Papers, 1870–1877. Department of Archives and Manuscripts, Louisiana State University Library, Baton Rouge.

Nicholls, Francis T., Letterbook, 1877. Department of Archives and Manuscripts, Louisiana State University Library, Baton Rouge.

Palfrey, William T., Papers, 1865–1866. Department of Archives and Manuscripts, Louisiana State University Library, Baton Rouge.

Sheridan, Philip H., Papers, 1865–1877. Manuscript Division, Library of
    Congress.
Sherman, John, Papers, 1876–1877. Manuscript Division, Library of Congress.
Sherman, William T., Letters/David F. Boyd Family Papers, 1865–1877. De-
    partment of Archives and Manuscripts, Louisiana State University Library,
    Baton Rouge.
Sherman, William T., Miscellany, 1865–1877. Department of Archives and
    Manuscripts, Louisiana State University Library, Baton Rouge.
Sherman, William T., Papers, 1874–1877. Manuscript Division, Library of
    Congress.
Stanton, Edwin M., Papers, 1865–1867. Manuscript Division, Library of Con-
    gress (microfilm copy in Ohio Historical Society, Columbus).
Taliaferro, James G., and Family Papers, 1865–1876. Department of Archives
    and Manuscripts, Louisiana State University Library, Baton Rouge.
Warmoth, Henry Clay, Papers, 1869–1872. Department of Archives and Manu-
    scripts, Louisiana State University Library, Baton Rouge.
Warmoth, Henry Clay, Papers, 1865–1877. Southern Historical Collection, Li-
    brary of the University of North Carolina at Chapel Hill (microfilm copy in
    Louisiana State University Library, Baton Rouge).
Wilson, Henry, Papers, 1866. Manuscript Division, Library of Congress.

Records in the National Archives

Record Group 60: Records of the United States Department of Justice
    Letters Received by the Justice Department from Louisiana, 1871–1884 (Mi-
        crocopy M-940, reels 1, 2, 3, 6).
    Letters Sent by the Justice Department, Instructions to U.S. Attorneys and
        Marshals, 1867–1904 (Microcopy M-701, reel 3).
Record Group 94: Records of the United States Army Adjutant General's Office
    Annual Reports of Military Divisions and Departments (Microcopy M-619,
        reel 828; Microcopy M-666, reels 44, 98, 138, 184, 243, 385).
    AGO File 2747 of 1871: Correspondence Relating to Events at the Louisiana
        Custom House (Microcopy 666, reel 27).
    AGO File 4882 of 1872: Correspondence Relating to the Louisiana Election of
        1872 and the Use of Troops to Support the Kellogg Government (Micro-
        copy M-666, reel 93).
    AGO File 3579 of 1874: Correspondence Relating to the Operations of
        Troops in Alabama, Louisiana, and South Carolina, During and After the
        Election of 1874 (Microcopy M-666, reels 169–173).
    AGO File 4788 of 1876: Correspondence Relating to the Operations of
        Troops in the South During and After the Election of 1876 (Microcopy
        M-666, reels 298–300).
    Letters Sent, AGO (Main Series), 1876–1877 (Microcopy M-565, reels 37,
        41, 47).
    Returns from U.S. Military Posts (Microcopy M-617, reel 18, Alexandria,
        1865–1875; reel 86, Baton Rouge, 1865–1877; reel 423, Greenville,

1864–1869; reels 523, 524, Jackson Barracks, 1865–1877; reel 791, Monroe, 1865–1877; reels 843, 844, New Orleans, 1865–1877; reel 1169, Shreveport, 1865–1876).

U.S. Army Yellow Fever Files, 1865–1877.

Record Group 108: Letters Sent by the Headquarters of the U.S. Army (Main Series), 1828–1903

Letters Sent, volume 24, 1873–1875 (Microcopy 857, reel 8).

Record Group 391: Records of United States Army Regiments
  Headquarters, 3rd Infantry. Letters and Telegrams Sent, 1877.

Record Group 393: Records of United States Army Continental Commands
  Military Division of the Southwest and Department of the Gulf
    Letters and Telegrams Sent, 1868–1870.
  Military Division of the Southwest and Military Division of the Gulf
    Letters Sent, 1865–1866.
    Letters Received, 1866.
  Military Division of the South
    Letters and Telegrams Sent, 1869–1875.
  Military Division of the Missouri
    General Sheridan's Letters, 1869–1877.
    Letters and Telegrams Sent, 1869–1875.
  Military Division of the Gulf
    General Orders, 1865–1866.
    Telegrams Sent, 1865–1866.
  Military Division of the Gulf and Department of the Gulf
    Letters Sent, 1866–1867.
  Department of the South and South Carolina
    Letters Received, 1877.
  Department of the Gulf and Military Division of West Mississippi
    Letters Sent, 1865.
    Special Orders, 1865.
  Department of the Gulf and Fifth Military District
    General and Special Orders, 1865–1866, 1868–1870.
    Telegrams Sent, 1866–1868.
  Fifth Military District
    Letters and Telegrams Sent, 1867–1868.
    Letters Received, 1867–1868.
    Letters Received, Civil Affairs, 1867–1868.
    Letters Sent, Civil Affairs, 1868.
    Telegrams Received, Civil Affairs, 1867–1868.
    Telegrams Sent, Civil Affairs, 1867–1868.
    Telegrams Received, 1867–1870.
  Department of the Gulf
    General Orders and Circulars, 1874–1877.
    Journal of Events, 1873–1877.
    Letters Received, 1873–1877.
    Letters Sent, 1871–1877.

Monthly Returns, 1865–1877.
Special Orders, 1873–1877.
Telegrams Received, 1865–1867, 1871–1877.
Telegrams Sent, 1871–1877.
Department of Louisiana
General Orders, 1865–1870.
Letters Received, 1868–1870.
Letters Sent, 1865–1866.
Department of Louisiana and Texas
General Orders, 1865–1866.
Department of Texas
Letters Received, 1870–1871.
Letters Sent, 1870–1871.
Miscellaneous Letters, 1870–1871.
District of Baton Rouge
Letters and Telegrams Sent and Received, 1876.
District of Eastern Louisiana
General Orders, 1865.
Letters Sent, 1865.
District of LaFourche
Letters Received, 1864–1865.
District of Louisiana
Letters Received, 1866–1869.
Letters Sent, 1866–1869.
Special Orders, 1866–1869.
Post of New Orleans
Letters Received, 1865–1866.

United States Government Publications

39th Congress, 1st Session
Senate Executive Documents, No. 2, Serial 1237 (Conditions of the South, 1865).
Senate Executive Documents, No. 12, Serial 1237 (Officers and Men of the Regular Army, 1866).
Senate Executive Documents, No. 13, Serial 1237 (Major Generals and Brigadier Generals of Volunteers).
Senate Executive Documents, No. 27, Serial 1238 (Freedmen's Bureau in Louisiana).
House Executive Documents, No. 71, Serial 1256 (Number of Troops in the South and Volunteer Troops in Service, 1866).
House Reports, No. 30, Serial 1273 (Congressional Investigation of Southern Affairs).

39th Congress, 2nd Session
Senate Executive Documents, No. 6, Serial 1276 (Freedmen's Bureau Report).

House Executive Documents, No. 1, Serial 1285 (Report of the Secretary of War, 1866).

House Executive Documents, No. 8, Serial 1287 (Military Telegrams, 1866).

House Executive Documents, No. 68, Serial 1292 (Report of the Military Commission on the New Orleans Riot of July 30, 1866).

House Reports, No. 16, Serial 1304 (Report on the New Orleans Riot of July 30, 1866).

40th Congress, 1st Session

Senate Executive Documents, No. 14, Serial 1308 (Military Letters, Orders and Telegrams, 1867).

House Executive Documents, No. 20, Serial 1311 (Military Telegrams, 1867).

40th Congress, 2nd Session

House Executive Documents, No. 1, Serial 1324 (Report of the Secretary of War, 1867–1868).

House Executive Documents, No. 172, Serial 1339 (Hancock–Grant Correspondence, 1868).

House Executive Documents, No. 209, Serial 1341 (Military Orders and Removals in Louisiana, 1867).

House Executive Documents, No. 291, Serial 1343 (Military Orders and Elections in the Southern States).

House Executive Documents, No. 342, Serial 1346 (Military Orders, 1867).

House Miscellaneous Documents, No. 43, Serial 1349 (Hancock's Removal).

40th Congress, 3rd Session

Senate Executive Documents, No. 15, Serial 1360 (Disturbances in Louisiana, 1868).

House Executive Documents, No. 1, Serial 1367 (Report of the Secretary of War, 1868–1869).

House Reports, No. 33, Serial 1388 (Organization of the Army).

41st Congress, 2nd Session

Senate Executive Documents, No. 38, Serial 1405 (Buildings Occupied by the Quartermaster's Department).

House Executive Documents, No. 1, Serial 1412 (Report of the Secretary of War, 1869–1870).

House Miscellaneous Documents, No. 154, Serial 1435 (Louisiana Elections, 1869).

41st Congress, 3rd Session

Senate Executive Documents, No. 16, Parts 1 & 2, Serial 1440 (Outrages by Disloyal Persons).

House Executive Documents, No. 1, Serial 1446 (Report of the Secretary of War, 1870–1871).

42nd Congress, 2nd Session

House Executive Documents, No. 1, Serial 1503 (Report of the Secretary of War, 1871–1872).

House Executive Documents, No. 209, Serial 1513 (War Department Correspondence).

House Executive Documents, No. 274, Serial 1515 (Military Telegrams).

House Executive Documents, No. 211, Serial 1527 (Military Telegrams).

House Reports, No. 92, Serial 1543 (Use of the Army in Louisiana).

42nd Congress, 3rd Session

Senate Reports, No. 457, Serial 1549 (Investigation into Louisiana Elections).

House Executive Documents, No. 1, Serial 1558 (Report of the Secretary of War, 1872–1873).

House Executive Documents, No. 91, Serial 1565 (Military Correspondence).

43rd Congress, 1st Session

House Executive Documents, No. 1, Serial 1597 (Report of the Secretary of War, 1873–1874).

House Executive Documents, No. 229, Serial 1614 (Telegrams Relating to the Brooks–Baxter Controversy).

House Reports, No. 384, Serial 1624 (The Military Establishment).

43rd Congress, 2nd Session

Senate Executive Documents, No. 13, Serial 1629 (Correspondence Pertaining to Louisiana).

Senate Executive Documents, No. 17, Serial 1629 (Military Telegrams).

Senate Miscellaneous Documents, No. 45, Serial 1630 (Affairs in Louisiana).

Senate Miscellaneous Documents, No. 46, Serial 1630 (Communication of Michael Hahn).

Senate Miscellaneous Documents, No. 47, Serial 1630 (Affairs in Louisiana).

Senate Reports, No. 626, Serial 1632 (Credentials of Pinchback).

House Miscellaneous Documents, No. 1, Serial 1635 (Report of the Secretary of War, 1874–1875).

House Reports, No. 101, Parts 1 and 2, Serial 1657 (Affairs in Louisiana).

House Reports, No. 261, Parts 1 and 2, Serial 1660 (Election Investigations).

44th Congress, 1st Session

House Executive Documents, No. 1, Serial 1674 (Report of the Secretary of War, 1875–1876).

House Miscellaneous Documents, No. 181, Serial 1706 (Disposition of U.S. Army Troops).

House Reports, No. 816, Serial 1716 (Report on Federal Officers).

44th Congress, 2nd Session

Senate Executive Documents, No. 2, Serial 1718 (Louisiana Election of 1876).

Senate Miscellaneous Documents, No. 14, Serial 1723 (Louisiana Election of 1876).

Senate Reports, No. 701, Volumes 1–3, Serials 1735, 1736, 1737 (Louisiana Election of 1876).

House Executive Documents, No. 1, Serial 1742 (Report of the Secretary of War, 1876–1877).

House Executive Documents, No. 30, Serial 1755 (Use of the Military in the South).

House Miscellaneous Documents, No. 34, Volumes 1–3, Serials 1765, 1766, 1767 (Election of 1876 in Louisiana).

House Reports, No. 156, Serial 1769 (Louisiana Election of 1876).

45th Congress, 2nd Session
House Executive Documents, No. 1, Serial 1794 (Report of the Secretary of War, 1877–1878).

House Executive Documents, No. 55, Serial 1806 (Distribution of U.S. Army Troops).

House Executive Documents, No. 97, Serial 1809 (Election Investigations).

45th Congress, 3rd Session
House Executive Documents, No. 1, Serial 1843 (Report of the Secretary of War, 1878).

House Miscellaneous Documents, No. 31, Volumes 1–5, Serials 1864, 1865 (Problems Following the Election of 1876).

67th Congress, 2nd Session
Senate Executive Documents, No. 263, Serial 7985 (Federal Aid in Domestic Disturbances, 1787–1922).

Richardson, James D., comp. *A Compilation of the Messages and Papers of the Presidents, 1789–1897*. 10 vols. Washington: Government Printing Office, 1896–1899.

War Department. *A Report on Barracks and Hospitals, with Descriptions of Military Posts*. Surgeon General's Office, Circular No. 4. Washington: Government Printing Office, 1870.

———. *War of the Rebellion: Official Records of the Union and Confederate Armies*. 128 Parts in 70 Volumes. Washington: Government Printing Office, 1880–1901.

Newspapers

Army and Navy Journal, 1866–1877.
Alexandria *Caucasian*, 1874–1875.
Alexandria *Democrat*, 1865–1877.
Alexandria *Rapides Gazette*, 1871–1873, 1876.
Amite *Independent*, 1875–1876.
Baton Rouge *Tri-Weekly Advocate*, 1869–1871.
Baton Rouge *Weekly Advocate*, 1869–1872, 1876.
Bellvue *Bossier Banner*, 1869–1877.
Brashear [Morgan City] *News*, 1875.
Colfax *Chronicle*, 1876–1877.
Donaldsonville *Chief*, 1871–1874, 1876–1877.
Franklin *Planter's Banner*, 1868–1872.
Lake Providence *Carroll Record*, 1868–1869.

Monroe *Ouachita Telegraph*, 1866–1867, 1869–1877.
Morgan City *Attakapas Register*, 1876–1877.
Natchitoches *People's Vindicator*, 1874–1877.
New Iberia *Sugar Bowl*, 1870–1877.
New Orleans *Bee*, 1865–1872.
New Orleans *Bulletin*, 1874–1875.
New Orleans *Crescent*, 1865–1869.
New Orleans *Daily Picayune*, 1865–1877.
New Orleans *Democrat*, 1876–1877.
New Orleans *Republican*, 1867–1877.
New Orleans *Times*, 1865–1877.
New York *Times*, 1865–1877.
New York *Tribune*, 1866.
Opelousas *Courier*, 1869–1877.
Opelousas *Journal*, 1869–1877.
Plaquemine *Iberville South*, 1869–1870, 1876–1877.
Rayville *Richland Beacon*, 1872–1877.
Shreveport *Times*, 1871–1877.
Shreveport *Daily South-Western*, 1865–1869, 1871.
Shreveport *South-Western*, 1865–1871.
Thibodaux *Sentinel*, 1869–1877.
Vermilionville [Lafayette] *Lafayette Advertiser*, 1869–1870, 1873–1874.
Vermilionville [Lafayette] *Louisiana Cotton Boll*, 1873–1870.

Autobiographies, Memoirs, Diaries, and Travel Accounts

Badeau, Adam. *Grant in Peace*. Hartford: S. S. Scranton, 1887.
Beale, Howard K., ed. *Diary of Gideon Welles*, 3 vols. New York: W. W. Norton, 1960.
Biddle, Ellen M. *Reminiscences of a Soldier's Wife*. Philadelphia: Lippincott, 1907.
Butler, Benjamin F. *Butler's Book*. Boston: Thayer, 1892.
Custer, Elizabeth B. *Tenting on the Plains*. New York: Charles L. Webster, 1887.
Dixon, William H. *White Conquest*. 2 vols. London: Chatto & Windus, 1876.
Forsyth, George A. *The Story of a Soldier*. New York: Harper & Bros., 1900.
Grant, Ulysses S. *Personal Memoirs of U.S. Grant*. 2 vols. New York: Charles L. Webster, 1886.
Hancock, Almira R. *Reminiscences of Winfield Scott Hancock*. New York: Charles L. Webster, 1887.
Hoar, George F. *Autobiography of Seventy Years*. 2 vols. New York: Charles Scribner's Sons, 1903.
Hoffman, Wickham. *Camp, Court, and Siege*. New York: Harper & Bros., 1877.
King, Edward. *The Great South*. Hartford: American, 1879.
Latham, Henry. *Black and White, A Journal of a Three Months' Tour in the United States*. London: Macmillan, 1867.

Nordhoff, Charles. *The Cotton States in the Spring and Summer of 1875*. New York: D. Appleton, 1876.

Post, Marie C. [ed.] *The Life and Memoirs of Comte Regis de Trobriand*. New York: E. P. Dutton, 1910.

Reid, Whitelaw. *After the War: A Tour of the Southern States, 1865–1866*. Edited by C. Vann Woodward. New York: Harper & Row, 1965.

Roe, Frances M. A. *Army Letters from an Officer's Wife*. New York: D. Appleton, 1909.

Sheridan, Philip H. *Personal Memoirs of P. H. Sheridan*. 2 vols. New York: Charles L. Webster, 1888.

———. *Personal Memoirs of P. H. Sheridan*. 2 vols. Enlarged and edited by Michael V. Sheridan. New York: D. Appleton, 1902.

Taylor, Richard. *Destruction and Reconstruction: Personal Experiences of the Late War*. Edited by Richard Harwell. New York: Longmans, Green, 1955.

Trowbridge, John T. *A Picture of the Desolated States and the Work of Restoration, 1865–1868*. Hartford: L. Stebbins, 1868.

Warmoth, Henry C. *War, Politics, and Reconstruction: Stormy Days in Louisiana*. New York: Macmillan, 1930.

Williams, T. Harry, ed. *Hayes: The Diary of a President, 1875–1881, Covering the Disputed Election, the End of Reconstruction, and the Beginning of Civil Service*. New York: David McKay, 1964.

Miscellaneous

Appleton's Annual Cyclopedia and Register of Important Events of the Year 1866 (and succeeding volumes, 1867–1877). New York: D. Appleton, 1867–1884.

Basler, Roy P., ed. *The Collected Works of Abraham Lincoln*. 9 vols. New Brunswick, N.J.: Rutgers University Press, 1955.

The Civil Record of Major General Winfield S. Hancock During His Administration in Louisiana and Texas. New Orleans[?]: n.p., 1871.

Lathrop, Barnes F., ed. "An Autobiography of Francis T. Nicholls, 1834–1881," *Louisiana Historical Quarterly*, XVII (April, 1934), 246–67.

McPherson, Edward. *The Political History of the United States During the Period of Reconstruction, 1865–1870*. 2nd ed. Washington: Solomons & Chapman, 1875; rpr., New York: Negro Universities Press, 1969.

Padgett, James A., ed. "Some Letters of George S. Denison, 1854–1866: Observations of a Yankee on Conditions in Louisiana and Texas," *Louisiana Historical Quarterly*, XXIII (October, 1940), 1,132–240.

Prichard, Walter, ed. "The Origin and Activities of the 'White League' in New Orleans," *Louisiana Historical Quarterly*, XXIII (April, 1940), 525–43.

Richardson, Frank L. "My Recollections of the Battle of the Fourteenth of September, 1874, in New Orleans, La.," *Louisiana Historical Quarterly*, III (October, 1920), 498–501.

Sioussat, St. George L., ed. "Notes of Colonel W. G. Moore, Private Secretary to President Johnson, 1866–1868," *American Historical Review*, XIX (October, 1913), 98–132.

Thorndike, Rachel S., ed. *The Sherman Letters: Correspondence Between General and Senator Sherman from 1837 to 1891*. New York: Charles Scribner's Sons, 1894.

SECONDARY SOURCES

Books

Barnard, Harry. *Rutherford B. Hayes and His America*. Indianapolis: Bobbs-Merrill, 1954.

Baird, John A., Jr. *Profile of a Hero: Absalom Baird, His Family, and the American Military Tradition*. Philadelphia: Dorrance, 1977.

Beale, Howard K. *The Critical Year: A Study of Andrew Johnson and Reconstruction*. New York: Harcourt, Brace, 1930.

Belz, Herman. *Reconstructing the Union: Theory and Policy During the Civil War*. Ithaca, N.Y.: Cornell University Press, 1969.

Benedict, Michael L. *A Compromise of Principle: Congressional Republicans, and Reconstruction, 1863–1869*. New York: W. W. Norton, 1974.

Bentley, George R. *A History of the Freedmen's Bureau*. Philadelphia: University of Pennsylvania Press, 1955.

Birkhimer, William E. *Military Government and Military Law*. 2nd ed., rev. Kansas City, Mo.: Franklin Hudson, 1904.

Blassingame, John W. *Black New Orleans, 1860–1880*. Chicago: University of Chicago Press, 1973.

Bowers, Claude G. *The Tragic Era: The Revolution After Lincoln*. Cambridge Mass.: Houghton Mifflin, 1929.

Buck, Paul H. *The Road to Reunion, 1865–1900*. Boston: Little, Brown, 1937.

Burr, Frank A., and Richard J. Hinton. *The Life of Gen. Philip H. Sheridan*. Providence, R.I.: J. A. & R. A. Reid, 1888.

Caldwell, Stephen A. *A Banking History of Louisiana*. Baton Rouge: Louisiana State University Press, 1935.

Capers, Gerald M. *Occupied City: New Orleans Under the Federals, 1862–1865*. Lexington: University of Kentucky Press, 1965.

Carter, Hodding. *The Angry Scar*. New York: Doubleday, 1959.

Cash, Wilbur J. *The Mind of the South*. New York: Alfred A. Knopf, 1941.

Caskey, Willie M. *Secession and Restoration of Louisiana*. Baton Rouge: Louisiana State University Press, 1938.

Cornish, Dudley T. *The Sable Arm: Negro Troops in the Union Army, 1861–1865*. New York: W. W. Norton, 1966.

Coulter, E. Merton. *The South During Reconstruction, 1865–1877*. Baton Rouge: Louisiana State University Press, 1947.

Current, Richard N. *Three Carpetbag Governors*. Baton Rouge: Louisiana State University Press, 1967.

Dabbs, Jack A. *The French Army in Mexico, 1861–1867*. The Hague: Mouton, 1963.

Davison, Kenneth E. *The Presidency of Rutherford B. Hayes*. Westport, Conn.: Greenwood Press, 1972.

Dorris, Jonathan T. *Pardon and Amnesty Under Lincoln and Johnson*. Chapel Hill: University of North Carolina Press, 1953.

DuBois, W. E. B. *Black Reconstruction in America*. New York: Harcourt, Brace, 1935.

Dufour, Charles L. *The Night the War Was Lost*. New York: Doubleday, 1960.

Dunning, William A. *Essays on the Civil War and Reconstruction*. New York: Macmillan, 1897.

————. *Reconstruction, Political and Economic, 1865–1877*. New York: Harper & Bros., 1907.

Ficklen, John R. *History of Reconstruction in Louisiana (Through 1868)*. John Hopkins University Studies in Historical and Political Science, vol. XXVIII. Baltimore: John Hopkins University Press, 1910.

Fischer, Roger A. *The Segregation Struggle in Louisiana, 1862–1877*. Urbana: University of Illinois Press, 1974.

Foner, Jack D. *The United States Soldier Between Two Wars: Army Life and Reforms, 1865–1898*. New York: Humanities Press, 1970.

Franklin, John Hope. *Reconstruction After the Civil War*. Chicago: University of Chicago Press, 1961.

Gerteis, Louis S. *From Contraband to Freedman: Federal Policy toward Southern Blacks, 1861–1865*. Westport, Conn.: Greenwood Press, 1973.

Gillette, William. *Retreat from Reconstruction, 1869–1879*. Baton Rouge: Louisiana State University Press, 1979.

Graber, Doris A. *The Development of the Law of Belligerent Occupation, 1863–1914*. Columbia Studies in History, Economics, and Public Law, Number 543. New York: Columbia University Press, 1949.

Grivas, Theodore. *Military Governments in California, 1846–1850*. Glendale, Cal.: Arthur H. Clarke, 1963.

Hanna, Alfred J., and Kathryn A. Hanna. *Napoleon III and Mexico*. Chapel Hill: University of North Carolina Press, 1971.

Harrington, Fred H. *Fighting Politician: Major General N. P. Banks*. Philadelphia: University of Pennsylvania Press, 1948.

Henry, Robert S. *The Story of Reconstruction*. Indianapolis: Bobbs-Merrill, 1938.

Hesseltine, William B. *Ulysses S. Grant, Politician*. New York: Dodd, Mead, 1935.

Heyman, Max L. *Prudent Soldier: A Biography of Major General E. R. S. Canby, 1817–1873*. Glendale, Cal.: Arthur H. Clarke, 1959.

Holzman, Robert S. *Stormy Ben Butler*. New York: Macmillan, 1954.

Hyman, Harold M. *Era of the Oath: Northern Loyalty Tests During the Civil War and Reconstruction*. Philadelphia: University of Pennsylvania Press, 1954.

Johnson, Ludwell H. *Red River Campaign: Politics and Cotton in the Civil War*. Baltimore: John Hopkins University Press, 1958.

Kendall, John S. *History of New Orleans*. 3 vols. Chicago: Lewis, 1922.

Kerby, Robert L. *Kirby Smith's Confederacy: The Trans-Mississippi South, 1863–1865.* New York: Columbia University Press, 1972.

Klingberg, Frank W. *The Southern Claims Commission.* University of California Publications in History, vol. L. Berkeley: University of California Press, 1955.

Landry, Stuart O. *The Battle of Liberty Place.* New Orleans: Pelican, 1955.

Leckie, William H. *The Buffalo Soldiers: A Narrative of the Negro Cavalry in the West.* Norman: University of Oklahoma Press, 1967.

Lewis, Lloyd. *Captain Sam Grant.* Boston: Little, Brown, 1950.

Lonn, Ella. *Reconstruction in Louisiana After 1868.* New York: G. P. Putnam's Sons, 1918.

McCrary, Peyton. *Abraham Lincoln and Reconstruction: The Louisiana Experiment.* Princeton: Princeton University Press, 1978.

McGinty, Garnie W. *Louisiana Redeemed: The Overthrow of Carpetbag Rule, 1876–1880.* New Orleans: Pelican, 1941.

McKitrick, Eric L. *Andrew Johnson and Reconstruction.* Chicago: University of Chicago Press, 1964.

McPherson, James M. *The Struggle for Equality: Abolitionists and the Negro in the Civil War and Reconstruction.* Princeton: Princeton University Press, 1964.

Messner, William F. *Freedmen and the Ideology of Free Labor: Louisiana, 1862–1865.* University of Southwestern Louisiana History Series, Number 12. Lafayette: Center for Louisiana Studies, 1978.

Milton, George F. *The Age of Hate: Andrew Johnson and the Radicals.* New York: Coward-McCann, 1930.

Nankivell, John H., comp. and ed. *History of the Twenty-fifth Regiment United States Infantry, 1869–1926.* Denver: Smith-Brooks, 1927; rpr., New York: Negro Universities Press, 1969.

Nevins, Alan. *Hamilton Fish: The Inner History of the Grant Administration.* New York: Dodd, Mead, 1937.

O'Connor, Richard. *Sheridan the Inevitable.* Indianapolis: Bobbs-Merrill, 1953.

Parton, James. *General Butler in New Orleans.* New York: Mason Bros., 1864.

Patrick, Rembert W. *The Reconstruction of the Nation.* New York: Oxford University Press, 1967.

Perkins, Dexter. *A History of the Monroe Doctrine.* Boston: Little, Brown, 1955.

Perman, Michael. *Reunion Without Compromise: The South and Reconstruction, 1865–1868.* Cambridge: Cambridge University Press, 1973.

Polakoff, Keith I. *The Politics of Inertia: The Election of 1876 and the End of Reconstruction.* Baton Rouge: Louisiana State University Press, 1973.

Randall, James G., and David H. Donald. *The Civil War and Reconstruction.* 2nd ed., rev. Lexington, Mass: D. C. Heath, 1969.

Randall, James G. *Constitutional Problems Under Lincoln.* rev. ed. Urbana: University of Illinois Press, 1964.

Reed, Emily H. *Life of A. P. Dostie; or, The Conflict in New Orleans.* New York: W. P. Tomlinson, 1868.

Ripley, C. Peter, *Slaves and Freedmen in Civil War Louisiana.* Baton Rouge: Louisiana State University Press, 1976.

Rister, Carl C. *Border Command: General Phil Sheridan in the West*. Norman: University of Oklahoma Press, 1944.

Sanger, Donald B., and Thomas R. Hay. *James Longstreet*. Baton Rouge: Louisiana State University Press, 1952.

Sefton, James E. *The United States Army and Reconstruction, 1865–1877*. Baton Rouge: Louisiana State University Press, 1967.

———. *Andrew Johnson and the Uses of Constitutional Power*. Boston: Little, Brown, 1980.

Shugg, Roger W. *Origins of Class Struggle in Louisiana*. Baton Rouge: Louisiana State University Press, 1939.

Simkins, Francis B., and Robert H. Woody. *South Carolina During Reconstruction*. Chapel Hill: University of North Carolina Press, 1932.

Singletary, Otis A. *Negro Militia and Reconstruction*. Austin: University of Texas Press, 1957.

Taylor, Joe Gray. *Louisiana Reconstructed, 1863–1877*. Baton Rouge: Louisiana State University Press, 1974.

Thomas, Benjamin P., and Harold M. Hyman. *Stanton: the Life and Times of Lincoln's Secretary of War*. New York: Alfred A. Knopf, 1962.

Trefousse, Hans L. *Ben Butler: The South Called Him Beast!* New York: Twayne, 1957.

———. *Impeachment of a President: Andrew Johnson, the Blacks, and Reconstruction*. Knoxville: University of Tennessee Press, 1975.

Trelease, Allen W. *White Terror: The Ku Klux Klan Conspiracy and Southern Reconstruction*. New York: Harper & Row, 1971.

Tucker, Glenn. *Hancock the Superb*. Indianapolis: Bobbs-Merrill, 1960.

Vincent, Charles. *Black Legislators in Louisiana During Reconstruction*. Baton Rouge: Louisiana State University Press, 1976.

Weigley, Russell F. *History of the United States Army*. New York: Macmillan, 1967.

West, Richard S., Jr. *Lincoln's Scapegoat General: A Life of Benjamin F. Butler, 1818–1893*. Boston: Houghton Mifflin, 1965.

White, Howard A. *The Freedmen's Bureau in Louisiana*. Baton Rouge: Louisiana State University Press, 1970.

Wiley, Bell I. *Southern Negroes, 1861–1865*. New Haven, Conn.: Yale University Press, 1965.

Williams, T. Harry. *Hayes of the Twenty-third: The Civil War Volunteer Officer*. New York: Alfred A. Knopf, 1965.

Winters, John D. *The Civil War in Louisiana*. Baton Rouge: Louisiana State University Press, 1963.

Woodward, C. Vann. *The Burden of Southern History*. rev. ed. Baton Rouge: Louisiana State University Press, 1968.

———. *Reunion and Reaction: The Compromise of 1877 and the End of Reconstruction*. Boston: Little, Brown, 1966.

Articles

Binning, F. Wayne. "Carpetbaggers' Triumph: The Louisiana State Election of
1868," *Louisiana History*, XIV (Winter, 1973), 21–39.
Bone, Fanny Z. L. "Louisiana in the Disputed Election of 1876," *Louisiana Historical Quarterly*, XIV (July, 1931), 408–440; XIV (October, 1931), 549–66;
XV (January, 1932), 93–116; XV (April, 1932), 234–67.
Burns, Frances P. "White Supremacy in the South: The Battle for Constitu-
tional Government in New Orleans, July 30, 1866," *Louisiana Historical Quar-
terly*, XVIII (July, 1935), 581–616.
Capers, Gerald M. "Confederates and Yankees in Occupied New Orleans,
1862–1865," *Journal of Southern History*, XXX (November, 1964), 405–426.
Carpenter, Allen H. "Military Government of Southern Territory, 1861–1865,"
American Historical Association *Annual Report for the Year 1900*. 2 vols. Wash-
ington: Government Printing Office, 1901, I, 465–98.
Carpenter, John A. "Atrocities in the Reconstruction Period," *Journal of Negro
History*, XLVII (October, 1962), 234–47.
Carrigan, Jo Ann. "Yankees Versus Yellow Jack in New Orleans, 1862–1866,"
Civil War History, IX (September, 1963), 248–60.
Clendenen, Clarence C. "President Hayes' 'Withdrawal' of the Troops—An
Enduring Myth," *South Carolina Historical Magazine*, LXX (October, 1969),
240–50.
Dabney, Thomas E. "The Butler Regime in Louisiana," *Louisiana Historical
Quarterly*, XXVII (April, 1944), 487–526.
Davis, Donald W. "Ratification of the Constitution of 1868—Record of Votes,"
Louisiana History, VI (Summer, 1965), 301–305.
DeLatte, Carolyn E. "The St. Landry Riot: A Forgotten Incident of Recon-
struction Violence," *Louisiana History*, XVII (Winter, 1976), 45–59.
Dufour, Charles L. "The Age of Warmoth," *Louisiana History*, VI (Fall, 1965),
335–64.
Fischer, Roger A. "A Pioneer Protest: The New Orleans Street Car Controversy
of 1867," *Journal of Negro History*, LIII (July, 1968), 219–33.
Fletcher, Marvin E. "The Negro Volunteer in Reconstruction, 1865–1866," *Mil-
itary Affairs*, XXXII (December, 1968), 124–31.
Freidel, Frank. "General Orders 100 and Military Government," *Mississippi Val-
ley Historical Review*, XXXII (March, 1946), 541–56.
Futtrell, Robert J. "Federal Military Government in the South, 1861–1865,"
Military Affairs, XV (Winter, 1951), 181–91.
Gabriel, Ralph H. "American Experience with Military Government," *American
Historical Review*, XLIX (July, 1944), 630–43.
Gonzales, John E. "William Pitt Kellogg: Reconstruction Governor of Loui-
siana, 1873–1877," *Louisiana Historical Quarterly*, XXIX (April, 1946),
394–495.
Grosz, Agnes S. "The Political Career of P. B. S. Pinchback," *Louisiana Histor-
ical Quarterly*, XXVII (April, 1944), 527–612.
Harris, Francis B. "Henry Clay Warmoth, Reconstruction Governor of Loui-

siana," *Louisiana Historical Quarterly*, XXX (April, 1947), 523–653.

Highsmith, William E. "Some Aspects of Reconstruction in the Heart of Louisiana," *Journal of Southern History*, XIII (November, 1947), 460–91.

Horowitz, Murray M. "Ben Butler and the Negro: 'Miracles are Occurring,'" *Louisiana History*, XVII (Spring, 1976), 159–86.

Hyman, Harold M. "Johnson, Stanton, and Grant: A Reconsideration of the Army's Role in the Events Leading to Impeachment," *American Historical Review*, LXVI (October, 1960), 85–100.

Johnson, Howard P. "New Orleans Under General Butler," *Louisiana Historical Quarterly*, XXIV (April, 1941), 434–536.

Lestage, H. Oscar. "The White League in Louisiana and its Participation in Reconstruction Riots," *Louisiana Historical Quarterly*, XVIII (July, 1935), 617–95.

Lowrey, Walter M. "The Political Career of James Madison Wells," *Louisiana Historical Quarterly*, XXXI (October, 1948), 995–1,123.

McDaniel, Hilda M. "Francis Tillou Nicholls and the End of Reconstruction," *Louisiana Historical Quarterly*, XXXII (April, 1949), 357–513.

May, J. Thomas. "The Freedmen's Bureau at the Local Level: A Study of a Louisiana Agent," *Louisana History*, IX (Winter, 1968), 5–19.

Otten, James T. "The Wheeler Adjustment in Louisiana: National Republicans Begin to Reappraise Their Reconstruction Policy," *Louisiana History*, XIII (Fall, 1972), 349–67.

Pitre, Althea D. "The Collapse of the Warmoth Regime, 1870–1872," *Louisiana History*, VI (Spring, 1965), 161–87.

Rawley, James A. "The General Amnesty Act of 1872: A Note," *Mississippi Valley Historical Review*, XLVII (December, 1960), 480–84.

Reynolds, Donald E. "The New Orleans Riot of 1866 Reconsidered," *Louisiana History*, V (Winter, 1964), 5–27.

Richter, William L. "Longstreet: From Rebel to Scalawag," *Louisiana History*, XI (Summer, 1970), 215–30.

———. "Tyrant and Reformer: General Griffin Reconstructs Texas, 1865–1866," *Prologue*, X (1978), 224–41.

Roske, Ralph J. "Visiting Statesmen in Louisiana, 1876," *Mid-America*, XXXIII (April, 1951), 89–102.

Russ, William A., Jr. "Disfranchisement in Louisiana (1862–1870)," *Louisiana Historical Quarterly*, XVIII (July, 1935), 557–80.

———. "Was There a Danger of a Second Civil War during Reconstruction?," *Mississippi Valley Historical Review*, XXV (June, 1938), 39–58.

Seip, Terry L. "Municipal Politics and the Negro: Baton Rouge, 1865–1880," in Mark T. Carleton, et al., eds., *Readings in Louisiana Politics*. Baton Rouge: Claitor's, 1975, pp. 242–66.

Simpson, Amos E., and Vaughn B. Baker. "Michael Hahn: Steady Patriot," *Louisiana History*, XIII (Summer, 1972), 229–53.

Smith, Justin H. "American Rule in Mexico," *American Historical Review*, XXIII (January, 1918), 287–302.

Swinney, Everette. "Enforcing the Fifteenth Amendment, 1870–77," *Journal of*

Southern History, XXVIII (May, 1962), 202–218.

Tarbell, Ida M. "How the Union Army Was Disbanded," *Civil War Times Illustrated*, VI (December, 1967), 4–9, 44–47.

Taylor, Joe Gray. "New Orleans and Reconstruction," *Louisiana History*, IX (Summer, 1968), 189–208.

Tregle, Joseph G., Jr. "Thomas J. Durant, Utopian Socialism, and the Failure of Presidential Reconstruction in Louisiana," *Journal of Southern History*, XLV (November, 1979), 485–512.

Tucker, Robert C. "The Life and Public Service of E. John Ellis," *Louisiana Historical Quarterly*, XXIX (July, 1946), 679–770.

Tunnell, T. B., Jr. "The Negro, the Republican Party, and the Election of 1876 in Louisiana," *Louisiana History*, VII (Spring, 1966), 101–116.

Weigley, Russell F. "Philip H. Sheridan, a Personality Profile," *Civil War Times Illustrated*, VII (July, 1968), 5–9, 46–48.

Wetta, Frank J. "'Bulldozing the Scalawags': Some Examples of the Persecution of Southern White Republicans in Louisiana During Reconstruction," *Louisiana History*, XXI (Winter, 1980), 43–58.

Williams, T. Harry. "General Banks and the Radical Republicans in the Civil War," *New England Quarterly*, XII (June, 1939), 268–80.

———. "The Louisiana Unification Movement of 1873," *Journal of Southern History*, XI (August, 1945), 349–69.

Woodward, Earl F. "The Brooks and Baxter War in Arkansas, 1872–1874," *Arkansas Historical Quarterly*, XXX (Winter, 1971), 315–36.

Theses and Dissertations

Binning, F. Wayne. "Henry Clay Warmoth and Louisiana Reconstruction." Ph.D. dissertation, University of North Carolina, 1969.

Constantin, Roland P. "The Louisiana 'Black Code' Legislation of 1865." M.A. thesis, Louisiana State University, 1956.

Highsmith, William E. "Louisiana During Reconstruction." Ph.D. dissertation, Louisiana State University, 1953.

Kelly, Larry J. "Requests, Requisitions, and Refusals, Occupied New Orleans, 1862–1865." M.A. thesis, Louisiana State University, 1965.

Kirkland, John Robert. "Federal Troops in the South Atlantic States During Reconstruction, 1865–1877." Ph.D. dissertation, University of North Carolina, 1967.

Leavens, Finnian P. "*L'Union* and the *New Orleans Tribune* and Louisiana Reconstruction." M.A. thesis, Louisiana State University, 1966.

Mills, Wynona G. "James Govan Taliaferro: Louisiana Unionist and Scalawag." M.A. thesis, Louisiana State University, 1968.

Nichols, C. Howard. "Francis Tillou Nicholls, Bourbon Democrat." M.A. thesis, Louisiana State University, 1959.

Pfanz, Harry W. "Soldiering in the South During the Reconstruction Period, 1865–1877." Ph.D. dissertation, Ohio State University, 1958.

Pope, Ida W. "The Coushatta Massacre." M.A. thesis, McNeese State College, 1968.

Richter, William L. "The Army in Texas During Reconstruction, 1865–1870." Ph.D. dissertation, Louisiana State University, 1970.

Tunnell, Ted. "Anvil of the Revolution: The Making of Radical Louisiana, 1862–1877." Ph.D. dissertation, University of California, Berkeley, 1978.

Ulrich, William J. "The Northern Military Mind in Regard to Reconstruction, 1865–1872: The Attitude of Ten Leading Union Generals." Ph.D. dissertation, Ohio State University, 1959.

Reference Works

Cullum, George W. *Biographical Register of the Officers and Graduates of the United States Military Academy at West Point, New York, 1802–1867.* 2 vols. New York: D. Appleton, 1868.

Dyer, Frederick H. *A Compendium of the War of the Rebellion.* 3 vols. New York: Thomas Yoseloff, 1959.

Heitman, Francis B. *Historical Register and Dictionary of the United States Army, 1789–1903.* 2 vols. Washington: Government Printing Office, 1903.

Prucha, Francis P. *A Guide to the Military Posts of the United States, 1789–1895.* Madison: State Historical Society of Wisconsin, 1964.

Thian, Raphael P., comp. *Notes Illustrating the Military Geography of the United States.* Washington: privately printed, 1881.

Warner, Ezra J. *Generals in Blue: Lives of the Union Commanders.* Baton Rouge: Louisiana State University Press, 1964.

———. *Generals in Gray: Lives of the Confederate Commanders.* Baton Rouge: Louisiana State University Press, 1959.

Index